Visual QuickStart Guide

Quicken 6

for Windows

Steven Schwartz

Peachpit Press

Visual QuickStart Guide
Quicken 6 for Windows
Steven Schwartz

Peachpit Press
2414 Sixth Street
Berkeley, CA 94710
510/548-4393
800/283-9444
510/548-5991 (fax)

Find us on the World Wide Web at: http://www.peachpit.com

Peachpit Press is a division of Addison Wesley Longman

Editor: Jeremy Judson
Copyeditor: Janet Schwartz
Cover design: The Visual Group
Production: Steven Schwartz

Colophon
This book was created with Adobe PageMaker 6.0 on a Radius 81/110. The fonts used were Concorde and Kabel from Adobe.

ISBN 0-201-68860-3

9 8 7 6 5 4 3 2 1

Printed and bound in the United States of America

♻ Printed on recycled paper

Table of Contents

Table of Contents

Preface

About This Book

The intent of this book (and every other title in the *Visual QuickStart* series) is to get you up and running as quickly as possible. This book makes only a few assumptions about you:

- You understand the fundamentals of using a computer, such as how to use a mouse and how to choose menu commands. You do not have to be an expert computer user.
- Windows 3.1*x* or Windows 95 is installed on your computer.
- You have installed Quicken 6 for Windows on your PC.

Quicken and Quicken Deluxe

There are two varieties of Quicken 6 for Windows: Quicken and Quicken Deluxe. The components and features available to you depend on the version of Quicken that you purchased. Both versions are covered in this book.

Features that are only available in Quicken Deluxe are listed in **Table 1.1** and are noted throughout the book by a tiny CD icon, as shown here.

Table 1.1. Features Unique to Quicken Deluxe

Feature
Quicken Home Inventory
Financial Address Book
Expert Financial Advice
Tax Deduction Finder
Debt Reduction Planner
Mutual Fund Finder
Investor Insight
Credit Report

Parts of the Book

This book is divided into six parts, each representing a different functional area of Quicken. They are:

- *Part I: Getting Started.* Explains basic Quicken concepts, how to set up your accounts and transaction categories, and prepares you for using Quicken's on-line features.

- *Part II: Entering and Editing Transactions.* Using the register and financial calendar to create transactions, writing checks, and using the Financial Address book.
- *Part III: Financial Planning and Management.* Budgeting, creating loans, using the financial calculators, setting and monitoring goals, tracking personal possessions, managing investments, and tax planning and reporting.
- *Part IV: Reports and Graphs.* Creating standard or customized reports and graphs, and printing from Quicken components.
- *Part V: On-Line Activities.* Using Quicken Live to connect to the Internet, on-line banking and bill payment, and portfolio tracking with Investor Insight.
- *Part VI: Advanced Quicken.* Customizing Quicken and real-world Quicken solutions.
- *Appendices.* Quicken keyboard shortcuts, using file-handling commands, and ordering supplies.

About the Author

I began writing professionally in 1978 as a contributing editor for *Nibble*, a popular Apple II magazine. In the past 19 years, I've written hundreds of reviews and computer-related articles, in addition to more than 30 books. I was also the chief methodologist and a founding editor for *Software Digest*, the Business Applications Editor for

MACazine, and Technical Services Director for Funk Software.

I have a Ph.D. in psychology and live with my family and pets in the little town of Lizard Spit, Arizona (but I am seriously considering a move to the neighboring village of Coyote Butte).

Acknowledgments

I want to extend my special thanks to several people who made important contributions to this book:

- Maria Langer (another Peachpit author) for lending her extensive accounting experience to Chapter 23, "Quicken Solutions."
- Brent Prouty of Intuit for providing essential software and other materials without which several chapters could not have been written.
- Jeremy Judson of Peachpit Press for outstanding editorial supervision.
- Kaethin Prizer of Peachpit Press for stepping in at the last moment while Jeremy took a well-deserved vacation. (Sure... *Editors* get vacations. I haven't had one in years!)
- John Horn of Peachpit Press for making sure that the production process went without a hitch.

Part I: Getting Started

Introducing Quicken 6

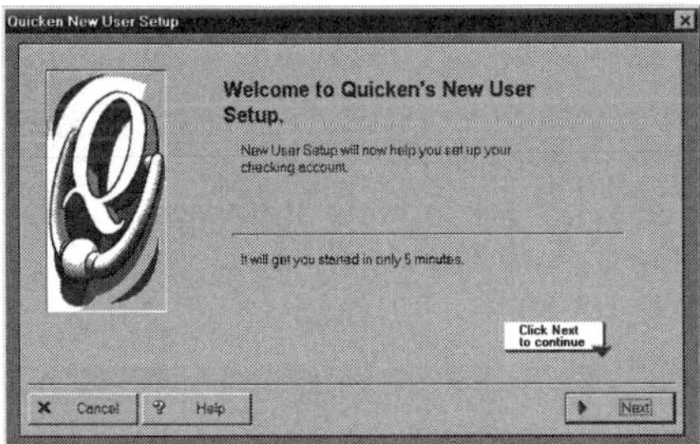

Figure 1.1 *A series of Quicken New User Setup dialog boxes guides you through the setup process.*

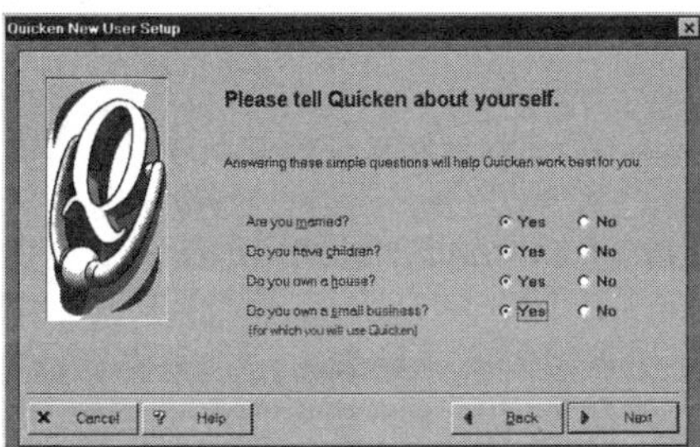

Figure 1.2 *The answers you give to these questions will determine your initial set of transaction categories.*

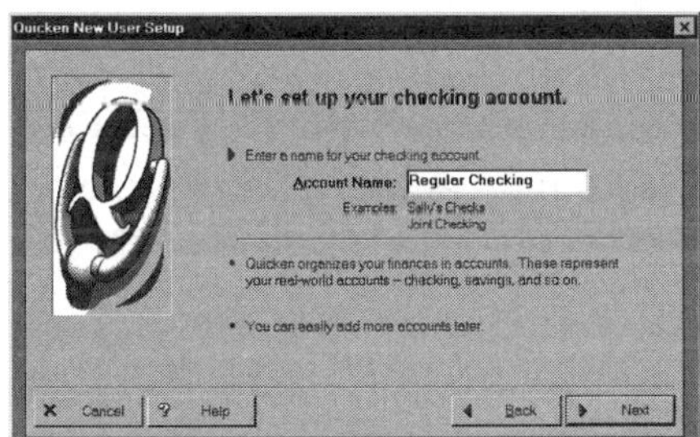

Figure 1.3 *Name the account.*

In this chapter, you will run Quicken for the first time and set up your first account; learn about the Quicken interface and the many ways in which you can get help; and receive several useful tips that will make it easier to work with the program.

First Time Setup

The first time you run Quicken after installing it, a series of dialog boxes appears in which you choose categories for classifying transactions and create your first account (a checking account). Before beginning, get the most recent bank statement for the account, if it is available.

After responding to the information requests in each dialog box, click Next to continue. You can click Back to return to the previous dialog box or Help for more information about the current dialog box. To end the process or begin again, click Cancel.

To set up Quicken:

1. Click the Next button to begin the setup process (see **Figure 1.1**).
2. Answer each question by clicking a Yes or No button (see **Figure 1.2**).
3. Enter a name for the account (see **Figure 1.3**), such as First American checking, National Republic 2058-1249, or Checking.

4. If you have a recent statement for the account, click Yes (see **Figure 1.4**); otherwise, click No.

   Information from the statement is used to set an opening balance for the account. If you want to track the account back to the beginning of the year, you can use the *first* statement of the year instead of the most recent one.

5. If you answered Yes to the question in Step 4, the dialog box shown in **Figure 1.5** appears. Enter the ending date and ending balance from the statement. (If you do not have a statement, the account is created with an initial balance of zero and today as the starting date.)

6. A summary of the information you entered appears (see **Figure 1.6**). Check to see that it is correct, and click Next.

7. To conclude the setup, click Done in the final dialog box. To see a short presentation on Quicken's features, click Overview.

Now that you have created your first account, you are ready to begin using Quicken. You can enter transactions for the checking account, create other accounts (for savings and investments), or work with other Quicken features.

✔ **Tips**

■ The information entered during the setup is preliminary only. You can adjust the opening balance and add, edit, or delete categories any time you wish.

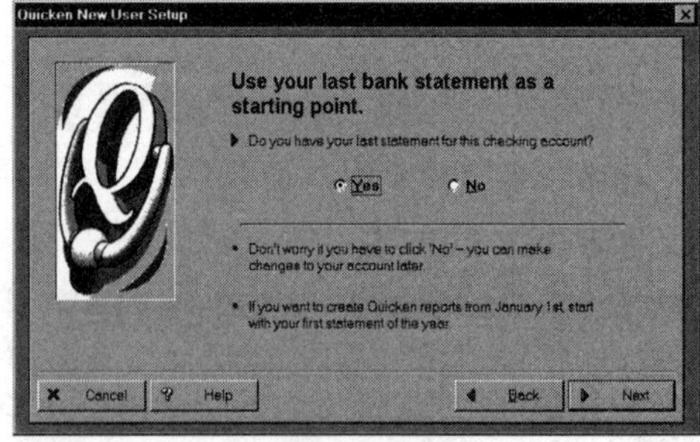

Figure 1.4 *If you have a statement for the account, click Yes.*

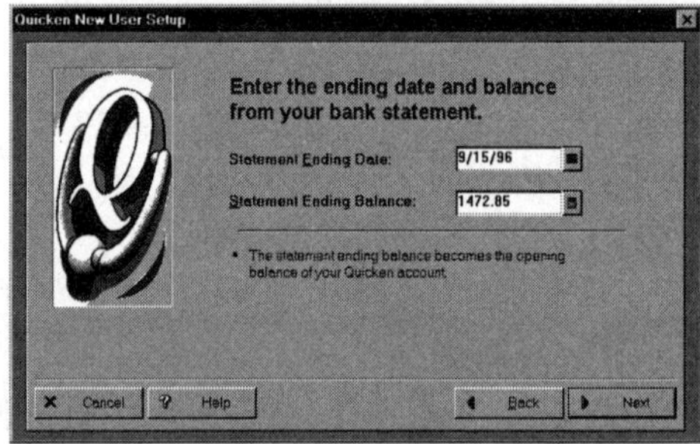

Figure 1.5 *Enter the ending date and balance from the account statement.*

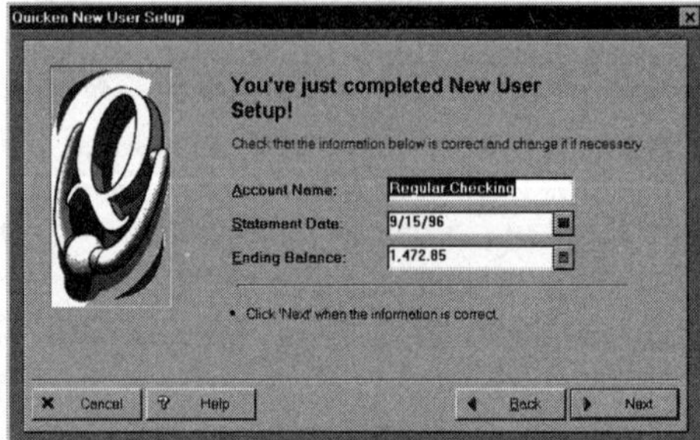

Figure 1.6 *If necessary, you can make changes in this summary dialog box.*

- If you like, you can add other users. You may, for example, want to record separate sets of expenses and income for a small business, your spouse, or your children. However, this makes sense only if each person or business entity has separate accounts.

  To add another user, choose New from the File menu. A similar set of dialog boxes steps you through the setup process (see **Figure 1.7**). A separate data file is created for each user.

  If you prefer to use the Quicken New User Setup dialog boxes, hold down Ctrl Shift while selecting New from the File menu.

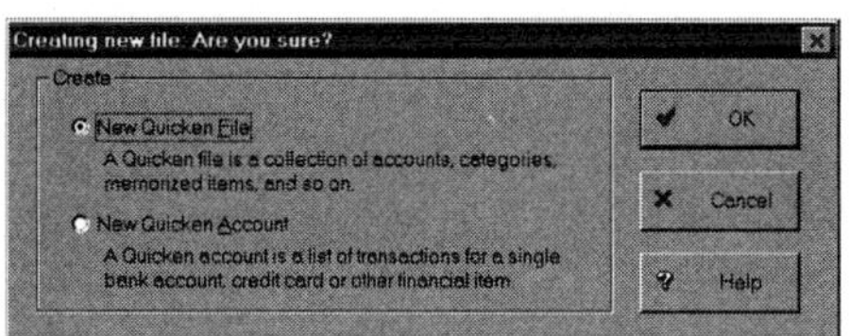

Figure 1.7 *You can choose New from the File menu to create a new Quicken file or a new account.*

Updating Old Quicken Data

If you've used a previous version of Quicken, you can update the data file by opening it with Quicken 6.

- If you only defined a single user in your previous version of Quicken for Windows, Quicken 6 will automatically find and open the old data file.
- If you defined multiple users in your previous version of Quicken for Windows, choose the Open command from the File menu and open each of the old data files.

The updating process is not reversible. As a precaution, Quicken 6 saves copies of the original data files in the OLDFILES or QW5FILES folder, found inside the new Quicken folder.

The Quicken Interface

Quicken 6 has many display options and interface features that make it easy to perform and learn about program activities (refer to the numbered items in **Figure 1.8**).

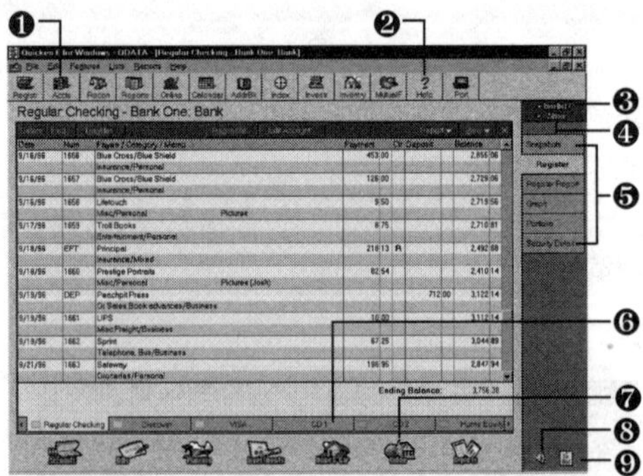

Figure 1.8 *Parts of the Quicken window.*

❶ *Top Iconbar.* Click an icon to work with a particular Quicken component or feature.

❷ *Help.* Click this button to request help for the current window. This is the same as choosing Help on this Window from the Help menu or pressing F1.

❸ *How Do I?* Click this button to get help with common tasks that you can perform in the current window (see **Figure 1.9**).

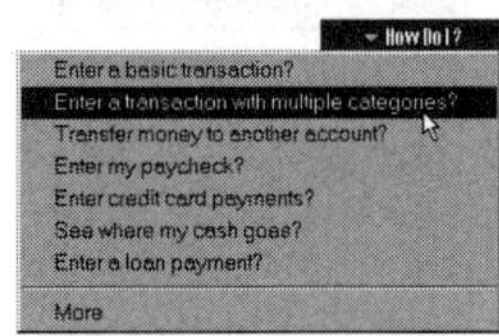

Figure 1.9 *Click the How Do I? button to receive instructions for performing a task in the current window.*

❹ *Advice.* Click this button to display a list of financial help topics (see **Figure 1.10**).

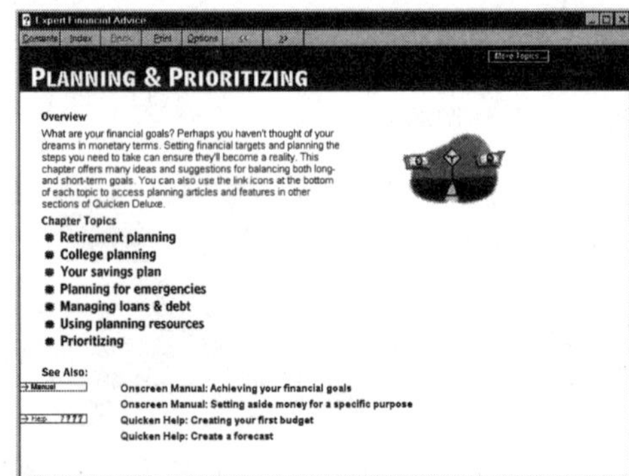

Figure 1.10 *Expert financial advice is available in Quicken Deluxe.*

❺ *QuickTabs.* As you use different program features, a QuickTab is added to this list for each open window. Click a tab to move its window to the front. When you close a window, its QuickTab is removed.

❻ *Account List.* When working in a register window (refer to **Figure 1.8**), all accounts are listed at the bottom of the window. Click an account name to open its register. If you've defined more accounts than can fit beneath the register, click the arrow icons at the left and right edges of the list to view the other accounts.

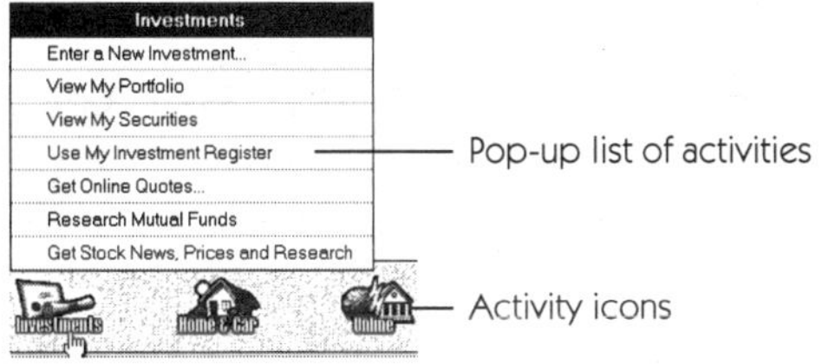

Figure 1.11 *You can choose an activity to perform by clicking an activity icon and then selecting an option from the pop-up list that appears.*

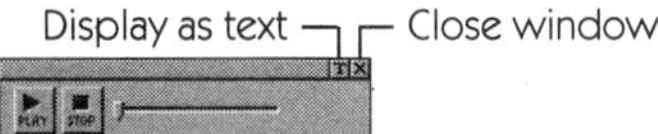

Figure 1.12 *Audio clips are available to help you understand many Quicken activities.*

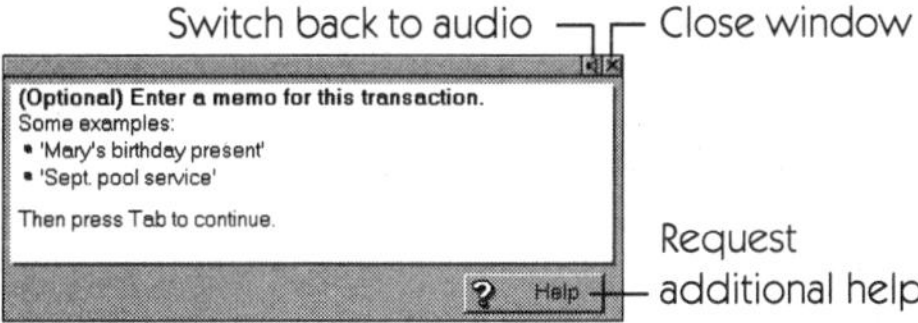

Figure 1.13 *Click the text icon shown in Figure 1.12 to view a text version of the information or to summon further help.*

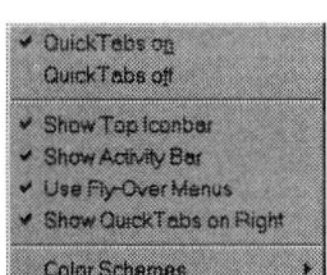

Figure 1.14 *Right-click in a blank area of the Quicken window to choose options for customizing the display.*

7 *Activity Bar.* Most Quicken activities can be grouped into one of seven categories. Click an activity icon to display a pop-up activity list (see **Figure 1.11**). If flyover menus are enabled (discussed in the Tips below), an activity list automatically appears whenever the cursor is moved over an activity icon.

8 *Audio Speaker.* Click this icon (see **Figures 1.12** and **1.13**) for audio instructions related to what you are currently doing. These audio, text, and video windows are known as *QCards.*

9 *To Do! Button.* Click this button to open the Quicken Reminders window.

✔ Tips

- You can customize the display by right-clicking in any blank area of the window. The pop-up menu in **Figure 1.14** appears. Menu options enable you to turn QuickTabs on or off, as well as specify whether they appear on the left or right side of the window; show or hide the top iconbar and the activity bar; turn flyover menus (for the activity bar icons) on or off; and set a color scheme for the display.
- To gain additional space for displaying registers and reports, you can turn off the top iconbar and/or the activity bar.
- You can set Quicken's color scheme to match your mood. Simply choose a setting from the Color Schemes submenu (refer to **Figure 1.14**).

Getting Help

Quicken offers many ways to get help with setting up the program, learning how features work, and improving your financial picture. You can choose help options from any of the following lists.

To get general help and tips:

1. Choose Contents or Index from the Help menu (see **Figure 1.15**), or click the Index button in the iconbar.
2. To search for help by keyword, click the Find tab in the Help Topics: Quicken Help dialog box (refer to **Figure 1.15**).

3. Click the Show Me symbol in a help window (see **Figure 1.16**) to view a video on a help topic (see **Figure 1.17**).
4. Choose Quicken Tips from the Help menu to learn to use Quicken more productively, as shown in **Figure 1.18**. These tips also appear each time you run Quicken.

   To learn how to implement a given tip, click the More Info button. To view all of the tips at once, click the Contents button.
5. Choose Quicken Overview from the Help menu to view a brief tour of Quicken 6. This is the same as clicking the Overview button during first-time setup, as described in pages 3–4.

6. Quicken Deluxe contains many detailed examples of how to use Quicken in real-world situations. Open the Examples icon in the Contents section of the Help file.

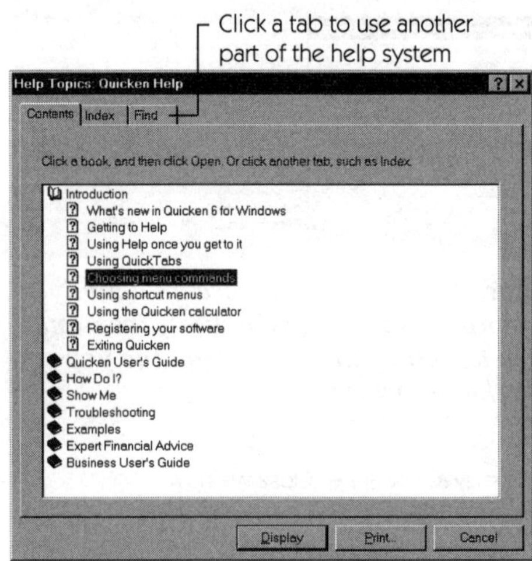

Figure 1.15 *Select a help topic to view by double-clicking it or by clicking Display.*

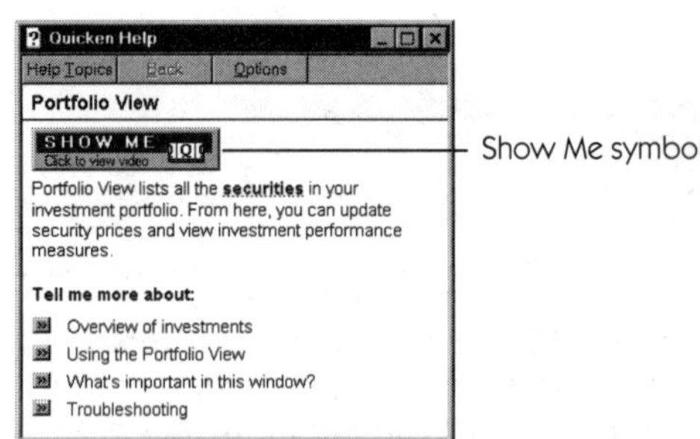

Figure 1.16 *If you have Quicken Deluxe, you can click the Show Me symbols to view instructional videos. (The Quicken CD must be in your CD-ROM drive.)*

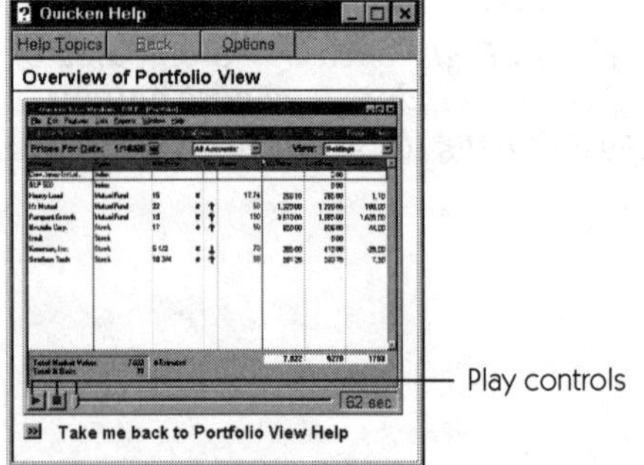

Figure 1.17 *Use the play controls to stop, pause, or restart a video.*

Getting Help

DELUXE

DELUXE

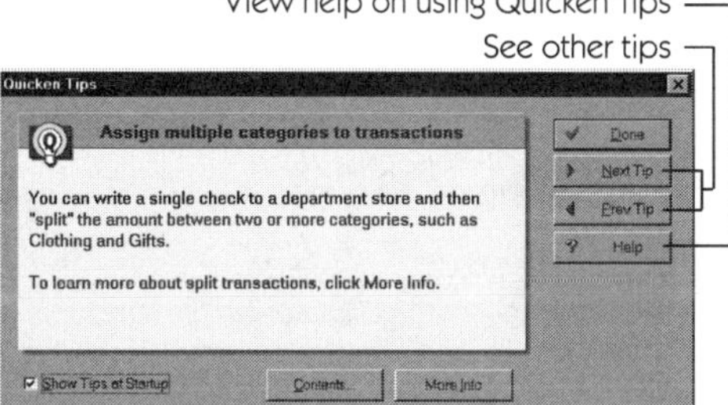

Figure 1.18 *The Quicken Tips window appears each time you start the program. To avoid this, remove the check mark from Show Tips at Startup.*

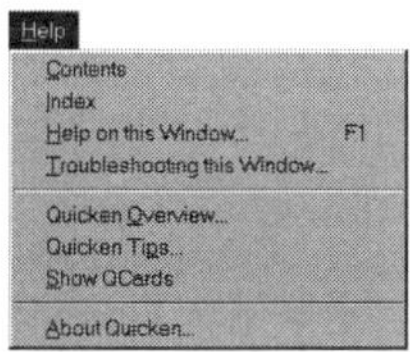

Figure 1.19 *The Help menu.*

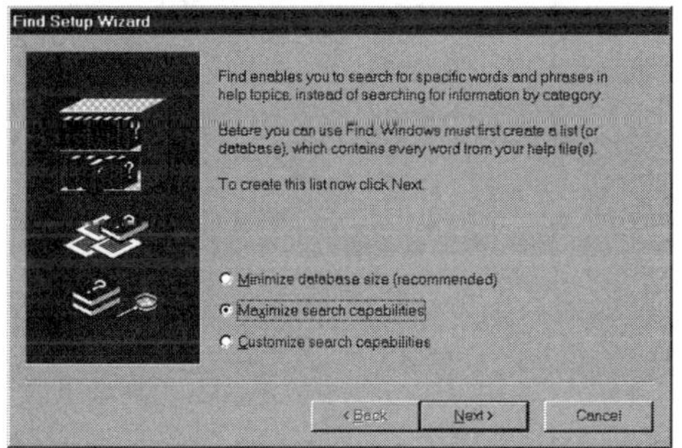

Figure 1.20 *Use the Find Setup Wizard to set search capabilities for a Windows Help file.*

To get help for the current window:

1. Press F1, choose Help on this Window from the Help menu (see **Figure 1.19**), or click the Help button on the top iconbar.
2. Click the How Do I? button (above the QuickTabs) to see instructions for performing common tasks in the current window.
3. Choose Troubleshooting this Window from the Help menu for help with resolving problems in the current window.

To get other types of help:

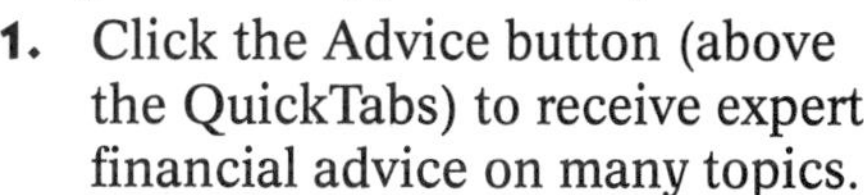

1. Click the Advice button (above the QuickTabs) to receive expert financial advice on many topics.
2. Choose Show QCards to make audio or video help automatically appear for program components.

   In most cases, however, it is best to turn this feature off. You can manually summon QCard help by clicking the speaker icon in the bottom-right corner of any program window.

✔ Tips

- You can view *any* Quicken help feature—including audio and video help—by choosing Contents from the Help menu.
- You can improve your ability to locate keywords in Help. The first time that you click the Find tab, the Find Setup Wizard appears (see **Figure 1.20**). Choose Maximize search capabilities.

  You can maximize the search capabilities for *any* help file.

General Quicken Tips

Here are several general tips that can make it easier to begin using Quicken.

- Most Quicken components are linked to one another. The more information you enter (such as assets and liabilities, for example), the more informative and complete your financial picture will be.
- You can edit, add, or delete transaction categories whenever you like. However, you'll find it more convenient to refine the categories before entering massive amounts of data. Similarly, if you decide to use *classes* (to separate business and personal expenses or those of a husband and wife, for example), the sooner you begin using them, the fewer transactions you'll need to edit. Categories and classes are discussed in Chapter 3.
- If you want to get maximum utility from Quicken reports, prepare to track *all* expenses, including cash purchases. A $100 ATM withdrawal may result in a dozen or more purchases. If you lump them together as a single Cash or Miscellaneous expense, you may discover that your largest class of expenditures is unclassified. And by failing to track cash purchases, totals for many categories (such as gasoline and groceries, for example) may appear much smaller than they really are.

  If many of your transactions are cash-based, you may want to create a Cash account (see **Figure 1.21**) to track cash expenditures. Unlike other types of accounts, a cash account need not be associated

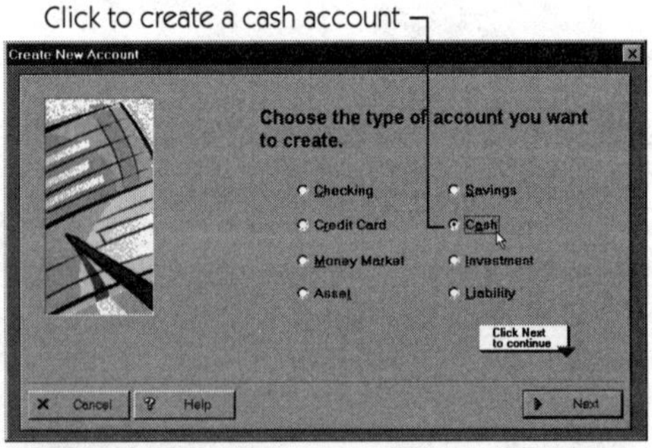

Click to create a cash account

Figure 1.21 *Not all accounts are linked with a bank or similar institution. You can create a cash account that operates out of your pocket.*

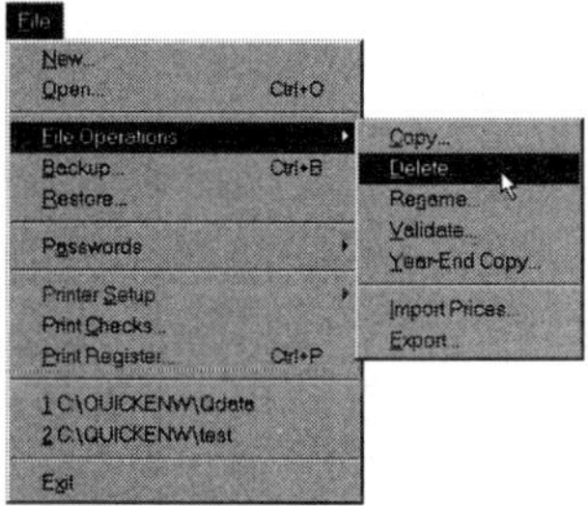

Figure 1.22 *Choose Delete from the File Operations submenu of the File menu.*

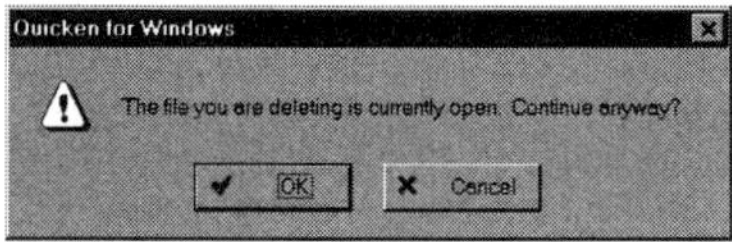

Figure 1.23 *Confirm the deletion, or click Cancel if you change your mind.*

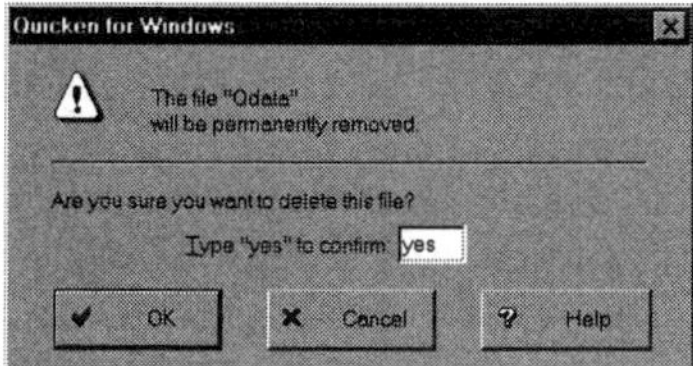

Figure 1.24 *To confirm the deletion, type Yes in the text box and click OK. Any other response leaves the file intact.*

with a bank or brokerage firm. It can be operated out of a wallet, purse, or a petty cash box.

- On the other hand, if you aren't interested in tracking expenses by category, you may elect to use only a handful of categories. The amount of detail tracked is up to you.
- If you find that your initial account and category setup are not satisfactory, you can easily start over again. Choose File ⇨ File Operations ⇨ Delete (see **Figure 1.22**), and then delete Qdata (the default Quicken data file), as shown in **Figures 1.23** and **1.24**. The next time you start Quicken, you can repeat the setup process (as described previously in "First Time Setup").

  If you think that you might change your mind, make a backup copy of the data file before you delete it. Choose Backup from the File menu.

Quicken Accounts

About Files and Accounts

In Quicken, an *account* can be a bank or investment account (e.g., checking, savings, credit cards, stocks, or bonds), an asset account (e.g., a list of property or collectibles), or a liability account (e.g., a mortgage or an auto loan). Funds can be transferred between accounts, and you can create reports that simultaneously present data from one or all of the accounts.

The first time you run Quicken, a file named Qdata is created. As you create accounts for checking, savings, and investments, the account data is stored in Qdata. Taken as a whole, the account balances show your current financial picture and enable Quicken to calculate your net worth.

As explained in Chapter 1, you can create separate files for multiple users or businesses. For example, you might create a second data file for a spouse or a small business. Accounts that you define for that person or business are stored in a new data file. The relationship between data files and accounts is shown in **Figure 2.1**.

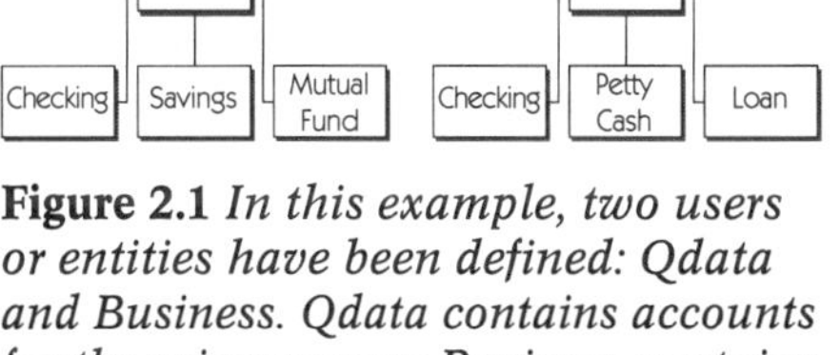

Figure 2.1 *In this example, two users or entities have been defined: Qdata and Business. Qdata contains accounts for the primary user; Business contains accounts for a small business. Qdata and Business are separate files, each with their own accounts.*

✔ Tips

- Let your real-world accounts determine whether you should define one or several data files. If you have separate personal and business checking accounts, for example, they can be stored in separate files. If business and personal money is co-mingled, on the other hand, a single data file is usually indicated. (You can still separate business and personal transactions by using categories and classes, as explained in Chapter 3.)

- When an accountant discusses accounts, he or she is usually talking about expense and income classifications, such as electricity and office supplies. In Quicken, these accounts are called *categories*, as explained in Chapter 3.

Types of Quicken Accounts

As shown in **Figure 2.2**, Quicken 6 offers the following types of accounts:

- *Checking*. Bank, credit union, and savings & loan checking accounts; debit cards.
- *Credit Card*. Credit cards, charge cards, lines of credit, and equity lines.
- *Money Market*. Bank, mutual fund, and brokerage money market accounts.
- *Asset*. Business equipment and personal property, real estate, CDs, treasury bills, accounts receivable, precious metals, and collectibles.
- *Savings*. Bank, credit union, and savings & loan savings accounts.
- *Cash*. Cash-based account, such as a petty cash account for a small business or a record of out-of-pocket purchases.
- *Investment*. Brokerage accounts, mutual funds, individual stocks and bonds, IRAs, and employer retirement accounts.

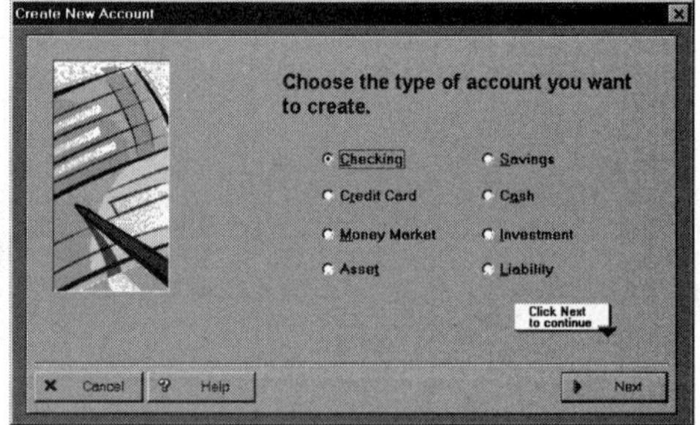

Figure 2.2 *The types of accounts supported by Quicken are shown in the Create New Account dialog box.*

- *Liability*. Loans and other accrued liabilities, such as taxes owed.

✔ **Tip**

- For more help in determining the proper type of account to create, refer to "Creating a New Account" (below) and "Setting up my investments" in Quicken Help.

Creating a New Account

In Chapter 1, you learned how to create a checking account as part of the setup process. In this section, I'll explain how to create other types of accounts.

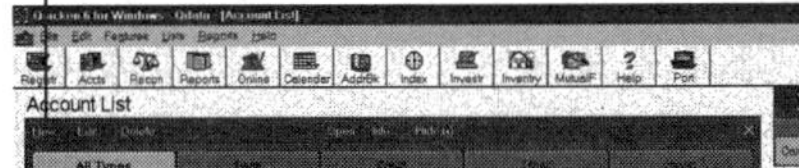

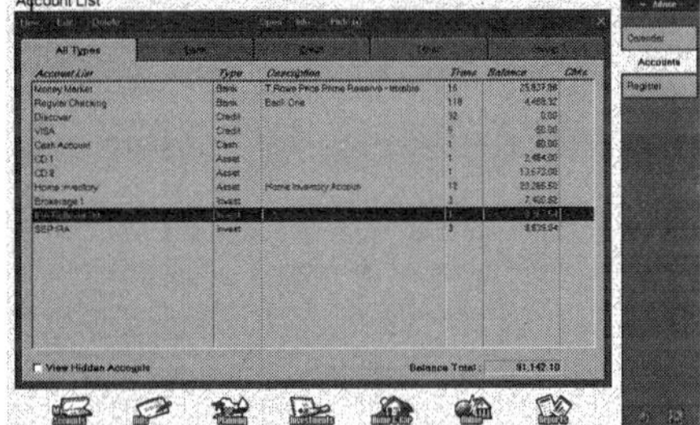

Figure 2.3 *The Account List shows all accounts that have been defined for an individual or business.*

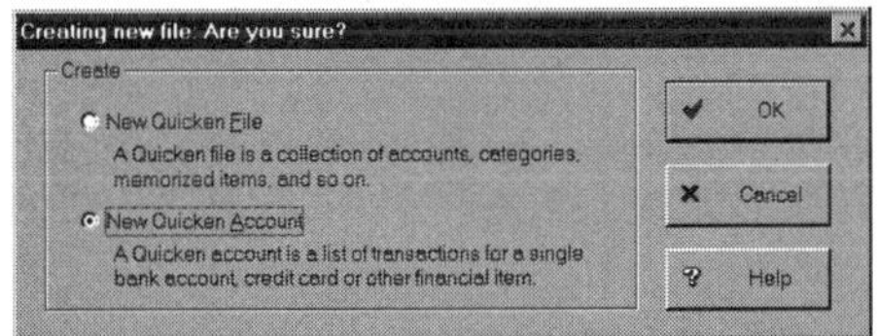

Figure 2.4 *The Creating New File dialog box can be used to create a new account or a new Quicken data file.*

To create a new account:

1. Each account is linked to a single data file (Qdata, for example). If the appropriate data file is not already open, do so now. Choose Open from the File menu, or press Ctrl O.
2. Display the Account List (see **Figure 2.3**), and click the New button at the top of the window.

   or

2. Choose New from the File menu. In the dialog box that appears (see **Figure 2.4**), click the New Quicken Account radio button, and then click OK.

   The Create New Account dialog box appears, as previously shown in **Figure 2.2**.
3. Click the radio button for the type of account you want to create, and click Next.
4. Fill in the information requested by the remaining dialog boxes, and click Done.

The following sections explain how to create the different types of accounts.

Checking Accounts

For instructions on creating a checking account, refer to "First Time Setup" in Chapter 1. To enter additional general information about the account, click Info in the final dialog box (see **Figure 2.5**). To declare the account to be tax-deferred or to link all transactions out of or into the account with a specific tax schedule, click the Tax button (see **Figure 2.6**).

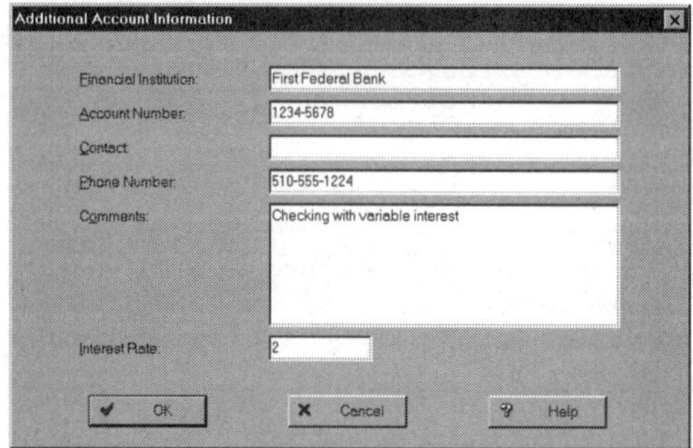

Figure 2.5 *The information entered in the Additional Account Information dialog box is optional. It is provided for your convenience.*

Credit Card Accounts

Creating an account for a credit card, charge card, line of credit, or equity line (a home equity line of credit, for example) differs little from creating a checking account.

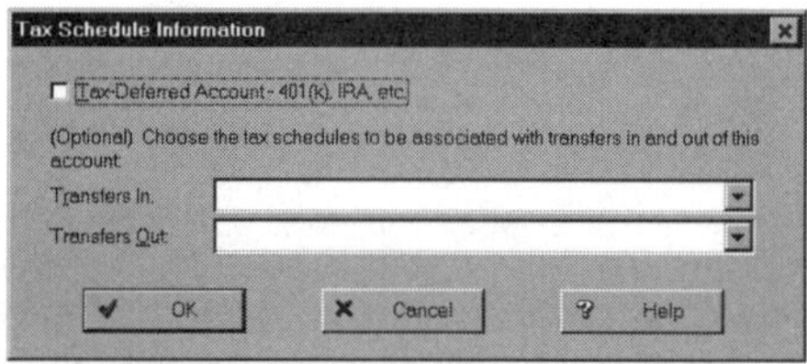

Figure 2.6 *Specifying a tax-deferred status for an account.*

A credit card account cannot be tax-deferred. After clicking the Tax button, however, you can still choose tax schedules for incoming and outgoing transfers, if appropriate. The other difference is that you can enter a credit limit, if there is one (see **Figure 2.7**).

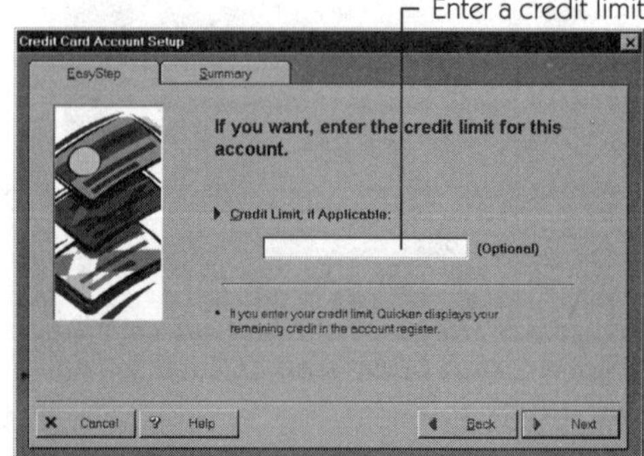

Figure 2.7 *If you specify a credit limit for a credit card account, Quicken shows the available credit in the account's register.*

Savings Accounts

Quicken savings accounts enable you to track deposits, withdrawals, and interest credited to a bank, savings and loan, or credit union savings account. The process of creating a savings account is identical to that of creating a checking account. For instructions, refer to "Checking Accounts" in this section and "First Time Setup" in Chapter 1.

Money Market Accounts

A Quicken money market account works like a checking or savings account. In its register, you can write checks (assuming that you have that privilege with the account), record interest received (as deposits), and so on. The setup process for a money market account is the same as that for a checking account.

If the account is part of a brokerage firm or mutual fund account (serving as a temporary parking place for an uninvested cash balance), you may prefer to set up the account as a linked checking account, as described below.

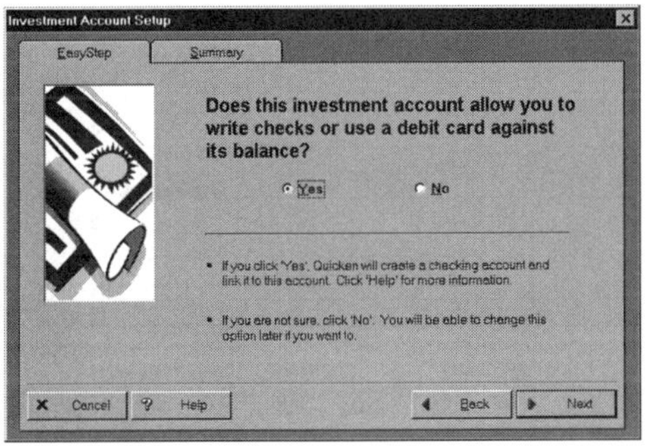

To create a linked money market account:

1. Create a new account by following Steps 1–2 on page 15 ("To create a new account").

   The Create New Account dialog box appears, as previously shown in **Figure 2.2**.

2. Click the Money Market radio button, and then click Next.

3. In the next dialog box (see **Figure 2.8**), click Yes to indicate that there is a linked money market account.

4. If the linked money market account is being created now, click New Quicken Account, and enter the requested balance information (see **Figure 2.9**).

   or

4. If the linked money market account already exists, click Existing Quicken Account, and choose the account from the drop-down list.

Figure 2.8 *Click "Yes" to create a linked checking/money market account.*

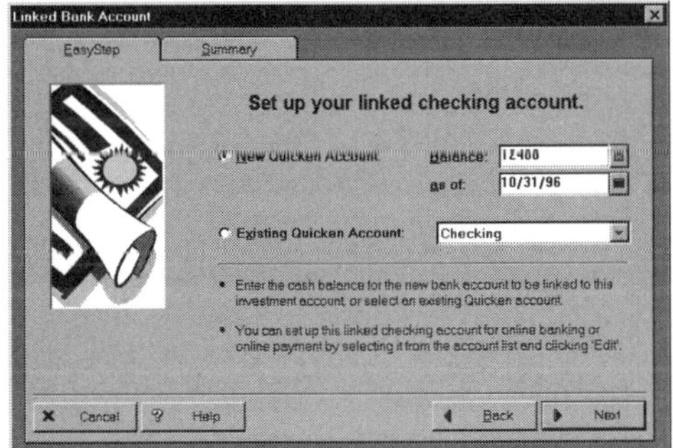

Figure 2.9 *Indicate whether the Quicken money market account has already been created or that it needs to be created now.*

5. Click Next. Continue responding to dialog boxes until you reach the Summary dialog box, as shown in **Figure 2.10**.
6. Review the summary information for the linked investment and money market accounts, make any necessary changes, and click Done.
7. Now describe the securities in the account, as requested by the next series of dialog boxes.

   For additional details about setting up an investment account, see "Investment Accounts," later in this chapter.

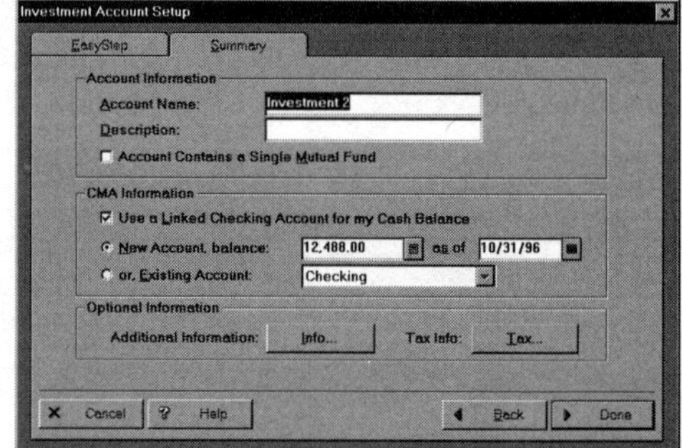

Figure 2.10 *This final dialog box presents information on the linked money market account.*

Cash Accounts

Unlike most other accounts, a cash account (see **Figure 2.11**) is not linked to a financial institution. If a business you own has a petty cash fund, you can create a Quicken cash account to track its expenditures.

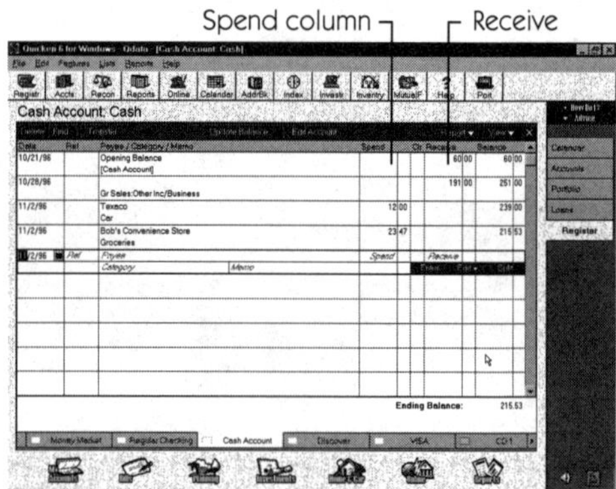

Figure 2.11 *Cash accounts use simplified accounting. Every transaction represents an amount spent or received.*

Cash accounts are often useful for individuals, too. If you regularly pay for items with cash (rather than by check or credit card), you are a candidate for a cash account. Perhaps you make ATM withdrawals so you'll have money to buy gasoline, meals, and so on. If you do not create a cash account to track these out-of-pocket purchases, the alternative is to create a split transaction for every ATM withdrawal to show how the money was spent.

Creating a cash account is identical to creating a credit card account. The only numerical information you must have ready is the amount of cash on hand (i.e., the opening balance).

Investment Accounts

You use investment accounts to record investments that fluctuate in price, such as stocks, bonds, and mutual funds. Any investment account can be a portfolio (containing one or more stocks, bonds, and mutual funds—normally from the same brokerage firm or mutual fund company), or it can be devoted to a single mutual fund. Quicken calls these *regular investment accounts* and *mutual fund accounts*, respectively.

Either type of account can be taxable or nontaxable and can have a linked checking or debit card account (which is used to pay for purchases and holds a cash balance from sales). You should note that a mutual fund account can later be changed to a regular investment account, but that the reverse is not true.

To create an investment account:

1. Follow Steps 1–2 in "To create a new account" on page 15. Click the Investment radio button, and then click Next.
2. Name the account, and indicate whether there is a linked checking or debit account.

   If you indicated that there is a linked checking or debit account, click New Quicken Account, and enter the account balance and starting date (if a new account), as shown in **Figure 2.12**.

   If the linked account already exists, click Existing Quicken Account, and choose the account from the drop-down list.

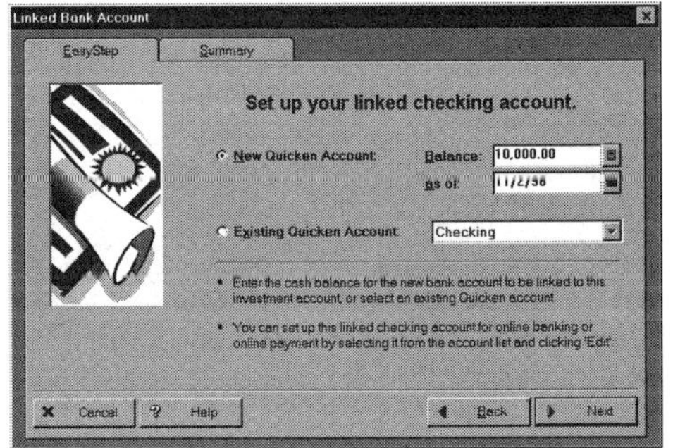

Figure 2.12 *Creating a linked checking account for an investment account.*

3. Specify whether you are creating a regular investment account or a single mutual fund account (see **Figure 2.13**).
4. In the next dialog box, click Yes or No to indicate whether the account is tax-deferred. Click Next to continue.
5. Summary information appears. After reviewing it, click Done.
6. If this is a regular investment account, Quicken presents a new series of dialog boxes in which you enter information about each security in the account, such as the type of investment (stock, bond, or mutual fund) and purchase data.

   or

6. If this is a single mutual fund account, the Set Up Mutual Fund Security dialog box appears (see **Figure 2.14**). Enter the requested information, and then click OK.

   Double-click the mutual fund's account name in the Account List. The Create Opening Share Balance dialog box appears, as shown in **Figure 2.15**.

   If you don't need the historical information for each purchase, sale, and dividend or interest distribution, fill in the blanks with data that represents the current state of the account. On the other hand, if you prefer to have a record of the historical data, you can create the necessary transactions in the account register.

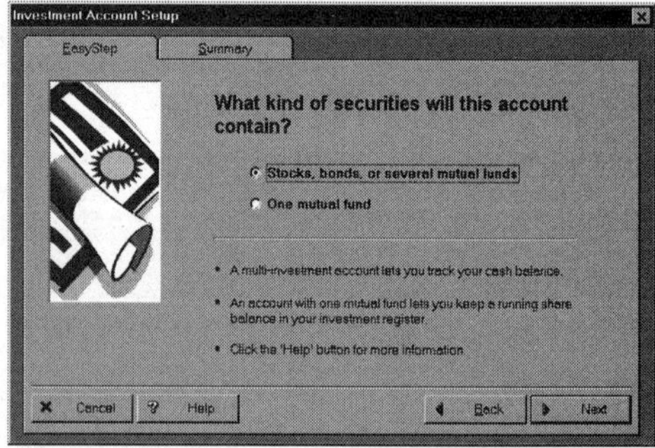

Figure 2.13 *Indicate the type of investment account you want to create.*

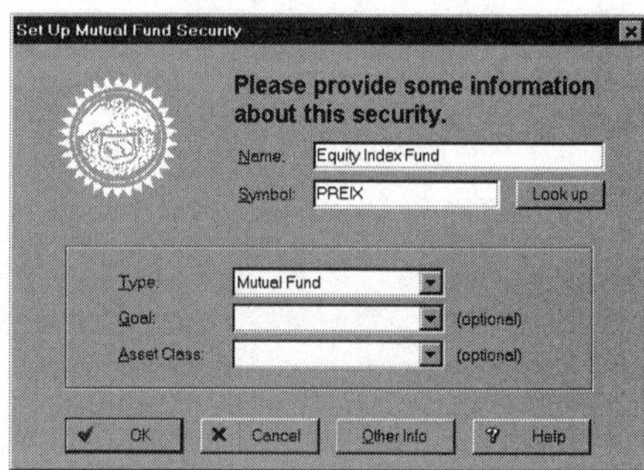

Figure 2.14 *Enter a name for the mutual fund and its trading symbol. The Type should be Mutual Fund.*

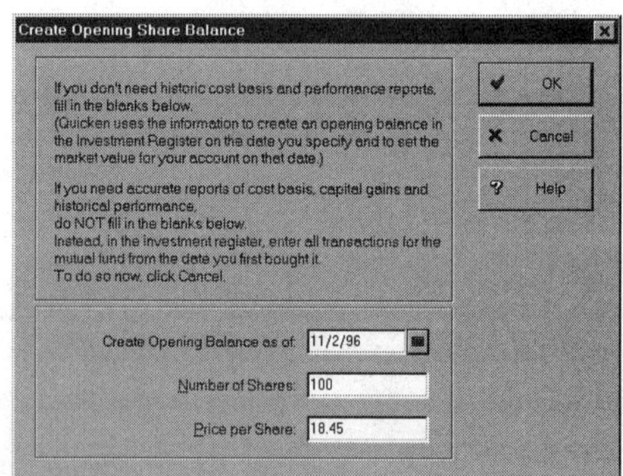

Figure 2.15 *If you like, you can create an opening balance for the account.*

Asset Accounts

Asset accounts are used to track the non-cash, non-investment items that you own, such as real estate, precious metals, collectibles, and personal property. An asset account can contain a single asset (such as a bank CD or a coin collection) or a group of related items, such as business equipment.

The process of creating an asset account is identical to that of creating a checking account. For instructions, refer to "Checking Accounts" in this section and "First Time Setup" in Chapter 1. You will be asked to provide the current value of the item(s) in the account rather than an opening balance.

Liability Accounts

You use liability accounts to record money that you owe to others. For home users of Quicken, the most common form that a liability account takes is that of a loan, such as a mortgage or an auto loan.

When creating a loan-related liability account, you have two options:

- Choose Features ⇨ Paying Bills ⇨ Loans, or press Ctrl H. Click the New button in the Loans window that appears (see **Figure 2.16**), and define the new loan. When you are finished, Quicken creates a liability account for the loan. (For information on creating loans, see Chapter 11.)
- Create a new liability account by following the steps described earlier in this chapter in "Creating a New Account."

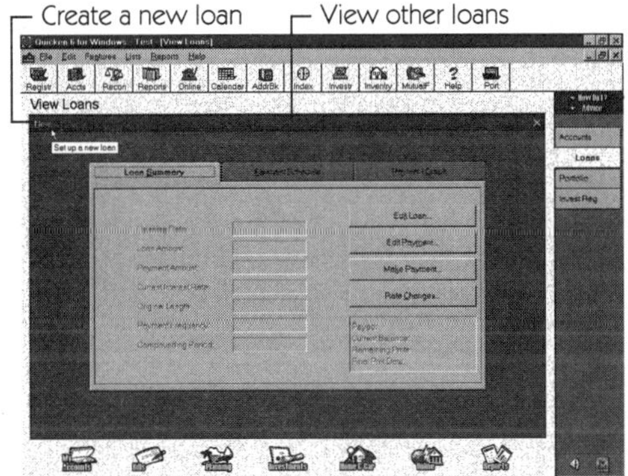

Figure 2.16 *Loans are created in the New Loans window. To view the details for an existing loan, choose it from the drop-down list at the top of the window.*

After specifying the amount you owe and a starting date, the summary dialog box in **Figure 2.17** appears. Verify the information, and click Done.

The dialog box in **Figure 2.18** now appears. Click Yes to enter the loan data, enabling Quicken to calculate the payments, interest expenses, and so on.

Not every liability account is a loan—particularly if you own a business. For example, you can track employee payroll taxes for which you are responsible. If you are a landlord, you can set up a liability account for security deposits that you are holding.

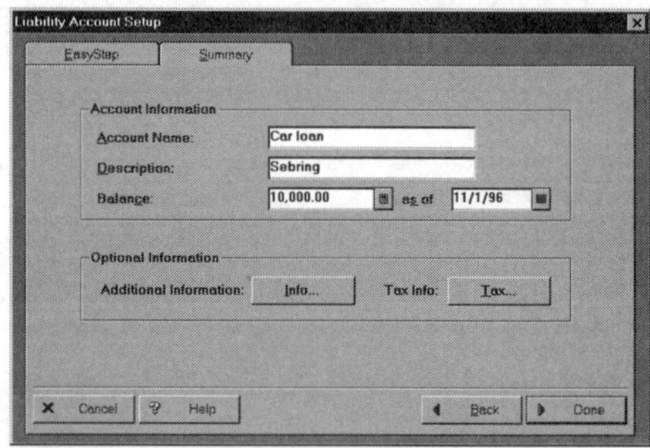

Figure 2.17 *A summary of the information entered for the account is presented in this dialog box.*

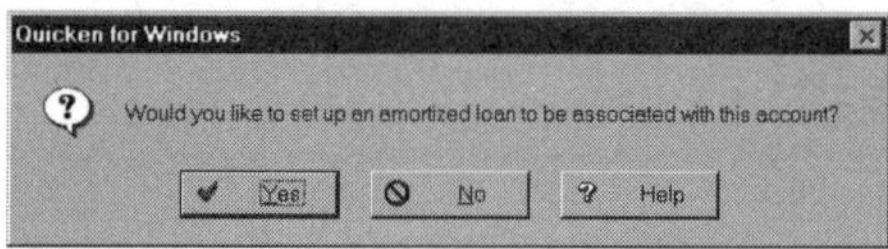

Figure 2.18 *Click Yes to enter loan information for this liability account.*

✔ Tips

- The *right* account type isn't always obvious. Some kinds of investments (such as collectibles, CDs, and treasury bills) can be tracked with an asset or an investment account, for example. For additional help with selecting an account type, see Quicken Help.
- DELUXE If you use Quicken Home Inventory (see **Figure 2.19**) to make a record of your personal property, an asset account is automatically created for those items.
- To track equity in an item (a house, for example), you must create two accounts: a liability account for the loan balance and an asset account in which you record the asset's current value. The difference between the two is your equity.

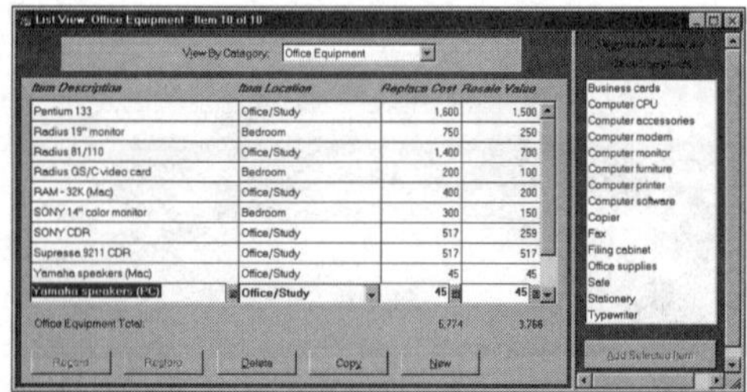

Figure 2.19 *All items entered in Quicken Home Inventory become part of an asset account named Home Inventory.*

Working with Accounts

In order to work with a given account (to record new transactions or generate a report, for example), you must open the account's register.

To work with an account:

1. Display the Account List window (see **Figure 2.20**).

   You can choose Account from the Lists menu, press Ctrl A, click the Accounts QuickTab or the Accts button in the top iconbar (if visible), or click the My Accounts icon in the activity bar and choose View All of My Accounts from the pop-up menu.

2. Click one of the tabs at the top of the window to display a list that includes the account that you want. (To display all accounts, click the All Types tab.)

3. In the account list, double-click the desired account. The account register opens.

When you are done working with an account, you can close its window by clicking the close box. If you want to work with another account, do not close the register window. Instead, follow the tip below.

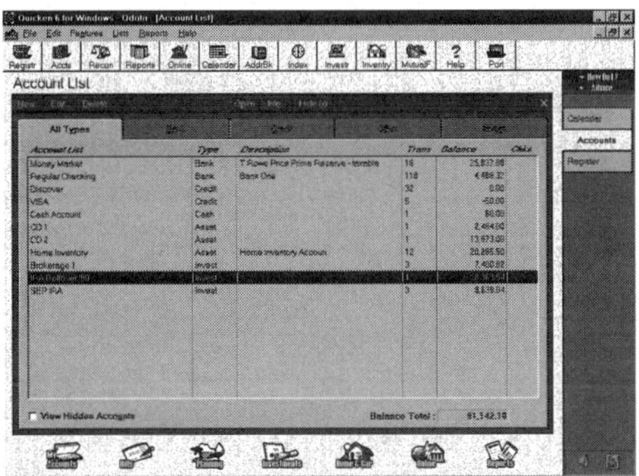

Figure 2.20 *The Account List window.*

✔ Tip

- Whenever a register window is open, all accounts are listed as tabs at the bottom of the window (see **Figure 2.21**). To view the register for a another account, click its tab. If all accounts do not fit at the bottom of the window, click the right or left arrow to scroll through the account list.

Figure 2.21 *The names of all accounts appear at the bottom of every register. Click an account name to work in the chosen register.*

Editing Account Information

Account information can change over time. Depending on the account type, you may be able to change its name, account number, interest rate, tax status, and so on.

To edit account information:

1. Display the Account List window (refer to **Figure 2.20**).

   You can choose Account from the Lists menu, press Ctrl A, click the Accounts QuickTab or the Accts button in the top iconbar (if visible), or click the My Accounts icon in the activity bar and choose View All of My Accounts from the pop-up menu.

2. Click one of the tabs at the top of the window to display a list that includes the account that you want to edit. (To display all accounts, click the All Types tab.)
3. In the list, select the account that you want to edit.
4. Click the Edit button at the top of the window, choose Edit ⇨ Account ⇨ Edit, or press Ctrl E. An Edit dialog box appears (see **Figure 2.22**).
5. Make any necessary changes, and then click Done.

✔ **Tip**

- Most items in the account information dialog box have no affect on Quicken's financial calculations. The items that *do* have such an affect are tax schedule information and designating a linked checking account for an investment.

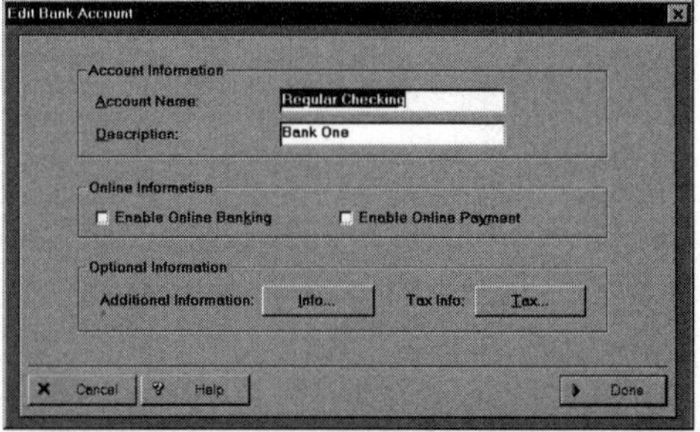

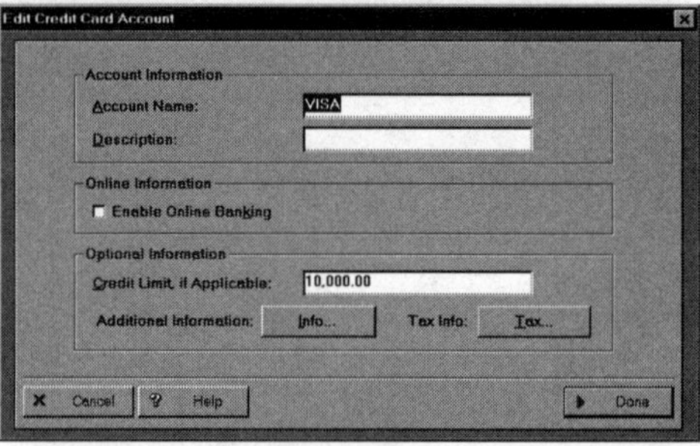

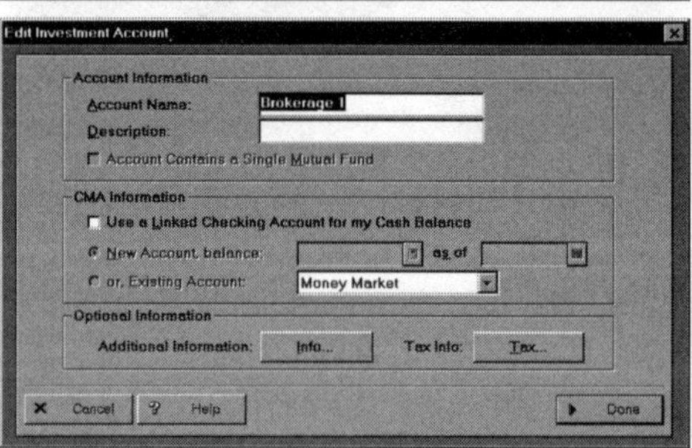

Figure 2.22 *The information that you can change varies by account type. The Edit dialog boxes shown here are for a checking account (top), credit card account (middle), and an investment account (bottom).*

Hiding/Deleting Accounts

To prevent an account from being used in reports or contributing to your net worth, you can hide or delete it.

Hiding an account merely makes it invisible. All account data is still stored in Quicken and can be made visible at any time with a button click.

Deleting an account, on the other hand, is a permanent action. All information about the account and its transactions are removed from your hard disk. To restore a deleted account, you must have a backup of the data.

To hide an account:

1. Display the Account List window (refer to **Figure 2.20**).

   You can choose Account from the Lists menu, press Ctrl A, click the Accounts QuickTab or the Accts button in the top iconbar (if visible), or click the My Accounts icon in the activity bar and choose View All of My Accounts from the pop-up menu.

2. Click one of the tabs at the top of the window to display a list that includes the account that you want to hide. (To display all accounts, click the All Types tab.)

3. In the list, select the account that you want to hide.

4. Click the Hide (x) button at the top of the window.

   If the check box for View Hidden Accounts is checked (found at the bottom of the Account List window, as shown in **Figure 2.23**), hidden accounts are marked with a hand icon. If this option is not checked,

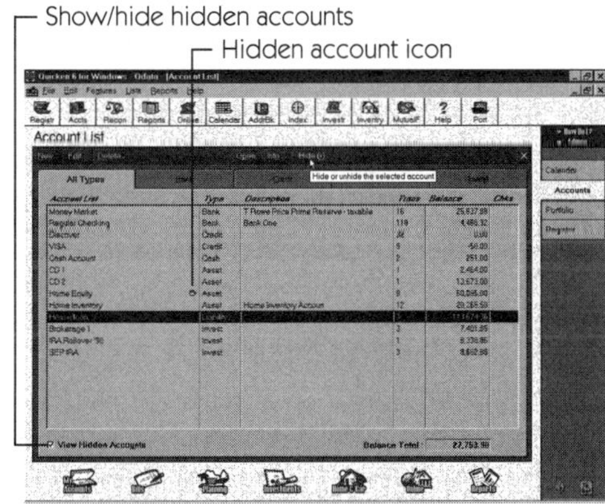

Figure 2.23 *You can hide or display selected accounts.*

Hiding/Deleting Accounts

hidden accounts are not shown nor do their totals contribute to the Balance Total for the list.

To delete an account:

1. Perform Steps 1–2 from "To hide an account" on the previous page.
2. If the account that you want to delete is currently hidden, make sure that View Hidden Accounts is checked (found at the bottom of the Account List window).
3. In the list, select the account that you want to delete.
4. Click the Delete button at the top of the window, choose Edit ⇨ Account ⇨ Delete (see **Figure 2.24**), or press Ctrl D. The dialog box shown in **Figure 2.25** appears.
5. To confirm the deletion, type "Yes" and click OK. If you change your mind, click Cancel or the close box.

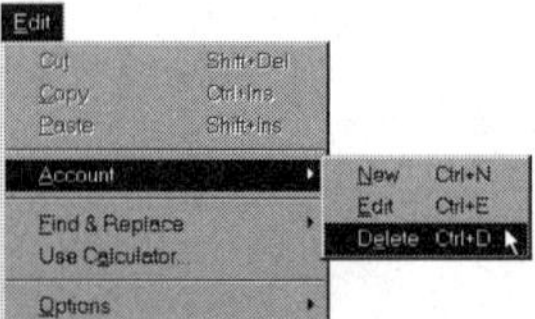

Figure 2.24 *Choose the Delete command to delete the selected account.*

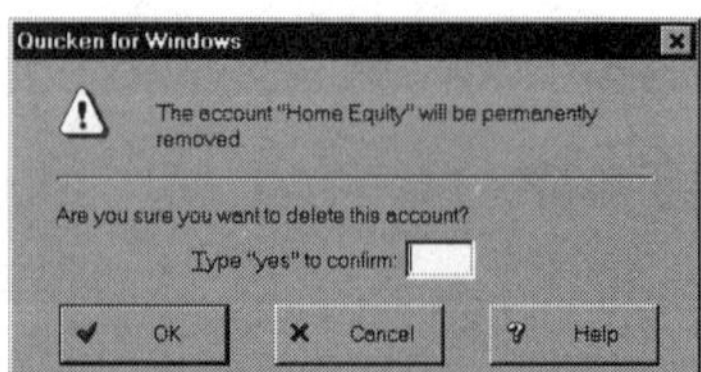

Figure 2.25 *You must confirm an account deletion.*

✔ Tips

- The Hide (x) button works as a toggle. If a selected account is hidden, clicking Hide (x) changes its status to visible.
- Because deleting an account is irreversible, you are advised to first make a backup of your data or to export the data for that account. If you later discover that the account should not have been deleted, you can use the Restore or the Import command to restore the account. See Appendix B for instructions.

3 Categories and Classes

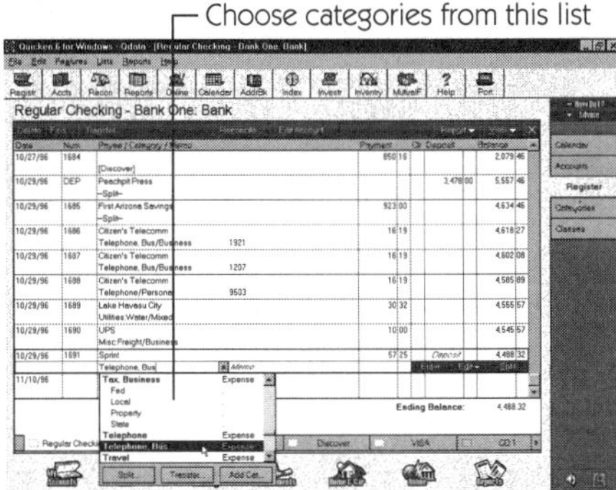

Figure 3.1 *When entering transactions, you can choose categories from a pop-up list.*

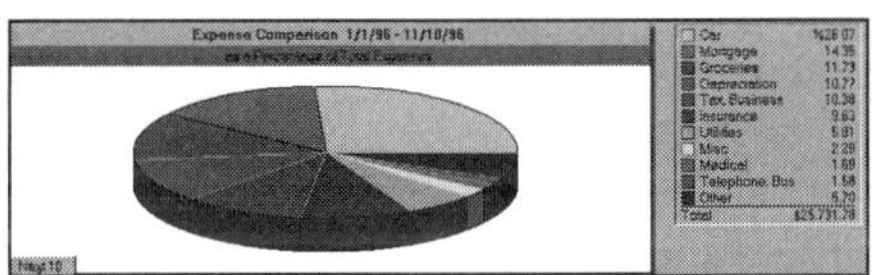

Figure 3.2 *This pie chart shows year-to-date expenses by category.*

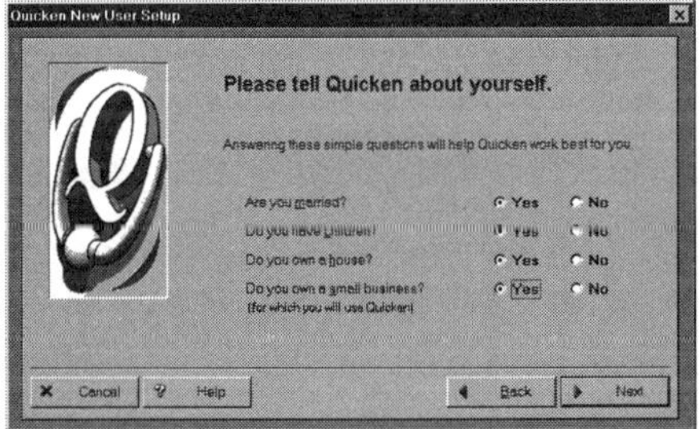

Figure 3.3 *Answers that you give to these questions determine your starting categories.*

About Categories

You use expense and income *categories* to classify each transaction that you enter in a Quicken account register. A purchase at the grocery store could be assigned to a Food or a Groceries category, as shown in **Figure 3.1**. When you fill up your gas tank, the expense might be classified as Auto or Gasoline. Categories come into play when you create budgets, reports, and graphs (see **Figure 3.2**).

When you first set up Quicken 6 (see **Figure 3.3**), you choose an initial set of categories. As is the case with most parts of Quicken, however, you can edit, add, and delete categories as your classification needs become more apparent.

If you want more detail for a certain type of expense or income, you can create *subcategories*. For example, a Food category could have two subcategories: Groceries and Dining Out. On the other hand, if you don't need the additional detail offered by subcategories, you can either delete the unnecessary ones or customize your reports so that certain subcategories are ignored.

✔ Tip

- If you have experience with accounting, don't be confused by the term "categories." In accounting parlance, the category list is your *chart of accounts*.

The Category & Transfer List

Use the Category & Transfer List (see **Figure 3.4**) to view or modify current categories. To display the list, choose Category/Transfer from the Lists menu or press Ctrl C.

Activities that you can perform in the Category & Transfer List include:

- Add new categories (user-defined or Quicken-provided).
- Delete or edit categories.
- Link a category to a specific line of an IRS tax schedule.
- Define *supercategories* to group related budget items.
- Create line-item reports for any category.

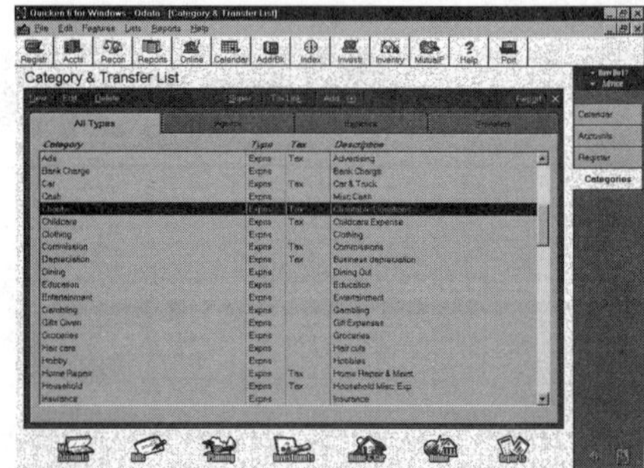

Figure 3.4 *Use the Category & Transfer List to make changes to categories.*

Adding New Categories

Although the standard Quicken categories include many common income and expense classifications, everyone's situation is different. You can create additional categories or choose them from the ones provided by Quicken.

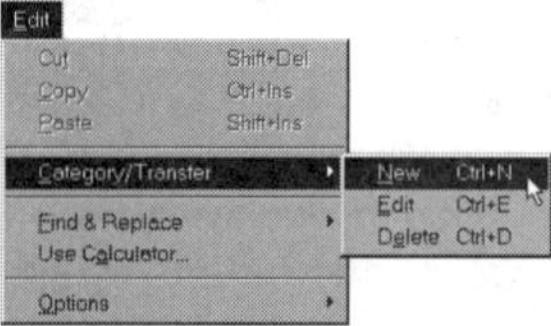

Figure 3.5 *You can work with categories by choosing commands from the Edit menu.*

To add a user-defined category:

1. Open the Category & Transfer List window.
2. Click the New button at the top of the window, choose Edit ⇨ Category/Transfer ⇨ New (see **Figure 3.5**), or press Ctrl N. The Set Up Category dialog box appears (see **Figure 3.6**).
3. Type a name for the new category (or subcategory) in the Name box.
4. *Optional:* Type a description for the category or subcategory.

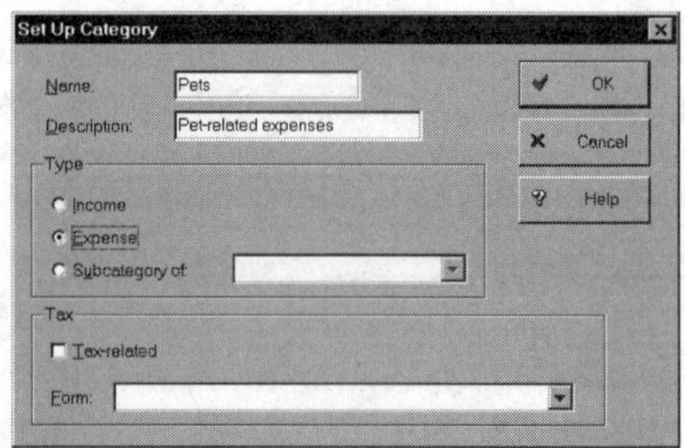

Figure 3.6 *You create new categories and subcategories in the Set Up Category dialog box.*

5. In the Type section of the dialog box, click a radio button to indicate whether this is a new income category, an expense category, or a subcategory of an existing category.

   If it is a subcategory, choose the parent category from the drop-down list. (As a writer, I have defined several subcategories of Gross Sales so I can distinguish different types of income, such as Article Fees, Book Advances, and Royalties.)

6. If this is a tax-related category or subcategory, click the Tax-related check box and choose a specific tax form and line from the Form drop-down list.

7. Click OK to add the new category.

Quicken also provides several sets of predefined categories: Standard, Married, Homeowner, Business, Children, and Investment. You can add selected categories and subcategories from these sets to your current category list.

To add a Quicken-provided category:

1. Open the Category & Transfer List window.

2. Click the Add button at the top of the window. The Add Categories dialog box appears (see **Figure 3.7**).

3. Choose a set of categories from the Available Categories drop-down list.

4. To select a category, click it in the left side of the dialog box. A check mark now precedes its name. Select additional categories, as desired.

5. *Optional:* To simultaneously mark all categories in a set, click the Mark All button.

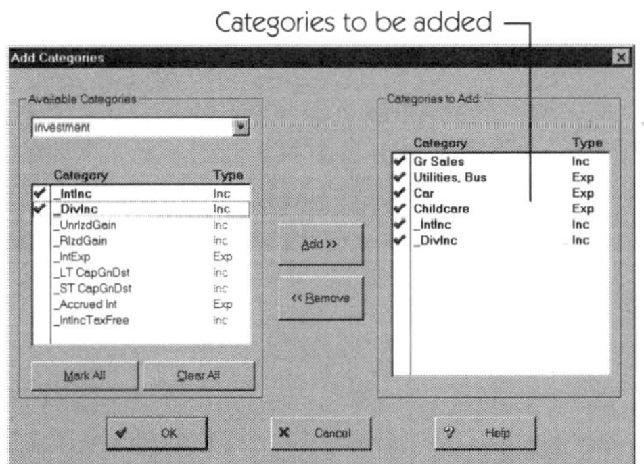

Figure 3.7 *To add predefined categories or subcategories, click Add to open the Add Categories dialog box (shown here).*

6. Click the Add button to move the selected items into the Categories to Add section of the dialog box.
7. Repeat Steps 3–6, as necessary.
8. Click OK to accept the category additions.

Deleting Categories

You may find that some categories are irrelevant to your financial situation. For example, self-employed persons usually have no need for salary-related income categories. To help eliminate clutter in the category list, you can delete these categories.

When you delete categories or subcategories, you should note the following:

- You cannot delete a category that contains subcategories. You must first delete the subcategories, promote them to categories, or change them into subcategories of a different category.
- When deleting a category, all transactions that were assigned to that category become undefined. You will have to manually assign other categories to those transactions. See "Editing Transactions" in Chapter 5 for details.
- When you delete a subcategory, all transactions that were assigned to the subcategory are reassigned to the parent category.

To delete a category or subcategory:

1. Open the Category & Transfer List window.
2. Select a category or subcategory to delete.

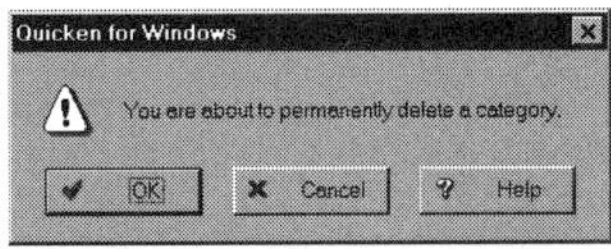

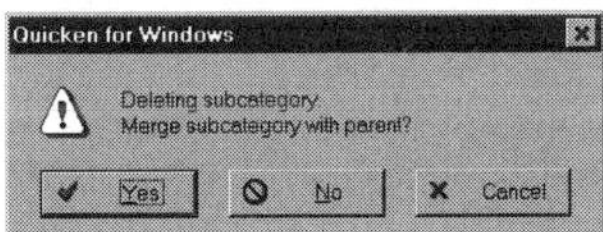

Figure 3.8 *Different dialog boxes appear when you try to delete a category (top) or a subcategory (bottom).*

3. Click the Delete button at the top of the window, choose Edit ⇨ Category/Transfer ⇨ Delete (refer to **Figure 3.5**), or press Ctrl D. One of the dialog boxes shown in **Figure 3.8** appears, depending on whether a category or subcategory is being deleted.
4. To delete a category that has no subcategories, click OK.

   or

4. To delete a subcategory, click Yes to reassign all affected transactions to the parent category; click No to simply delete the subcategory. In the latter instance, all affected transactions become undefined.

To change a subcategory into a category or move it to another category, see "Editing Categories," below.

Editing Categories

You can rename a category or change virtually any part of its definition by following these instructions:

To edit a category:

1. Open the Category & Transfer List window.
2. Select a category or subcategory to edit.
3. Click the Edit button at the top of the window, choose Edit ⇨ Category/Transfer ⇨ Edit (refer to **Figure 3.5**), or press Ctrl E. The dialog box shown in **Figure 3.9** appears.
4. Make the desired changes, and then click OK.

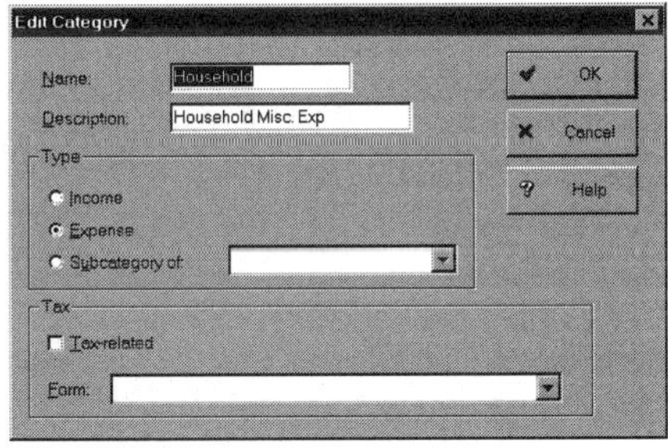

Figure 3.9 *The Edit Category dialog box is identical to the Set Up Category dialog box shown in Figure 3.6.*

The Category & Transfer List

When editing categories or subcategories, you should note the following:

- If you rename a category, any transactions that are presently assigned to that category are automatically given the new category name.
- It is permissible to change a category from an expense to an income item and vice versa.
- You can demote a category to a subcategory, promote a subcategory to a category, or choose a different parent category for a subcategory.
- A category's tax-related status can be altered by associating it with a different line item or toggling the state of the Tax-related check box.

Defining Category Tax Links

You can make it easy to generate tax reports by marking selected categories as tax-related and then specifying the appropriate line item from a particular tax form. Many standard Quicken categories and subcategories are already marked as tax-related. For example, IRA contributions are linked to a line on Form 1040 (see **Figure 3.10**). All tax-related categories are listed with the word "Tax" in the Tax column of the Category & Transfer List window.

You can set the tax-related status of a new category when you define it. To change the tax-related status of an existing category, refer to "Editing Categories," earlier in this chapter.

You can also assign tax links to categories with the Tax Link Assistant. Click the Tax Link button, and follow the directions in the Tax Link Assistant dialog box (see **Figure 3.11**).

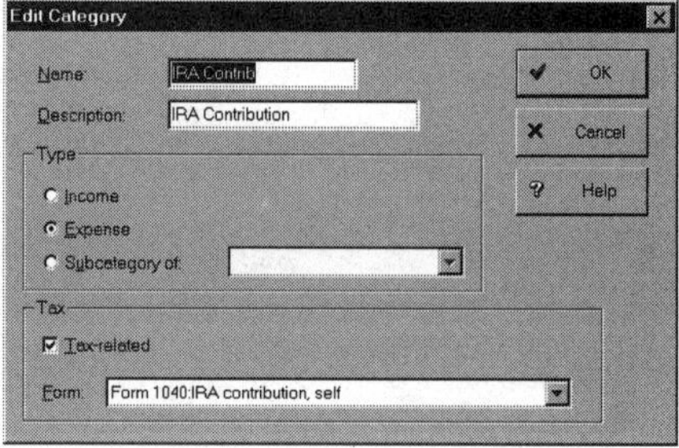

Figure 3.10 *Use the Edit command to examine or change the tax-related status of a category, as well as the line item to which the category is linked.*

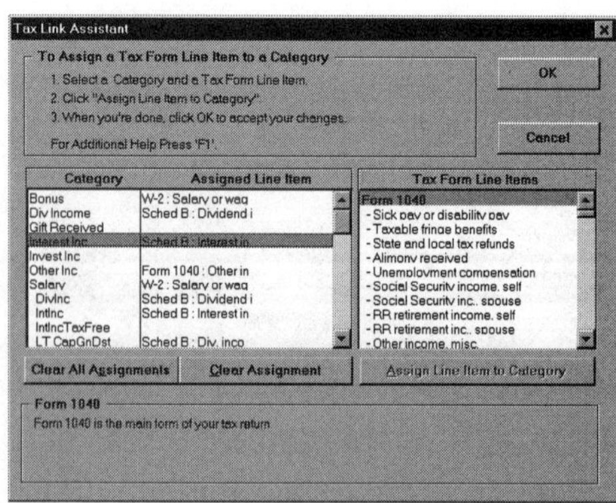

Figure 3.11 *The Tax Link Assistant can be used to view and change the tax links for categories.*

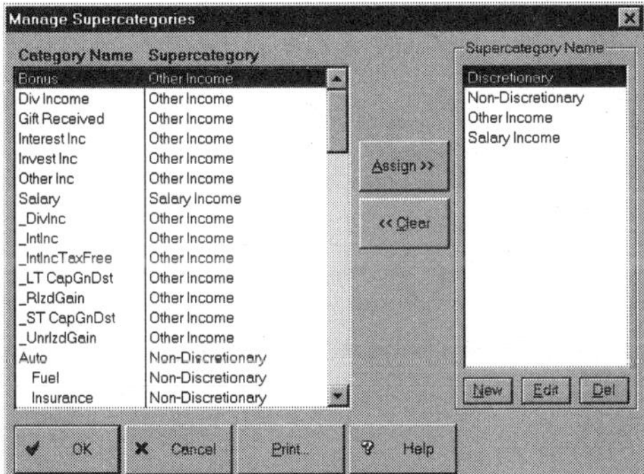

Figure 3.12 *You can add, edit, and delete supercategories in the Manage Supercategories dialog box.*

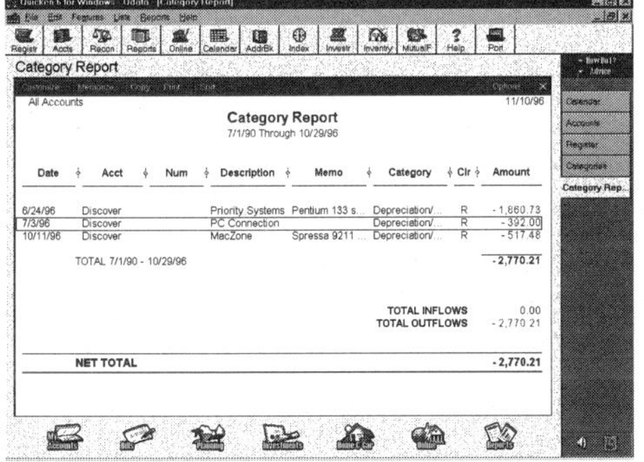

Figure 3.13 *You can quickly generate a report on any expense or income category.*

Working with Supercategories

Supercategories (see **Figure 3.12**) are category groupings that are used in budgeting. Rather than just set budget goals for individual categories (such as Dining Out, Charitable Contributions, and Entertainment), you could assign the three categories to a supercategory called Discretionary Expenses and set a total budget amount for that supercategory.

To work with supercategories, click the Super button. To learn more about supercategories, see Chapter 10.

Creating Category Reports

You can create a basic report on any expense or income category by selecting the category in the Category & Transaction list, and then clicking Report (see **Figure 3.13**). To learn more about creating, customizing, and printing reports, see Part IV, Chapters 17–18.

✔ Tips

- Investment category names begin with an underscore character, such as _RlzdGain.
- Category descriptions are optional. If you enter a description, it can be used in report headers.
- You can merge two categories by changing the category you want to eliminate into a subcategory of the category that you will keep. Then delete the subcategory, and click the Merge button in the dialog box that appears (refer to the bottom part of **Figure 3.8**).
- To learn how to assign categories to transactions and create new categories "on the fly," see Chapter 5.

About Classes

You can use *classes* as another way to group transactions. In those situations where creating additional data files does not work, classes are often the solution.

Suppose that you have a home business and you use the same checking and credit card accounts for all purchases. You can create Home and Business classes to distinguish the two types of expenses.

When you assign a category to a transaction, you can also assign a class to it by typing [/], followed by a class name. A computer repair might be categorized as Repairs/Business, while kitchen repairs would be Repairs/Home. You can use classes to handle expenses and income for each family member, rental properties that you own or manage, or maintenance expenses for several cars, for instance.

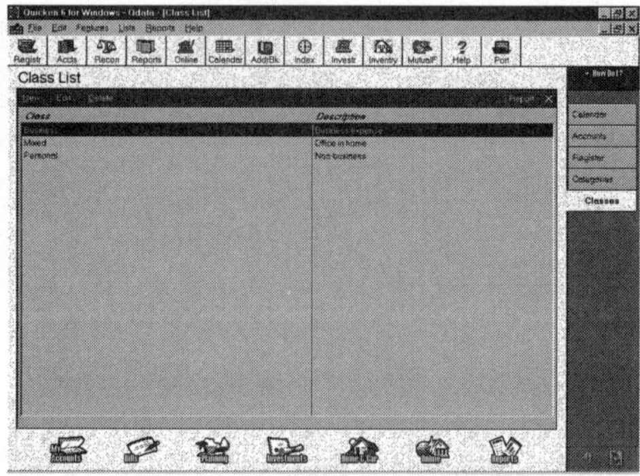

Figure 3.14 *The Class List displays the currently defined classes. Class-related activities are performed in this window.*

Creating Classes

Quicken does not provide class sets that you can load. You must create them yourself. Classes are created, edited, or deleted in the Class List (see **Figure 3.14**).

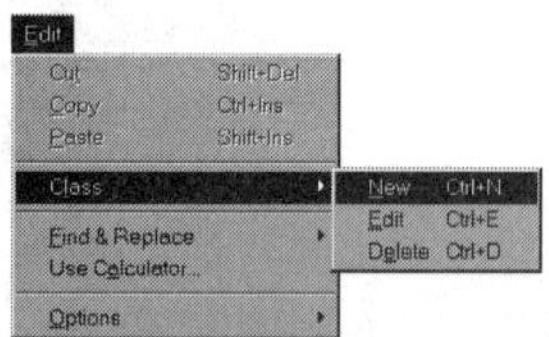

Figure 3.15 *Whenever the Class List is displayed, you can select editing commands from the Class submenu of the Edit menu.*

To create a new class:

1. Choose Class from the Lists menu or press [Ctrl][L]. The Class List appears.
2. Click the New button at the top of the Class List window, choose Edit ⇨ Class ⇨ New (see **Figure 3.15**), or press [Ctrl][N]. The Set Up Class dialog box appears, as shown in **Figure 3.16**.

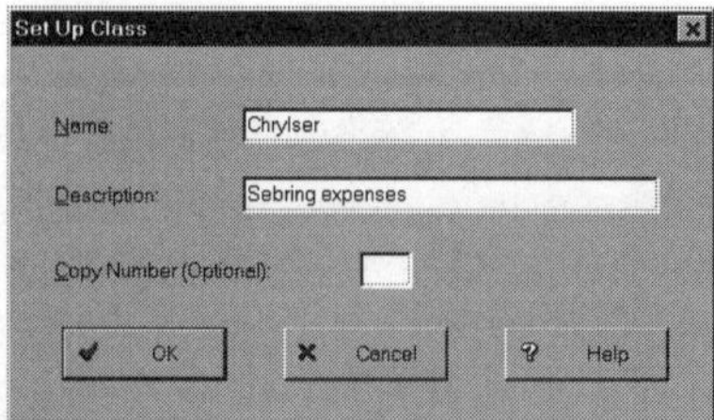

Figure 3.16 *To define a class, the only requirement is that you give it a name.*

3. Enter a name and—optionally—a description for the new class.
4. If you're a Canadian user of QuickTax, you can track tax-related transactions for two taxpayers in the same Quicken file by entering numbers in the Copy Number text box. Click Help for information on using this feature.
5. Click OK to create the new class.

Editing a Class

If you'd like to change a class name or description, select it in the Class List, and then click the Edit button, choose Edit ⇨ Class ⇨ Edit, or press Ctrl E. A dialog box that is identical to the Set Up Class dialog box appears. Make the desired changes, and then click OK. If the original class name has been assigned to transactions, those transactions are automatically renamed.

Deleting a Class

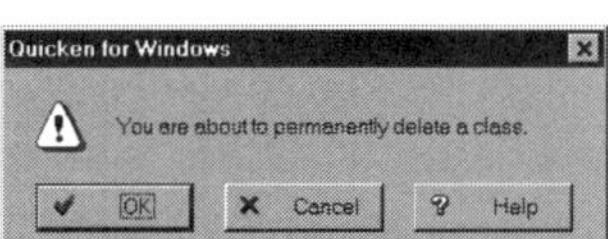

Figure 3.17 *To delete the selected class, click OK.*

If you no longer need a given class, you can delete it. Select the class in the Class List, and then click the Delete button, choose Edit ⇨ Class ⇨ Delete, or press Ctrl D. Click OK in the dialog box that appears (see **Figure 3.17**).

✔ **Tip**

- If possible, begin each class name with a different letter. As you type a class name for a transaction, Quicken tries to complete it based on the letter(s) entered.

About Classes

4

Preparing to Go On-Line

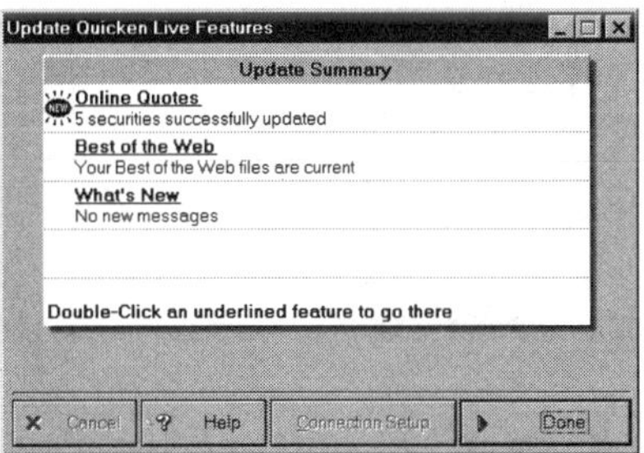

Figure 4.1 *It only takes a few moments to use Quicken Live to download current stock quotes, new Best of the Web sites, and so on. This dialog box shows the results.*

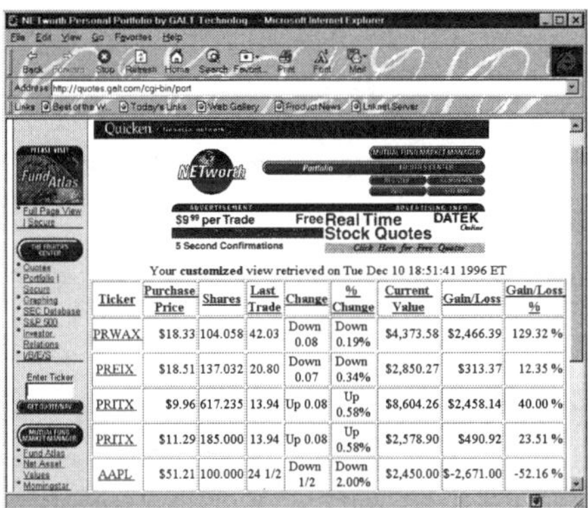

Figure 4.2 *You can use the Quicken Financial Network to track a personal stock and mutual fund portfolio.*

Quicken's On-Line Features

Like many current programs, Quicken has direct links to the Internet (see **Figure 4.1**). If you have a modem, you can use the following on-line features:

- *Quicken Live.* Quicken tips, Best of the Web (Internet sites of interest to Quicken users), free stock and mutual fund quotes, Quicken Financial Network (see **Figure 4.2**), the Quicken Store, and on-line program updates. See Chapter 19.
- *Investor Insight.* Capture prices, news stories, charts, and reports on up to 500 stocks and mutual funds. See Chapter 20.
- *Mutual Fund Finder.* Download quarterly updates to the mutual fund database. See Chapter 15.
- *On-line banking and bill paying.* Manage multiple bank accounts and pay bills on-line. See Chapter 21.

Quicken Live Setup

Quicken's on-line features require an Internet account. The account can be with an Internet service provider (ISP), an information service such as America Online or CompuServe, or you can use the limited account that is included free with Quicken. Before you can use the Internet features, you must configure Quicken, as described below. (If your computer has an external modem, turn it on before beginning the configuration process.)

To configure Quicken for the Internet:

1. The first time that you use Quicken Live, the setup process automatically begins.

   or

1. To manually set up Quicken, choose Features ➪ Online ➪ Quicken Live Setup ➪ Internet Connection Setup.

   The Internet Connection Setup dialog box appears, as shown in **Figure 4.3**.

2. Choose a connection method by clicking a radio button. Click Next.

The specific dialog boxes that appear next depend on the connection method chosen. Steps for using an existing dial-up connection are listed below. If you're using a different connection method, see the end of this section.

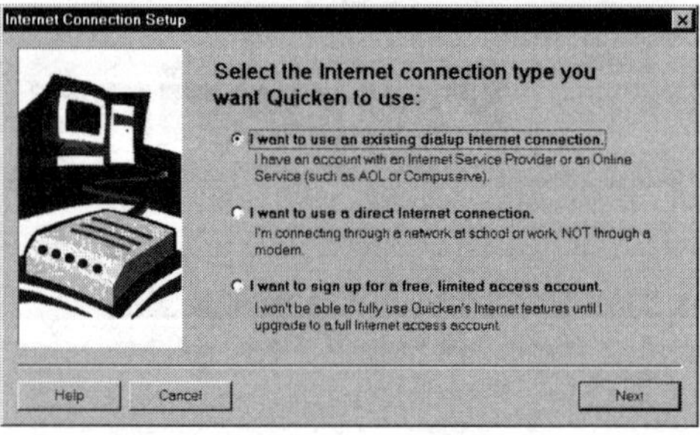

Figure 4.3 *Choose a connection method.*

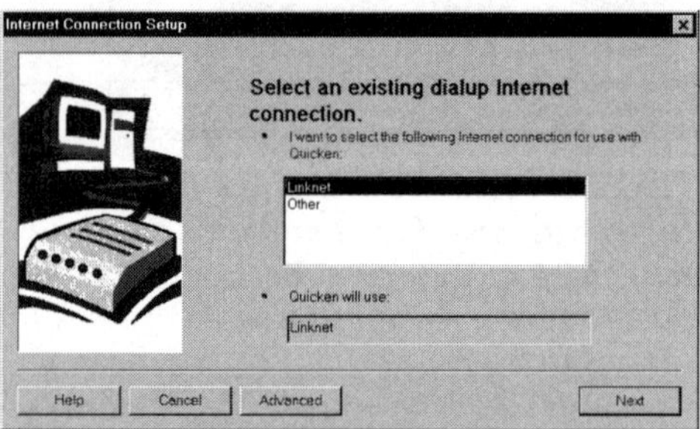

Figure 4.4 *Choose an existing connection or choose Other to create a new one.*

To configure Quicken to use an existing dial-up Internet connection:

1. Quicken scans your hard disk for existing Internet connections (see **Figure 4.4**). Select the connection to use or choose Other to create a new one. Click Next to continue.
2. If you chose Other in Step 1, the Edit Existing Dialup Connection Information dialog box appears. Contact your ISP to obtain the necessary information.
3. A dialog box lists all browser programs that are installed on your computer (see **Figure 4.5**). Select a browser to use with Quicken.

   A *browser* is a program that enables you to view text, graphics, and multimedia content from the part of the Internet known as the World Wide

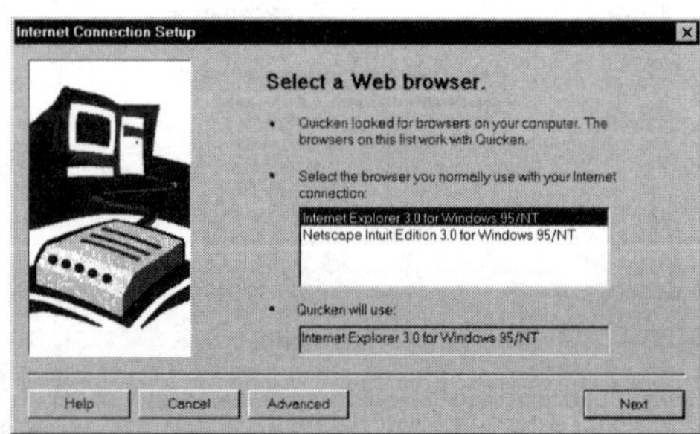

Figure 4.5 *Select a Web browser to use with Quicken.*

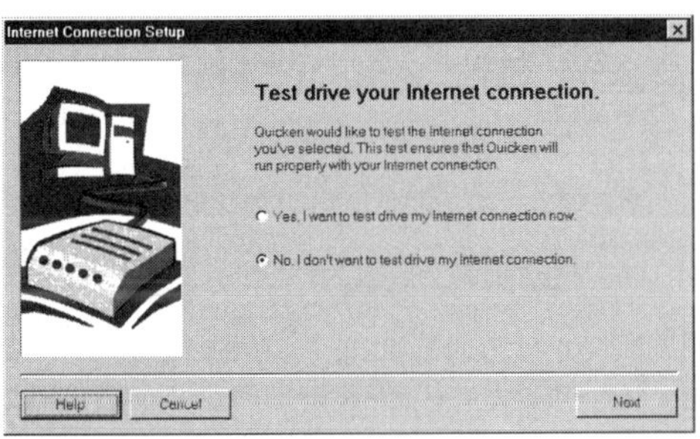

Figure 4.6 *You can test the connection, if you wish.*

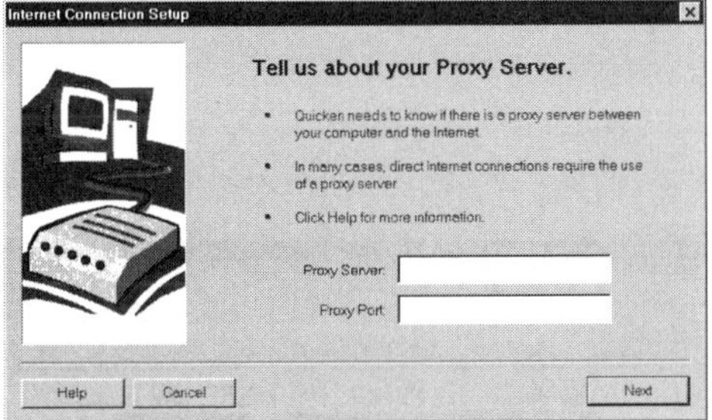

Figure 4.7 *If your Internet work is done from behind a firewall, enter proxy information in this dialog box.*

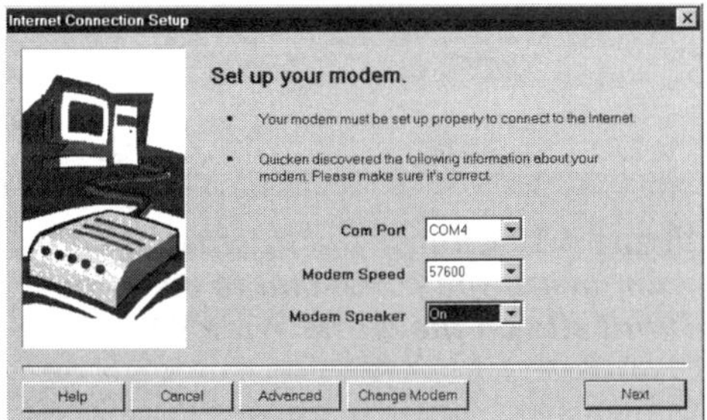

Figure 4.8 *After testing your modem, this dialog box lists its port and speed.*

Web. During the general installation procedure, Quicken installs a special edition of Netscape Navigator that you can use.

4. *Optional:* The next dialog box offers the opportunity to test the Internet connection, as shown in **Figure 4.6**. Click Yes to test; click No if you are sure that the connection will work.

5. The final dialog box appears, informing you that the setup is complete. Click Done.

Using a Direct Connection

If you are directly connected to the Internet over a local area network (LAN), the installation procedure jumps to Step 3 (choosing a browser).

Next, the dialog box in **Figure 4.7** appears. Contact your network administrator to learn whether proxies are used to connect to different parts of the Internet and, if so, the correct information to enter in the dialog box. The setup continues with Step 4.

Using a Free Account

If you don't have an Internet account, you can use the free, limited-access account from Intuit. The initial dialog boxes explain how to set up the account and ask for your name and address.

Next, Quicken checks for a connected modem and then tests its capabilities (see **Figure 4.8**). Make any necessary changes and click Next.

Select a phone number to use when connecting to the free account and then choose a browser.

✔ Tips

- If you already have a working Internet connection, you can safely skip the test in Step 4.
- If you connect to the Internet through an information service (America Online or CompuServe, for example), be sure to read Help. There are some limitations of which you should be aware, as shown in **Figure 4.9**. (Search Help for the name of your information service.)
- If you choose the free, limited-access account, you may only be allowed to use Netscape. Other installed browsers may not be listed.
- When you choose the free account, a new command is added to the Quicken Live Setup submenu. Choose Internet Account Administration to learn how to switch from a free account to a full-access Internet account (see **Figure 4.10**).
- To change your account setup or connection method, choose the Internet Connection Setup command again.
- If you are already on-line when Quicken Live is launched, the dialing phase is skipped and you stay on-line after Quicken has done its work. If Quicken makes the Internet connection, on the other hand, it automatically disconnects at the end of the session. (Note that this may not be true if you connect through an information service.)

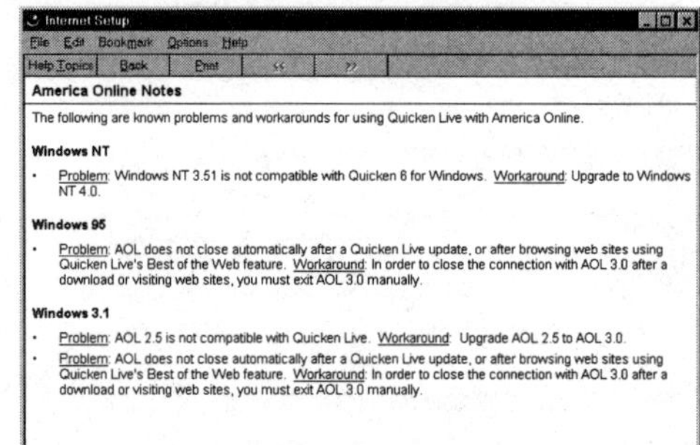

Figure 4.9 *Quicken Help contains trouble-shooting tips for America Online and most other information services.*

Figure 4.10 *Choose the Internet Account Administration command to visit this Intuit site on the World Wide Web.*

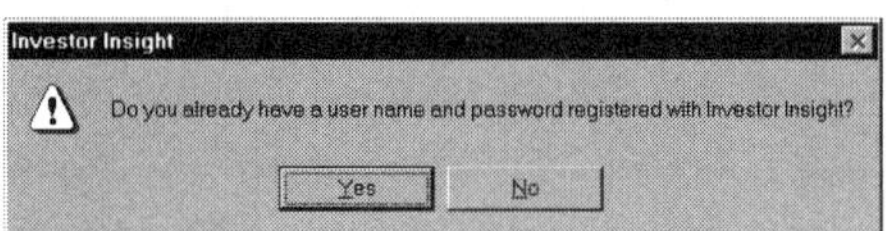

Figure 4.11 *Click No to begin your trial subscription to Investor Insight.*

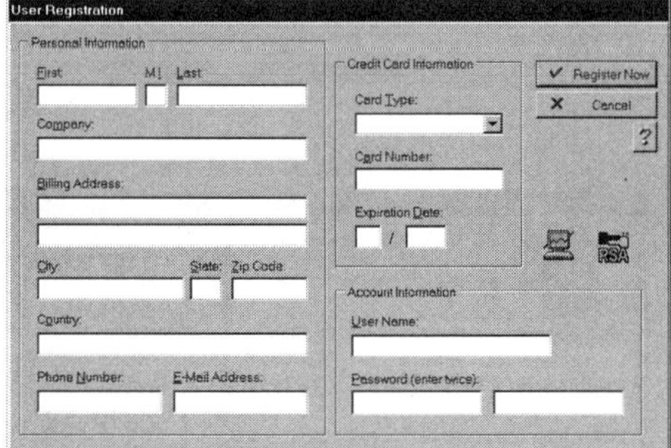

Figure 4.12 *Enter billing information, including a user I.D. and password of your choice.*

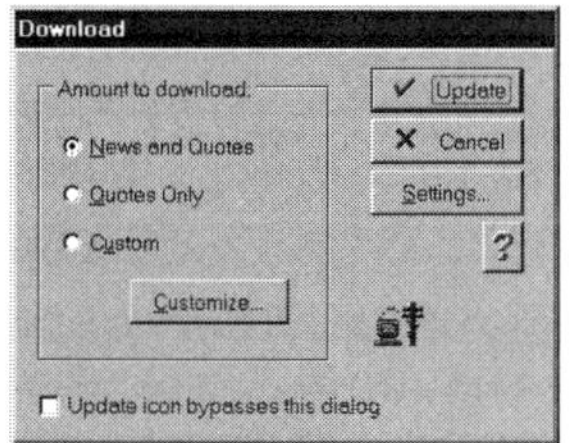

Figure 4.13 *Select the kinds of data that you want to download.*

Investor Insight Setup

Quicken Deluxe includes a 30-day free trial of Investor Insight, a service from which you can download quotes, historical data, company reports, and financial news.

To sign up for Investor Insight:

1. Launch Investor Insight and click the Update button in the iconbar. The dialog box shown in **Figure 4.11** appears.
2. Click No (indicating that you are not currently registered).
3. Review the Subscription Agreement and click Accept. The User Registration dialog box appears (see **Figure 4.12**).
4. Complete the form and click Register Now. The Download dialog box appears (see **Figure 4.13**).
5. *Optional:* Click the Settings button to verify that the on-line connection method is correct.
6. To complete your first download, click the Update button in the Download dialog box (refer to **Figure 4.13**).

Mutual Fund Finder Setup

You only need to go on-line in Mutual Fund Finder to download quarterly updates for the mutual fund database. (There is a fee for updates.) Although you can connect to the Quicken Financial Network via Mutual Fund Finder, you can also connect through Quicken Live. A separate on-line setup is not required for Mutual Fund Finder; setting up the connection for Quicken Live is sufficient.

On-Line Banking and Bill Paying Setup

If you set up an on-line banking account with your financial institution and pay any required fees, you can manage your accounts on-line—downloading transactions and balances, comparing the downloaded transactions to the ones recorded in Quicken, and transferring money between accounts.

At this writing, only 41 U.S. banks offer on-line banking. To see if your bank is among them, choose Features ⇨ Online ⇨ Online Banking Setup ⇨ Financial Institutions (see **Figure 4.14**). To make sure that the list is current, click the Update List button.

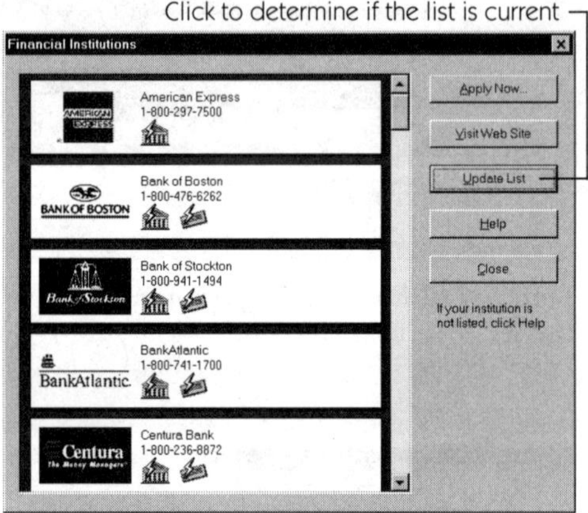

Figure 4.14 *This dialog box lists the financial institutions that offer on-line banking.*

With on-line bill paying, you can use Quicken to automatically pay certain bills each month and inquire about payments. Unlike on-line banking, this service is available to all Quicken users, regardless of where they bank. If your bank does not offer on-line bill paying, it can be handled through Intuit Services Corporation.

Preparing for on-line banking and/or bill paying is a three-step process. First, contact your financial institution to learn about their available services and fees. Second, submit an application to Intuit Services Corporation. Wait to receive the account information and a PIN (Personal Identification Number). Third, configure Quicken so it knows about your on-line account(s).

To set up on-line banking/bill paying:

1. Choose Features ⇨ Online ⇨ Online Banking Setup ⇨ Getting Started, or click the Online icon in the activity bar and choose Get

Figure 4.15 *The Get Started dialog box walks you through the on-line banking and bill paying setup process.*

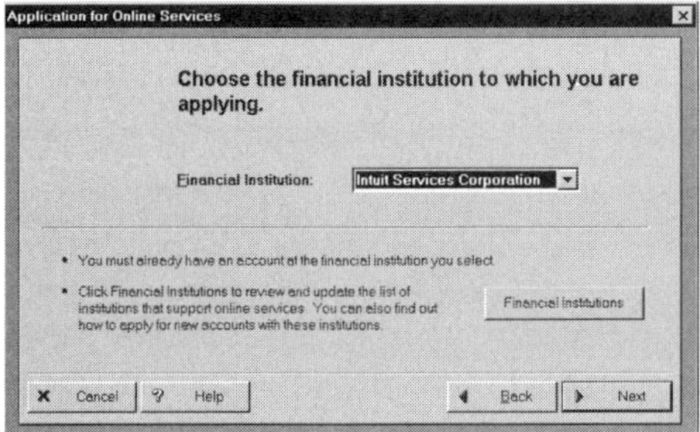

Figure 4.16 *If your bank doesn't offer on-line bill paying, choose Intuit Services Corporation as the financial institution.*

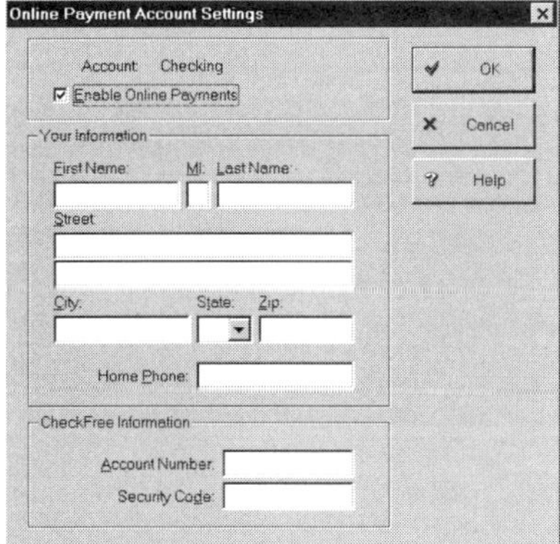

Figure 4.17 *To use the selected account with CheckFree, check the box to Enable Online Payments and enter the requested information.*

Started with Online Banking & Investment. The dialog box shown in **Figure 4.15** appears.

2. Click Apply for Online Services. Complete the series of dialog boxes and submit the data via modem.
3. After you receive your account information and PIN in the mail, run Quicken and choose Features ⇨ Online ⇨ Online Banking Setup ⇨ Getting Started.
4. Click Set Up Online Services and complete the series of dialog boxes that is presented.

✔ Tips

- If your bank isn't among the listed financial institutions, you can get on-line bill paying through Intuit Services Corporation, as shown in **Figure 4.16**.
- If you used CheckFree as your bill-paying service in a previous version of Quicken, you can continue do so in this version. (New users, on the other hand, should use the on-line payment feature.)

  To enable CheckFree for one or more accounts, choose Features ⇨ Online ⇨ CheckFree ⇨ Set Up Account (see **Figure 4.17**). Then choose Features ⇨ Online ⇨ CheckFree ⇨ Set Up Modem.

Part II: Entering and Editing Transactions

5

Using the Account Registers

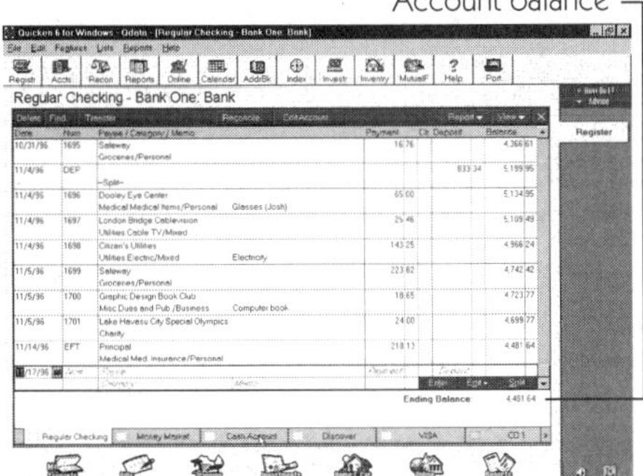

Figure 5.1 *A Quicken account register looks like a checkbook register.*

About Registers

Every account has its own *register* in which you record transactions, such as checks, ATM withdrawals, deposits, and transfers between accounts. A checking account register is shown in **Figure 5.1**.

Because the register is like a checkbook register, you'll immediately understand most parts of the register window. Each transaction is recorded on a separate line. As you add new transactions, the register automatically updates the account balance in the bottom-right corner of the register window.

Opening a Register

Whether you want to add new transactions for an account or edit existing ones, you must first open the register window for the account. Because working with registers is a common Quicken activity, there are many ways to open a register.

To open a register:

- Click the Register button in the iconbar.
- Choose Features ⇨ Banking ⇨ Use Register (or press Ctrl R). The register that is currently selected in the Account List opens.
- Choose Use My Register from the My Accounts icon on the activity bar (see **Figure 5.2**).

Figure 5.2 *To quickly open a register window, choose Use My Register from the My Accounts pop-up menu.*

- You can open any register by choosing its account from the Account List (see **Figure 5.3**). Open the Account List by choosing Account from the Lists menu, pressing Ctrl A, clicking the Accounts button in the iconbar, or clicking My Accounts in the activity bar and choosing View All of My Accounts.

  To open an account register, you can either double-click the account name or select the account and click the Open button.

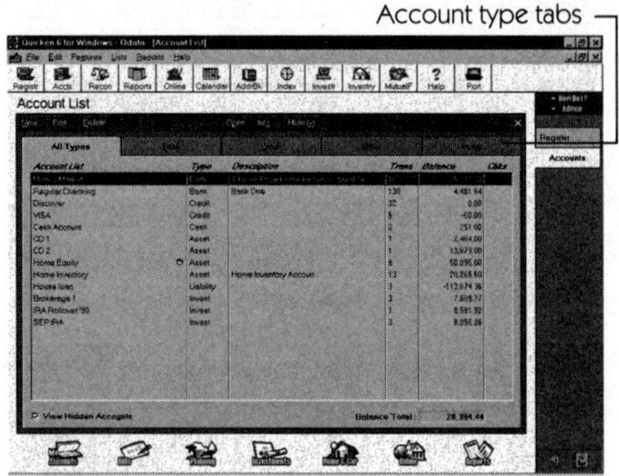

Figure 5.3 *The Account List shows the names and balances of all your Quicken accounts. To restrict the account list to only those of a particular type, click a tab at the top of the window.*

Switching to Another Register

At the bottom of the register window is a list of all account registers. To switch to another register, click its tab. If the register you want to work with is not visible, click an arrow on the left or right side of the account tab list to bring the account name into view.

Sorting a Register

By default, each register lists its transactions in date order. If two or more transactions share the same date, they are listed in order of their amounts.

Although this is satisfactory for normal use, there are some instances when it can be beneficial to change the sort order for a register. If you sort by check number, for example, all like types of transactions are grouped together. This makes it simple to find all deposits and ATM withdrawals.

To change the order of a register, click the View button and make a selection from the menu that appears, as shown in **Figure 5.4**.

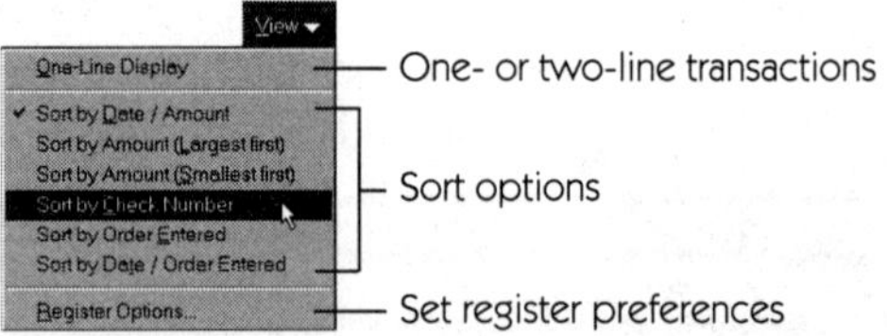

Figure 5.4 *You can use the View menu to set a sort order for a register, switch between a two-line and one-line display, and set register preferences.*

Entering Transactions

You can enter any kind of transaction into an account register. Checks that you intend to print can be entered in the Write Checks window, but they can also be entered directly into a register.

As you record a transaction, you can type the entries, choose them from lists, press keyboard shortcuts, or combine these actions. Press Tab to move from field to field within a transaction.

To enter a new transaction:

1. Open the account register.
2. At the bottom of the register is a blank record that you use to enter all new transactions. Click it to make it the active transaction. (To jump directly to the blank transaction, choose Edit ⇨ Transaction ⇨ New or press Ctrl N.)
3. Enter a date for the transaction.

   You can type a date, moving from section to section by pressing → or ←. You can also click the icon in the Date field and choose the date from the calendar that appears (see **Figure 5.5**).
4. Use the Num field to record a transaction number or type. Use numbers where there is a real-world counterpart, such as a check number. Otherwise, select a code to indicate a transaction type.

   To pick a code (see **Figure 5.6**), you can type its first letter, click it with the mouse, or press the arrow keys. The standard codes are Next Check Num (the number of the next check in sequence), ATM

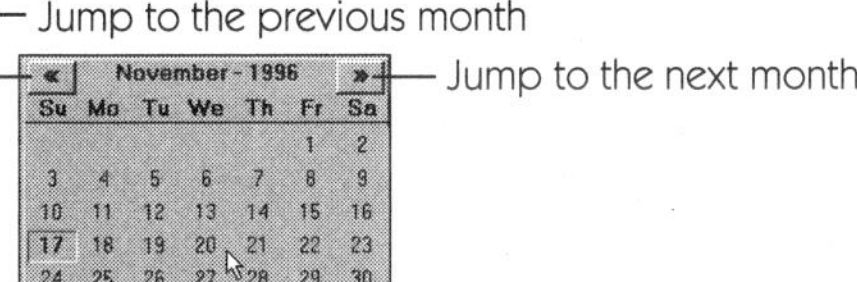

Figure 5.5 *Choose a date by clicking it. You can move a month forward or backward by clicking an arrow button.*

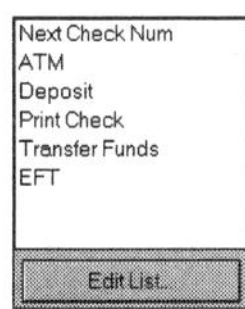

Figure 5.6 *Select a transaction code from the list attached to the Num field.*

(automated teller withdrawal), Deposit, Print Check (a check to be printed with Quicken), Transfer Funds (transfer funds between your accounts), and EFT (electronic funds transfer).

5. In the Payee field, type the name of the payee or who the money was received from (in the case of a deposit). As you type, Quicken tries to complete the entry for you by selecting a name from the list of memorized transactions, as shown in **Figure 5.7**. If an appropriate transaction isn't found, simply continue typing.

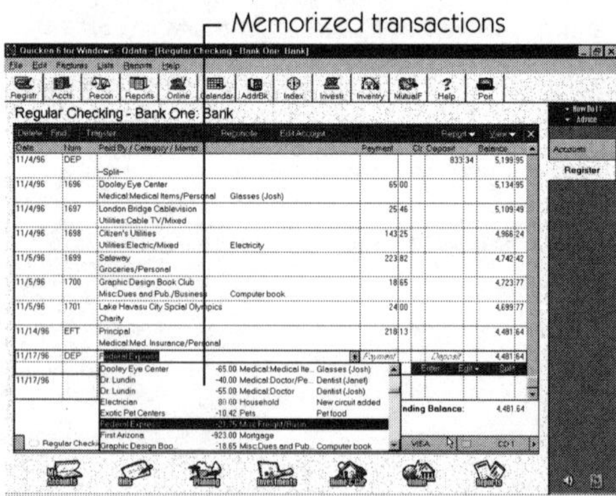

Figure 5.7 *Quicken attempts to fill in the Payee and Payment/Deposit fields with data from the most recent transaction for that person or company.*

6. Enter the transaction amount in the Payment or Deposit field, as appropriate.

7. Select a category for the transaction from the pop-up list, as shown in **Figure 5.8**. You can click the category name or type its first letter or two.

   If you also want to assign a *class* to the transaction, type a / after the category name, and then type the first letter or two of the class name. (To learn about classes, see Chapter 3.)

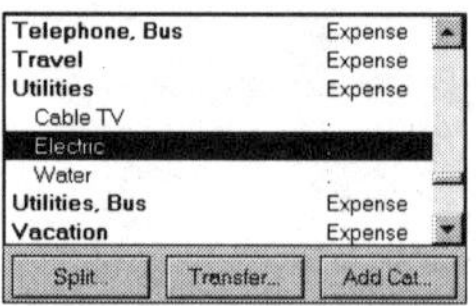

Figure 5.8 *Assign a category to each transaction by selecting it from this pop-up list.*

8. *Optional:* You can enter a note—such as a description of a purchased item—in the Memo field.

9. To record the transaction, click the Enter button or press Return. If necessary, Quicken sorts the transaction list to place the new entry in the proper position.

A few types of transactions require special handling, as described in the following sections.

Postdated Transactions

Occasionally, you may write checks that are dated in the future. Quicken allows such postdated transactions.

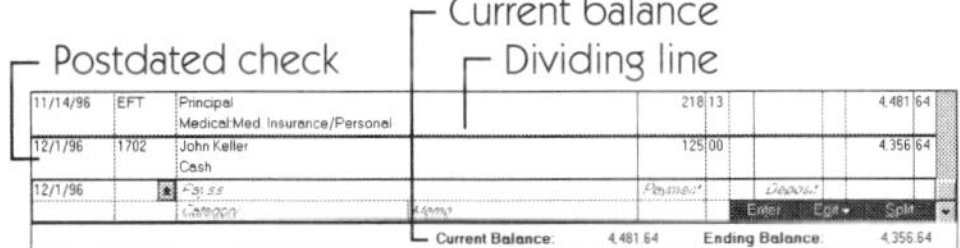

Figure 5.9 *Postdated transactions are separated from the others by a thick line.*

Other than entering a future date, nothing special is required to create a postdated transaction. However, there are two ways in which such transactions are distinguished from the others (see **Figure 5.9**). First, the earliest postdated transaction is marked with a thick colored bar. Second, *two* account balances are shown. Current Balance doesn't include postdated transactions; Ending Balance does include these transactions. When the date of a postdated transaction passes, it becomes a normal transaction.

Split Transactions

Some transactions can be allocated to several categories rather than just one. For example, you might buy clothing and office supplies at a department store. Or your paycheck can be divided among your salary and the taxes that have been withheld. To allocate a transaction to multiple categories, you create a *split transaction*.

Figure 5.10 *Enter and edit split transactions in the Split Transaction Window. To assist you, the window keeps track of the unallocated balance.*

To create a split transaction:

1. After entering all data for a transaction *except its category,* click the Split button at the right end of the transaction or click Split in the Category pop-up window. The Split Transaction window appears (see **Figure 5.10**).
2. You use the numbered lines to enter the distinct categories that comprise the total transaction. In each line, choose a category from the pop-up list, enter an optional

memo, and type an amount for the category. As you complete each line, Quicken calculates the remaining (unallocated) amount.

3. When you are done, click Finished.
4. Complete and save the transaction.

Transfers Between Accounts

If you are moving money directly between two accounts (savings and checking, for example), choose Transfer Funds in the Num field, select the account you are transferring to or from in the Category field (see **Figure 5.11**), and enter the amount in the Payment or Deposit field, as appropriate. The change is reflected in both accounts.

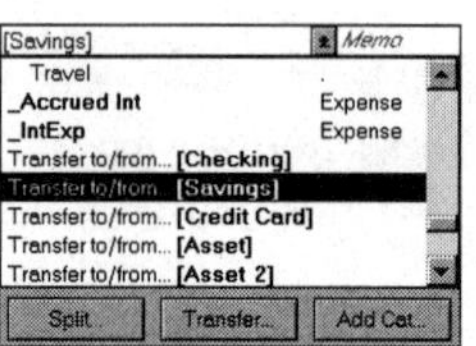

Figure 5.11 *One common type of transfer is that of moving funds between savings and checking accounts.*

Another way to record a transfer is to click the Transfer button. The Transfer dialog box appears (see **Figure 5.12**). Fill in the blanks, and then click OK.

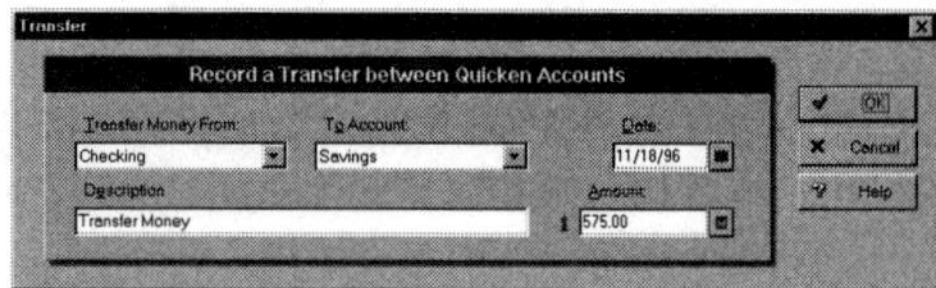

Figure 5.12 *To avoid possible confusion, you may find it easier to use the Transfer dialog box to record your transfers.*

If you are writing a check to move funds between accounts, you can also record it as two separate transactions: a check from your checking account and a deposit to your savings account, for instance.

Do not confuse account transfers with *electronic funds transfers* (EFT). The latter refers to a direct transfer between your and someone else's account. For example, you may have an insurance payment that is automatically withdrawn each month and transferred to the insurance company's account. Similarly, you may have made arrangements to have your salary deposited directly into your checking account. In both of these cases, enter EFT in the Num field.

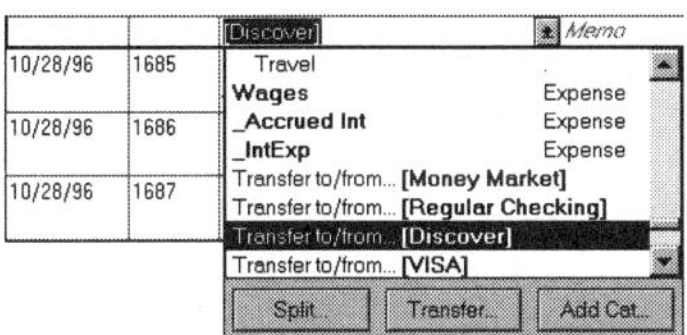

Figure 5.13 *To define a transfer, choose a Transfer to/from category.*

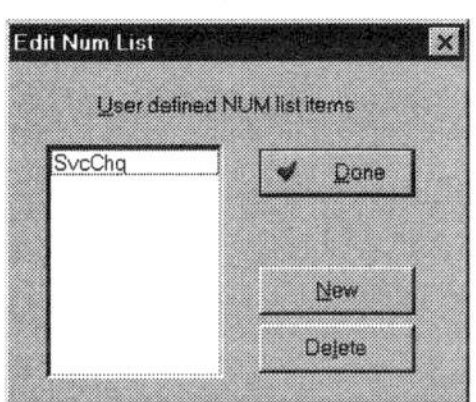

Figure 5.14 *You can add new entries to the Num field's pop-up list.*

Figure 5.15 *This simple calculator is great for totaling multiple-item deposits. As you enter additional numbers, the total appears in the field.*

Entering a Credit Card Payment

To make a credit card payment, enter a normal transaction in the checking account register. In the Category field, select the name of the credit card, such as Transfer to/from... [Discover], as shown in **Figure 5.13**. The amount is deducted from your checkbook, as well as from the credit card balance.

✔ Tips

- You can increase or decrease a date or check number by pressing [+] or [-].
- To quickly enter special dates, you can press a letter key. Press [T] for today's date, [M] for the first day of the current month, [H] for the last day of the month, [Y] for the first day of the current year, or [R] for the last day of the year. See Appendix A for other keyboard shortcuts you can use in a register window.
- You can change the Num field's pop-up list. You may note, for example, that there are no codes for withdrawals or bank service charges. To modify the list, click in any Num field and then click the Edit List button (see **Figure 5.14**).
- If you haven't added up all the items in a deposit, you can use the pop-up calculator beside the Deposit field (see **Figure 5.15**).
- When creating a split transaction, you can also enter *percentages* (rather than dollar amounts).
- To enter a paycheck as a split transaction, begin by entering the total (before deductions) as Salary. Then enter each deduction on a separate line as a negative amount.

Modifying Transactions

Quicken has many commands and procedures to help you modify transactions. Some mimic the activities that you routinely perform in your checkbook (voiding a check, for example); others are difficult or impossible to do with a paper check register or passbook.

These options include the following:

- Change the date, number, type, amount, category, or any other component of a transaction.
- Void or delete transactions.
- Reuse a transaction by copying and pasting.
- Search for transactions that match specific criteria.

Editing Transactions

You can edit any transaction. Click anywhere within the transaction, make the necessary changes, and then click Enter or press Return to record the changes.

Voiding or Deleting Transactions

To void a transaction, click anywhere within the transaction and choose Edit ⇨ Transaction ⇨ Void Transaction, choose Void Transaction from the Edit button's pop-up menu, or press Ctrl V.

To delete a transaction, click any field within the transaction, click the Delete button, and click Yes to confirm the deletion (see **Figure 5.16**).

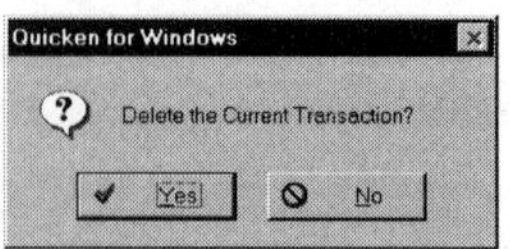

Figure 5.16 *You must confirm all transaction deletions.*

Reusing a Transaction

If you have several transactions that are very similar (two checks to the same phone company, for example), you can copy the initial transaction, paste it into the register, and then edit the copy. Quicken provides a special Copy command for this procedure that enables you to copy the entire contents of a transaction rather than just one field.

To copy a transaction, click anywhere within the transaction, and choose Edit ⇨ Transaction ⇨ Copy. To paste the transaction as a new record, click the blank transaction at the bottom of the register, and choose Edit ⇨ Transaction ⇨ Paste.

Searching for Transactions

When you want to quickly find a particular transaction or several that share something in common (such as all checks to Ace Hardware), you can use the Find command.

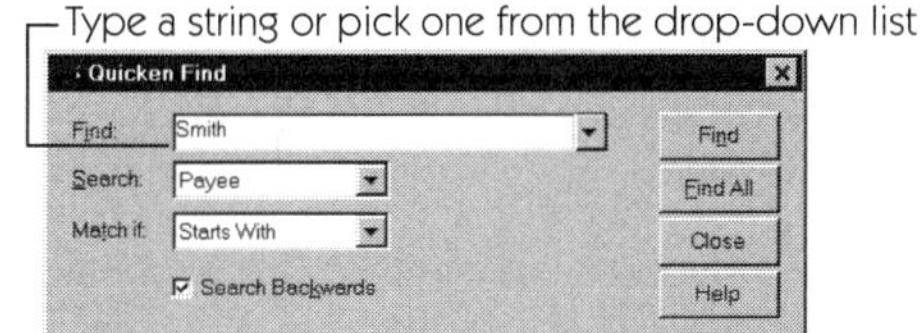

Figure 5.17 *To create a find request, enter a search string, the field to search, and the match conditions.*

To find transactions:

1. Click the Find button, choose Edit ⇨ Find & Replace ⇨ Find, or press Ctrl F. The Quicken Find dialog box appears (see **Figure 5.17**).
2. Type and/or choose search criteria.
3. To find individual matching transactions within the current account, click the Find button. The first match (if there is one) is selected. To see additional matches, click Find again. When you are done, dismiss the dialog box by clicking the Close button.

   or

3. To find all occurrences in all accounts, click Find All. A list of all matching transactions appears (see **Figure 5.18**). To jump to a found transaction, double-click it.

Figure 5.18 *After performing a Find All, the matching transactions are displayed in a Quicken Find List.*

✔ **Tips**

- Most editing procedures also can be performed by choosing commands from the Edit menu (see **Figure 5.19**), from the Edit button's menu (see **Figure 5.20**), or from the menu that appears when you right-click in a transaction field (see **Figure 5.21**).
- You may discover that you have assigned the wrong category to several transactions (classifying your monthly health insurance premiums as Insurance rather than as Medical Insurance, for instance).

  To simultaneously correct these transactions, choose Edit ⇨ Find & Replace ⇨ Recategorize. The Recategorize dialog box appears, as shown in **Figure 5.22**. Choose a Search Category from the drop-down list, click the Find All button, click all transactions that you want to recategorize, choose a Replace With category from the drop-down list, and then click Replace.

Memorizing Transactions

By default, Quicken remembers every transaction and records it in the Memorized Transaction List (see **Figure 5.23**). Memorized transactions can be used as the basis for new transactions in the account registers or the Financial Calendar. For example, if you have already written one check to a grocery store, when you next do business with the store, Quicken can recall the previous transaction. In many cases, all you have to do is edit the amount.

Normally, you will want to take full advantage of Quicken's memorization

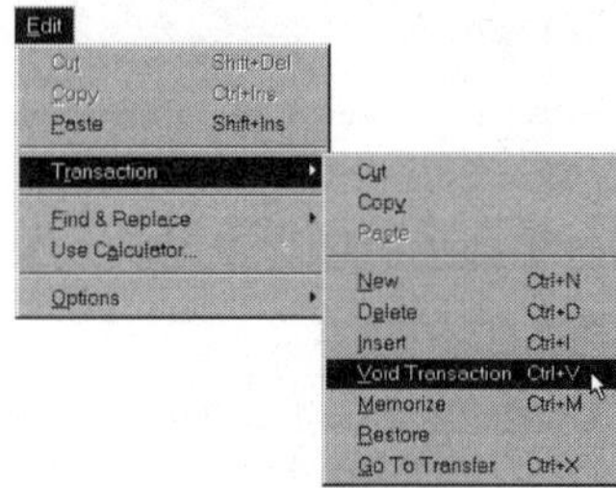

Figure 5.19 *Basic editing commands and their keyboard shortcuts can be found in the Transaction submenu of the Edit menu.*

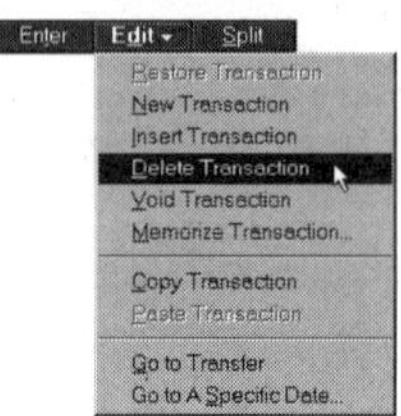

Figure 5.20 *You can also choose general transaction commands from the Edit button's menu.*

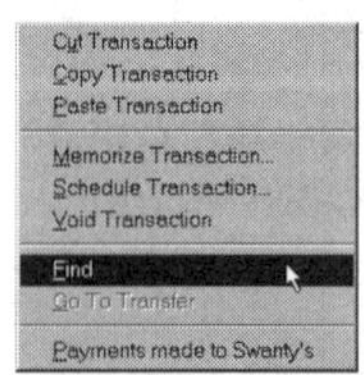

Figure 5.21 *This menu appears when you right-click a transaction field.*

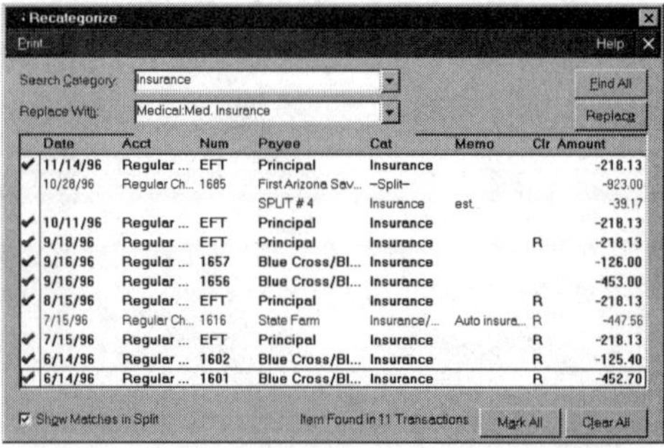

Figure 5.22 *You can simultaneously change the category for several records.*

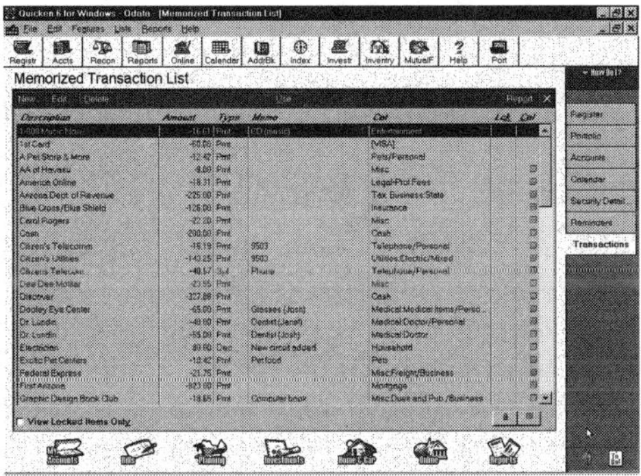

Figure 5.23 *The Memorized Transaction List records the most recent transaction to each payee.*

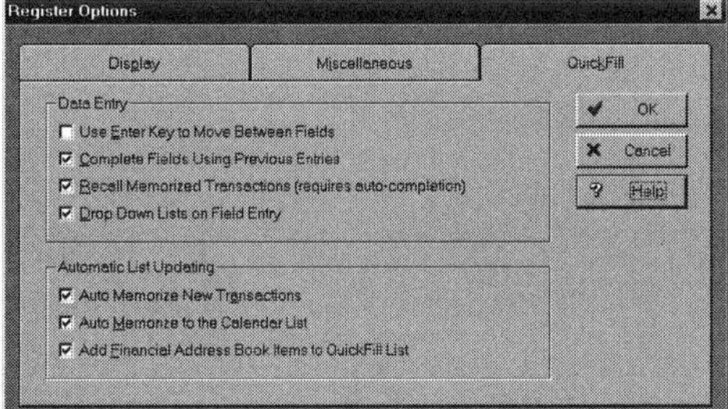

Figure 5.24 *Set memorization options in the QuickFill section of the Register Options dialog box.*

capabilities, enabling you to eliminate as much unnecessary data entry as you can. If you set Register Options to memorize transactions, you make them instantly available to you as drop-down lists in the Payee field of account registers and in the Financial Calendar.

To set memorization options:

1. Choose Edit ⇨ Options ⇨ Register. The Register Options dialog box appears (see **Figure 5.24**).
2. Click the QuickFill tab at the top of the dialog box.
3. To enable memorization, check the option to Auto Memorize New Transactions.
4. To automatically add new memorized transactions to the scrolling list in the Financial Calendar, check the Auto Memorize to the Calendar List option.
5. To use memorized transactions in the Payee field in account registers, check the options to Recall Memorized Transactions and Complete Fields Using Previous Entries.
6. Click OK to save the changes.

You can also use the Memorized Transaction List window to edit, delete, and lock memorized transactions, and to manually create new ones.

To edit a memorized transaction:

1. Choose Memorized Transaction from the Lists menu or press Ctrl T. The Memorized Transaction List window appears, as shown previously in **Figure 5.23**.
2. Select a transaction to edit and click the Edit button. The Edit

Memorized Transaction dialog box appears (see **Figure 5.25**).

3. Make the required changes and click OK. (Note that you can edit or set an address for a transaction only if its type is Print Check.)

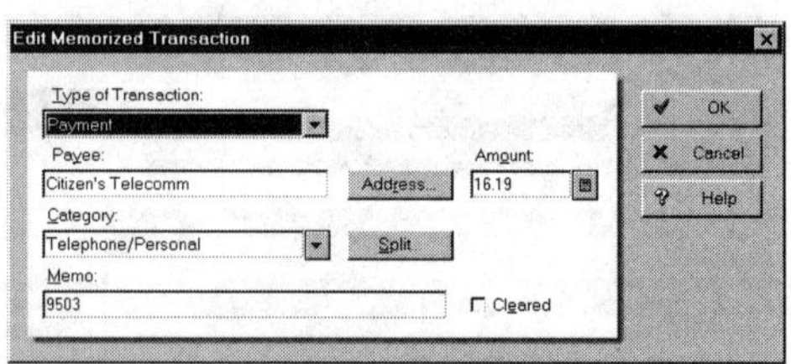

Figure 5.25 *When you open the Edit Memorized Transaction dialog box, all the data for the selected transaction is displayed. You can change any of the fields, as necessary.*

To remove a transaction from the Memorized Transactions List, select it, click the Delete button at the top of the window, and click OK in the confirmation dialog box that appears.

By default, all memorized transactions are available for inclusion in the list that appears in the Financial Calendar. However, you may elect to eliminate some transactions from that list.

To add or remove transactions from the list in the Financial Calendar:

1. Choose Memorized Transaction from the Lists menu or press Ctrl T. The Memorized Transaction List window appears, as shown previously in **Figure 5.23**.
2. Select a transaction.
3. Click once in the Cal column to add or remove the icon. When the icon is present, the transaction appears in the scrolling list in the Financial Calendar window.

You may also want to lock some memorized transactions by clicking in the Lock column. Locking a transaction prevents the amount from being overwritten by any newer transaction to the same payee.

To manually create a new memorized transaction, click the New button and fill in the information requested in the Create Memorized Transaction dialog box (see **Figure 5.26**).

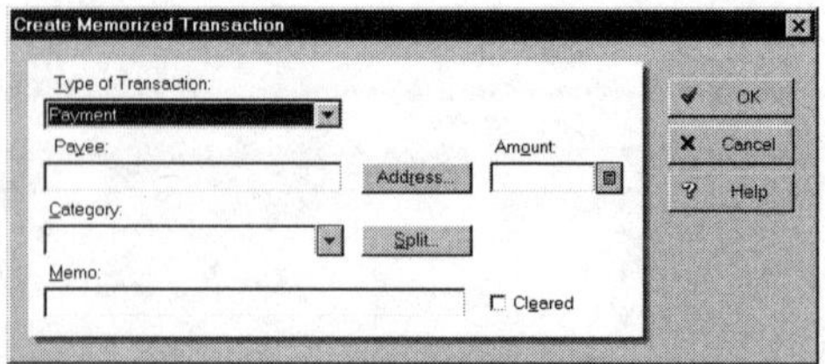

Figure 5.26 *You can use the Create Memorized Transaction dialog box to manually create a new memorized transaction.*

6 Writing Checks

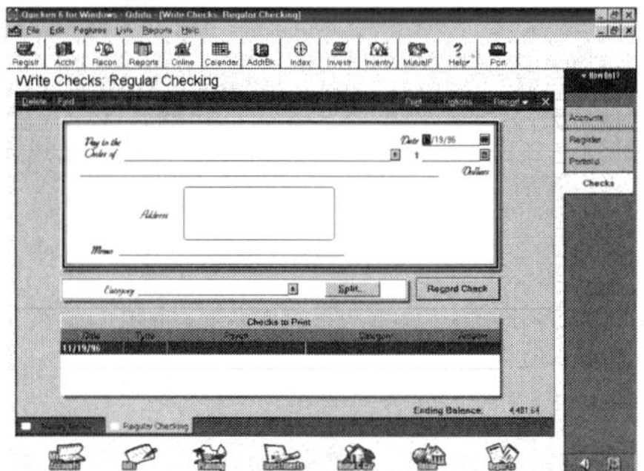

Figure 6.1 *The Write Checks window shows a blank check. It does not display a check number because Quicken prints on pre-numbered checks.*

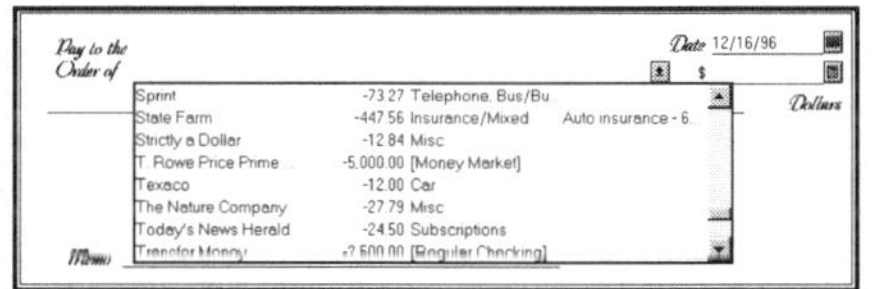

Figure 6.2 *You can select a payee and related information from this drop-down list of memorized transactions.*

About Writing Checks

Checks that you intend to print with Quicken are created in the Write Checks window (see **Figure 6.1**). You record handwritten checks in your checking or money market account register.

To write a check (for printing):

1. Open the Write Checks window. You can do this by choosing Features ⇨ Paying Bills ⇨ Write Checks, pressing Ctrl W, or clicking the Bills icon on the activity bar and choosing Write a Check to Print.
2. All accounts with check-writing privileges are listed at the bottom of the window. Click a tab to pick an account.
3. If necessary, change the date. By default, today's date is used—the day on which the check is entered in Quicken.
4. Type the name of the payee or choose it from the drop-down list of memorized transactions, as shown in **Figure 6.2**. As you type, Quicken attempts to select the correct payee for you.
5. Enter an amount for the check. Quicken translates the amount to a text string and enters it for you on the next line.
6. *Optional:* Enter a mailing address in the Address text box. To insert the payee's name into the address, type a ' on the first line.

7. *Optional:* Enter a memo that will appear on the check, such as an account number or the name of the item being purchased.
8. Select a category for the check. Use the same procedures that you use when working in a register. To record a split transaction, click the Split button.
9. Click Record Check. The check is recorded in the account register and is listed in the Checks to Print area of the Write Checks window (see **Figure 6.3**). Until you actually print the checks, they accumulate in this window. When these transactions are viewed in the register, the word Print is listed in the Num field.

For information on printing checks, see Chapter 18.

✔ Tips

- If a check to be printed does not need an address, you can create the check in the account register. Select the Print Check option in the Num field.

- Any address entered as part of a check is copied to the Financial Address Book.
- The contents of the memo field may be visible through the envelope window. To add a memo that cannot be seen, choose Edit ⇨ Options ⇨ Write Checks, and then check the option to Allow Entry of Extra Message on Check (see **Figure 6.4**).
- The Write Checks window provides other pop-up devices that you may find useful (see **Figure 6.5**).

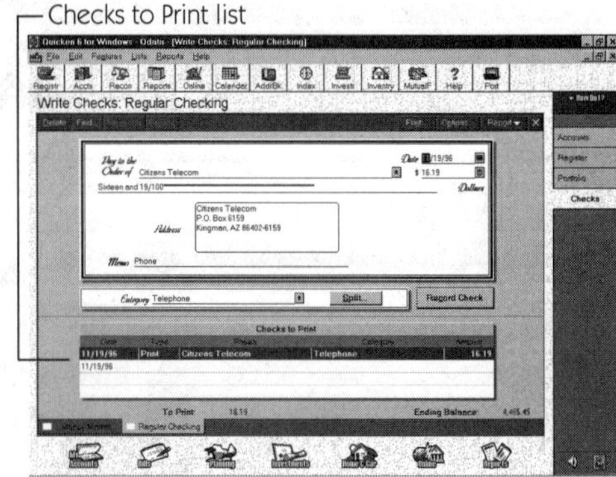

Figure 6.3 *Checks that are waiting to be printed are listed at the bottom of the Write Checks window.*

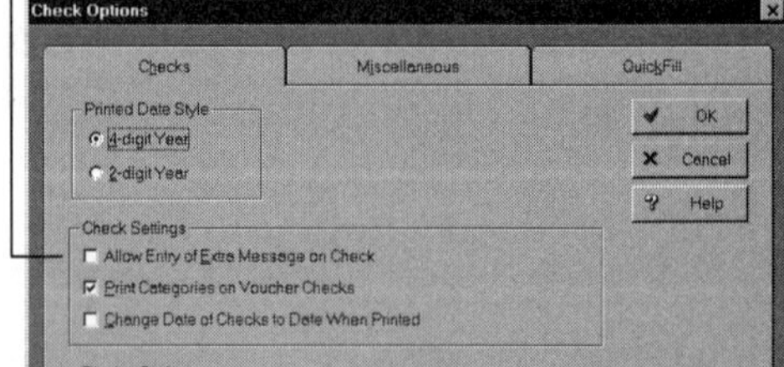

Figure 6.4 *You set preferences for writing checks in the Check Options dialog box.*

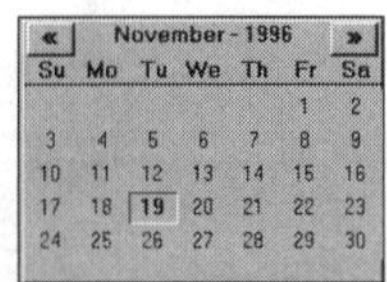

Figure 6.5 *The Date and Amount fields both contain pop-up utilities. You can select a date from the calendar (left) or total items for the check with the calculator (right).*

Editing and Deleting Checks

Until it has been printed, you can edit or delete any check—regardless of whether it was created in the Write Checks window or in a register.

Editing a Check

To edit a check in the Write Checks window, select it in the list at the bottom of the window, make the changes, and then click Record Check. To edit the check in the register, use normal editing procedures, and click Enter or press [Return] to save the changes.

Deleting a Check

To delete a check in the Write Checks window, select it in the list at the bottom of the window and choose Edit ⇨ Transaction ⇨ Delete, click the Delete button, or press [Ctrl][D]. To delete a check in a register, select it and then follow any of the same procedures.

To confirm the deletion, answer Yes to the prompt that appears (see **Figure 6.6**).

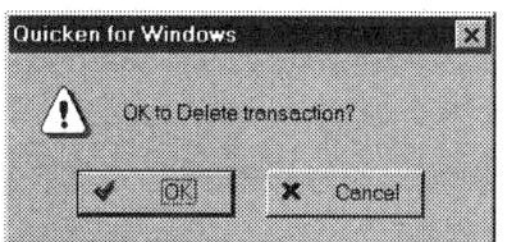

Figure 6.6 *You must confirm the deletion of a check.*

Tip

- If you want to *void* a previously issued check, you must do so in the account register. For assistance, see "Voiding or Deleting a Transaction" in Chapter 5.

7 Financial Calendar

Figure 7.1 *The Financial Calendar is patterned after a desk calendar. Each day lists transactions that were paid or are due.*

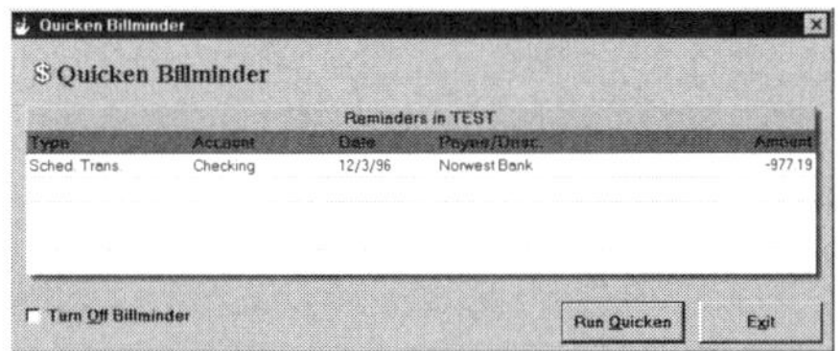

Figure 7.2 *When enabled, Billminder automatically pops up at the start of each Windows session in which bills are pending or due. You can launch Quicken by clicking Run Quicken.*

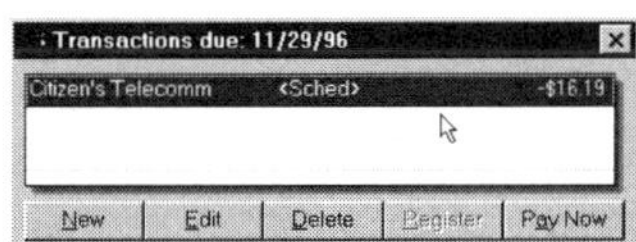

Figure 7.3 *This dialog box shows that the phone bill is due.*

About the Financial Calendar

The Financial Calendar (see **Figure 7.1**) is used to schedule one-time and recurring transactions and to create notes for appointments, special occasions, and the like.

Scheduled transactions can be set to occur automatically (entering a transaction for your cable bill on the 12th of each month, for example). Each time that day of the month occurs, the transaction is recorded in the appropriate register. If the amount of a bill varies, you can either be prompted before it is recorded or you can edit the automatically generated transaction.

If you prefer to pay bills in batches (a real convenience when printing checks), you can define transaction groups and pay everyone in the group at the same time. You can create up to 12 transaction groups.

There are three ways that Quicken can notify you of upcoming bills:

- Billminder (see **Figure 7.2**) can inform you of upcoming transactions when you start Windows.
- If you have instructed Quicken to prompt before entering a scheduled transaction, the Scheduled Transactions Due window displays all transactions that are now due (see **Figure 7.3**).
- The Reminders window (see **Figure 7.4**) lists all upcoming transactions.

To open the Financial Calendar, you can do any of the following:

- Choose Features ⇨ Paying Bills ⇨ Financial Calendar.
- Click the Calendar icon in the top iconbar.
- Click the Bills icon in the activity bar and then choose Schedule a Future Payment.

When the calendar is open, you can double-click any date to view the details of the transactions that were recorded on or are scheduled for that date. To move a month at a time in either direction, click the Prev Month or Next Month buttons at the top of the window. To go directly to a specific date, click Go To Date and enter a date in the dialog box that appears (see **Figure 7.5**).

✔ Tips

- If you prefer using the dialog box-based transactions of the Financial Calendar to using the registers, you can create all transactions in the Financial Calendar.
- Although most scheduled transactions are payments (utility bills, for example), you can also schedule *deposits*. A scheduled deposit can remind you to go to the bank every week to deposit your paycheck. Or if you have a forced savings plan, you can create a scheduled transaction in which you deposit a set amount into a savings account or money market fund.
- You can use [+] and [-] keys to move one day forward or backward in the Go To Date dialog box.

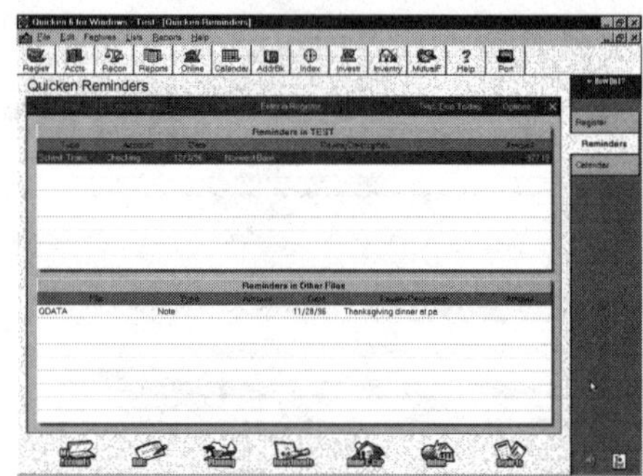

Figure 7.4 *The Reminders window shows all scheduled transactions and notes for all defined Quicken files. (In this example, there are two Quicken data files.)*

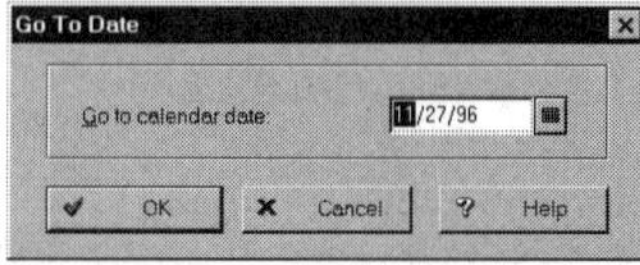

Figure 7.5 *The fastest way to view any date several months in the future or the past is to enter it in the Go To Date dialog box.*

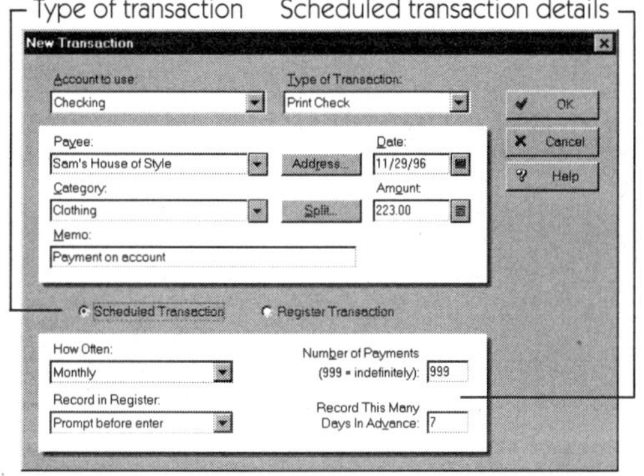

Figure 7.6 *The radio button selected in the center of the New Transaction dialog box determines whether this is a one-time or a recurring transaction.*

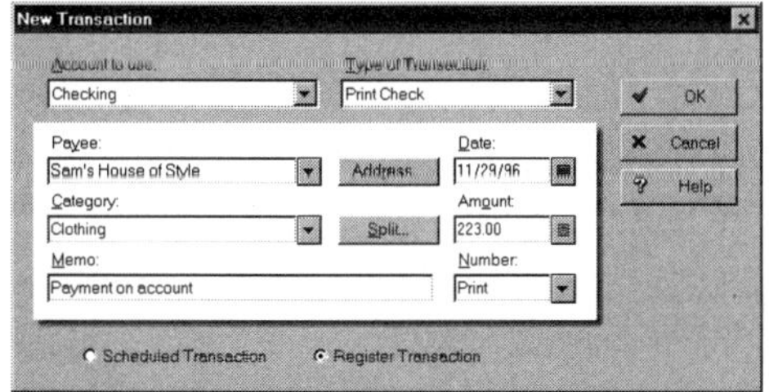

Figure 7.7 *When creating a one-time (or register) transaction, the bottom half of the dialog box automatically disappears.*

Creating Transactions

You can create one-time (register) transactions or recurring (scheduled) transactions in the Financial Calendar. The procedures differ little.

To schedule a transaction:

1. If an example of the transaction can be found in the list of memorized transactions to the right of the calendar, drag the transaction onto the date when it will next occur.

   or

1. If the transaction is not in the list, drag the item marked “Use this for a NEW one!” onto the date when the transaction will next occur.

   The New Transaction dialog box appears (see **Figure 7.6**). If the dragged item was a memorized transaction, the fields of the dialog box are filled in with details from the original transaction. If the NEW item was dragged onto the date, the transaction details are blank.

2. In the top part of the dialog box, fill in the standard information for the transaction. If this is a one-time transaction, the data entered should be the same as what you would enter in an account register. If this is a recurring transaction and the amount varies from one payment to the next, enter an average amount.

3. If this is a one-time payment, click the Register Transaction radio button. The dialog box collapses, as shown in **Figure 7.7**. Click OK to complete the transaction.

   or

3. If this is a recurring transaction, click the Scheduled Transaction radio button and continue entering data, as described in the following steps (refer to **Figure 7.6**).
4. Choose a transaction frequency from the How Often drop-down list.
5. Choose an option from the Enter in Register pop-up list. If you want to automatically record the payment in the register each time that it is due, choose Automatically enter. (Note that you can still edit such a transaction after it is created by changing the amount, for example).

   If you want to receive notification before the transaction is recorded, choose Prompt before enter. When the transaction is due, the Scheduled Transactions Due window appears (refer to **Figure 7.3**).
6. Enter a number in the Number of Payments text box. (Enter 999 for a transaction that will recur indefinitely, such as a utility payment.)
7. Since bills must often be paid by a due date, enter the number of days in advance of the due date that the transaction should be recorded. (To avoid a hefty penalty, I want to be reminded to write a check to my cable company a week in advance of the due date, for example.)
8. Click OK.

✔ **Tip**

■ To quickly locate a memorized transaction in the list, click in the list and type the first letter or two of the payee's name.

- You can make payments by check in the Financial Calendar in two ways. If you will handwrite the check, choose Payment in the Type of Transaction field and Next Check Num in the Number field. On the other hand, if you intend to print the check with Quicken, specify Print Check in the Type of Transaction field.

Recording Scheduled Transactions

Quicken has several methods of notifying you when transactions are due or pending: the Billminder dialog box, the Scheduled Transactions Due dialog box, the To Do! icon, and the Reminders window.

The Billminder Dialog Box

If any transactions are due or imminent, you are notified by Billminder at the start of the Windows session (see **Figure 7.8**). To launch Quicken, click the Run Quicken button.

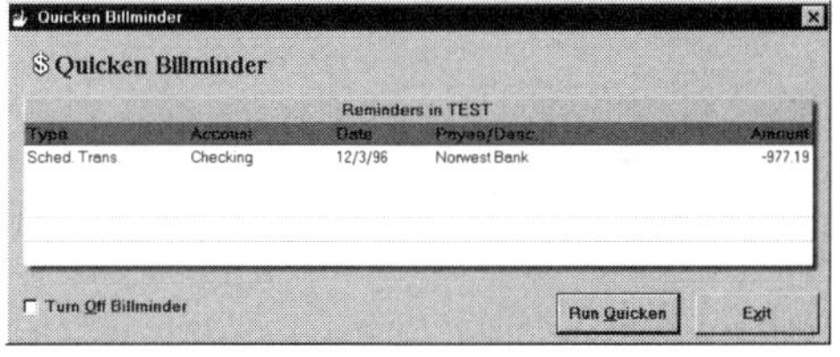

Figure 7.8 *If the Billminder option has been turned on in the Reminder Options dialog box, you are notified of due and pending transactions even when Quicken isn't running!*

The Scheduled Transactions Due Dialog Box

If some transactions are due today, the Scheduled Transactions Due dialog box automatically appears at the start of the Quicken session (see **Figure 7.9**). Select all transactions that you want to handle in the same way and then click Record to enter the transactions in their registers, Edit to change the amounts or other data, Skip Payment to ignore the transactions this time, or Done to dismiss the dialog box (usually with the intent of recalling it later).

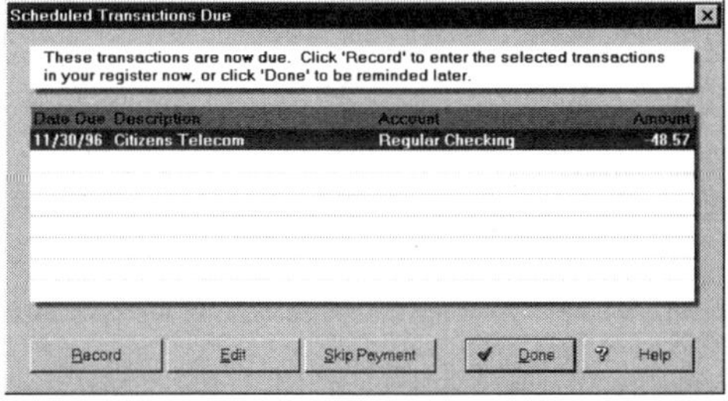

Figure 7.9 *When the Scheduled Transactions Due dialog box appears, you can enter the selected transactions in the appropriate register(s) by clicking Record.*

The To Do! Icon

The To Do! icon blinks if there are pending transactions or notes. Click the icon to open the Reminders window (see **Figure 7.10**). You can immediately record any listed transaction by clicking Enter in Register. The Record Scheduled Transaction dialog box appears (see **Figure 7.11**). Edit the transaction data as necessary and click Record.

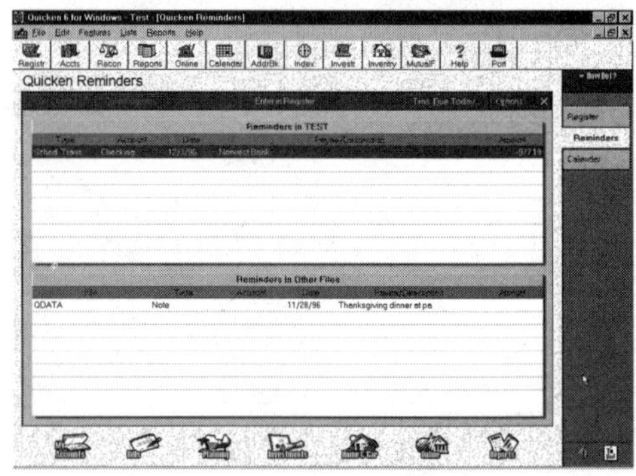

Figure 7.10 *Pending transactions and notes are listed in the Reminders window.*

Handling Transactions Early

In addition to recording due transactions in the Scheduled Transactions Due dialog box and pending transactions in the Reminders window, you can pay *any* bill that is listed in the Financial Calendar in advance of its scheduled transaction or due date.

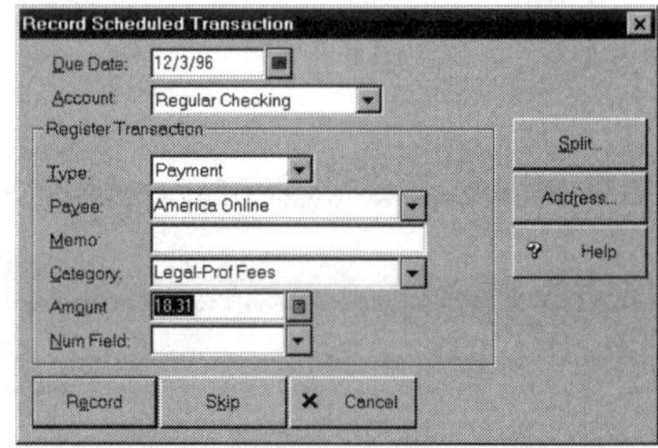

Figure 7.11 *The Record Scheduled Transaction dialog box contains the same fields as those of a register.*

To pay a bill early:

1. In the Financial Calendar window, double-click the date in which the pending transaction is listed. The Transactions Due dialog box appears (see **Figure 7.12**).
2. Select the transaction, and click Pay Now. The Record Scheduled Transaction dialog box appears, as previously shown in **Figure 7.11**.
3. Make any necessary changes and click Record.

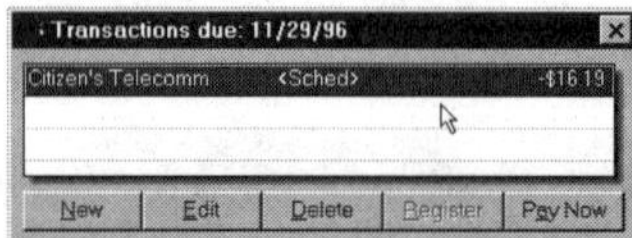

Figure 7.12 *To pay a bill before its scheduled payment date, select it and click Pay Now.*

✔ Tips

- Remember that recording a scheduled transaction merely enters it in the appropriate register. If you pay by check, for example, you must still print or handwrite the check.
- You can also display the Scheduled Transactions Due dialog box by clicking the Txns. Due Today button in the Reminders window.

Transaction Groups

If you prefer to pay bills in batches, you can create transaction groups which enable you to simultaneously handle many transactions. If you check the due dates on your bills, you may find several that are all due on the first of the month, for example.

To create a transaction group:

1. Choose Scheduled Transaction from the Lists menu or press Ctrl J. The Scheduled Transaction List appears.
2. Click the New Button. The Create Scheduled Transaction dialog box appears.
3. Click the Group button. The Create Transaction Group dialog box appears (see **Figure 7.13**).
4. Choose an account from which the payments will be made, click the Regular radio button, name the group (Utilities, for example), and enter the remaining details as you would for a normal transaction.
5. Click OK. The Assign Transactions to Group dialog box appears (see **Figure 7.14**).
6. Select transactions to include in the group.
7. Click Done.

To pay/record a group transaction, select it in the Scheduled Transaction List and click the Pay button. The Record Transaction Group dialog box appears (see **Figure 7.15**). Make any necessary changes and click Record. If amounts differ from one month to the next, open the register(s) and edit the transactions.

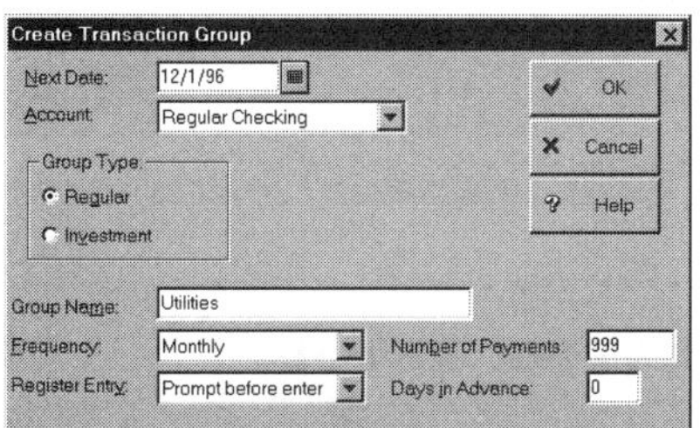

Figure 7.13 *Use the Create Transaction Group dialog box to define new groups.*

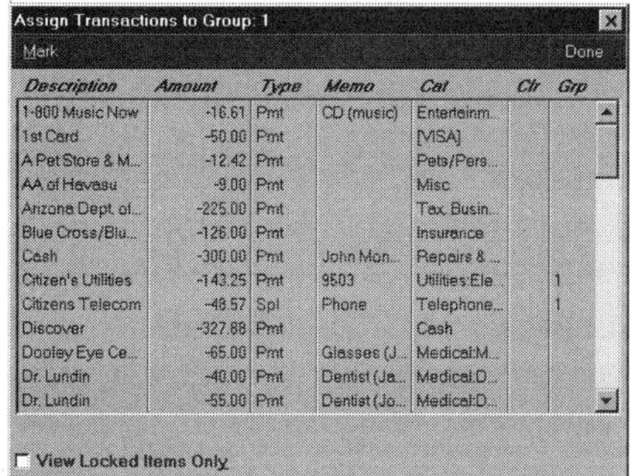

Figure 7.14 *Select group members in the Assign Transactions to Group dialog box.*

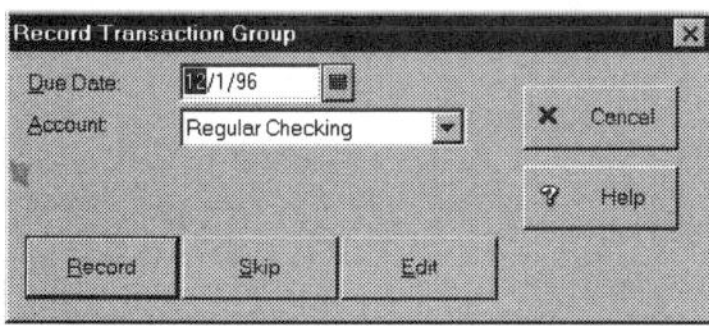

Figure 7.15 *Use the Record Transaction Group dialog box to send the group's transactions to the register(s).*

Creating Notes

You can also record general reminders in the calendar that may or may not have anything to do with a payment or with your finances. Colored notes can be attached to any date to remind you of an appointment, birthday, or other important event. Notes are also listed in the Quicken Reminders window (refer to **Figure 7.10**). You can only have one note per date.

To create a note:

1. Select the date to which you want to attach a note.
2. Click the Note button or right-click the date and choose Note from the pop-up menu. The Note window appears (see **Figure 7.16**).
3. Enter the text for the note.
4. Choose a color for the note from the Note Color pop-up list.
5. Click Save to store the note. A tiny colored note icon appears on the selected date.

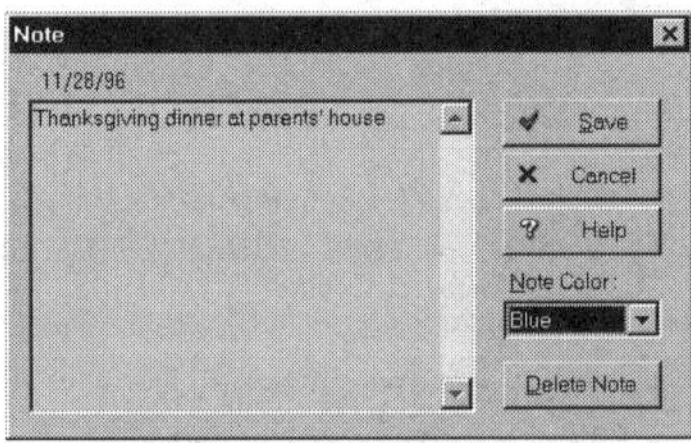

Figure 7.16 *You can create and delete notes in the Note window.*

To open a note, click it once. To delete a note, open it and click the Delete Note button in the Note window.

✔ **Tip**

- You may want to classify notes by color. You can use blue notes for financial matters, green for appointments, and pink for birthdays, anniversaries, and other special occasions, for instance.

Setting Calendar Options

You set calendar options by clicking the View and Options buttons.

View Button

Click the View button to reveal the View pop-up menu (see **Figure 7.17**). Most of the commands are toggles; a check mark indicates that the command is in effect. Here is what each command accomplishes:

- *Show Recorded Transactions in Calendar.* Choose this command to show all transactions that have been recorded on each date (either in the calendar or in a register).
- *Show Scheduled Transactions in Calendar.* Choose this command to show upcoming transactions that you have scheduled.
- *Show Account Graph.* Choose this command to display a bar graph of account balances at the bottom of the Financial Calendar window (see **Figure 7.18**).
- *Show Memorized Transaction List.* Choose this command to list all memorized transactions to the right of the calendar. Enabling this option lets you base new transactions on old ones.
- *Edit Memorized Transaction List.* Choose this command to display the Memorized Transaction List so you can add, edit, or delete entries (see **Figure 7.19**). Changes that you make in this window are reflected in the transaction list that accompanies the Financial Calendar.

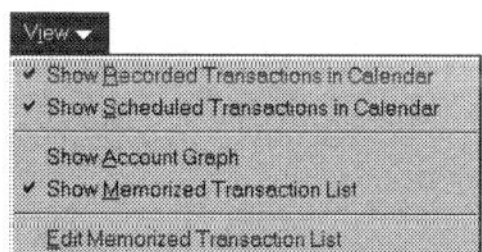

Figure 7.17 *The View pop-up menu.*

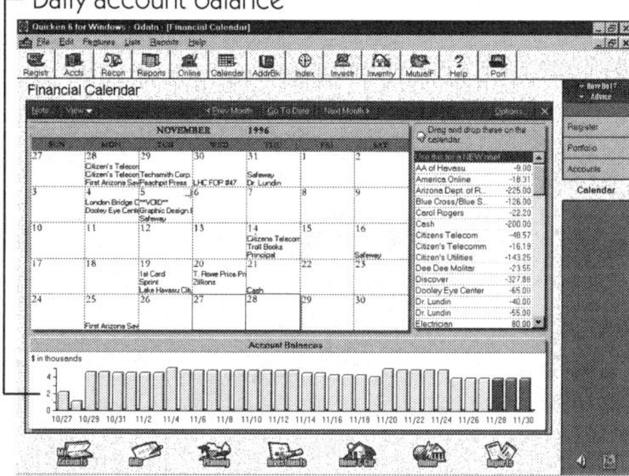

Figure 7.18 *The graph shows how your account balances change from day to day.*

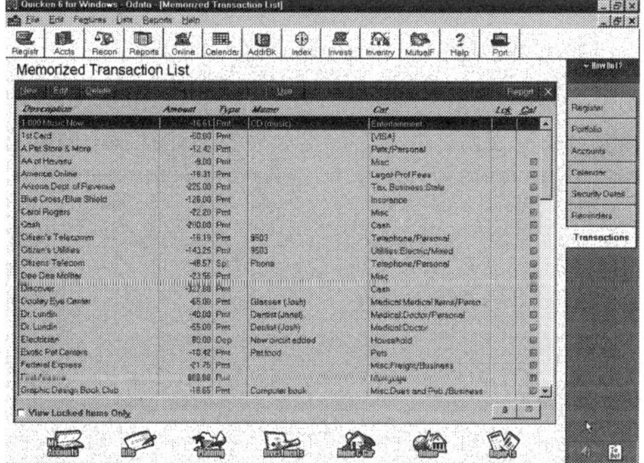

Figure 7.19 *To create a new memorized transaction, click New. To edit or remove a transaction, select it and click the Edit or Delete button.*

Options Button

To set additional options for the Financial Calendar, click the Options button at the top of the window. The Calendar Options dialog box appears (see **Figure 7.20**).

To select accounts to include in the account graph, click the Accounts tab. To set QuickFill options that affect the calendar, click the QuickFill tab (see **Figure 7.21**). For an explanation of QuickFill options, see “Memorizing Transactions” in Chapter 5.

✔ Tips

- If you choose not to display the Memorized Transaction List, you can still create new transactions by double-clicking any date on the calendar. Click New in the dialog box that appears (see **Figure 7.22**) to display the New Transaction dialog box. To learn more about working with memorized transactions, see Chapter 5.
- You can reduce much of the clutter in the date boxes by turning off the option to Show Recorded Transactions in Calendar.
- When you set the option to Show Account Graph, the graph displays the total daily balance of all included accounts. The graph is more informative if you restrict the included accounts to the ones from which you pay bills. Usually, this will be your checking account.

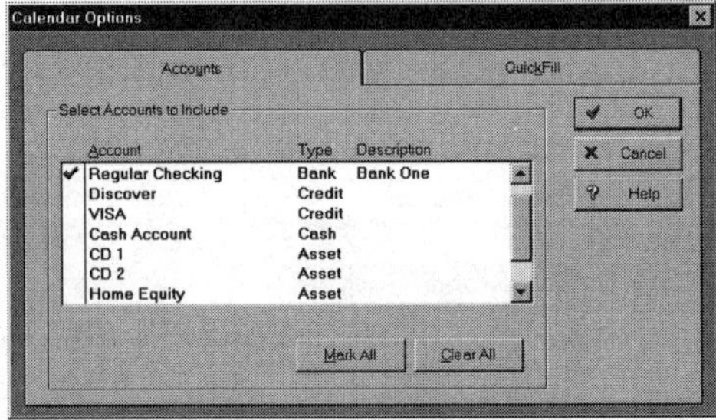

Figure 7.20 *The Calendar Options dialog box has two sections: Accounts (shown here) and QuickFill (see Figure 7.21).*

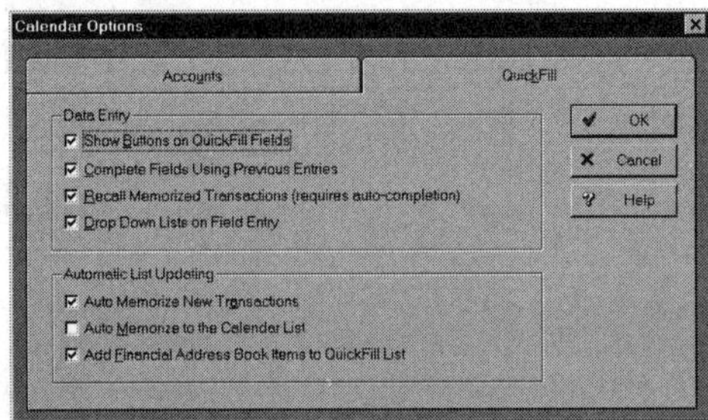

Figure 7.21 *The QuickFill section of the Calendar Options dialog box.*

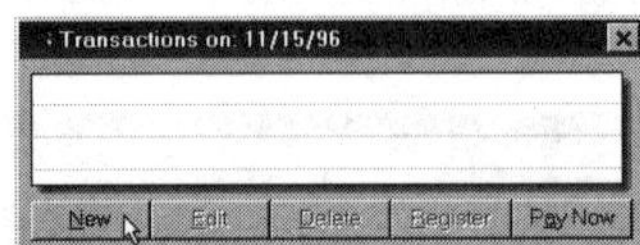

Figure 7.22 *Click the New button to create a new transaction for the chosen date.*

Reconciling Accounts and Updating Balances

8

About Account Reconciliation and Balance Adjustments

If you ask someone why they purchased Quicken, one common answer is: "So I can balance my checking account." And, of course, Quicken excels at this task. While balancing a paper check register against a bank statement can take hours, the same process can usually be handled in minutes with Quicken.

If you mention reconciling an account to most people, they usually assume that you're talking about a checking account (or perhaps a money market account with check-writing privileges). In fact, Quicken enables you to reconcile or update the balance of *any* type of account.

In Quicken, you can reconcile checking, savings, money market, and credit card accounts. Although there is no reconciliation procedure for cash, asset, or liability accounts, you can update the balance for any of these accounts to reflect interest received, deposits made, and so on.

This chapter is organized according to account type. For help with performing a bank reconciliation or updating an account balance, look for that account type in the section headers.

Checking, Savings, and Money Market Accounts

A single procedure is used to balance checking, savings, and money market accounts against a statement.

To reconcile a checking, savings, or money market account:

1. Open the register of the account that you want to reconcile.
2. To begin the reconciliation, click the Recon button in the iconbar, click the Reconcile button at the top of the register window, choose Features ⇨ Banking ⇨ Reconcile, or click the My Accounts icon in the activity bar and choose Reconcile an Account. The Reconcile Bank Statement dialog box appears (see **Figure 8.1**).

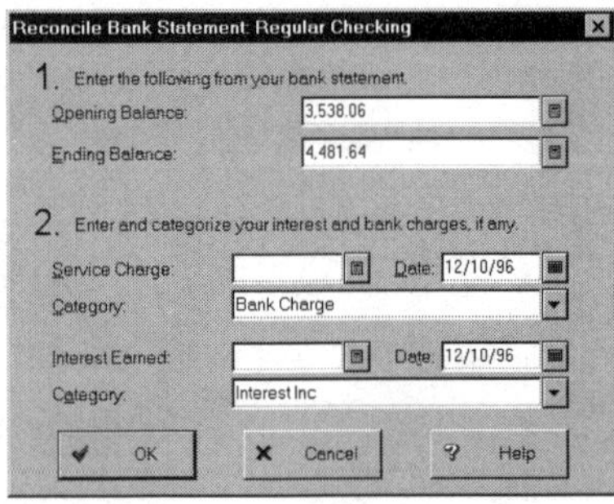

Figure 8.1 *All of the information needed for the Reconcile Bank Statement dialog box can be found on the statement.*

3. Check the Opening Balance entry to make sure that it agrees with the opening balance shown on the bank statement.
4. Enter the Ending Balance from the bank statement.
5. If the statement includes a service charge or interest, record these amounts in the Service Charge and Interest Earned text boxes. If necessary, change the category and date for each of these entries.
6. Click OK to continue. The Reconcile Bank Statement window appears (see **Figure 8.2**).
7. Click each item that—according to the statement—has cleared the bank. A cleared item is preceded by a check mark. (If you check an item by mistake, click it again to remove the check mark.)

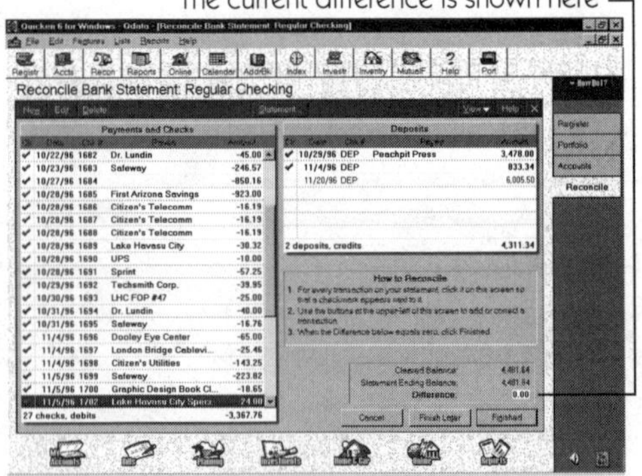

Figure 8.2 *Mark off all cleared transactions in the Reconcile Bank Statement window.*

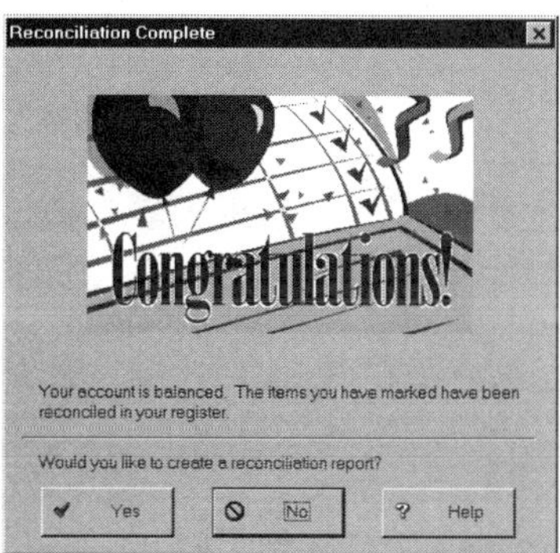

Figure 8.3 *You can now create a report or end the reconciliation process.*

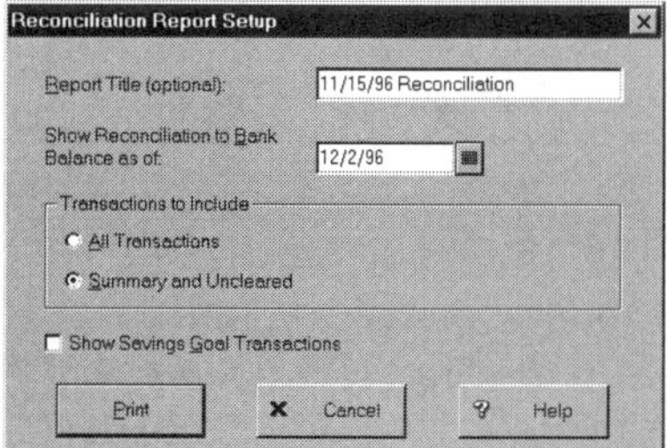

Figure 8.4 *Set report options in the Reconciliation Report Setup dialog box.*

8. As you mark items, Quicken updates the Difference figure in the lower-right corner of the window. When you have checked off all items on the statement, the Difference should be zero. If so, click Finished. If a difference still exists, see "Troubleshooting Reconciliation Problems," later in this chapter.
9. If the account balances, the Reconciliation Complete dialog box appears (see **Figure 8.3**). Click Yes to create a reconciliation report or No to end the process.
10. If you clicked Yes in Step 9, the Reconciliation Report Setup dialog box appears (see **Figure 8.4**). Enter a report title, set options, and click Print. The Print dialog box appears. For help with printing, see Chapter 18.

✔ Tips

- Service charges can be entered *en masse* in the Reconcile Bank Statement dialog box, or they can be recorded as separate or split transactions in the register. However, be sure not to record the service charge in *both* places.
- If you are having trouble finding transactions in the Reconcile Bank Statement window, you can alter the sort order. Click the View button, and choose Sort by Check Number or Sort by Date.
- You can mark any contiguous set of transactions as cleared by clicking the first transaction, holding down the Shift key, and clicking the last transaction.

Credit Card Accounts

The process of reconciling a credit card account with a monthly statement is very similar to the one for checking, savings, and money market accounts.

To reconcile a credit card account:

1. Open the register of the account that you want to reconcile.
2. To begin the reconciliation, click the Recon button in the iconbar, click the Reconcile button at the top of the register window, choose Features ⇨ Banking ⇨ Reconcile, or click the My Accounts icon in the activity bar and choose Reconcile an Account. The Credit Card Statement Information dialog box appears (see **Figure 8.5**).
3. Enter the total of all new purchases and cash advances in the Charges, Cash Advances text box. (However, do not include finance charges in this amount.)
4. Enter the total of all payments made and credits issued to your account in the Payments, Credits text box.
5. Enter the new balance in the Ending Balance text box.
6. If the statement lists a finance charge, enter it in the Finance Charges text box and then assign a category to the charge.
7. Click OK. The Reconcile Credit Card Statement window appears (see **Figure 8.6**).
8. Click each item that appears on the credit card statement (whether you intend to pay the full balance or not).

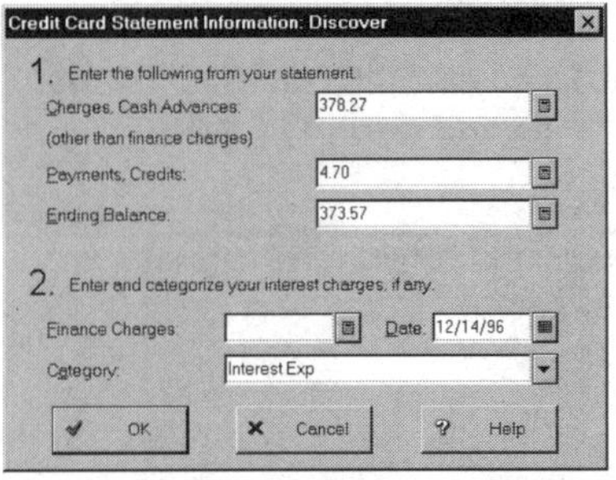

Figure 8.5 *Enter amounts from your statement in the Credit Card Statement dialog box.*

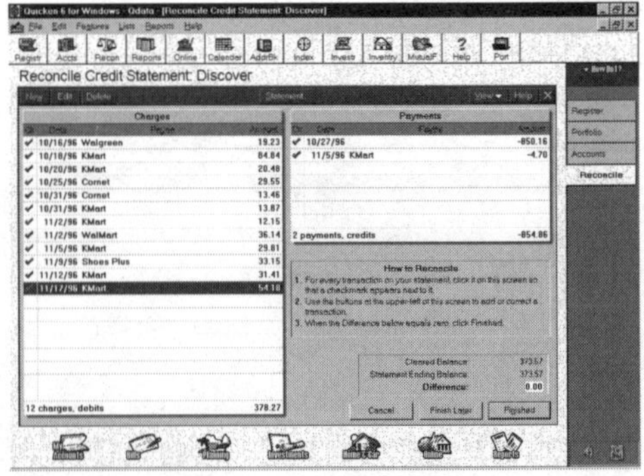

Figure 8.6 *Check off each transaction that appears on the statement.*

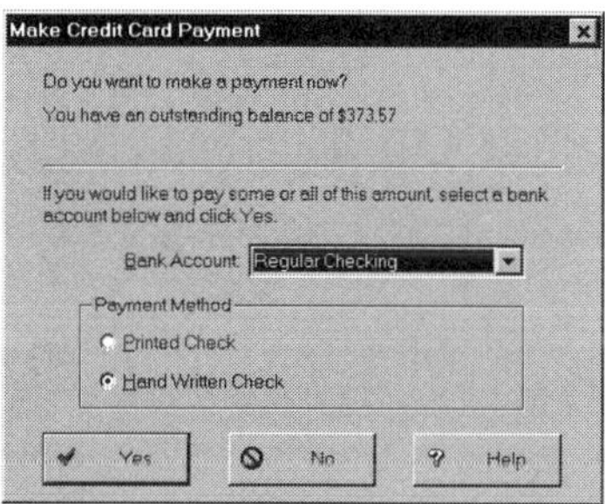

Figure 8.7 *Use the Make Credit Card Payment dialog box to issue a check for all or part of the account balance.*

9. As you mark items, Quicken updates the Difference figure in the lower-right corner of the window. When you have checked off all items on the statement, the Difference should be zero.

   Click the Finished button. The Make Credit Card Payment dialog box appears (see **Figure 8.7**).

10. If you want to pay off some or all of the account balance, select the account from which the funds will be drawn, click a button to indicate the manner in which the check will be generated, and click the Yes button. A transaction for the full amount is entered in your check register. If you only want to make a partial payment, edit the transaction to show the correct amount.

    or

10. If you do not want to make a payment at this time, click No.

✔ **Tip**

- The tips at the end of the previous section ("Checking, Savings, and Money Market Accounts") and those in "Troubleshooting Reconciliation Problems" at the end of this chapter also apply to credit card reconciliations. For example, you can edit transaction amounts, eliminate duplicates, and enter missing transactions. (However, there are no sort commands that you can use to reorder credit card transactions. They are simply listed in date order.)

Troubleshooting Reconciliation Problems

Reconciliation doesn't always go without a hitch—especially the first time. Here are some suggestions that you may find helpful:

- If this is your first attempt at reconciling a checking or credit card account in Quicken, click the Help button in the first dialog box that appears. This is especially important if you are balancing an on-line credit card account.
- If you discover that you made an error in the Reconcile Bank Statement or Credit Card Statement dialog box, click the Statement button at the top of the window, make the necessary changes, and click the OK button.
- If a transaction amount does not agree with the amount shown on the statement, select the item and click Edit at the top of the window. You are taken to that transaction in the register (see **Figure 8.8**). Change the amount and click the Return to Reconcile button below the transaction.
- If the statement shows a transaction that you haven't recorded in the register, click New at the top of the window to create the transaction. When you are finished, click Return to Reconcile and then mark the transaction.
- If you find a duplicate transaction, you can delete it by selecting it and then clicking the Delete button at the top of the window.

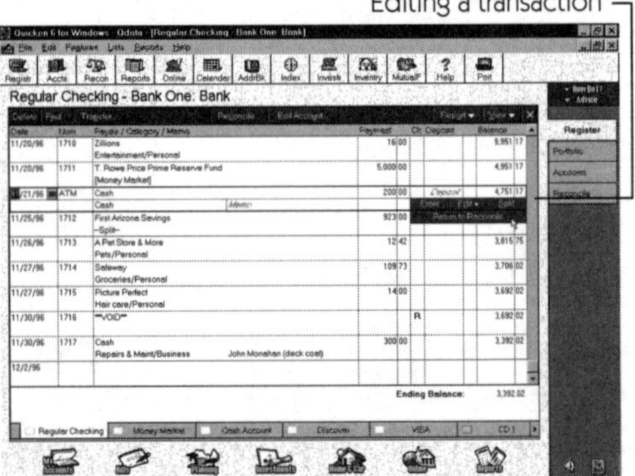

Figure 8.8 *Edit the transaction, click Enter to record it, and then click Return to Reconcile.*

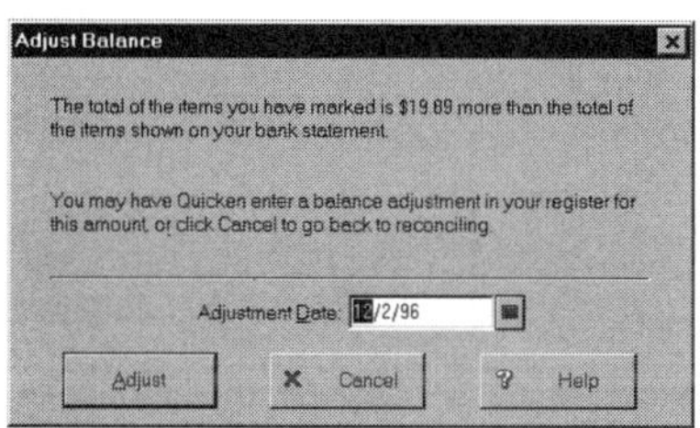

Figure 8.9 *To adjust the account balance by the amount shown, verify the Adjustment Date and click Adjust.*

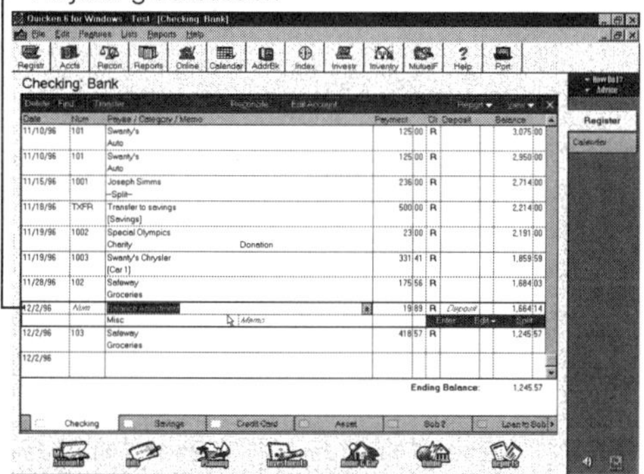

Figure 8.10 *The adjusting transaction is named Balance Adjustment.*

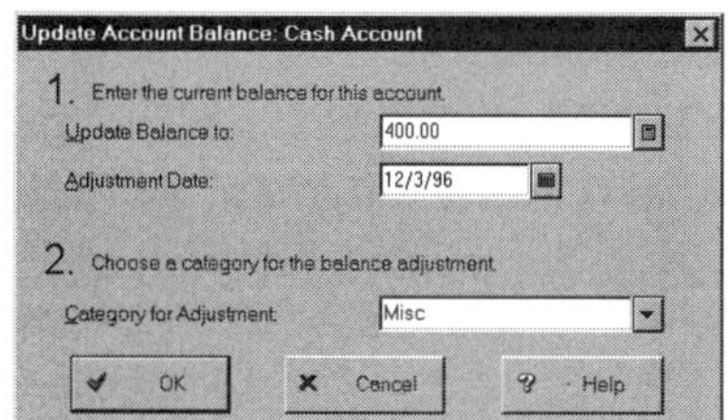

Figure 8.11 *To adjust a cash, asset, or liability account register, enter the new balance. Quicken determines the adjusting transaction that is necessary.*

- To temporarily leave a reconciliation, click Finish Later. You can pick up where you left off when it's more convenient.
- If you can't reconcile an account but the difference is small, you can accept the bank statement as correct and let Quicken adjust the account balance. Click Finished. The Adjust Balance dialog box appears (see **Figure 8.9**). Enter a date for the adjustment and click Adjust. An adjusting transaction is entered in the register, as shown in **Figure 8.10**. If you later find the error, you can correct it and delete the adjusting transaction.

Cash, Asset, and Liability Accounts

If you examine the Features menu when a cash, asset, or liability account is displayed, you'll note that there is no Reconcile command. In its place is Update Balance. Use this command to make an adjustment to the account that reflects the current balance.

To update a cash account's balance:

1. Choose Features ⇨ Banking ⇨ Update Balance or click the Recon button in the top iconbar. The Update Account Balance dialog box appears (see **Figure 8.11**).
2. Enter the new balance in the Update Balance to text box. If necessary, change the date.
3. Choose a category for the adjustment.
4. Click OK. An adjusting entry appears in the account register.

Financial Address Book

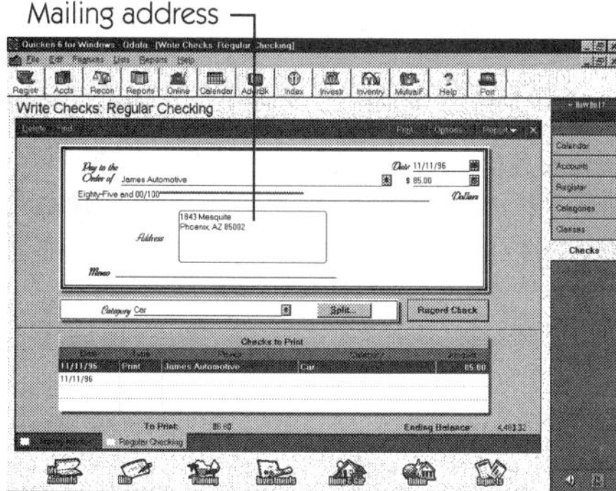

Figure 9.1 *When writing a check, you can include the recipient's address.*

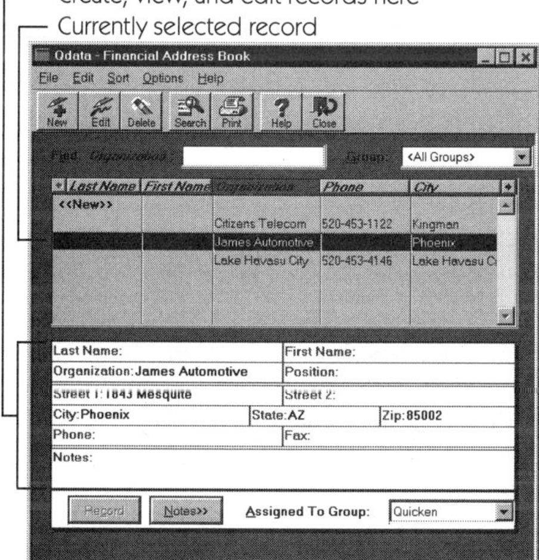

Figure 9.2 *The fields for the selected record are shown in the bottom part of the window.*

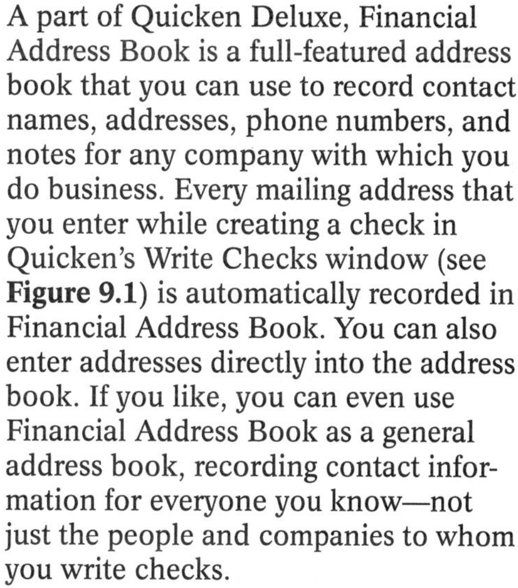

About Financial Address Book

A part of Quicken Deluxe, Financial Address Book is a full-featured address book that you can use to record contact names, addresses, phone numbers, and notes for any company with which you do business. Every mailing address that you enter while creating a check in Quicken's Write Checks window (see **Figure 9.1**) is automatically recorded in Financial Address Book. You can also enter addresses directly into the address book. If you like, you can even use Financial Address Book as a general address book, recording contact information for everyone you know—not just the people and companies to whom you write checks.

As shown in **Figure 9.2**, all records in the address book are displayed in a scrolling list in the top section of the window. When you select a person or company from this list, the record is displayed in the bottom half of the window where it can be examined or edited.

How Quicken and Financial Address Book Work Together

In general, there is two-way communication between Quicken and Financial Address Book. If you enter an address for a memorized transaction, scheduled transaction, or an on-line payee, the address information is automatically recorded in your address book. Changes made to addresses within Quicken are also sent to the address book. Deletions made within Quicken, however, are not communicated. To permanently remove these addresses, you must open the address book and delete them.

Addresses that you've entered directly into Financial Address Book can be automatically added to Quicken's QuickFill list by setting an option in Quicken (see **Figure 9.3**).

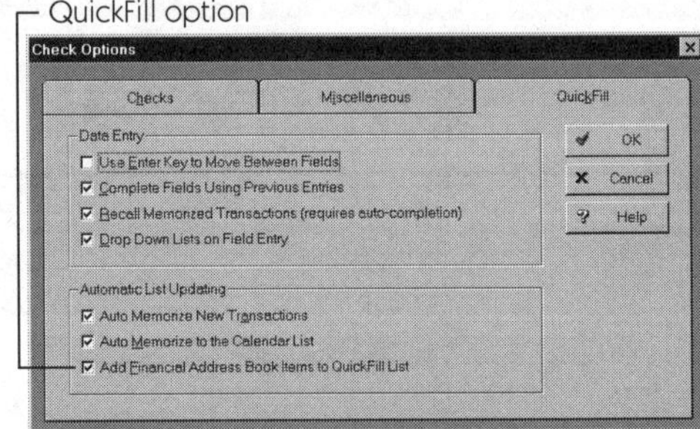

Figure 9.3 *To send addresses from the address book to Quicken, open the Check Options or Register Options dialog box and set the QuickFill option.*

Opening Financial Address Book

Financial Address Book is linked to and accessible from Quicken. Because it was designed as a stand-alone program, Financial Address Book can also be run separately; that is, Quicken need not be running in order for you to examine, add, or edit records in the address book.

The following sets of steps explain how to launch Financial Address Book from within Quicken and from the Windows desktop.

Figure 9.4 *You can launch Financial Address Book from the Home & Car activity bar icon.*

To open Financial Address Book from within Quicken:

- Choose Track Important Addresses from the Lists menu, or
- Click the Home & Car activity bar icon, and choose Track Important Addresses (see **Figure 9.4**).

To open Financial Address Book from the desktop:

- In Windows 95, choose Financial Address Book from the Start menu (see **Figure 9.5**).
- In Windows 3.1, open the Quicken program group and double-click the Financial Address Book icon.

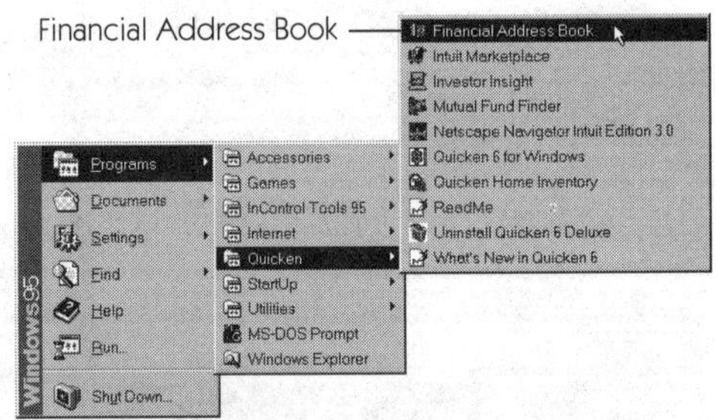

Figure 9.5 *When installing Quicken Deluxe on a PC running Windows 95, Financial Address Book is added to the Start menu (in the Quicken group).*

Creating and Editing Records

Financial Address Book has procedures for creating, editing, and deleting records, as described below.

Creating New Records

Addresses that you enter in the Write Checks window of Quicken are automatically entered in your address book. You can also enter new addresses directly into the address book.

To create a new address:

1. Choose New from the Edit menu, click the New button in the toolbar, or press Ctrl N.

   or

1. Click the **<<New>>** record at the top of the record list (see **Figure 9.6**).

   A blank record appears at the bottom of the window.

2. Enter the data for the record, assign it to a group, if desired (see "Working with Groups," later in this chapter), and then click Record to add it to the address book.

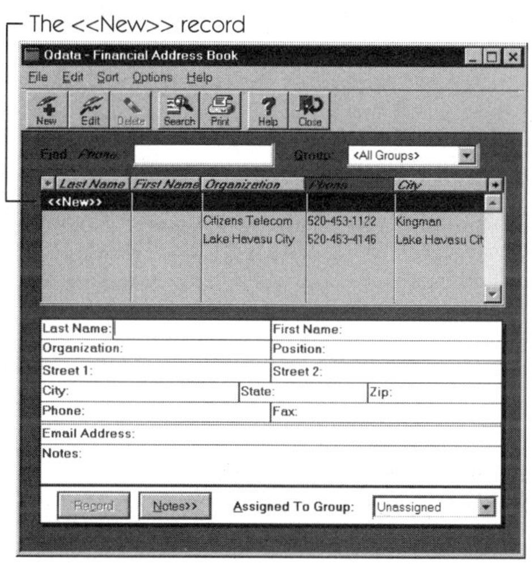

Figure 9.6 *You can create a new record by clicking the ever-present <<New>> record at the top of the list.*

Editing Records

You can modify the contents of any field in an existing record using normal editing procedures.

To edit a record:

1. Select the record you wish to edit from the scrolling list in the top part of the window.
2. Make the desired changes, and then click Record.

If you make changes to a record and then try to edit another one without clicking Record, the dialog box in **Figure 9.7** appears. Click Yes to save the changes or click No to ignore them.

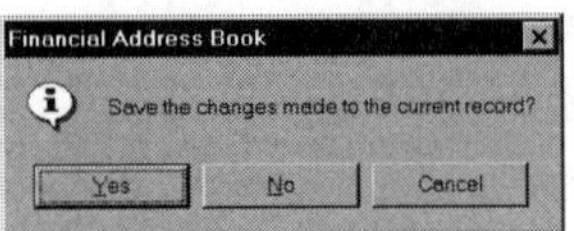

Figure 9.7 *After editing an address record, you must either click Record or verify the changes in this dialog box.*

Deleting Records

You can delete any record in the address book by selecting it and then choosing Delete from the Edit menu, clicking the Delete button, or pressing Ctrl D or Del. To confirm the deletion, click Yes in the dialog box that appears.

Swapping the Organization and Name Fields

When you write a check in Quicken that is payable to a person rather than to a company, there is a problem when the address is sent to Financial Address Book. Whatever you enter on the payee line is assumed to be a company. That data becomes the Organization field in the new record. Although you can edit the affected records in the address book, another option is to use the Move Organization into Names command.

To move Organization field data into the First and Last Names fields:

1. Select the incorrect record in the Financial Address Book window (see **Figure 9.8**).
2. Choose the Move Organization into Names command from the Edit menu or press Ctrl M. The person's full name is divided into first and last names, and they are entered in the appropriate fields in the bottom part of the window.
3. If the name has been split correctly, click Record.

Full name is in the Organization field

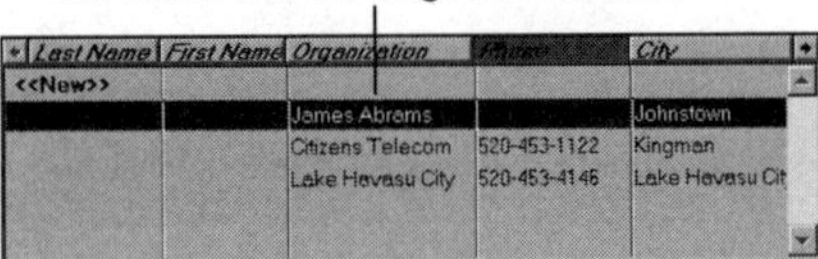

The name has been moved into the Name fields

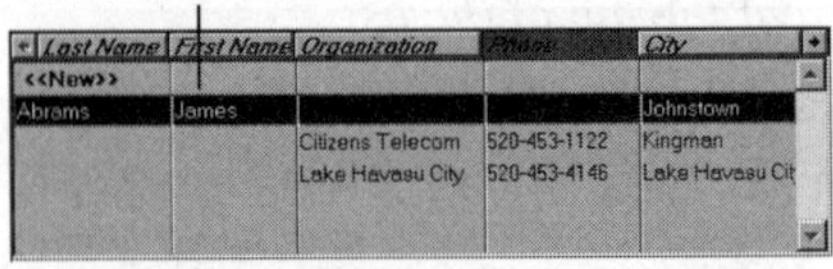

Figure 9.8 *Select the incorrect record (top), choose the Move Organization into Names command, and click Record. The address record is corrected (bottom).*

Working with Groups

Records can be classified according to some element they share in common with other records. You can use these *groups* to help you coordinate mass mailings, print group directories, and speed your searches. Financial Address Book provides several default groups to which records can be assigned, such as Family, Friends, and Work.

You should note the following when working with groups:

- Each record can be associated with only one group. You can have as many as 100 different groups.
- Any record created in Quicken in the Write Checks window is automatically assigned to the Quicken group.
- Records that are not currently assigned to a group are members of the Unassigned group.

You can select a group for each new record, as well as change the group assignment for any existing record.

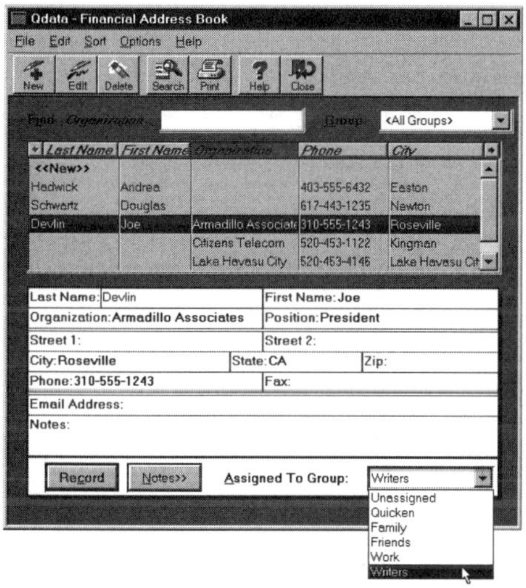

Figure 9.9 *Choose a group for the record from the Assigned to Group drop-down list.*

To choose a group for a new or existing record:

1. Create a new record or select an existing one.
2. Choose a group from the drop down list at the bottom of the window (see **Figure 9.9**).
3. Click the Record button.

   Regardless of the record's original group (if one was previously set), the record becomes part of the new group.

The following steps explain how to manage Financial Address book groups.

To create, edit, or delete a group:

1. Choose Set Up Groups from the Options menu. The Set Up Groups dialog box appears, as shown in **Figure 9.10**.
2. To create a new group, select the **<<New>>** entry in the Available Groups list, type a name in the Add New Group text box, and then click Record.
3. To change the name of an existing group, select it in the Available Groups list, type a new name or edit the current one in the Rename Selected Group To text box, and then click Record.
4. To delete a group, select it in the Available Groups list, and then click Delete.

   If the group currently has one or more members, the dialog box shown in **Figure 9.11** appears. Click Yes to reassign the affected records to the Unassigned group, or click No to cancel the deletion.

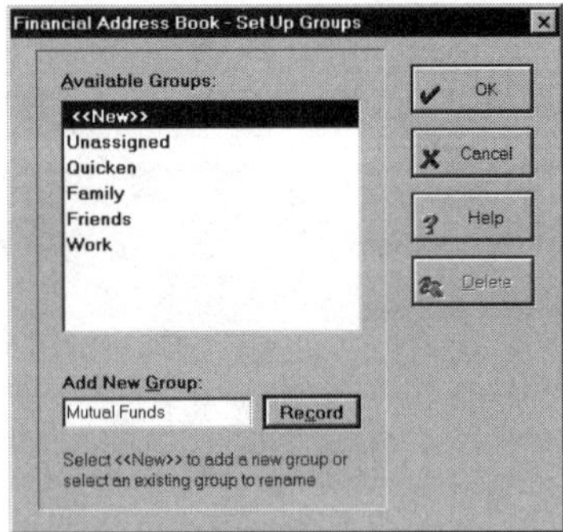

Figure 9.10 *You can create, rename, and delete groups in the Set Up Groups dialog box.*

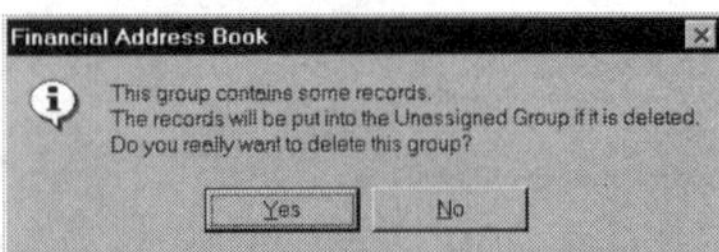

Figure 9.11 *You must confirm the deletion of any group that contains members.*

✔ **Tip**

- You cannot delete or rename the Quicken or the Unassigned group. The Quicken group is automatically assigned to all records created in Quicken. Records that are not assigned to a group are relegated to the Unassigned group. If you wish, you can assign the latter records to other groups.

Searching for Records

Financial Address Book offers a variety of search options that you can use to select records to view or print. You can conduct simple or complex searches.

Figure 9.12 *Simple searches can be conducted entirely within the Financial Address Book window.*

To view one or all groups:

- To display records from only one group, choose the group name from the Group drop-down list at the top of the dialog box (see **Figure 9.12**).
- To display all records, choose All Groups from the Group list.

To search for a specific record:

1. Choose a group to examine from the Group drop-down list. (To search the entire database, choose All Groups.)
2. Click the column heading of the field you want to search, such as Last Name or Organization.
3. Type a search string in the Find text box. As you type, Financial Address Book attempts to complete the search string for you and shows any matching records. Continue typing until the desired record is displayed.

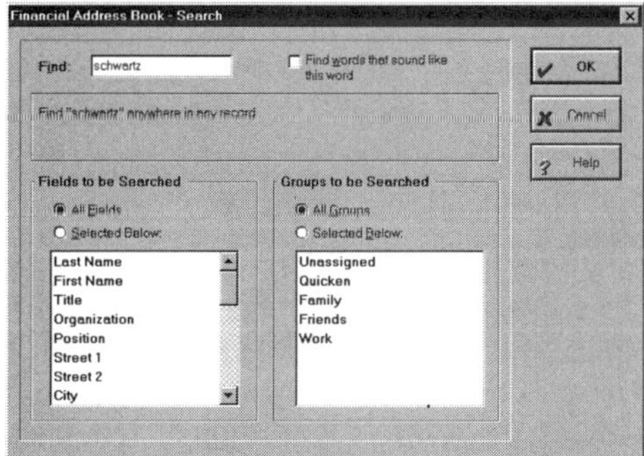

Figure 9.13 *You can use the Search dialog box to perform complex searches that include multiple groups and/or fields.*

To perform a complex search:

1. Click the Search button, choose Search from the Edit menu, or press Ctrl S. The Search dialog box appears (see **Figure 9.13**).
2. Select the group(s) and/or field(s) to be searched. (To select multiple groups or fields, Ctrl-click them.)
3. Enter a search string in the Find box.
4. Click OK.

✔ **Tips**

- When you perform a complex search and are not sure how to spell the keyword, enter an approximation of it in the Find box and check the option to "Find words that sound like this word."
- If you want to view several groups while hiding the others, use the Search dialog box. Select groups and click OK—without entering a keyword.

Printing

You can print the entire address book or selected addresses in five formats: address book, phone book, labels, Rolodex cards, or business envelopes.

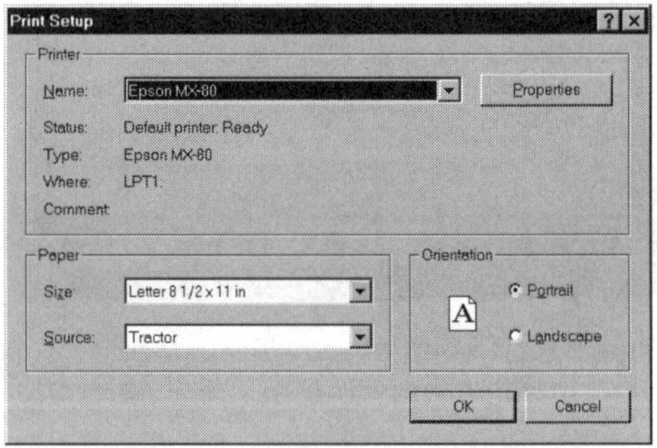

Figure 9.14 *Use the Print Setup box to select from all installed printers and to set options, such as the paper orientation.*

To print address records:

1. *Optional:* To print a record subset, Ctrl-click the records or perform a search.
2. *Optional:* Choose Print Setup from the Print menu, select an installed printer, and set options for the print job (see **Figure 9.14**).
3. Click the Print button, choose Print from the File menu, or press Ctrl P. The Print dialog box appears (see **Figure 9.15**).
4. Select a print format and paper type from the Print and On pop-up lists. To use a different font, size, or style, click the Change button.
5. Click OK. (Some print formats will present additional dialog boxes.)

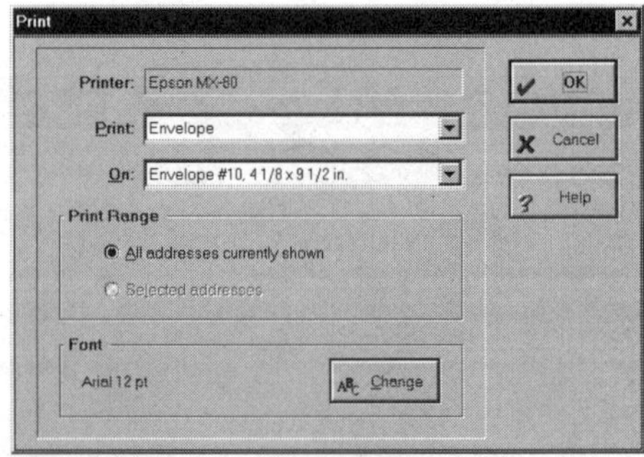

Figure 9.15 *Choose a print format and paper type in the Print dialog box.*

✔ **Tip**

- For an on-screen preview, choose Print Preview from the File menu.

Customizing the Display

You can change the appearance of Financial Address Book by selecting the fields that you want to use, choosing which columns to display, setting an order for them, sorting the address book by the contents of any column, and showing or hiding the iconbar.

Selecting Fields to Display

As shown previously in **Figure 9.2**, Financial Address Book initially displays only a dozen fields per record. Over twice that number are available for you to use, however. (Although the other fields are part of the address book database, they are considered *hidden*.)

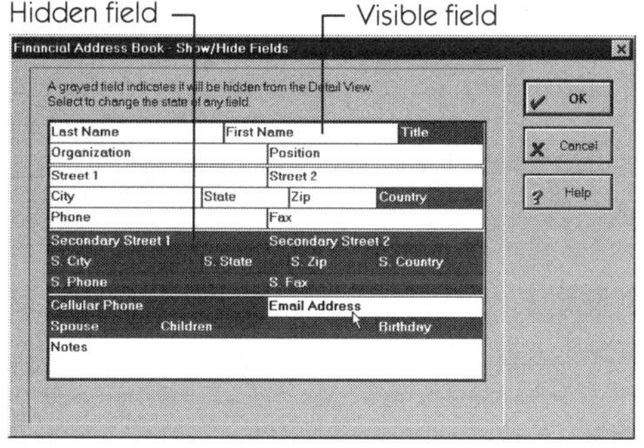

Figure 9.16 *Click a field in the Show/Hide Fields dialog box to toggle its state between hidden (gray) and visible (white).*

To show or hide fields:

1. Choose Show/Hide Fields from the Options menu. The dialog box shown in **Figure 9.16** appears.
2. Gray fields are currently hidden; white fields are displayed. To reverse the state of any field, click it once.
3. Click OK to accept the changes. The new fields will now be visible in the bottom portion of the Financial Address Book window.

You should note that some fields, such as Last Name and Organization, cannot be hidden.

Changing the Columns

The top half of Financial Address Book initially displays information for seven fields (Last Name, First Name, Organization, Phone, City, State, and Zip). These fields are important because you use them to sort and select records for viewing or editing. If you like, you can remove some of the original columns, add others, and set a new display order for the columns.

To change the selected columns or the column display order:

1. Choose Change Column Order from the Options menu. The dialog box shown in **Figure 9.17** appears. The current columns are listed in order in the Current List Column Order scrolling list box.
2. To remove a column, select it in the Current List Column Order list, and then click Remove.
3. To add a new column, select it in the Available Selections scrolling list box, and then click Append.
4. To change the order in which columns are displayed, select the column to move in the Current List Column Order list, and click Move Up or Move Down until the column is in the desired position.
5. Click OK to accept the changes.

If you want to start your column selection from scratch, click Clear. If you want to revert to the default set of columns in their original order, click the Default Button.

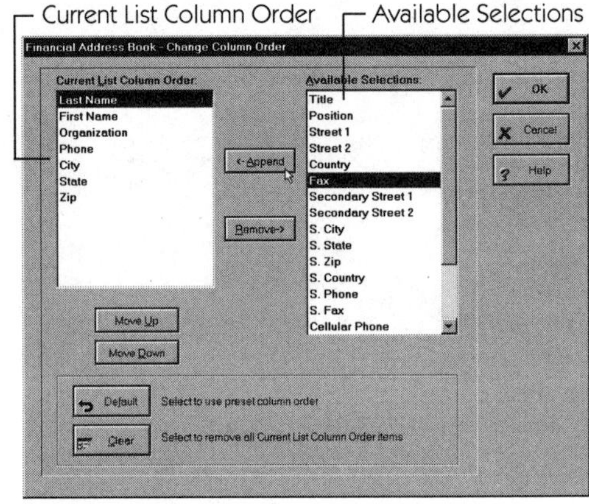

Figure 9.17 *The Change Column Order dialog box is used to choose columns to display and set an order for them.*

Sorting the Address Book

You can sort the address book by any visible (non-hidden) column. All sorts are in ascending order, either alphabetic or numeric—depending on the column chosen. You can use any of the following methods to sort the address book:

- Click the column heading by which you want to sort (Last Name, for example). If the desired column is

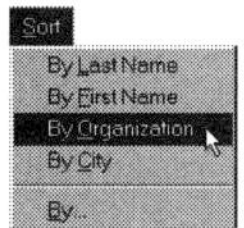

Figure 9.18 *You can sort by choosing a command from the Sort menu.*

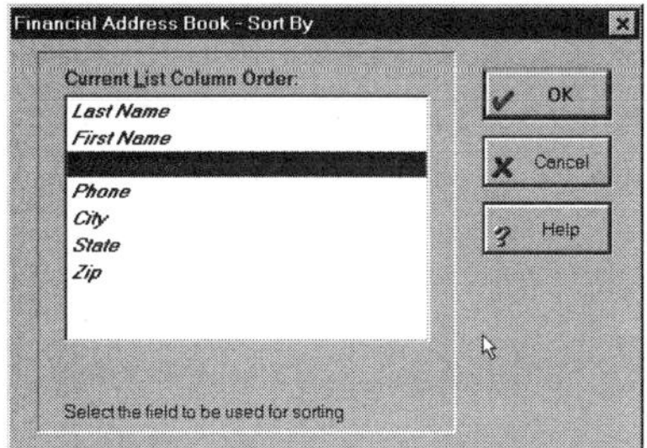

Figure 9.19 *You can sort by any visible column by selecting it in the Sort By dialog box.*

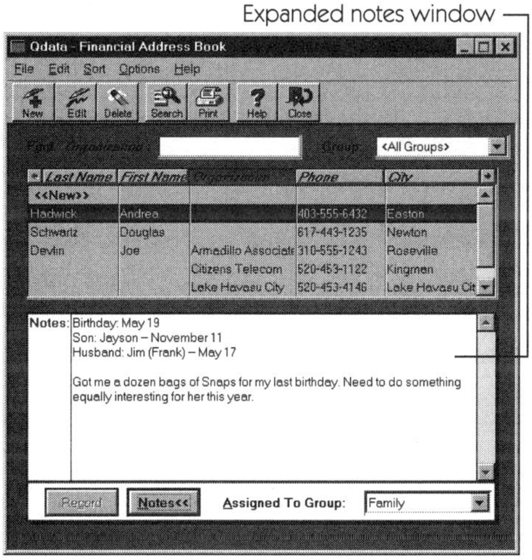

Expanded notes window

Figure 9.20 *To toggle between the normal Notes window and this expanded version, click the Notes button.*

off-screen, use the left or right scroll arrows to bring the column into view.

- To sort by Last Name, First Name, Organization, or City, choose the command from the Sort menu (see **Figure 9.18**).
- To sort by a visible field other than Last Name, First Name, Organization, or City, choose By from the Sort menu. The Sort By dialog box appears, as shown in **Figure 9.19**. Choose a sort field and click OK.

Showing or Hiding the Iconbar

The set of buttons at the top of the window can be displayed or hidden. To toggle the state of this iconbar, choose Show Iconbar from the Options menu.

✔ Tips

- You can change the size of the Financial Address Book window by clicking and dragging the bottom-right corner. This can be extremely helpful if you've added many additional columns or fields.
- When viewing or editing records, you can click the Notes button to make it easier to read lengthy notes (see **Figure 9.20**).

Part III: Financial Planning and Management

10 Budgeting

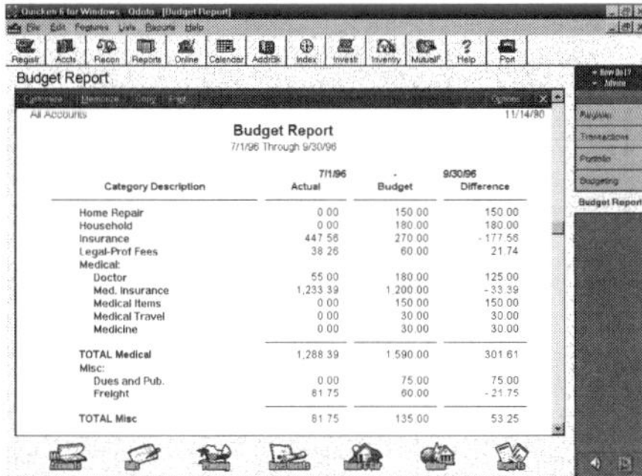

Figure 10.1 *You can create reports that show the differences between budgeted and actual spending.*

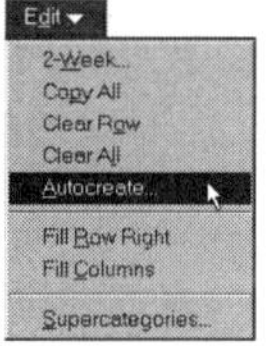

Figure 10.2 *Choose the Autocreate command to base the initial budget estimates on your actual income and expense figures.*

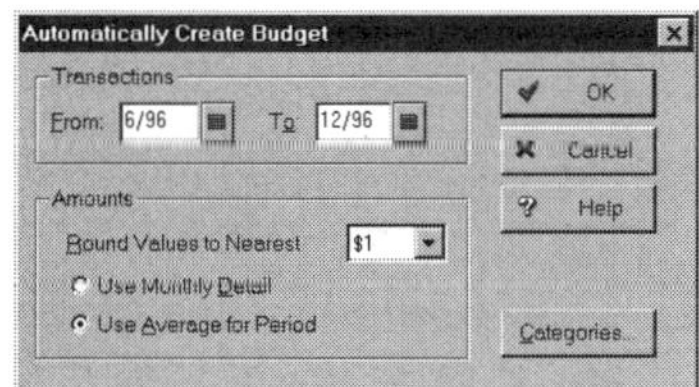

Figure 10.3 *Set budget-creation options in the Automatically Create Budget dialog box.*

About Budgeting

If you make a point of keeping your Quicken account registers current, you can generate reports that show how well you are doing for the year. If you live on a fixed income or routinely find that you are spending more than you make, however, you may find it helpful to create a *budget*. A budget enables you to compare your projected income and expenses against the actual amounts (see **Figure 10.1**).

Creating a Budget

A Quicken budget can be based on your actual income and expenses over a period of time (Autocreate Budget), created from scratch (Zero-Filled Budget), or copied from an existing budget (Copy Current Budget).

To generate an Autocreate budget:

1. Choose Features ⇨ Planning ⇨ Budget, or choose Budget My Spending from the Planning icon in the activity bar.

   The Budget window opens to an empty budget with two folders. The Inflows folder will hold your income budget categories; the Outflows folder stores expense categories.

2. Choose Autocreate from the Edit pop-up menu (see **Figure 10.2**). The Automatically Create Budget dialog box appears (see **Figure 10.3**).

3. Select a transaction date range on which to base the budget estimates.

   It is customary to base a budget on the previous year's income and expense figures. If this data is not available, you can use a date range from the current year for the initial estimates.

4. In the Amounts section of the dialog box, click Use Monthly Detail. The actual category expense and income figures for the selected period will be used as the budget estimates.

   or

4. Click Use Average for Period to instruct Quicken to calculate an average for each income and expense category over the specified period. (Unless your income and expenses vary on a seasonal basis, Use Average for Period is usually the best choice.)

5. At a minimum, budget estimates are calculated in single dollar amounts. If you prefer, you can increase the minimum by choosing an amount from the Round Values to Nearest pop-up list.

6. *Optional:* By default, Quicken includes all of your defined categories in the budget. To use only a subset of these categories, click the Categories button. The Select Categories to Include dialog box appears (see **Figure 10.4**).

   Checked categories will be used in the budget. Remove the check mark from any category that you wish to exclude. Click OK.

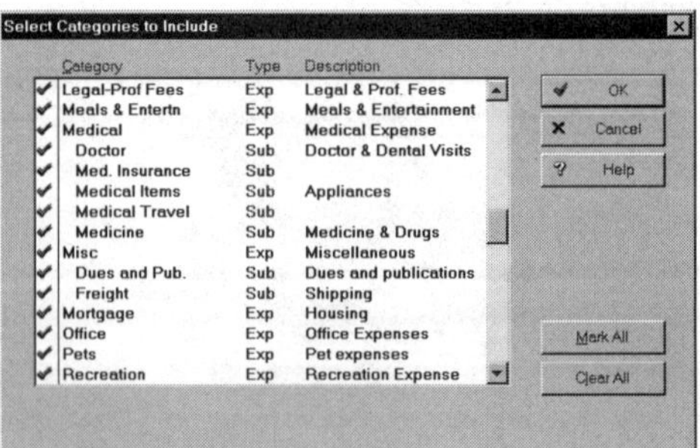

Figure 10.4 *If you only want to budget for specific categories, you can choose them in the Select Categories to Include dialog box.*

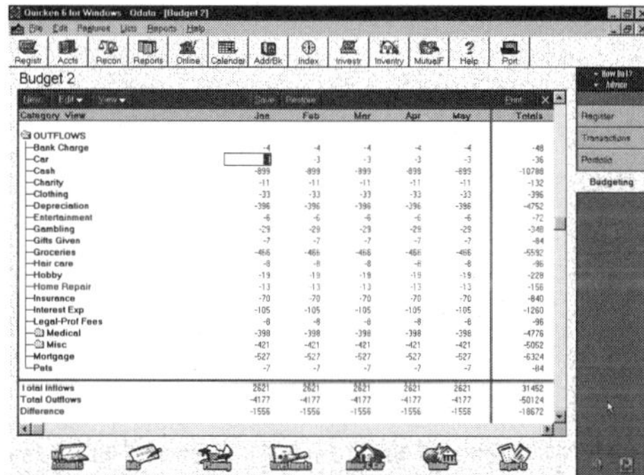

Figure 10.5 *An autocreated budget.*

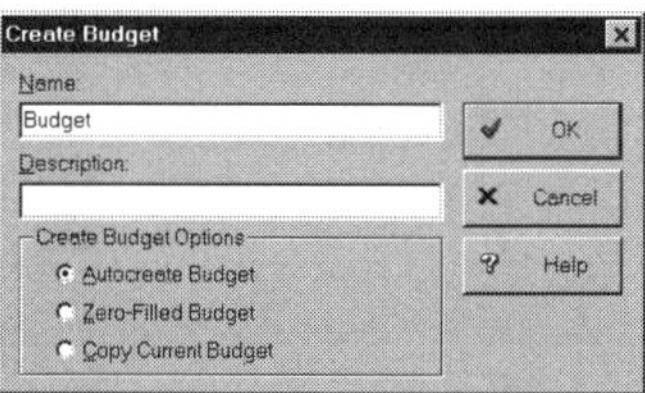

Figure 10.6 *Use the Create Budget dialog box to name and set options for new budgets.*

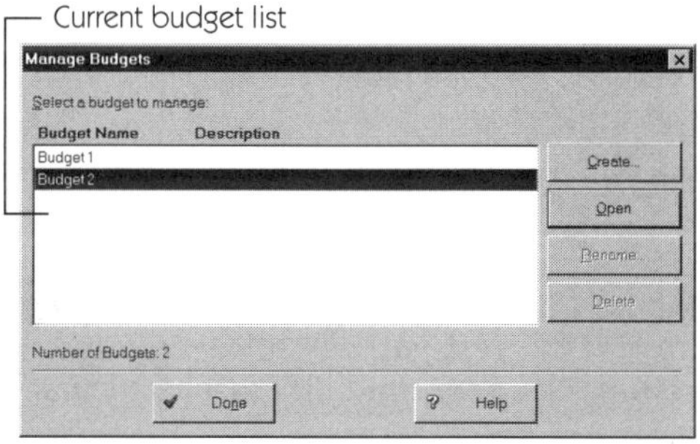

Current budget list

Figure 10.7 *Use the Manage Budgets dialog box when working with multiple Quicken budgets.*

7. Click OK to close the Automatically Create Budget dialog box. The initial budget is presented (see **Figure 10.5**).

To generate a zero-filled budget:

1. Choose Features ⇨ Planning ⇨ Budget. (As an alternative, you can also choose Budget My Spending from the Planning icon in the activity bar.)
2. Choose Zero Budget Categories from the View pop-up menu. The Inflows and Outflows folders expand to show all your categories, each containing a zero (0).

Whether it is autocreated or zero-filled, the initial budget is unlikely to meet your needs without some editing. See the following section ("Modifying a Budget") for details.

✔ Tips

- You are not restricted to only one budget. You can create others by clicking the New button. The Create Budget dialog box appears, as shown in **Figure 10.6**.

  To determine which of several budgets you want to use at the moment, choose Other Budgets from the View pop-up menu and select a budget name from the Manage Budgets dialog box (see **Figure 10.7**). Click Open.

- To create a new budget based on the currently open budget, click the New button and choose the option to Copy Current Budget (refer to **Figure 10.6**).

Modifying a Budget

Regardless of the method used to generate the initial budget, there is usually some cleanup work that needs to be done. Even if you based the budget on a whole year's data, you may know that your salary or insurance costs will be significantly different in the coming year, for example.

The Budget window (see **Figure 10.8**) is designed much like a spreadsheet. The budget categories are the rows, and the time periods (months, quarters, or years) are the columns. You can edit any budget amount by clicking its cell and then typing.

Other changes that you can make to a budget include altering your view by choosing elements to show or hide, renaming or deleting budgets, and saving changes or reverting to the most recently saved budget.

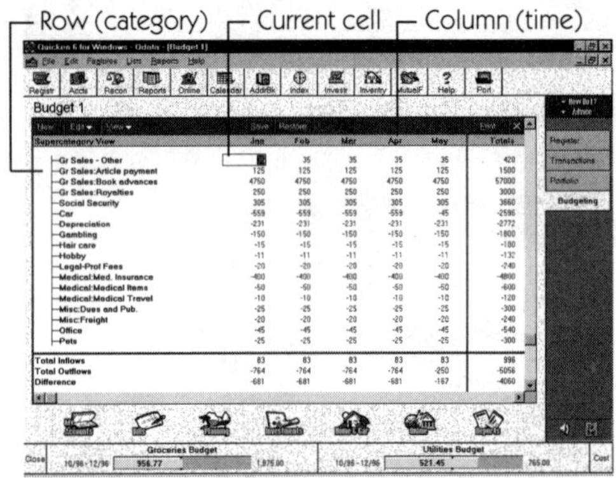

Figure 10.8 *The budget is displayed in a spreadsheet-like grid.*

Changing Budget Amounts

The following are some methods you can use to modify the budget amounts. Note that all editing commands can be selected by clicking the Edit button (as shown in **Figure 10.9**) or by right-clicking a budget cell.

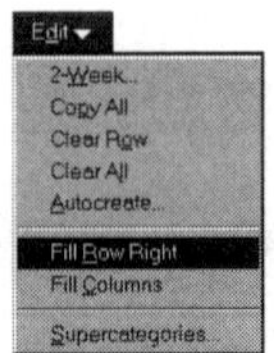

Figure 10.9 *In addition to directly editing any budget cell, you can select editing commands from the Edit button's menu.*

- You can click any budget cell and edit its data by typing.
- To copy the current cell's data into every cell to its right, click the Edit button and choose Fill Row Right.
- If you make a midyear change to several budget categories (you get a raise and pay off a car loan, for example), you can use the Fill Columns command to copy the current column to all remaining columns in the year.

- If some items are better budgeted on a two-week basis (rather than monthly), select a cell for that category and choose 2-Week from the Edit button menu.

Changing Your View of a Budget

Quicken provides several commands that you can use to change the Budget window display.

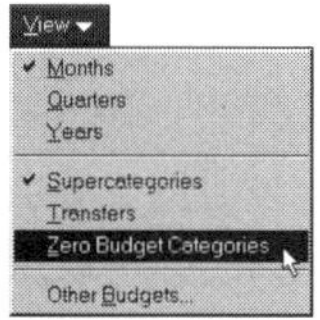

Figure 10.10 *Use the View menu to set display options for the current budget.*

To change the budget view:

1. Click the View button, as shown in **Figure 10.10**.
2. To set the time period for each budget column, choose Months, Quarters, or Years.
3. To hide or show supercategories, account transfers, or categories that have a budget of zero (0), choose the matching menu command. Each command is a toggle.

Renaming or Deleting a Budget

Quicken does not allow you to rename or delete the active budget. To accomplish either of these actions, you must first create an additional budget that you can switch to while renaming or deleting the other budget.

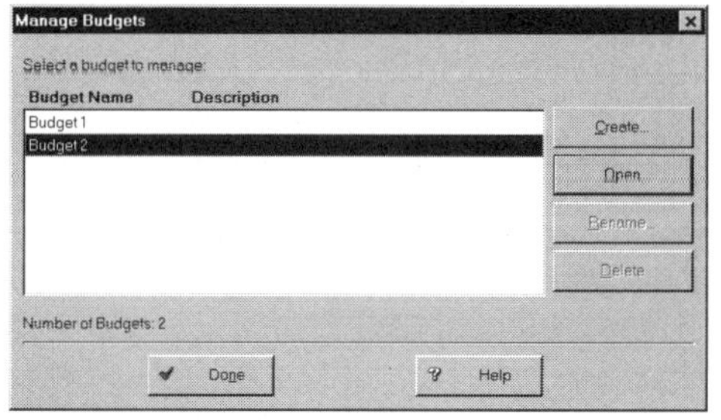

Figure 10.11 *If you have created several budgets, you must use the Manage Budgets dialog box to work with them.*

To rename or delete a budget:

1. If you have only one budget, create a second one by clicking the New button in the Budget window.
2. If the second budget isn't currently displayed, choose Other Budgets from the View menu. The Manage Budgets dialog box appears (see **Figure 10.11**). Select the second budget and click Open. The chosen budget becomes active.

3. Choose Other Budgets from the View menu. Select the original budget, and then click Delete or Rename, as desired.
4. To close the dialog box, click Done.

Saving and Restoring a Budget

Unlike other parts of Quicken, changes made to a budget are not automatically saved. To store a new budget or any changes made to an existing one, you *must* click the Save button.

To revert to the most recently saved budget (discarding all changes), click the Restore button.

✓ Tips

- When setting annual budget amounts, set the view to Years (see **Figure 10.12**). Any budget amount entered will automatically be divided by 12 when you switch to Months view or by 4 when examined in Quarters view.
- If you'd like to analyze your budget data in another program (a spreadsheet, for instance), choose Copy All from the Edit button menu. The entire budget is copied to the Windows clipboard, where it is available for pasting into the documents of other programs.
- When creating additional budgets, be sure to save them before switching to the original budget. If you forget to click Save, the new budget is discarded.

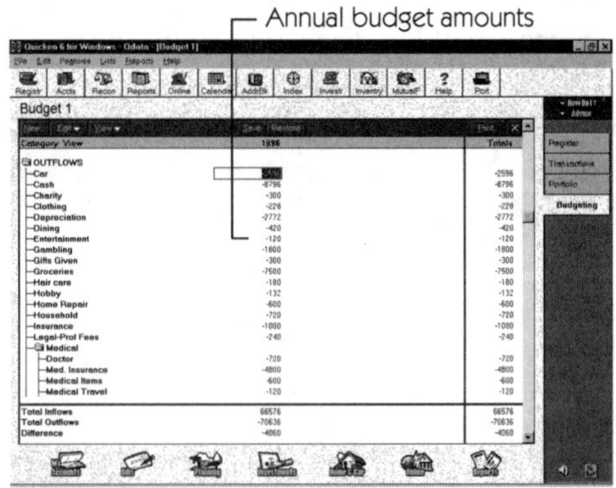

Figure 10.12 *A budget in Years view displays only the annual budget amount for each category.*

Using Supercategories

You use a *supercategory* to combine budget amounts for a selected subset of categories into one total. Quicken provides several predefined supercategories that you can use, such as Discretionary and Non-Discretionary, Other Income, and Salary Income.

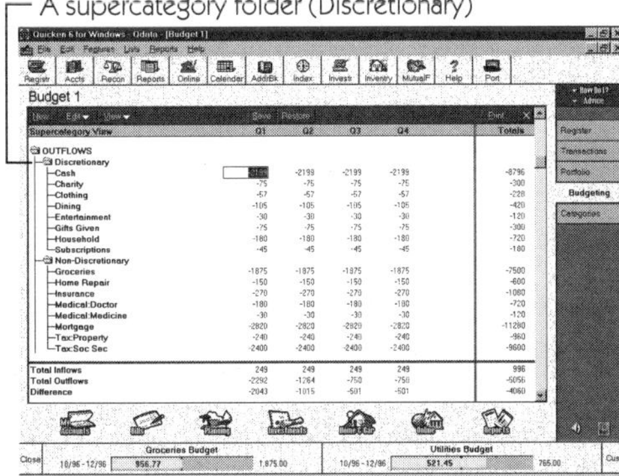

Figure 10.13 *Supercategories are displayed as folders in the Budget window.*

To display supercategories in the Budget window, choose Supercategories from the View button's menu. New folders for all defined supercategories are added to the Budget window, as shown in **Figure 10.13**. To return to the normal budget view, choose the same command again.

You can also create your own supercategories. For example, if you operate a small business, you could lump all business-related categories into Business Income and Business Expenses.

To create a supercategory:

1. Choose Category/Transfer from the Lists menu, or press Ctrl C.
2. Click the Super button at the top of the Category & Transfer list. The Manage Supercategories dialog box appears, as shown in **Figure 10.14**.
3. Click New to create a new supercategory.
4. With the new supercategory still selected, Ctrl-click to choose categories and subcategories that you want to assign to it.
5. Click the Assign button.
6. Click OK to accept the changes.

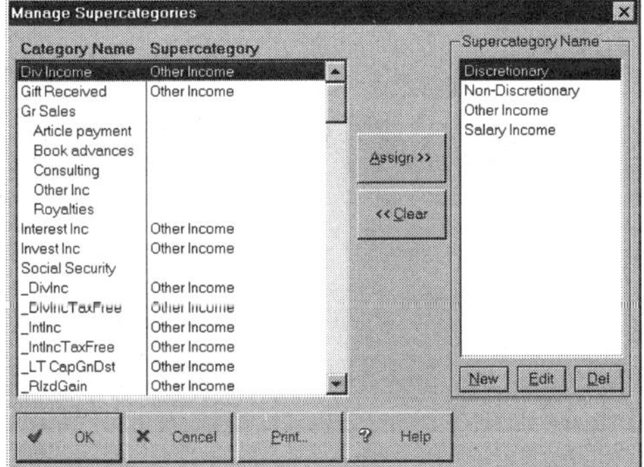

Figure 10.14 *You create, edit, and delete supercategories using the Manage Supercategories dialog box.*

To learn more about supercategories, see Chapter 3.

Creating a Budget Report

Of course, the point of creating a budget is to enable you to compare your *actual* spending against what you *intended* to spend (i.e., the budgeted amounts). This cannot be accomplished in the Budget window. Instead, you must create a report.

Here are some ways that you can generate a budget report:

- Choose Reports ➪ Other ➪ Budget.
- Choose Reports ➪ Home ➪ Monthly Budget.
- Click the Reports button in the iconbar. The Create Report dialog box appears (see **Figure 10.15**). Click the Home or Other tab, and then choose Monthly Budget or Budget.
- Choose EasyAnswer Reports from the Reports menu. The EasyAnswer Reports & Graphs dialog box appears (see **Figure 10.16**). Select "Did I meet my budget?," choose a time frame, and click the Show Report or Show Graph button.

Another way to monitor your budget is to display progress bars at the bottom of the Budget window (see **Figure 10.17**). To view the bars, choose Features ➪ Planning ➪ Progress Bars. To turn off the bars, choose the same command again or click the Close button to the left of the bars.

The information that is displayed is set separately for the left and right progress bars. Each bar can display a budget goal for a category, a supercategory budget, or a savings goal.

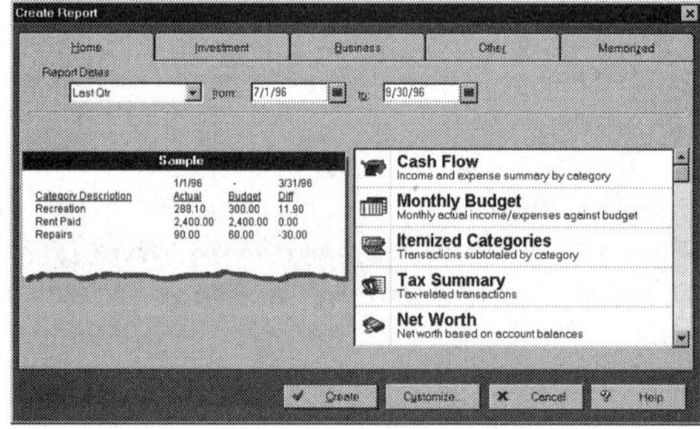

Figure 10.15 *You can create dozens of reports in the Create Report dialog box.*

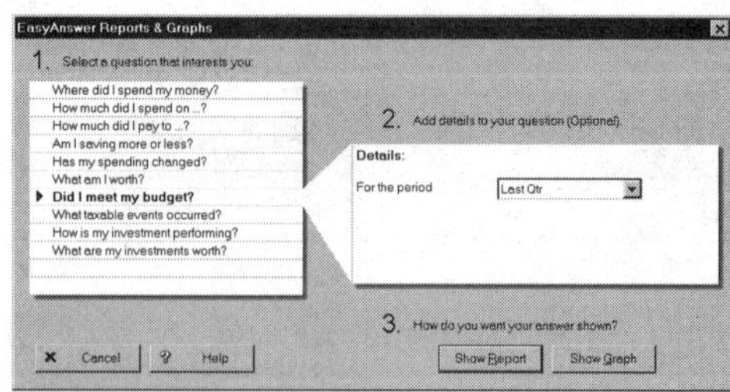

Figure 10.16 *The EasyAnswer Reports & Graphs dialog box.*

Figure 10.17 *A close-up of a progress bar.*

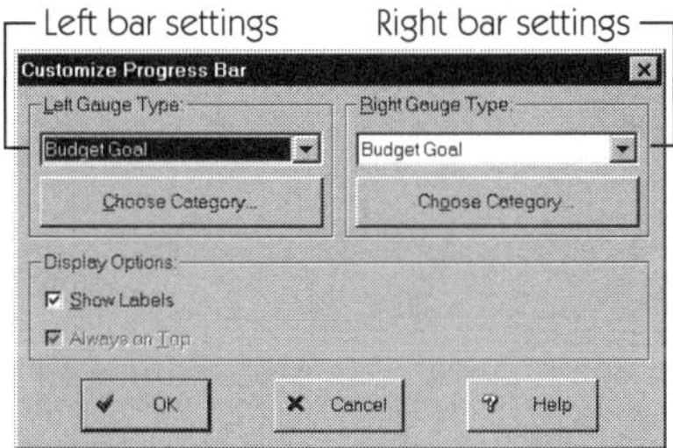

Figure 10.18 *Use the Customize Progress Bar dialog box to choose what will be shown in the left and right progress bars.*

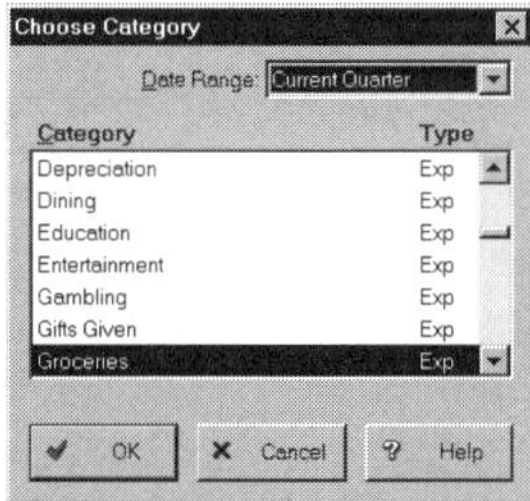

Figure 10.19 *Select a category and a date range to monitor.*

To set display options for a bar:

1. Click the Cust (Customize) button to the right of the bars. The Customize Progress Bars dialog box appears (see **Figure 10.18**).
2. Choose bar types from the Left Gauge Type and Right Gauge Type drop-down lists. (To display budget information in the bars, choose Budget Goal or Supercategory Budget.)
3. Click the button beneath the Left or Right Gauge Type to specify the category or supercategory to display. The dialog box shown in **Figure 10.19** appears.
4. Choose a category or supercategory, and then click OK.
5. When you are through setting options, click OK to dismiss the Customize Progress Bar dialog box.

✔ **Tip**

- You can print the current budget list, report, or graph by choosing the Print command from the File menu or by pressing Ctrl P.

Loans

About Loans

Quicken makes it easy to track loans, whether you are the borrower or the lender. You create a separate account for each loan. When you finish defining a loan in which you are the borrower (such as a mortgage on your house or an auto loan), Quicken automatically creates a *liability account*. Loans for which you are the lender are created as *asset accounts*.

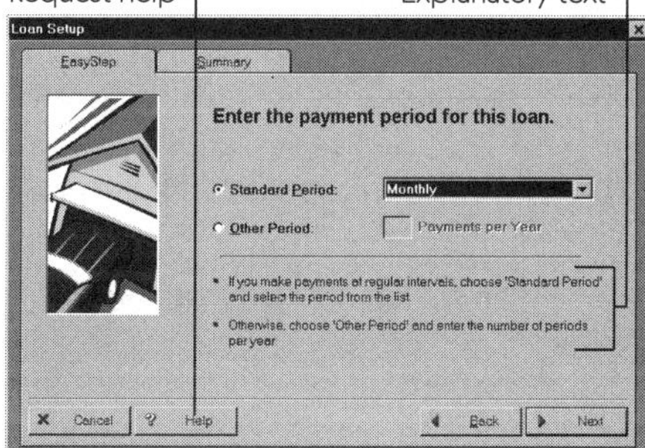

Figure 11.1 *Every EasyStep dialog box includes a Help button. Most of them also provide explanatory text.*

Creating a New Loan

To help you create a new loan, Quicken presents a series of EasyStep dialog boxes. The specific dialog boxes shown depend on how you answer the questions, including whether you are the borrower or the lender, whether the loan includes a balloon payment at the end, and so on. If you don't understand a given data request, read the explanatory text at the bottom of the dialog box or click the Help button (see **Figure 11.1**).

After responding to each prompt or question, click Next to continue. To return to the previous dialog box, click Back. To halt the process, click Cancel or the close box.

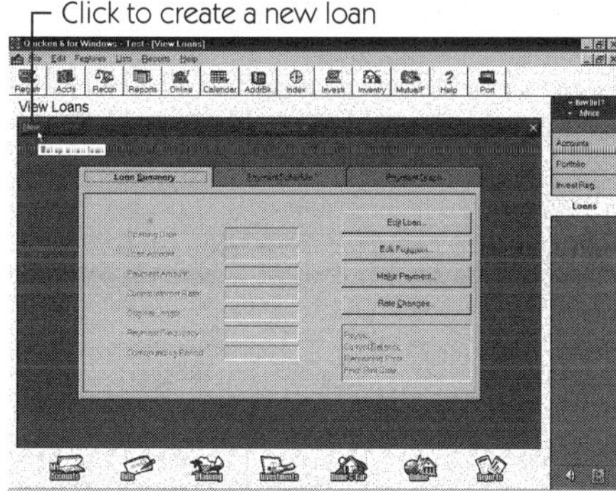

Figure 11.2 *All loans are created, viewed, and managed in the View Loans window.*

To create a loan (as the borrower):

1. Open the View Loans window (see **Figure 11.2**). Choose Features ⇨ Paying Bills ⇨ Loans, press Ctrl H, or click the Home & Car activity bar icon and choose Set Up or Track a Loan.

2. Click the New button at the top of the View Loans window. The New Loan dialog box appears. Click Next to continue.
3. Click the Borrow Money radio button (see **Figure 11.3**).
4. Because this is a new loan, click the New Account radio button. Enter a name for the loan account.

   The additional dialog boxes that appear will vary depending on the answers you give.
5. The final two EasyStep dialog boxes summarize the loan information entered (see **Figure 11.4**). Any necessary changes can be made here. Click Next and Done to finish the loan setup. The Setup Loan Payment dialog box appears (see **Figure 11.5**).
6. If loan payments include more than principal and interest (insurance and taxes, for example), click the Edit button. A standard Split Transaction window appears (see **Figure 11.6**). Enter the additional payment categories and amounts. Click Finished when you're done. The Full Payment total in the Setup Loan Payment dialog box updates to reflect the additional amount.
7. Select a payment type from the drop-down list. The standard choices are Payment (handwrite a check) and Print Check (print a check with Quicken). If you have on-line bill paying, you can also choose Online Pmt.
8. Click the Payment Method button. The Select Payment Method dialog box appears (see **Figure 11.7**).

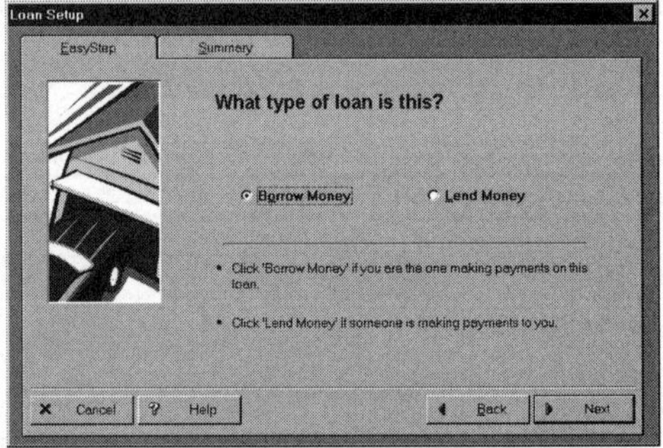

Figure 11.3 *Click a radio button to indicate the type of loan you are creating.*

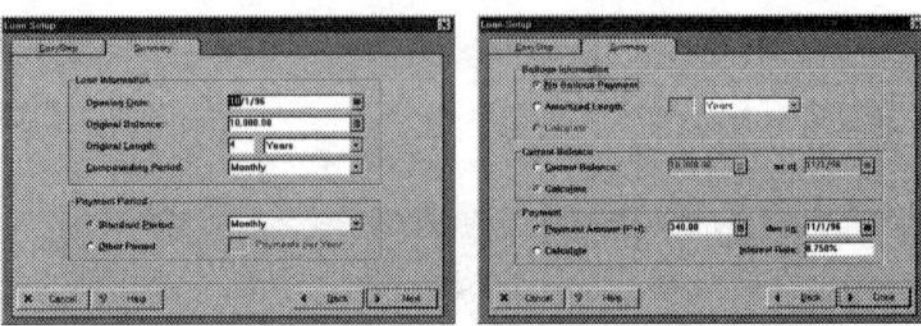

Figure 11.4 *The loan terms are displayed in this pair of Summary dialog boxes.*

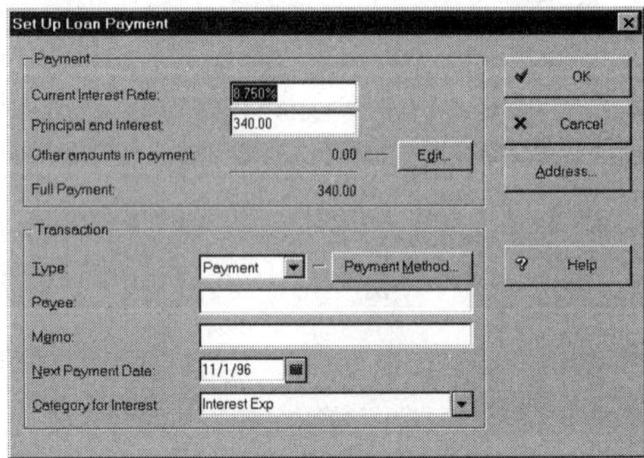

Figure 11.5 *You enter payment details in the Setup Loan Payment dialog box.*

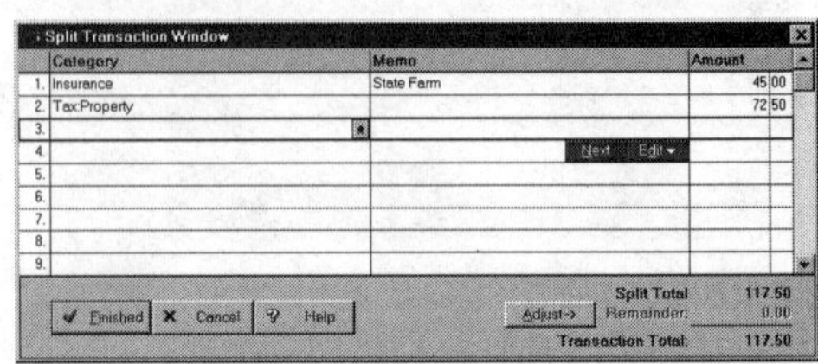

Figure 11.6 *Enter additional payment amounts in this split transaction window.*

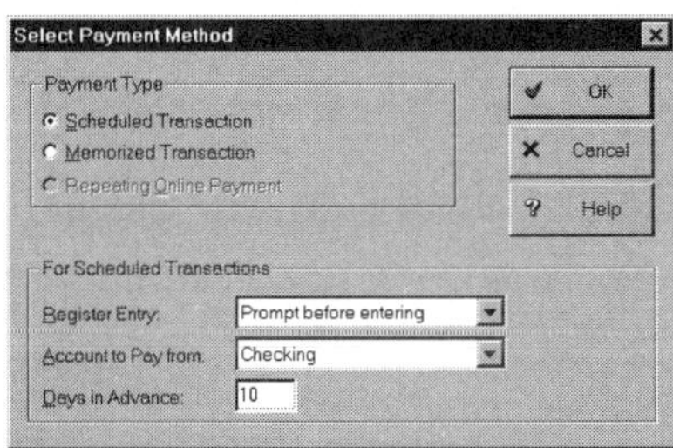

Figure 11.7 *Specify payment options in the Select Payment Method dialog box.*

Specify payment options, and click OK.

9. Enter the name of the lender in the Payee text box.
10. If you chose Print Check in Step 7, click the Address button so you can enter a mailing address for the payee.
11. Make any other necessary changes, and click OK.

The loan setup process is slightly different when you are the money lender, rather than the borrower.

To create a loan (as the lender):

1. Perform Steps 1–2 from "To create a loan (as the lender)."
2. Click the Lend Money radio button (refer to **Figure 11.3**).
3. Complete the remaining EasyStep dialog boxes and review the summary information for the loan.
4. Click Done to complete the loan setup. The Setup Loan Payment dialog box appears, as shown in **Figure 11.8**.
5. If loan payments include more than principal and interest, click the Edit button. A standard Split Transaction window appears (refer to **Figure 11.6**). Enter the additional payment categories and amounts. Click Finished when you are done. The Full Payment total in the Setup Loan Payment dialog box updates to reflect the additional amount.
6. Click the Payment Method button. The Select Payment Method dialog box appears. Specify payment options, and click OK.

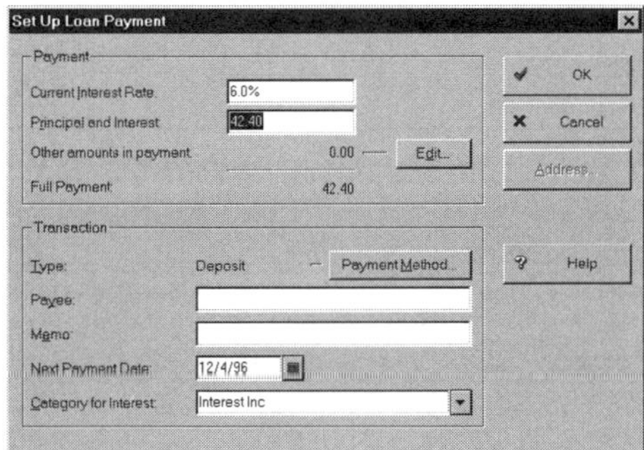

Figure 11.8 *Use the Setup Loan Payment dialog box to indicate how and by whom you will be paid.*

7. Enter the name of the borrower in the Payee text box.
8. Make any other necessary changes, and click OK.

✔ **Tips**

- If you aren't sure about the terms of your loan, review your loan documents or speak to your lender.
- A loan in which you are the borrower can be set up while you are creating a liability account. If you click Yes in the final dialog box of the liability account setup (see **Figure 11.9**), the same Loan Setup dialog boxes presented in this section appear. For additional details, refer to Chapter 2.

Viewing Loan Information

You use the View Loans window to view the details for any of your current loans, as well as change the terms or payment methods. After selecting a loan by clicking the Choose Loan button, you can do any of the following:

- View a summary of the loan terms by clicking the Loan Summary tab (see **Figure 11.10**).
- Examine the amortization table for the loan terms by clicking the Payment Schedule tab (see **Figure 11.11**).
- View a graph showing the loan balance and payment history over time by clicking the Payment Graph tab (see **Figure 11.12**).

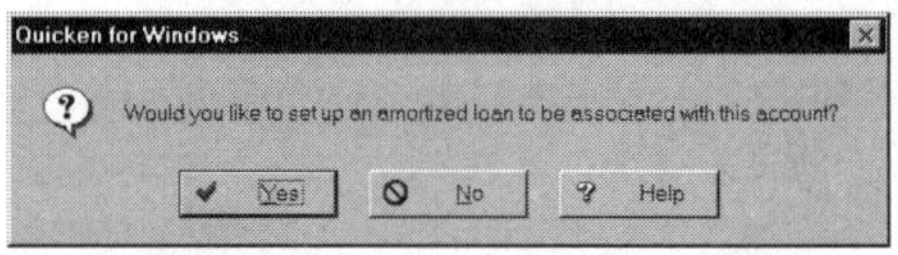

Figure 11.9 *Click Yes to use EasyStep to create a loan.*

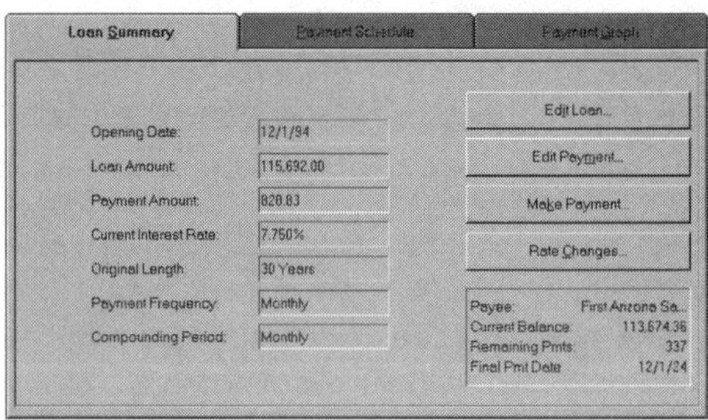

Figure 11.10 *The terms of the loan are displayed in the Loan Summary window.*

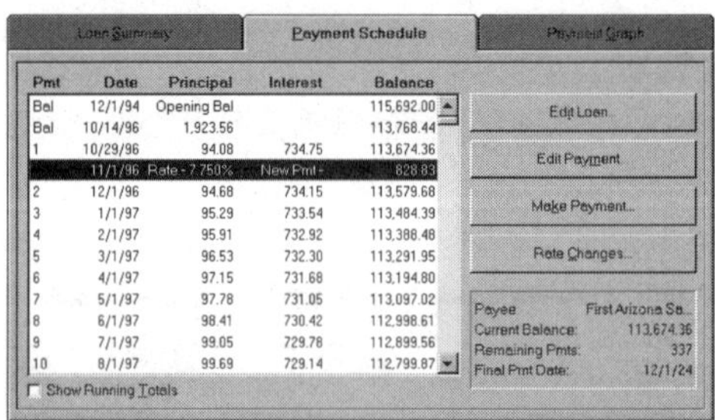

Figure 11.11 *The Payment Schedule window presents an amortization table for the selected loan.*

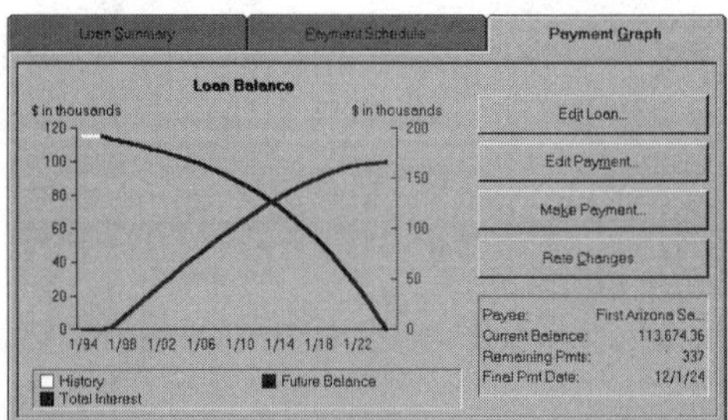

Figure 11.12 *Click the Payment Graph tab to view a line graph showing how the loan balance decreases as payments are made.*

Making Loan Payments

Depending on how you originally set up the loan in Quicken, there are two ways that you can make payments:

- If you set the payments to be automatically-entered scheduled transactions or if you use on-line bill paying, each payment is made and recorded automatically.
- If you specified another means of making payments, you can record each payment in the View Loans window, as described below.

To make a loan payment:

1. Open the View Loans window. Choose Features ⇨ Paying Bills ⇨ Loans, press Ctrl H, or click the Home & Car activity bar icon and choose Set Up or Track a Loan.
2. If the correct loan isn't already displayed, select it by clicking the Choose Loan button.
3. Click the Make Payment button. The Loan Payment dialog box appears, as shown in **Figure 11.14**.
4. To make a normal payment or a payment plus an additional amount, click Regular. The Make Regular Payment dialog box appears (see **Figure 11.15**).

   To pay the usual amount, review the settings and then click OK.

   To include an additional amount in the payment, click the Split button, enter the amount as a new line in the Split Transaction window, select the loan name as the category, and then click Adjust, Finished, and OK.

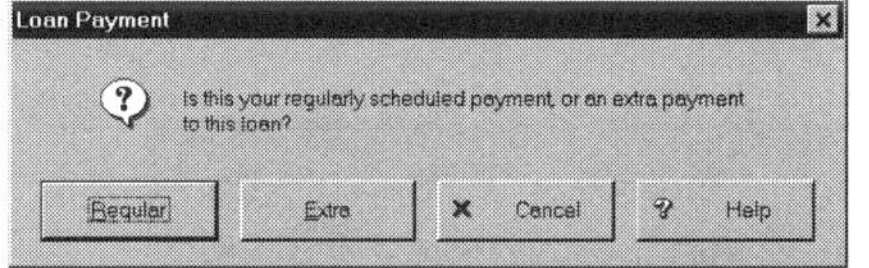

Figure 11.14 *Click Regular to make a normal payment (or a payment plus an additional amount). Click Extra to make a principal-only payment.*

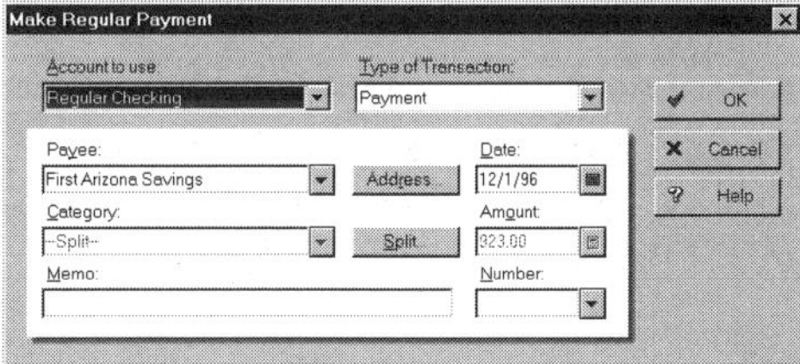

Figure 11.15 *If you are making the normal required loan payment, click OK.*

Making Loan Payments

or

4. To make a principal-only payment, click Extra. The Make Extra Payment dialog box appears (see **Figure 11.15**). Enter the amount of the payment, make any other necessary changes, and click OK.

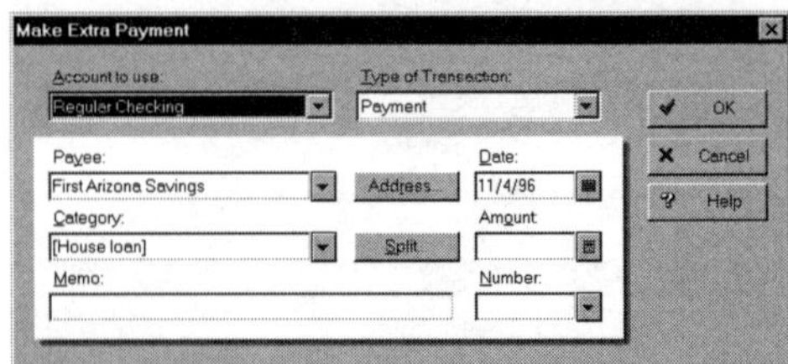

Figure 11.15 *When making an extra (principal-only) payment, enter an amount and click OK.*

Using the Loan Planner

If you are thinking about taking out a loan or lending someone else some money, you can quickly work out the financial details with the Loan Planner.

To use the Loan Planner:

1. Choose Features ⇨ Planning ⇨ Financial Planners ⇨ Loan. The Loan Planner dialog box appears (see **Figure 11.16**).
2. Choose the value for which you want to solve by clicking either the Loan Amount or Payment Per Period radio button.
3. Enter the loan details in the text boxes.
4. If necessary, click Calculate.

If you want to see the payment schedule for the proposed loan, click Schedule (see **Figure 11.17**).

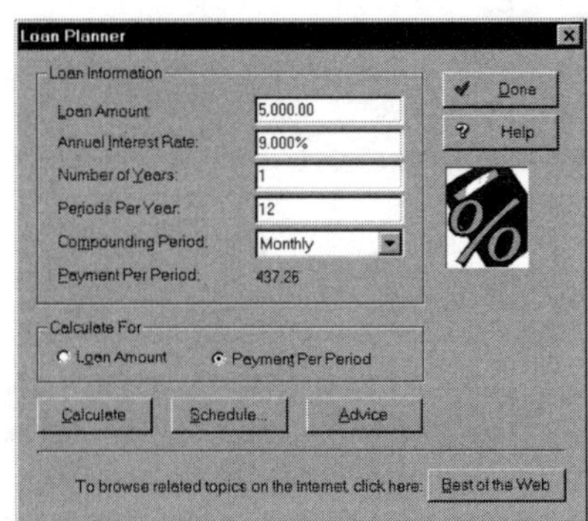

Figure 11.16 *The Loan Planner makes it easy to determine how much of a loan you can afford.*

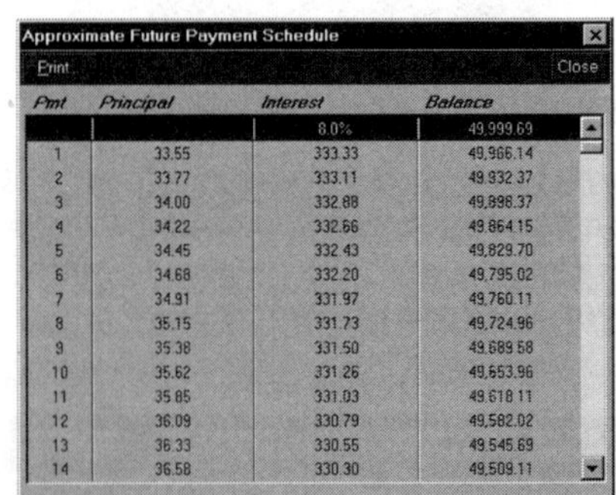

Pmt	Principal	Interest	Balance
		8.0%	49,999.69
1	33.55	333.33	49,966.14
2	33.77	333.11	49,932.37
3	34.00	332.88	49,898.37
4	34.22	332.66	49,864.15
5	34.45	332.43	49,829.70
6	34.68	332.20	49,795.02
7	34.91	331.97	49,760.11
8	35.15	331.73	49,724.96
9	35.38	331.50	49,689.58
10	35.62	331.26	49,653.96
11	35.85	331.03	49,618.11
12	36.09	330.79	49,582.02
13	36.33	330.55	49,545.69
14	36.58	330.30	49,509.11

Figure 11.17 *Click Schedule to see an approximate payment schedule (principal plus interest).*

Using the Financial Planning Calculators

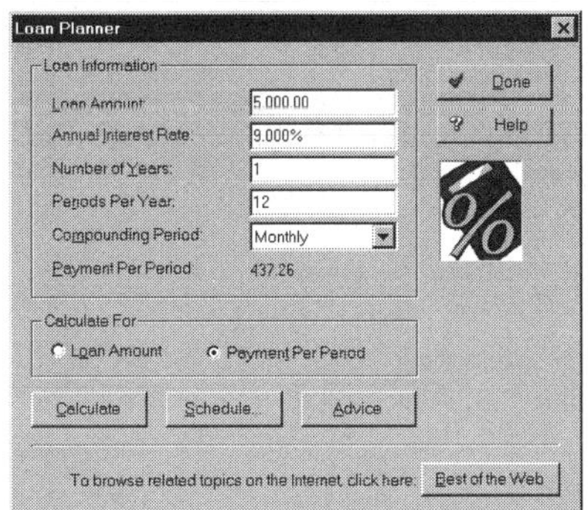

Figure 12.1 *Each planning calculator provides a series of text boxes in which you enter your financial data.*

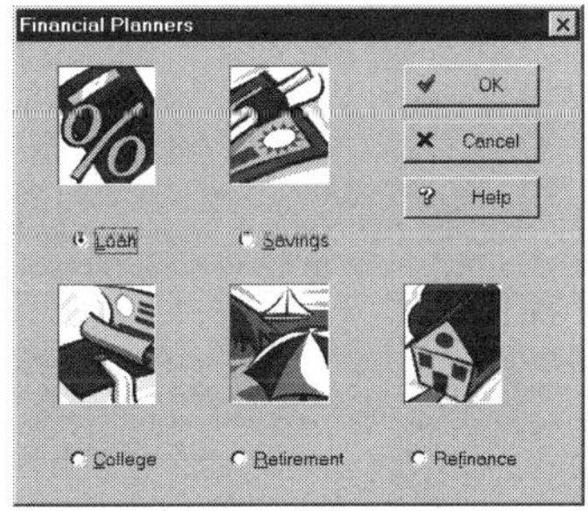

Figure 12.2 *You can also select a calculator by clicking a radio button in the Financial Planners window.*

About the Calculators

Hand calculators are great for simple math problems, but many of us are lost when it comes to financial calculations. To make it easy to answer common "what-if" questions, Quicken provides the following set of financial planning calculators (see **Figure 12.1**):

- Refinance Planner
- Loan Planner
- Investment Savings Planner
- College Planner
- Retirement Planner

By plugging in a few numbers, you can use the calculators to answer important financial questions, such as whether refinancing a mortgage will save money and how soon you will reach the break even point, and the amount of money you must save to finance your child's college education.

To use any of the planning calculators, choose Features ⇨ Planning ⇨ Financial Planners ⇨ *calculator name*. Each calculator opens in its own window. (Note that the Loan Planner is discussed only in Chapter 11.)

✔ Tip

- Another way to open a calculator is to click the Planning icon in the activity bar and choose Use Financial Planning Calculators (see **Figure 12.2**).

Refinance Planner

You can use Refinance Planner (see **Figure 12.3**) to determine whether this is a good time to refinance your mortgage. In addition to showing how much you can save each month, Refinance Planner also does a break even analysis, showing the number of months it will take to recoup any closing costs and points associated with the new loan.

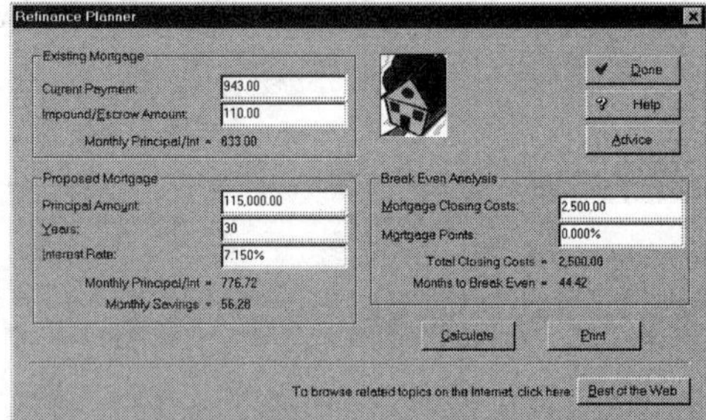

Figure 12.3 *The Refinance Planner.*

To use Refinance Planner:

1. Choose Features ⇨ Planning ⇨ Financial Planners ⇨ Refinance.
2. Enter the amount of your present monthly mortgage in the Current Payment text box.
3. In the Impound/Escrow Amount text box, enter the portion of your current monthly payment that is not applied to principal or interest. Typical costs that contribute to this item include homeowner's insurance, property taxes, and mortgage insurance. (If you aren't certain of this amount, contact your lender.)

   The figure shown for Monthly Principal/Interest is automatically calculated by subtracting the Impound/Escrow Amount from the Current Payment.
4. After contacting a lender, enter the figures for the proposed loan in the Proposed Mortgage and Break Even Analysis. Click Calculate.
5. *Optional:* If you want a record of the analysis, click Print (see **Figure 12.4**). To explore related topics on the World Wide Web, click Best of the Web. (To use the latter feature, you must first configure Quicken for on-line work. See Chapter 4.)

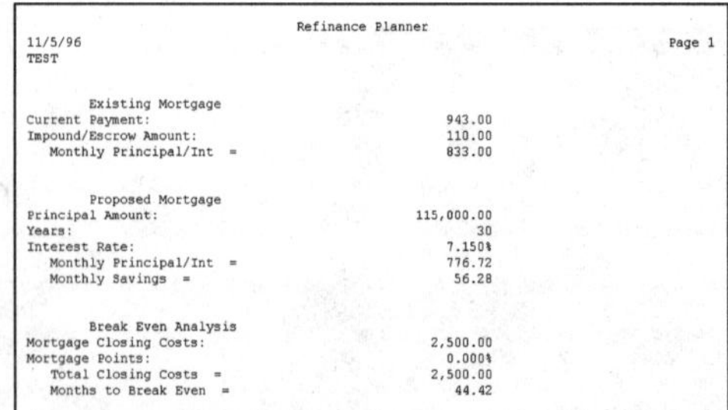

Refinance Planner

11/5/96 Page 1

TEST

Existing Mortgage

Current Payment:	943.00
Impound/Escrow Amount:	110.00
Monthly Principal/Int =	833.00

Proposed Mortgage

Principal Amount:	115,000.00
Years:	30
Interest Rate:	7.150%
Monthly Principal/Int =	776.72
Monthly Savings =	56.28

Break Even Analysis

Mortgage Closing Costs:	2,500.00
Mortgage Points:	0.000%
Total Closing Costs =	2,500.00
Months to Break Even =	44.42

Figure 12.4 *To make it easier to compare several possible loans, you can print each refinancing analysis. You can also use Window's Preview mode (shown here) to examine the report on-screen.*

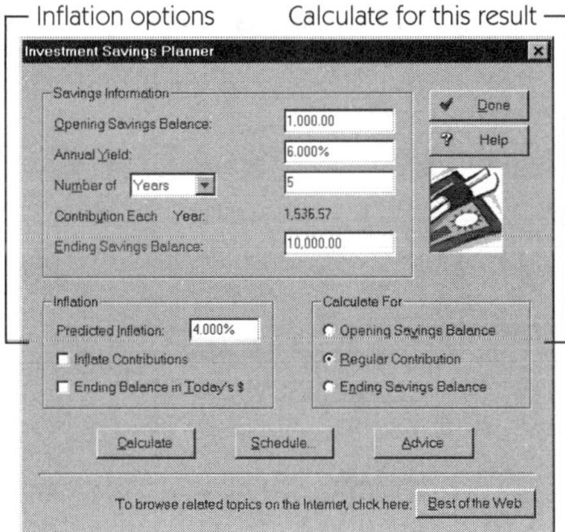

Figure 12.5 *The Investment Savings Planner.*

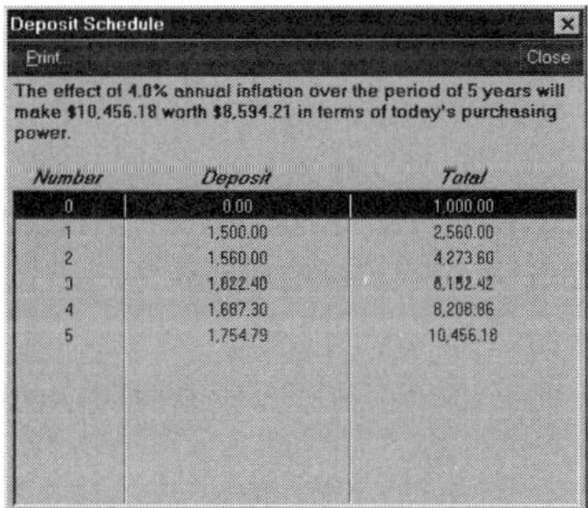
Deposit Schedule

Print Close

The effect of 4.0% annual inflation over the period of 5 years will make $10,456.18 worth $8,594.21 in terms of today's purchasing power.

Number	*Deposit*	*Total*
0	0.00	1,000.00
1	1,500.00	2,560.00
2	1,560.00	4,273.60
3	1,622.40	6,152.42
4	1,687.30	8,208.86
5	1,754.79	10,456.18

Figure 12.6 *Click the Schedule button to see how your account will grow over the term of the investment.*

Investment Savings Planner

The Investment Savings Planner (see **Figure 12.5**) helps you save for future goals. Assuming a fixed rate of interest and a given savings term, you can use Investment Savings Planner to solve for any of the following amounts:

- *Opening Balance*—the amount you must have in the account at the beginning.
- *Regular Contribution*—the amount you must contribute each period.
- *Ending Savings Balance*—the account total at the end of the savings term.

For example, if you enter an annual yield and the starting and ending balances, you can determine how much you will need to deposit each period.

To use Investment Savings Planner:

1. Choose Features ⇨ Planning ⇨ Financial Planners ⇨ Savings.
2. Choose an amount to solve for by clicking a radio button in the Calculate For section of the window.
3. Fill in the text boxes in the Savings Information section of the window.
4. *Optional:* You can adjust the results for the effects of anticipated annual inflation by entering a percentage for Predicted Inflation and clicking one or both of the check boxes in the Inflation section.
5. If necessary, click Calculate to compute the new results.
6. *Optional:* Click Schedule to view the account over the term of the investment (see **Figure 12.6**).

College Planner

College Planner (see **Figure 12.7**) is a variant of Investment Savings Planner, discussed on the previous page. You can solve for any of these amounts:

- *Annual College Costs*—the annual college costs you will be able to afford, given your current and planned savings,
- *Current College Savings*—the amount that must initially be in the account.
- *Ending Savings Balance*—the amount you must contribute each period in order to reach your goal.

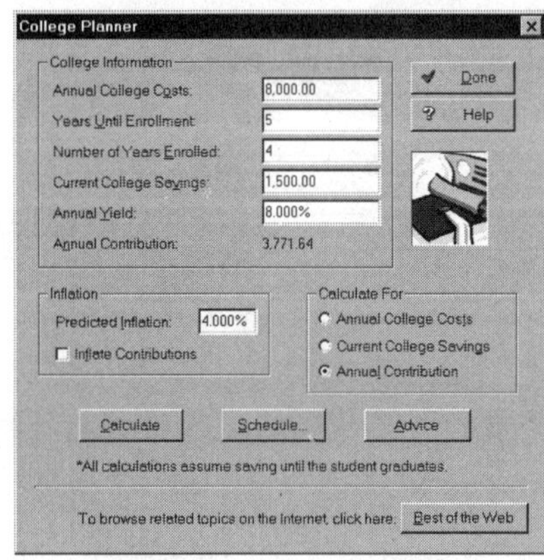

Figure 12.7 *The College Planner.*

To use College Planner:

1. Choose Features ⇨ Planning ⇨ Financial Planners ⇨ College.
2. Choose an amount to solve for by clicking a radio button in the Calculate For section of the window.
3. Fill in the text boxes in the College Information section of the window.
4. *Optional:* You can adjust the results for the effects of anticipated annual inflation by entering a percentage for Predicted Inflation and clicking the Inflate Contributions check box in the Inflation section.
5. If necessary, click Calculate to compute the new results.
6. *Optional:* Click Schedule to view the account from now through your child's college years, as shown in **Figure 12.8**.

Note that the calculations assume that you will continue to make annual deposits while your child is in college.

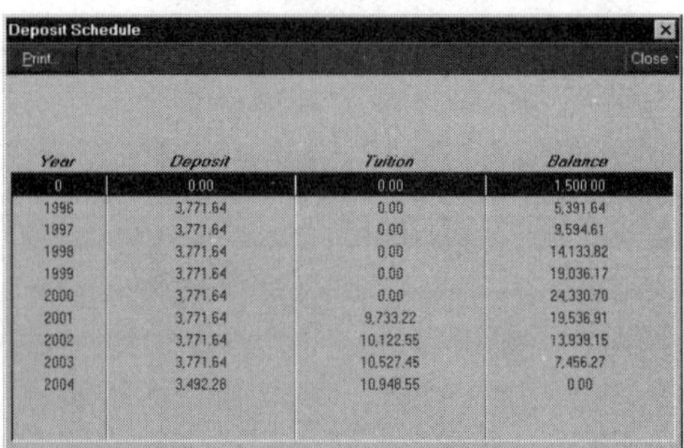

Deposit Schedule

Print   Close

Year	Deposit	Tuition	Balance
0	0.00	0.00	1,500.00
1996	3,771.64	0.00	5,391.64
1997	3,771.64	0.00	9,594.61
1998	3,771.64	0.00	14,133.82
1999	3,771.64	0.00	19,036.17
2000	3,771.64	0.00	24,330.70
2001	3,771.64	9,733.22	19,536.91
2002	3,771.64	10,122.55	13,939.15
2003	3,771.64	10,527.45	7,456.27
2004	3,492.28	10,948.55	0.00

Figure 12.8 *Click Schedule to view or print the proposed deposit schedule for the account.*

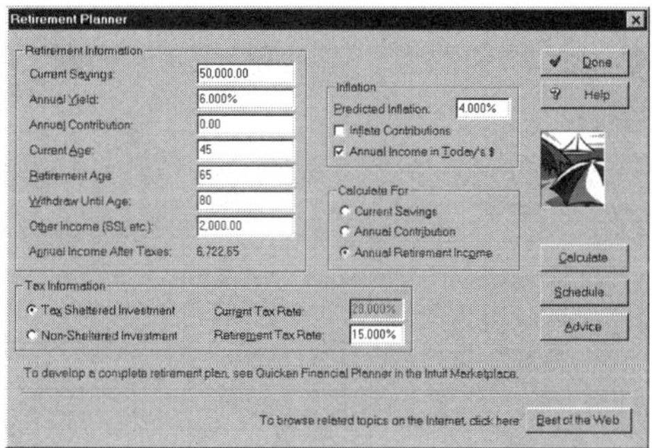

Figure 12.9 *The Retirement Planner.*

Retirement Planner

Because a comfortable retirement depends on such a large number of variables and may be many years in the future, Retirement Planner (see **Figure 12.9**) is a more complex calculator than the others. You can use it to solve for any of these amounts:

- *Current Savings*—the amount that must initially be in the account.
- *Annual Contribution*—the amount you must contribute each year in order to reach your goal.
- *Annual Retirement Income*—the annual amount available to you during your retirement years.

To use Retirement Planner:

1. Choose Features ⇨ Planning ⇨ Financial Planners ⇨ Retirement.
2. Choose an amount to solve for by clicking a radio button in the Calculate For section of the window.
3. Fill in the text boxes in the Retirement Information section of the window.
4. In the Tax Information section, click a radio button to indicate whether your retirement account(s) are currently tax-sheltered (in an IRA, for example) or are taxable. Change the tax rates, if necessary.
5. *Optional:* You can adjust the results for the effects of anticipated annual inflation by entering a percentage for Predicted Inflation and clicking one or both of the check boxes in the Inflation section.
6. If necessary, click Calculate to compute the new results.

7. *Optional:* Click Schedule to view the account from now through your retirement years (refer to **Figure 12.10**). To obtain a printout of the schedule and the calculation details (see **Figure 12.11**), click the Print button.

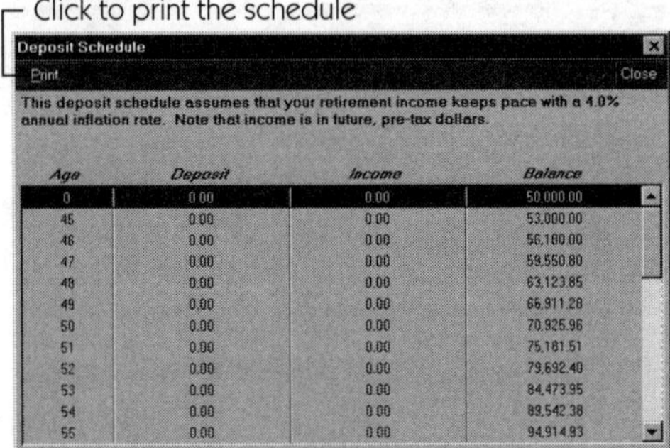

Figure 12.10 *Examine the schedule to see how your account will grow during the pre-retirement years, as well as how you will draw it down when you retire.*

✔ **Tips**

- The retirement calculations assume that each annual contribution is made at year-end and that withdrawals are made at the beginning of each year. You can substantially increase your retirement income by making all contributions at the *beginning* of each year, rather than at the end.
- If your retirement is many years away, you should be sure to check the option for Annual Income in Today's Dollars in the Inflation section. Then when you calculate Annual Retirement Income, the results are presented in terms of today's dollars. You can remove the check mark to see what the *actual* dollar amount will be.
- There are many opportunities to play "what if" with the Retirement Planner. If any of your assumptions are wrong (such as how long you will live, what the average annual rate of inflation will be, or the yield you can expect to achieve), the results may be dramatically under- or overstated.

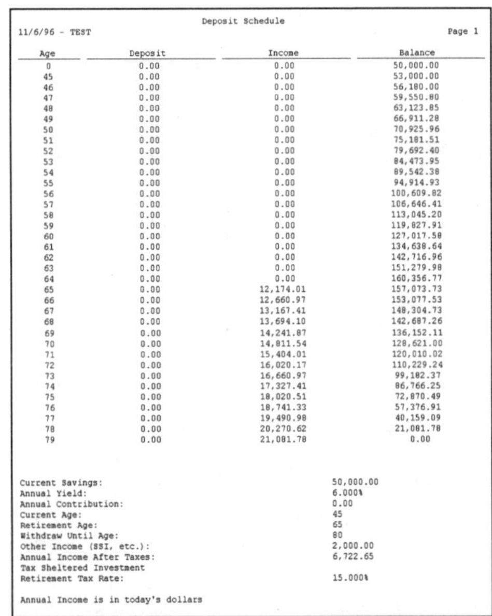
Deposit Schedule

11/6/96 - TEST Page 1

Age	Deposit	Income	Balance
0	0.00	0.00	50,000.00
45	0.00	0.00	53,000.00
46	0.00	0.00	56,180.00
47	0.00	0.00	59,550.80
48	0.00	0.00	63,123.85
49	0.00	0.00	66,911.28
50	0.00	0.00	70,925.96
51	0.00	0.00	75,181.51
52	0.00	0.00	79,692.40
53	0.00	0.00	84,473.95
54	0.00	0.00	89,542.38
55	0.00	0.00	94,914.93
56	0.00	0.00	100,609.82
57	0.00	0.00	106,646.41
58	0.00	0.00	113,045.20
59	0.00	0.00	119,827.91
60	0.00	0.00	127,017.58
61	0.00	0.00	134,638.64
62	0.00	0.00	142,716.96
63	0.00	0.00	151,279.98
64	0.00	0.00	160,356.77
65	0.00	12,174.01	157,073.73
66	0.00	12,660.97	153,077.53
67	0.00	13,167.41	148,304.73
68	0.00	13,694.10	142,687.26
69	0.00	14,241.87	136,152.11
70	0.00	14,811.54	128,621.00
71	0.00	15,404.01	120,010.02
72	0.00	16,020.17	110,229.24
73	0.00	16,660.97	99,182.37
74	0.00	17,327.41	86,766.25
75	0.00	18,020.51	72,870.49
76	0.00	18,741.33	57,376.91
77	0.00	19,490.98	40,159.09
78	0.00	20,270.62	21,081.78
79	0.00	21,081.78	0.00

Current Savings:	50,000.00
Annual Yield:	6.000%
Annual Contribution:	0.00
Current Age:	45
Retirement Age:	65
Withdraw Until Age:	80
Other Income (SSI, etc.):	2,000.00
Annual Income After Taxes:	6,722.65
Tax Sheltered Investment	
Retirement Tax Rate:	15.000%

Annual Income is in today's dollars

Figure 12.11 *The schedule printout also provides a record of your assumptions.*

Setting and Monitoring Financial Goals

13

A budget enables you to compare your actual income and expenses with the amounts you think you should be earning and spending. However, there is more to financial planning and monitoring than creating budgets. In this chapter, you'll learn how to accomplish the following tasks:

- Save for a goal.
- Check your credit rating.
- Create a debt reduction plan.
- Calculate your net worth.
- Track the equity in your home.
- Create financial forecasts.

Quicken also has several useful calculators that you can use to do financial planning. See Chapter 12 for details.

Saving for a Goal

Quicken can help you put aside money for a vacation, a new car, or any other expense. You can create *savings goals*—dummy savings accounts into which you transfer money from other accounts. (The money isn't actually transferred; it stays in the original accounts. Quicken simply marks the "saved" money as unavailable to you. In effect, a savings goal is Quicken's version of stashing small bills and change in a cookie jar.)

To create a savings goal:

1. Choose Features ⇨ Planning ⇨ Savings Goals, or click the Planning icon in the activity bar and choose

Save for an Upcoming Expense. The Savings Goals window appears.

2. Click the New button at the top of the window. The Create New Savings Goal dialog box appears (see **Figure 13.1**).
3. Enter the requested information and click OK. A new savings goal account is created and the Savings Goals window updates to show the new goal (see **Figure 13.2**). You can create additional goals by clicking the New button.

To make a contribution to or a withdrawal from a savings goal account, select the goal in the Savings Goals window and click the Contribute or Withdraw button at the top of the window. Enter the amount, date, and account to use for the transfer (see **Figure 13.3**).

To change or eliminate a goal, select the goal and click Edit or Delete. Click the Report button to create a transaction report for the selected goal.

✔ Tips

- To see the *real* balance for an account from which savings goal funds have been transferred, open the account register and choose Hide Savings Goals from the View drop-down menu.
- You can also track your progress by displaying a savings goal progress bar at the bottom of the Quicken window. See "To set display options for a bar" in Chapter 10 for information on creating progress bars.

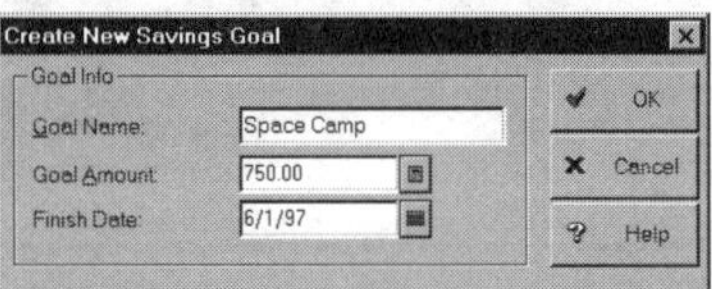

Figure 13.1 *Enter a name for the goal, the amount of the goal, and a date when the goal must be met.*

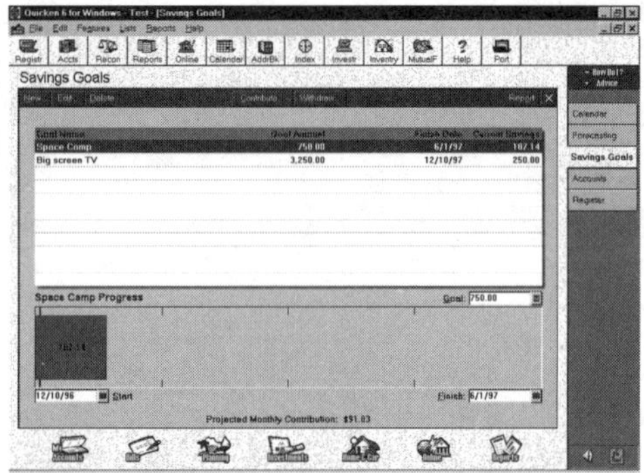

Figure 13.2 *You use the Savings Goals window to create, edit, delete, manage, and view the progress of savings goals.*

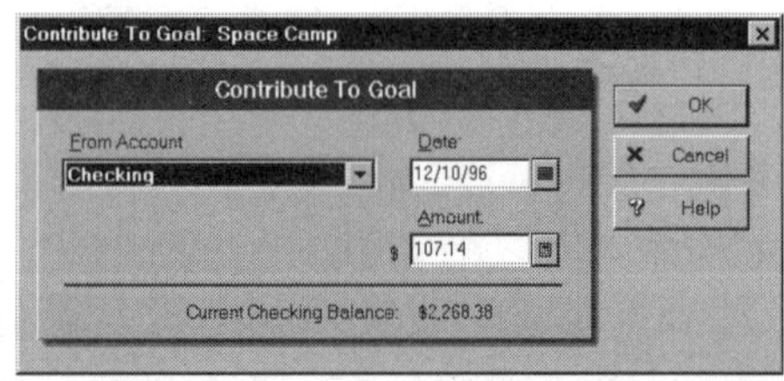

Figure 13.3 *To make a contribution to a savings goal, enter the data requested in the Contribute to Goal dialog box.*

Saving for a Goal

Applying for a Credit Report

Are you creditworthy? You may think so, but the next time you apply for a loan, mortgage, or a new credit card, you could be in for a surprise. Lenders weigh your credit history heavily when determining the amount of credit—if any—they are willing to extend to you.

You can't correct credit problems until you identify them. You can use Quicken to request a copy of your credit report.

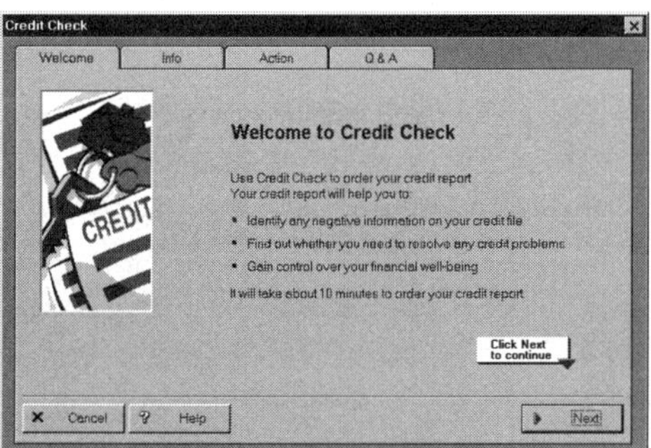

Figure 13.4 *This series of dialog boxes walks you through the application process. You can click tabs to jump directly to different sections, if you wish.*

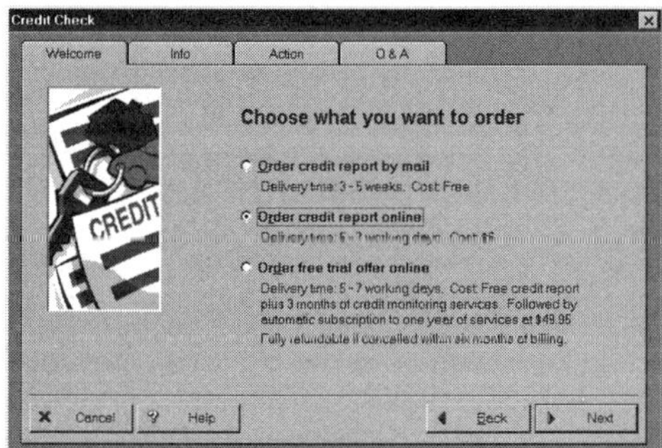

Figure 13.5 *You can apply for a free report by mail, an inexpensive report by modem, or enroll in a subscription credit monitoring service.*

To apply for a credit report:

1. Choose Features ⇨ Planning ⇨ Check My Credit Online, or click the Planning icon in the activity bar and choose Get a Personal Credit Report. The Credit Check dialog box appears, as shown in **Figure 13.4**.
2. After reading and responding to each dialog box, click the Next button. If you wish, you can jump to different parts of the application by clicking the tabs at the top of the dialog box.
3. As shown in **Figure 13.5**, there are three ways that you can apply for a credit report. Choose an option and then complete the application.
4. The final dialog box that appears depends on the type of report you requested (refer to **Figure 13.5**). Click the button to Send or Print the credit report request.

✔ Tip

- Click the Q & A tab to learn about credit reports and to review tips for repairing a bad credit rating.

Reducing Debt

If you are in debt and have Quicken Deluxe, you can use the Debt Reduction Planner to discover the fastest way to become debt free.

To use the Debt Reduction Planner:

1. Choose Features ⇨ Planning ⇨ Create a Debt Reduction Plan, or click the Planning icon in the activity bar and choose Create a Debt Reduction Plan. The Debt reduction dialog box appears.
2. Click Next to begin. Quicken lists all of your current debts, as shown in **Figure 13.6**. Click Add to enter information about a non-Quicken debt. To eliminate a debt from your plan, select it and click Remove. Click Update to re-import debt data from your Quicken accounts.
3. If information is missing for one or more of the accounts (the annual interest rate or minimum payment, for example), the Edit Debt Reduction dialog box appears (see **Figure 13.7**). Supply the requested data.
4. Quicken shows the current status of your debts. In the Order section of the dialog box, you can change the order in which the debts are paid off, if you wish.
5. If you have savings, you can apply some of it to the debts as a one-time payment.
6. In the Budget section of the dialog box, Quicken lists your largest expense categories. Enter amounts that you believe you can cut back.
7. Quicken creates the debt reduction plan (see **Figure 13.8**).

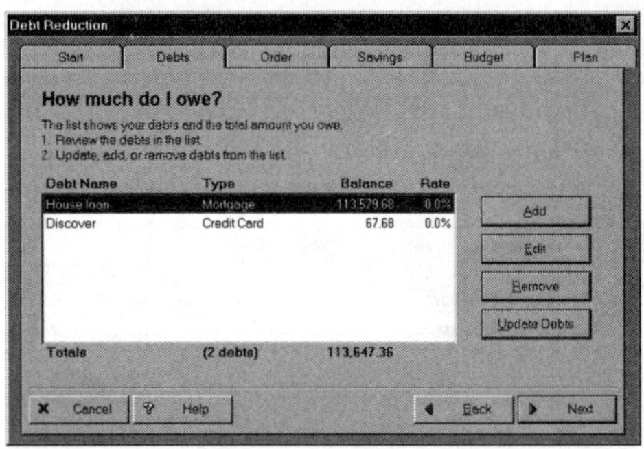

Figure 13.6 *Click Add to add a debt that is not recorded in Quicken. Click Remove to eliminate a debt that you do not want to include in your plan.*

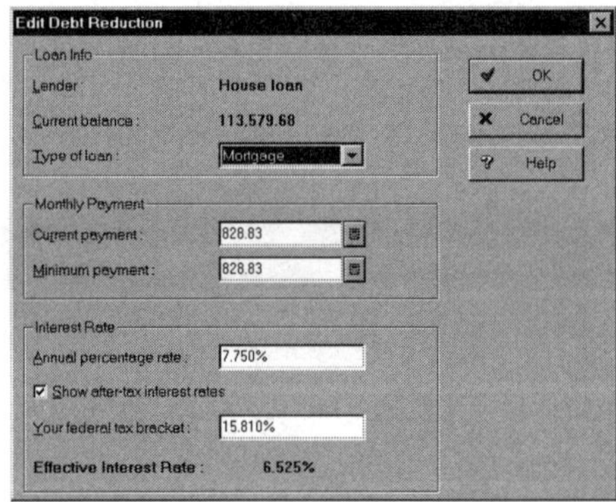

Figure 13.7 *Enter the additional information requested for each debt.*

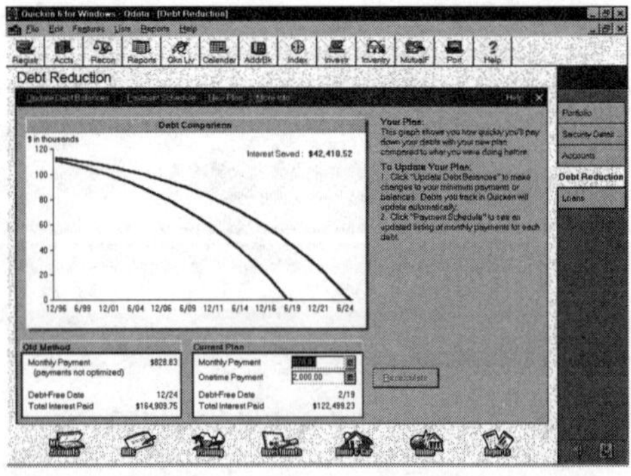

Figure 13.8 *Quicken presents the debt reduction plan. Refer to the on-screen instructions for updating the plan, displaying a payment schedule, and so on.*

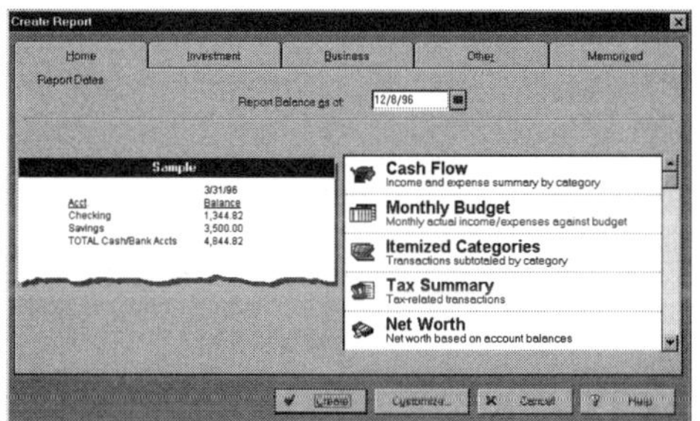

Figure 13.9 *Choose Net Worth as the type of report to create.*

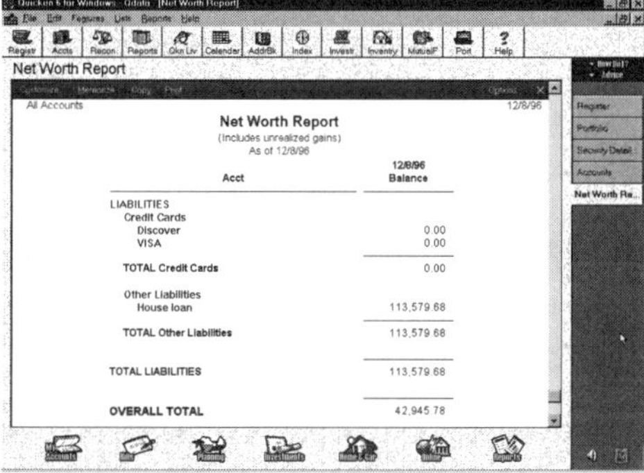

Figure 13.10 *This report shows how your accounts contribute to your net worth.*

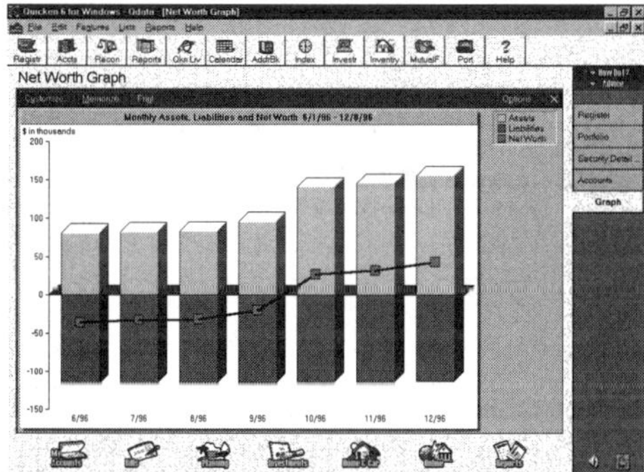

Figure 13.11 *Create a graph to see how your net worth changes over time.*

Calculating Your Net Worth

To determine your net worth, you subtract all liabilities (loans, credit card balances, and the like) from your total assets (investments, savings and checking accounts, personal property, real estate holdings, and so on). If you diligently record your financial data, you can easily determine your net worth.

The Net Worth Figure

If all you want to see is the single figure that represents your net worth, choose Account from the List menu or press Ctrl A. The Account List appears. Click the All Types tab at the top of the window. The figure shown for the Balance Total is your net worth.

Net Worth Report

You can create a standard report that shows how your assets and liabilities contribute to your net worth. Choose Reports ⇨ Home ⇨ Net Worth. The Create Report dialog box appears (see **Figure 13.9**). Make sure that Net Worth is selected and then click Create. The resulting report shows your current net worth (see **Figure 13.10**).

Net Worth Graph

Choose EasyAnswer Reports from the Reports menu. Choose "What am I worth?" from Section 1, and then click Show Graph. A bar graph (see **Figure 13.11**) shows your net worth over the specified period.

✔ Tip

- To see how your net worth changes over time, you can customize the Net Worth report by setting the interval to Month or Quarter.

Tracking Home Equity

The *equity* that you have in your home is its value minus whatever you still owe to the bank. On the day that you move in, your equity is simply the amount that you paid as a down payment. As the years pass and you pay off more of the loan principal, your equity in the property increases. Knowing your equity is useful when applying for a home equity loan or when you are thinking of selling the house.

To track home equity:

1. Create an asset account called Home Value or something similar. Enter the approximate price for which you could sell it as the asset's Value (see **Figure 13.12**).
2. If you haven't already done so, choose Features ⇨ Paying Bills ⇨ Loans and create a new loan for your mortgage. Doing so creates a liability account. As you make the monthly payments, the amount owed on this account decreases.
3. Click the Reports button, choose the Net Worth report in the Create Report dialog box, and click the Customize button.
4. Enter a new title for the report, such as Home Equity. Click the Accounts tab.
5. Select the Home Value and Home Loan accounts. (If you have other home asset or liability accounts—such as a second mortgage or an equity loan—include them, too.)
6. Click Create to generate the report (see **Figure 13.13**).

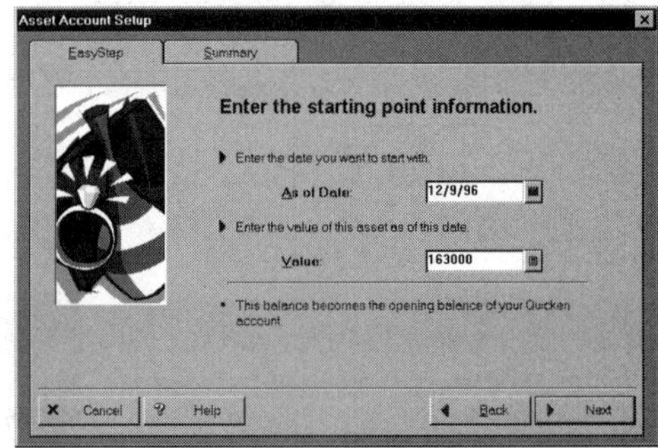

Figure 13.12 *Enter the approximate resale value of your house as its starting value. As market conditions change and you make improvements to the house, you can update the value.*

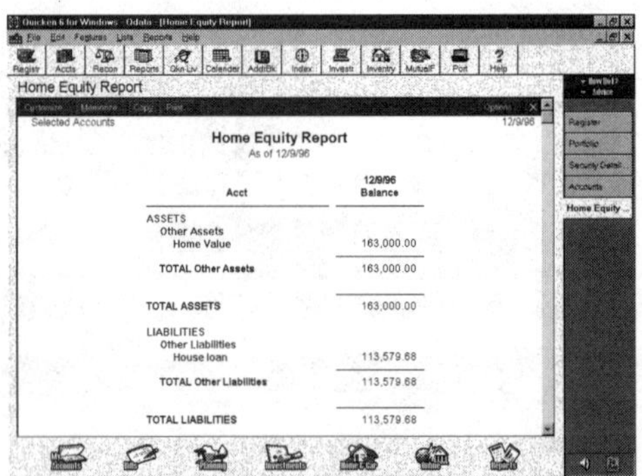

Figure 13.13 *Your equity is the difference between your home asset accounts and home liability accounts.*

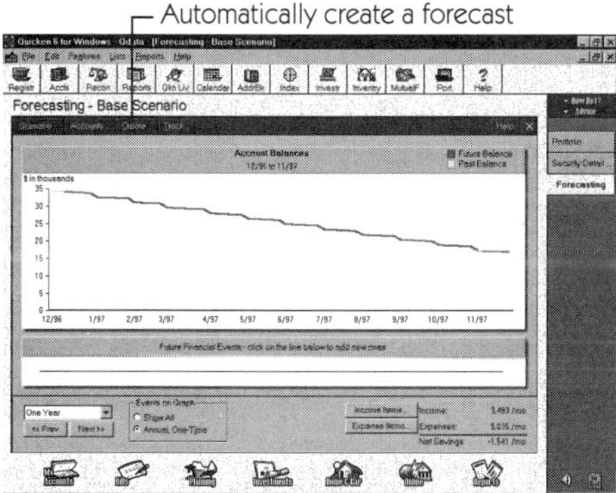

Figure 13.14 *The forecasting base scenario.*

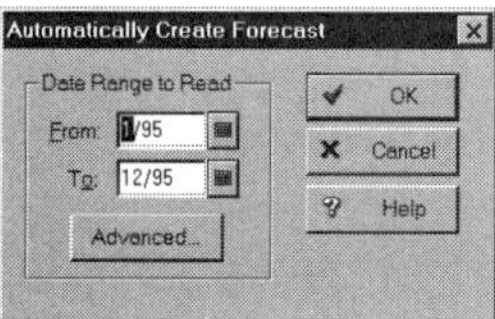

Figure 13.15 *At a minimum, you must specify the date range on which to base the forecast.*

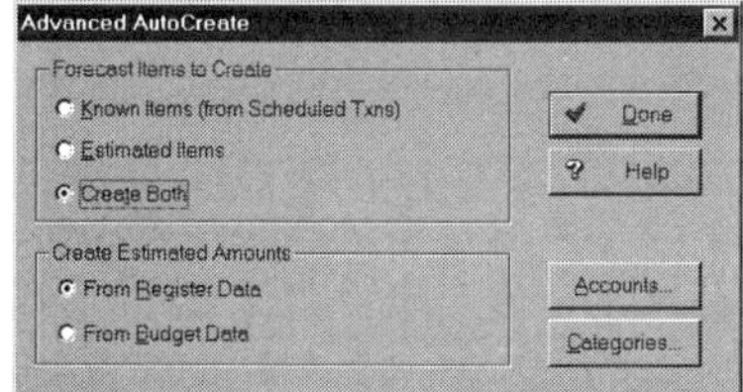

Figure 13.16 *You can fine tune an automatic forecast by specifying the types of base data to use, as well as the particular accounts and categories to consider.*

Financial Forecasting

Forecasting enables you to project your account balances into the future. A forecast is based on *known events* (scheduled transactions, plus others that have occurred three times in the last four months) and *estimates* (budget amounts and register items).

To create a forecast:

1. Choose Features ⇨ Planning ⇨ Forecasting. The Forecasting Base Scenario window appears (see **Figure 13.14**).
2. Click the Create button at the top of the window. The Automatically Create Forecast dialog box appears (see **Figure 13.15**).
3. Specify a date range on which to base the forecast.
4. *Optional:* Click the Advanced button to set additional options. The Advanced AutoCreate dialog box appears (see **Figure 13.16**).

   A forecast can be based on real data (scheduled transactions), estimates (taken from the current budget or register data averages), or on both types of data.

   To select specific accounts and/or categories to use when generating the forecast, click Accounts or Categories.

   Click Done when you are finished setting advanced options.
5. To create the forecast, click OK in the Automatically Create Forecast dialog box.

Viewing the Forecast

You can choose a different time interval for the forecast from the drop-down list in the lower-left corner of the Forecast window. Click the Next or Prev button to scroll to the next or previous time period. You can move the cursor over any point on the time line to see the forecast amount for that date.

The tiny triangles beneath the time line are your scheduled transactions and annual/one-time transactions. You can click any triangle to see the event that it represents. You can specify the types of transactions that are shown by clicking one of the Events on Graph radio buttons.

Making Adjustments

Although an automatic forecast is a good place to start, adjustments are often necessary. (The more appropriate the original data, the more likely that the forecast will be accurate.)

To add a new event, click an approximate date for the transaction on the line beneath the graph. The Create New Item dialog box appears (see **Figure 13.17**). Enter the requested information. To specify a category for the transaction and the number of occurrences, click More. The Edit Advanced Info dialog box appears (see **Figure 13.18**). The forecast updates when the dialog boxes are closed.

Click the Accounts button at the top of the window to specify the accounts that will be included in the forecast. As shown in **Figure 13.19**, I excluded my IRA/pension accounts since I cannot spend the principal or interest from those accounts.

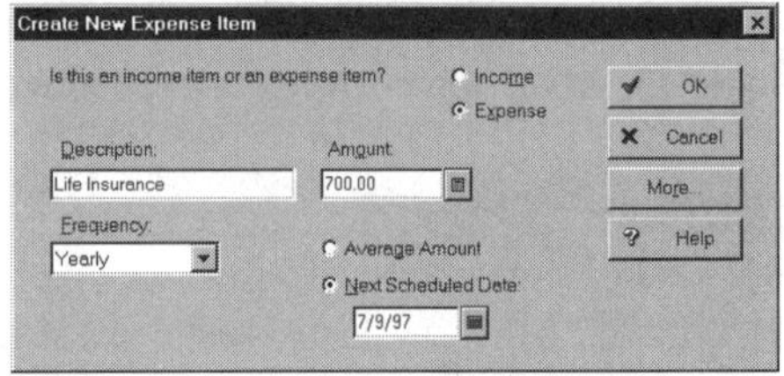

Figure 13.17 *New items can be expenses or income, as well as an average or specific amount (shown here).*

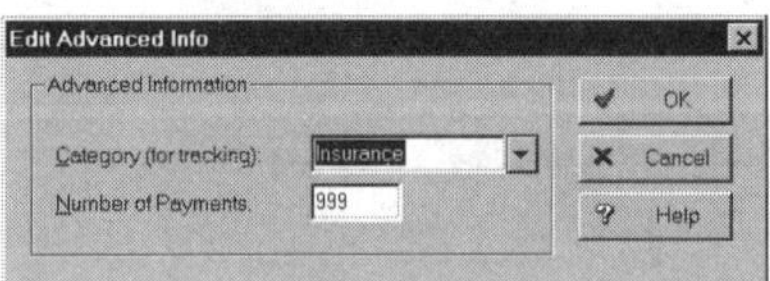

Figure 13.18 *You can specify a category and the number of occurrences for the transaction. (Enter 999 for a transaction that recurs indefinitely.)*

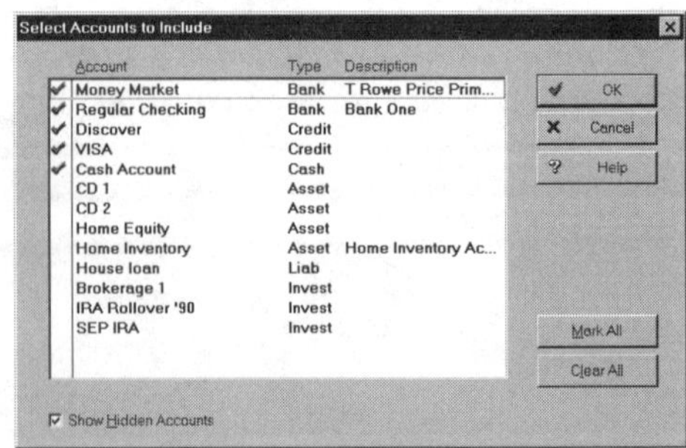

Figure 13.19 *Choose accounts from the Select Accounts to Include dialog box.*

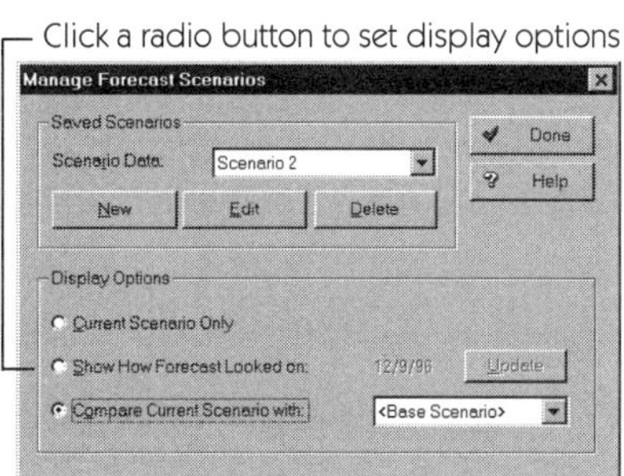

Figure 13.20 *In addition to creating, editing, and deleting scenarios, you can set display options for any scenario in the Manage Forecast Scenarios dialog box.*

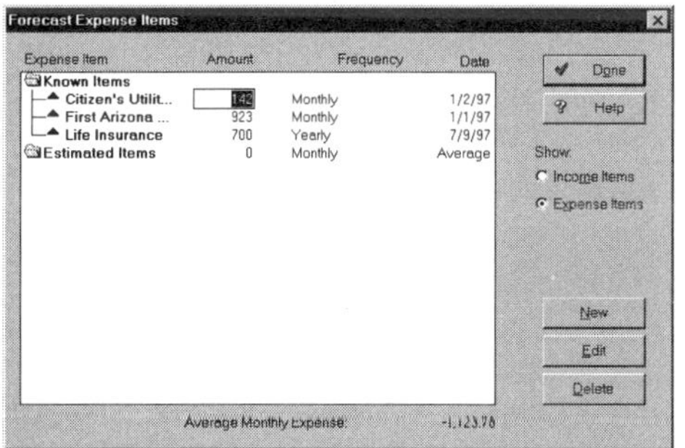

Figure 13.21 *Items can be added, deleted, or edited in the Forecast Items dialog box. You can switch between expenses and income items by clicking the appropriate radio button.*

You aren't restricted to one scenario. You can create additional scenarios and compare them, if you like. For example, I created a scenario which included the income I could make from writing a magazine article every month and then compared it to the base scenario.

Click Create to make additional automatic scenarios. To create a scenario that is a copy of another scenario or one that you will configure from scratch, click the Scenario button and then click New.

To compare two scenarios, click Scenario. The Manage Forecast Scenarios dialog box appears (see **Figure 13.20**). Choose a scenario from the Scenario Data drop-down list and then choose a comparison scenario from those listed at the bottom of the dialog box.

✔ Tips

- You can also create a new transaction by clicking the Expense or the Income button at the bottom of the Forecasting window. The Forecast Expense (or Income) Items dialog box appears (see **Figure 13.21**).
- The more data on which a forecast is based, the more accurate it will be. Unless income and expenses vary little from month to month, you may want to wait until you have between six months and a year's worth of data before generating forecasts.

Quicken Home Inventory

About Home Inventory

DELUXE

Home Inventory is a part of Quicken Deluxe that you can use to record a description, location, and value for your important possessions. Such a record can be extremely useful in the event of a major loss, such as a fire or burglary, and can help you determine if your insurance coverage is adequate.

Entries made in Home Inventory are recorded in Quicken. The first time you run Home Inventory, a Quicken asset account named Home Inventory is automatically created (see **Figure 14.1**). This account contributes to any net worth reports that you generate.

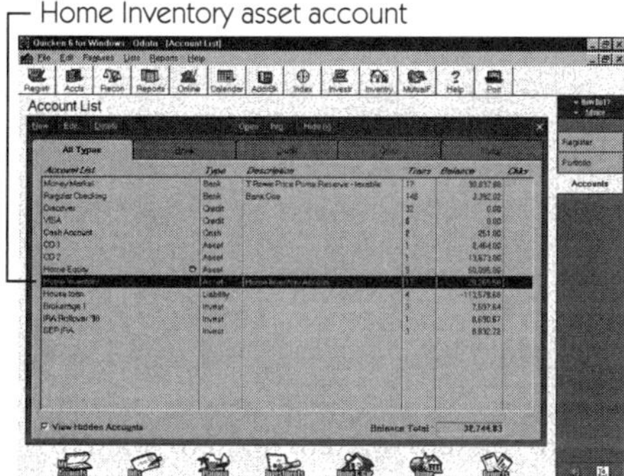

Figure 14.1 *The Home Inventory asset account tracks the total value of items recorded in Home Inventory. You can run Home Inventory by double-clicking its account name.*

Launching Home Inventory

You can start Home Inventory in any of the following ways:

- Click the Inventory button in the top iconbar.
- Choose Features ⇨ Planning ⇨ Quicken Home Inventory.
- Click the Home & Car icon in the activity bar and choose Record My Home Inventory from the pop-up menu that appears.
- On the Windows 95 taskbar, click the Start button and choose Quicken Home Inventory (see **Figure 14.2**).
- On the Windows 3.1 desktop, open the Quicken program group and double-click the Quicken Home Inventory icon.

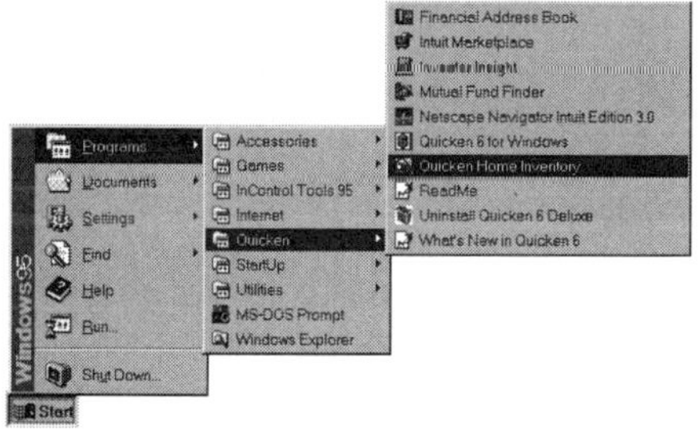

Figure 14.2 *Because Home Inventory is a stand-alone program, you can launch it from Quicken or from the Windows desktop, as shown here.*

Inventory Views

Home Inventory has two *views* in which you can create, edit, and enter records: list view and detail view.

List view (see **Figure 14.3**) shows only the essential information for each inventory item: Item Description, Item Category, Replacement Cost, Resale Value, and Location. As such, it is very useful for quickly creating a basic inventory. Later, you can switch to detail view and fill in the remaining fields for each record.

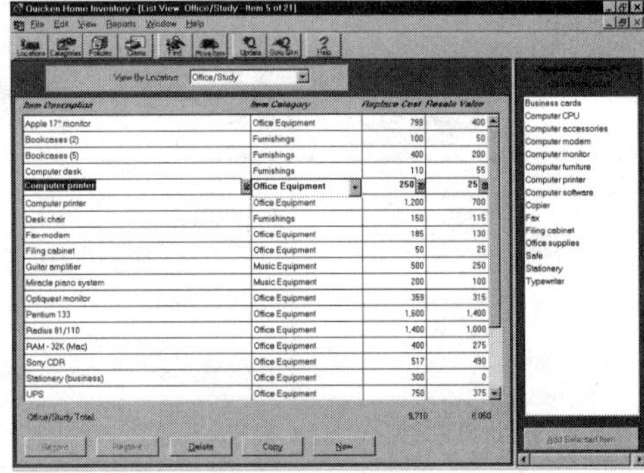

Figure 14.3 *Use list view to see all possessions that are in a particular location.*

As its name implies, you use detail view (see **Figure 14.4**) to enter and view detailed information about inventory items, such as the make and model, serial number, date and place of purchase, original price, and the insurance policy under which the item is covered.

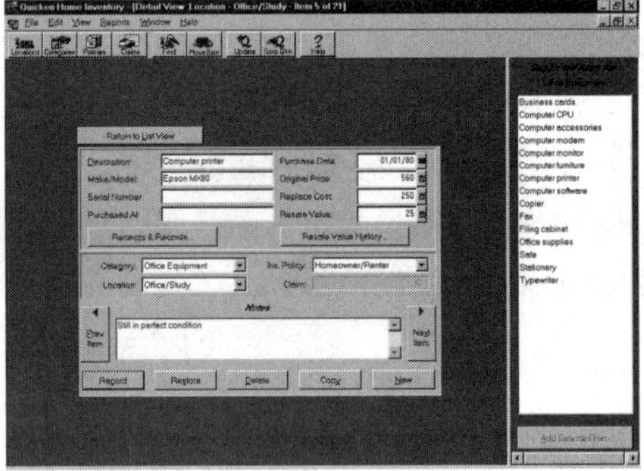

Figure 14.4 *Use detail view when you want to see or enter all the important data for an inventory item.*

Communicating with Quicken

Although you can invoke Home Inventory from Quicken and vice versa, it is also a stand-alone program that can be used whether Quicken is running or not. You can launch Quicken by clicking the Goto Qkn button in the iconbar, choosing Goto Quicken from the File menu, or by pressing Ctrl Q.

New inventory data is not automatically sent to Quicken. When you want to update the Home Inventory asset account, click the Update button in Home Inventory's iconbar or choose Update Quicken from the File menu.

✔ **Tip**

- You can create multiple inventory files (one for home and one for a business, for example). Choose New from the File menu.

About Home Inventory

Creating and Editing Records

You can create and edit records in list or detail view. Press Tab to move from field to field.

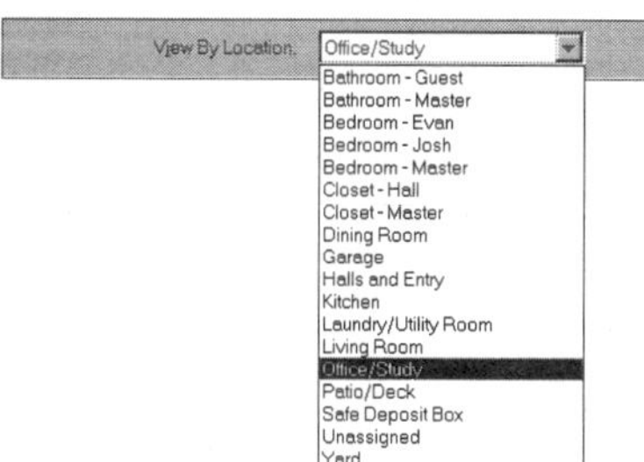

Figure 14.5 *The View by Location drop-down list.*

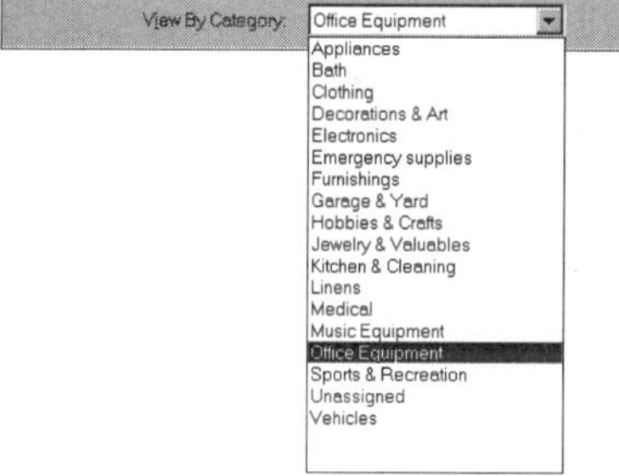

Figure 14.6 *The View by Category drop-down list.*

To create a new record in list view:

1. List view can display all items in the same location or in the same category. Choose By Location or By Category from the View menu to select a mode in which to work.
2. Click the drop-down list at the top of the window to choose a location (see **Figure 14.5**) or item category (see **Figure 14.6**), depending on the choice made in Step 1. The list changes to show all items in the same location or category.
3. Click the New button or click the first empty record at the bottom of the list.
4. Type a general description for the item in the Item Description field.
5. Choose a category from the Item Category field or a location from the Item Location field, depending on the choice made in Step 1.
6. Enter the approximate cost to replace the item.
7. By default, the item's approximate resale value is automatically calculated, based on a percentage of the replacement cost. You can edit this figure, if you wish.
8. To save the data for this record, click Record.

To create a new record in detail view:

1. Click the New button at the bottom of the detail view window.

2. Enter data by typing and choosing options from the drop-down lists. Press Tab to move from field to field.

3. *Optional:* To note sales receipts or insurance records for the item, click the Receipts and Records button (see **Figure 14.7**).

4. *Optional:* Click Resale Value History to view, edit, or create entries for the item's resale value.

5. Click Record to store the record.

You can edit any field of any record, as well as delete records. For example, you may want to adjust the resale value of all items once a year to reflect new depreciation or appreciation, as shown in **Figure 14.8**. To edit a record, click in the field that you want to edit, make the changes, and then click Record.

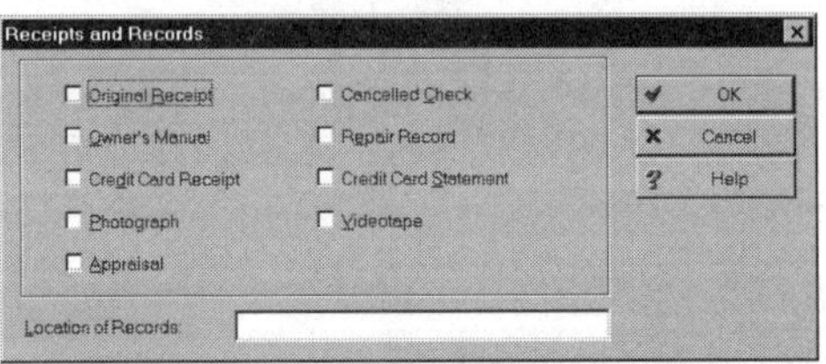

Figure 14.7 *Click check boxes to note any receipts or insurance records that you have for the current item.*

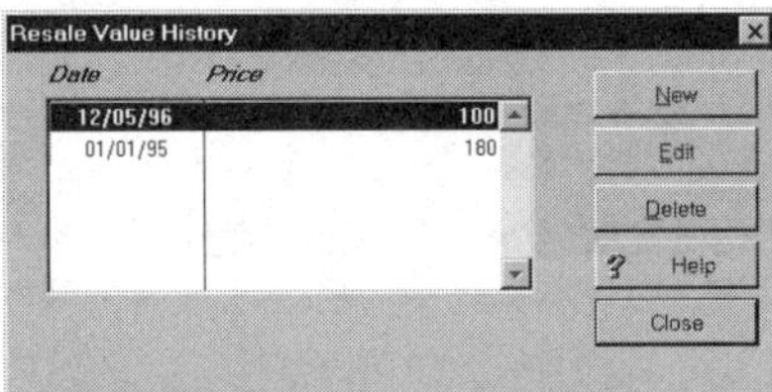

Figure 14.8 *Click the Resale Value History button to see a list of all resale values that you entered for an item. Click New to enter an additional value or Edit to change an existing value.*

✔ Tips

- You can freely switch between list and detail views while entering or editing records. To switch to detail view, choose Detail View from the View menu or click the button at the end of the Item Description field (see **Figure 14.9**). To switch from detail to list view, click the Return to List View button at the top of the window or choose List View from the View menu.
- You can right-click in any field to display a pop-up menu of editing commands (see **Figure 14.10**).
- Records are normally listed in the order in which they were created. To sort the current list, choose Alphabetize Register from the Edit menu.

Figure 14.9 *In list view, click the icon at the end of the Item Description field to work with the record in detail view.*

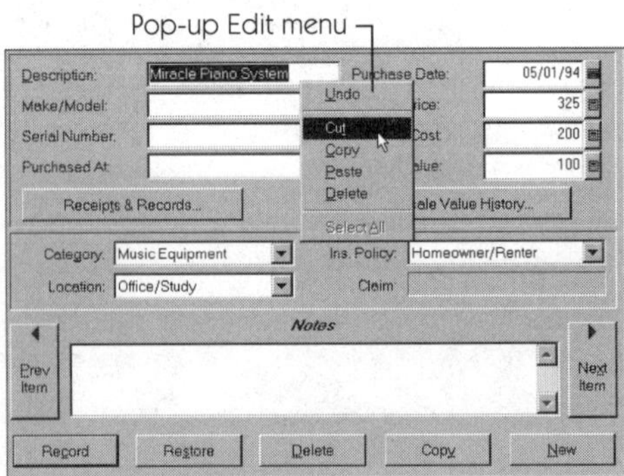

Figure 14.10 *While entering or editing data, you can right-click in a field to use a pop-up Edit menu.*

Editing Category, Location, Policy, and Claim Lists

Although they are fairly thorough, the standard category and location lists will probably require some modifications. You can edit the lists by adding, renaming, and deleting entries. You can use the same procedures to change the master list of insurance policies and claims.

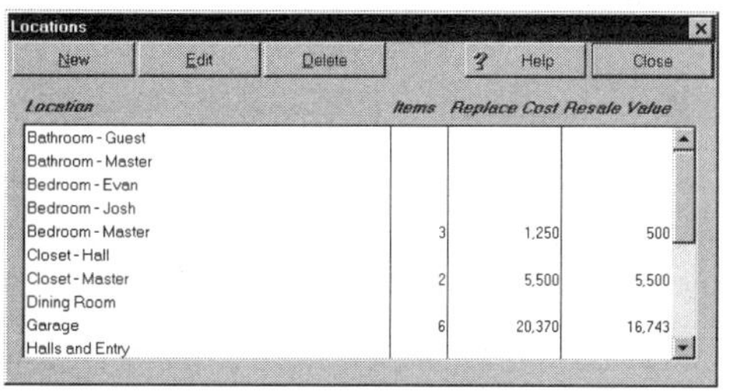

Figure 14.11 *The Locations dialog box.*

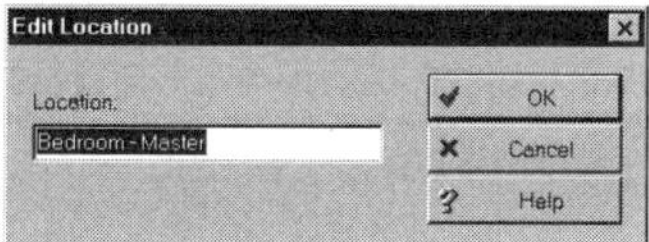

Figure 14.12 *To rename a location, edit the current name or type a new one.*

To edit a category, location, policy, or claims list:

1. Click the iconbar button for Locations, Categories, Policies, or Claims; or choose Location List, Category List, Policy List, or Claims List from the View menu. The appropriate dialog box appears, as shown in **Figure 14.11**.
2. To change the name of an entry, select it and click Edit (or double-click the entry). An Edit dialog box appears (see **Figure 14.12**). Edit the name or type a new one, and then click OK.
3. To create a new entry, click the New button. A New dialog box appears that is similar to the Edit dialog box. Type a name for the new entry and click OK.
4. To delete an entry, sclcct it and click Delete.
5. To record your changes, click the Close button.

If you move an item from one room or location to another, you may want to update the item's record.

To change an item's location:

1. Choose Move Item from the Edit menu or click the Move Item icon in the iconbar. The Move Item dialog box appears (see **Figure 14.13**).
2. The item list can be viewed by location or by insurance policy. Click the appropriate View By radio button on the right side of the dialog box.
3. Choose a location or policy to view from the drop-down list at the top of the dialog box.
4. Select the item(s) to move from the scrolling list on the left. To select multiple items, Ctrl-click them.
5. Select a new location for the item(s) from the scrolling list on the right.
6. Click Move.
7. To move additional items, repeat Steps 2–6; otherwise, click Close.

✔ Tips

- A more elaborate dialog box appears when you edit or create insurance policies and claims (see **Figure 14.14**).
- When moving an item to another location, you can view the item details by clicking the Item Info button in the Move Item dialog box.
- To quickly locate a particular item, click the Find button in the iconbar or choose Find from the Edit menu (see **Figures 14.15** and **14.16**).

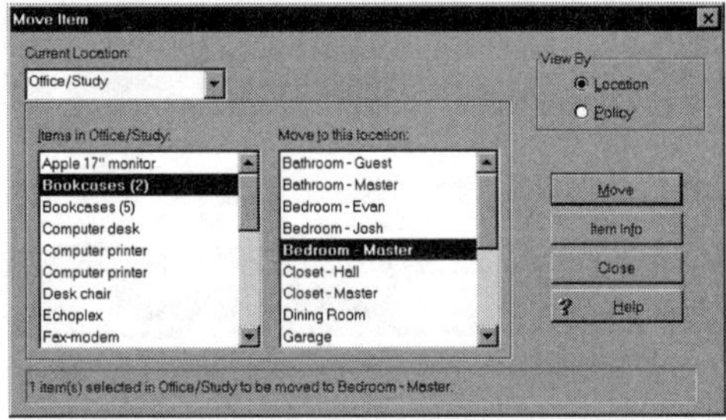

Figure 14.13 *The Move Item dialog box.*

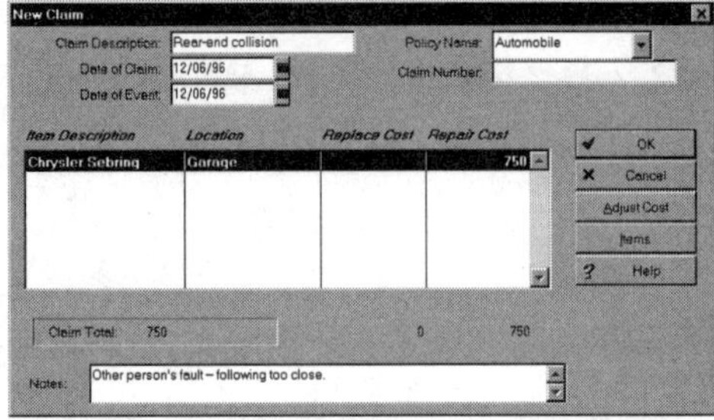

Figure 14.14 *Fill in the text boxes to create a new insurance claim. To set the claim amount or select the affected items, click the Adjust Cost or Items buttons.*

Figure 14.15 *Enter all or part of the item name you want to locate and click Find All. The List of Found Inventory Items dialog box appears (see Figure 14.16).*

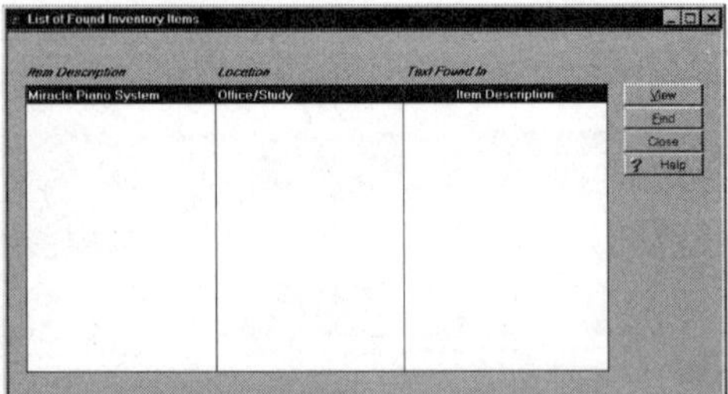

Figure 14.16 *To display the record for a found item, select it and click View.*

Figure 14.17 *The Reports menu.*

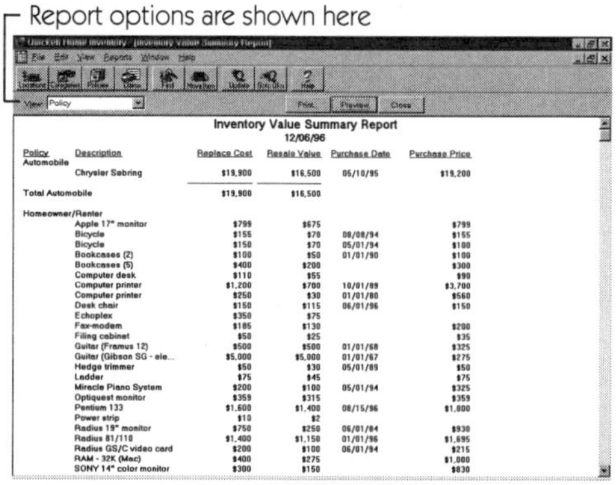

Report options are shown here

Figure 14.18 *A report example.*

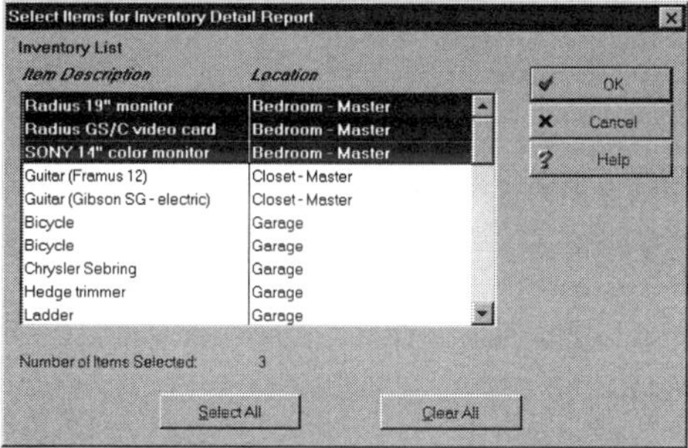

Figure 14.19 *You can base some reports on a subset of the data by* Ctrl*-clicking items.*

Creating Reports

As **Figure 14.17** shows, you can create three types of reports in Home Inventory: inventory lists, insurance coverage, and insurance claims. A summary or detail report can be generated for each of the three report types. You can print reports or examine them on-screen.

From the Reports menu, choose the title of the report you want to generate. A basic report is created and appears on-screen in a scrolling window, as shown in **Figure 14.18**.

To customize the report, you can choose options from drop-down menus at the top of the window. Depending on the report chosen, you can set options that enable you to view items grouped by category, location, or policy (Inventory Value Summary or Detail reports); include only selected items, as shown in **Figure 14.19** (Inventory Detail and Insurance Coverage Detail reports); and sort by location or category (Insurance Coverage Summary report).

After setting options, click the Preview button to examine the report on-screen. (Since a preview is an exact representation of the eventual printout, you can easily determine if there will be printing problems.) You can click buttons at the top of the preview window to zoom in and out, view other report pages, and change the font for the body text. When you are satisfied with the appearance of the report, click the Print button or choose Print from the File menu.

✔ **Tip**

- To learn more about printing and print options, see Chapter 18.

Setting Preferences

Like other Quicken components, you can customize the way that Home Inventory works. The Options dialog box in which preferences are set has three components (Suggested Item List, Display, and General), each represented by a tab.

To set preferences, choose Options from the Edit menu. The Options dialog box appears. Click the tab for the class of options that you want to set.

Suggested Item List Options

If "Use suggested values for new inventory items" is checked (see **Figure 14.20**) and you create a record based on an item in the Suggested Items list, the recommended replacement and resale prices are automatically entered. You can edit these amounts.

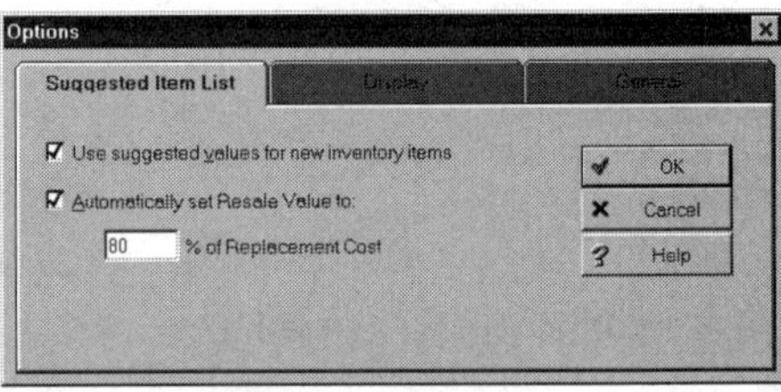

Figure 14.20 *The Options dialog box (Suggested Item List).*

If you set the option to "Automatically set resale value to *x*% of Replacement Cost," resale value is estimated for all inventory items. If you disable this option, Resale Value is set equal to Replacement Cost. (Note that you can change the percentage, as well as override the estimated value.)

Display Options

The first two options (see **Figure 14.21**) determine whether you receive auditory or visual warnings—or both—when you record or delete items. The next option adds sound effects when you click the Prev Item and Next Item buttons in detail view. The final option governs whether currency amounts are rounded to the nearest dollar or exact figures are used.

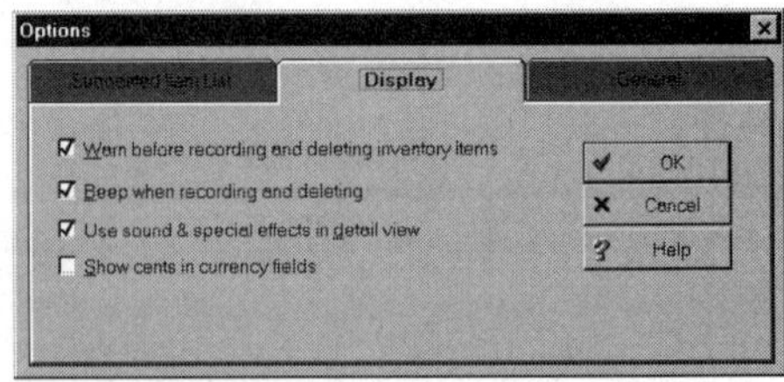

Figure 14.21 *The Options dialog box (Display).*

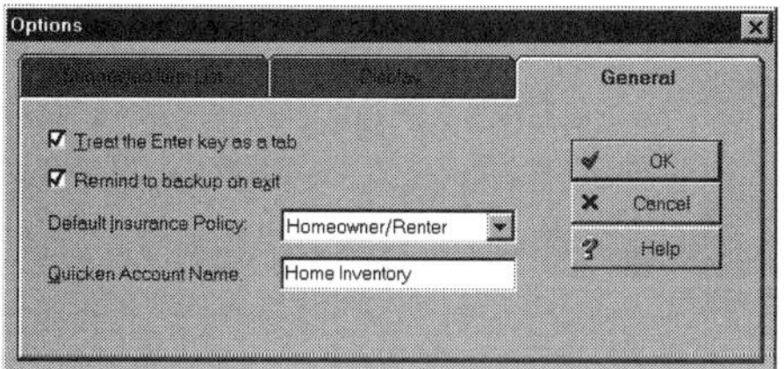

Figure 14.22 *The Options dialog box (General).*

General Options

Enable the first option (as shown in **Figure 14.22**) to use both Tab and Enter to move from field to field. When this option is not checked, Tab moves the cursor to the next field and Enter saves the current record.

If you want to back up your data at the end of each session, check the option to Remind to backup on exit. (To perform a backup, choose Backup from the File menu, select a destination disk and directory, and click OK.)

The final options enable you to specify a default insurance policy and the name of the Quicken asset account in which the total value of Home Inventory is recorded.

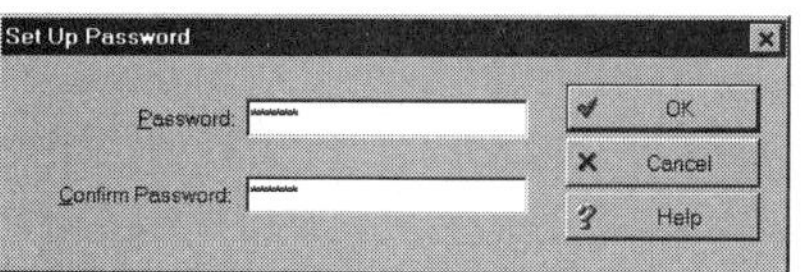

Figure 14.23 *To create a password for the current inventory file, type it twice in the Set Up Password dialog box.*

Using a Password

Although it is not listed in the Options dialog box, Home Inventory has an additional option that many users will find comforting. By choosing Password from the File menu, you can assign a password to your inventory file (see **Figure 14.23**).

Managing Investments

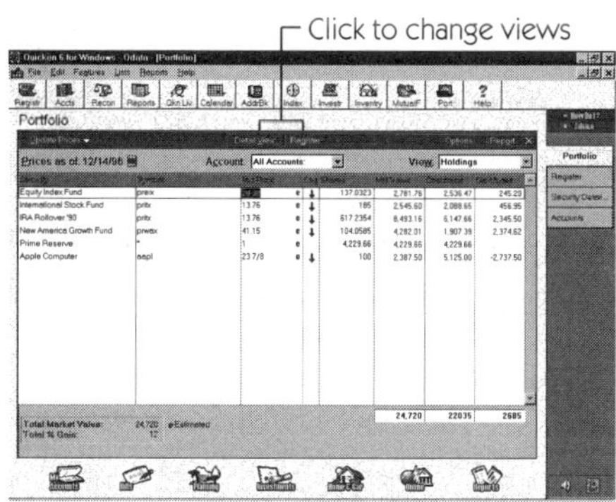

Figure 15.1 *The Portfolio window.*

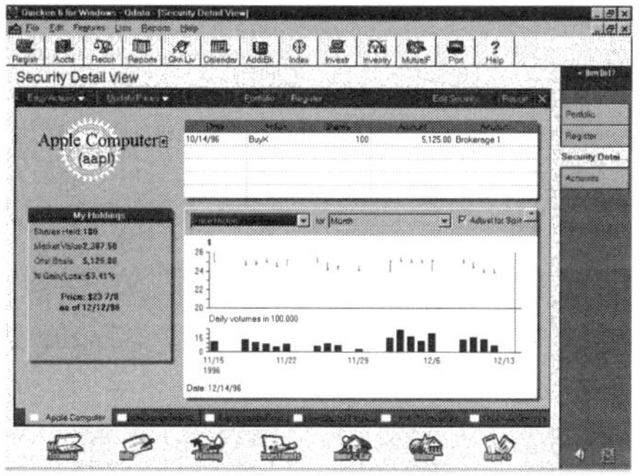

Figure 15.2 *Security Detail View.*

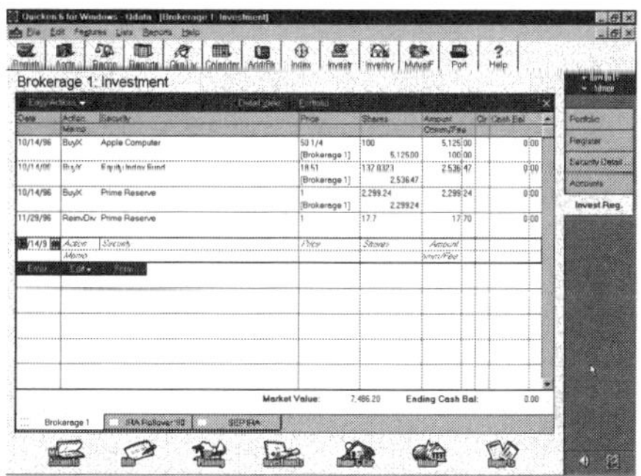

Figure 15.3 *An Investment Register.*

About Managing Investments

You can use investment accounts to store individual investments (a single mutual fund, for example) or investment portfolios (all stocks held in a brokerage account, for example). After setting up your investment accounts (see Chapter 2), you can work with and view investments in three Quicken components: the Portfolio window (see **Figure 15.1**), Security Detail View (see **Figure 15.2**), and Investment Registers (see **Figure 15.3**). Actions that you can perform in these components are as follows:

- *Portfolio window.* Shows current prices, gain/loss, and so on for the investments in your portfolio.
- *Security Detail View.* Graphically displays historical data for each investment.
- *Investment Registers.* Shows all transactions for a portfolio.

You can easily move between these three windows by clicking the Register, Portfolio, or Detail View buttons at the top of each window.

Quicken Deluxe includes two other investment utilities that you arc ccrtain to find useful: Mutual Fund Finder (helps you identify mutual funds that meet your investment criteria) and Investor Insight (an on-line subscription service for tracking security prices and financial news). See Chapter 20 for information on using Investor Insight.

The Portfolio Window

The main purpose of the Portfolio window (see **Figure 15.4**) is to display quotes, valuations, and other information about your investments. When you update prices with Quicken Live, the new figures are shown in this window.

To open the Portfolio window, do any of the following:

- Click the Portfolio (Port) button in the top iconbar.
- Choose Features ➪ Investments ➪ Portfolio View (or press Ctrl U).
- Click the Investments icon in the activity bar and choose View My Portfolio.
- If an Investment Register is open or you are in Security Detail View, click the Portfolio button at the top of the window.

To set display options, choose a setting from the Accounts drop-down list and specify the fields to show by choosing an option from the View drop-down list. Although you'll normally want to see the most recent data, you can view another date by clicking the Prices as of button. To sort the display, click a column heading.

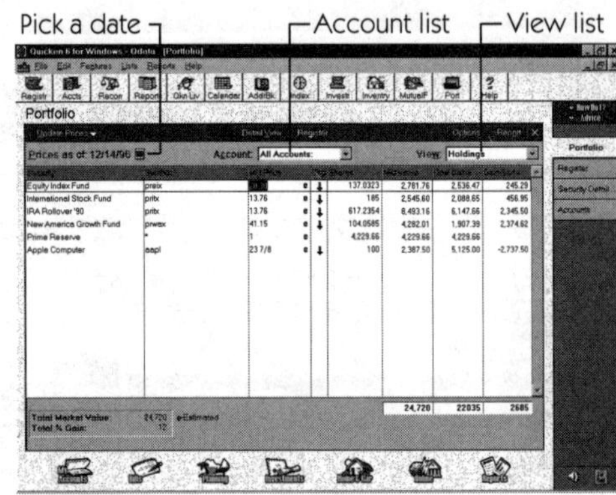

Figure 15.4 *Use the Portfolio window to view numeric price information for the securities in your portfolio.*

Updating Security Prices

To update your security prices, choose Get Online Quotes from the Update Prices drop-down menu. (See Chapter 19 for other methods of issuing the Update command.) If you don't have a modem, you can manually update the price for any security by clicking in the Last Price field and then typing.

Price History for: Apple Computer

New... Edit... Delete Print... Close

Date	Price	High	Low	Volume
12/13/96	23 1/4	23 7/8	23 1/4	795,500
12/12/96	23 7/8	24 1/4	23 7/8	776,800
12/11/96	24	24 1/4	23 3/4	1,458,600
12/10/96	24 1/2	25	24 1/4	1,645,400
12/9/96	25	25 3/8	24 13/16	1,416,500
12/6/96	25 1/8	25 3/8	24	2,048,100
12/5/96	25	25 1/4	25	1,269,100
12/4/96	25	25 3/8	24 7/8	1,703,800
12/3/96	25 1/8	25 1/2	25	2,460,100
12/2/96	25 1/8	25 1/8	23 7/8	1,562,300
11/29/96	24 1/8	24 5/8	24	377,600
11/27/96	24 1/2	24 5/8	24 1/8	795,000
11/26/96	24 1/4	25	24	1,008,800
11/25/96	25	25 1/2	25	704,900
11/22/96	25 1/4	25 1/4	24 1/2	928,400

Figure 15.5 *Click New to create a new price entry. To edit or delete a price, select it and click Edit or Delete, respectively.*

To view, edit, or print a price history, select a security and then choose Edit Price History from the Update Prices drop-down menu. The Price History window appears (see **Figure 15.5**).

Setting Options

To set other options for the Portfolio window, click the Options button at the top of the window. The Portfolio View Options dialog box appears. Here are a few of the more useful options that you can set:

- *Accounts tab.* Choose the investment accounts to display. In most cases, you'll want to see them all.
- *Miscellaneous tab.* As shown in **Figure 15.6**, return on investment calculations can be based on the period you have owned each security (Entire History), the current calendar year (This Year), the previous 365 days, or starting from a specific date. You can change this setting whenever you wish, note the new figures, and then restore the usual setting.

  If you want to sort securities by type, you can enable the Name/Type/Symbol or Name/Type option in the Layout area of the dialog box.

  If you have several holdings with the same securities, check the item to Copy Price Updates to All Securities with the Same Symbol.
- *Custom Views tab.* When you open the View drop-down list, you will note two views named Custom1 and Custom2. Use the Custom Views section of the dialog box (see **Figure 15.7**) to choose fields to display in these views.

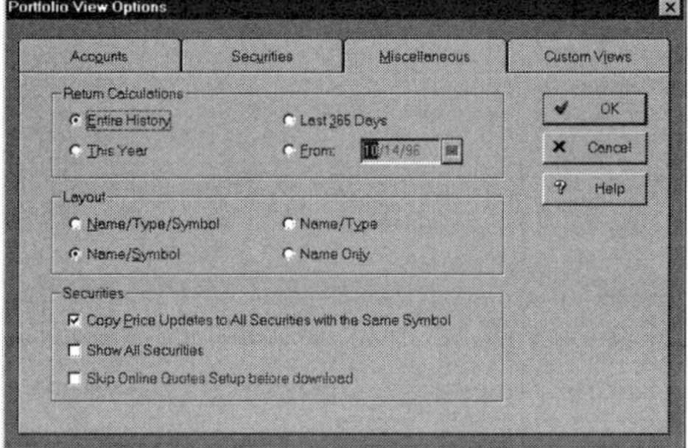

Figure 15.6 *Miscellaneous view options.*

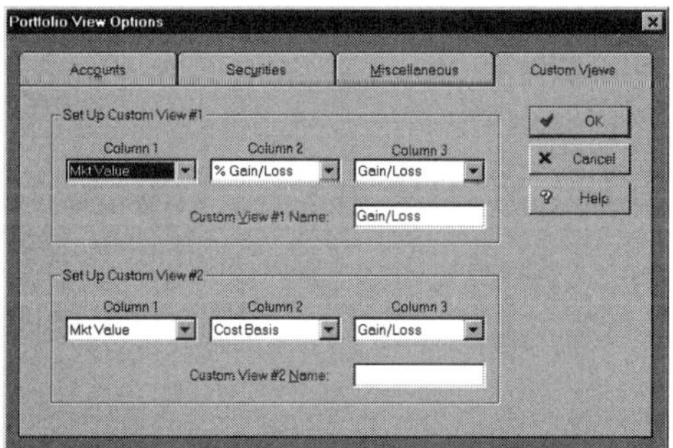

Figure 15.7 *You can create two custom views for displaying securities.*

The Portfolio Window

✔ **Tips**

- You can also follow stock indices and securities that you don't own. For instructions, see "On-Line Quotes" in Chapter 19.

- If you have Quicken Deluxe, you can import price history data for your securities from Investor Insight. See Chapter 20 for details.

Security Detail View

Use Security Detail View (see **Figure 15.8**) to view investment charts and enter transactions, such as buying and selling shares, recording dividends, adjusting a stock for a split, and so on.

You can examine only one security at a time. To choose a different one, click the button to the right of the current security's name. A drop-down list like the one shown in **Figure 15.9** appears. You can also choose a security to view by clicking a named tab at the bottom of the window.

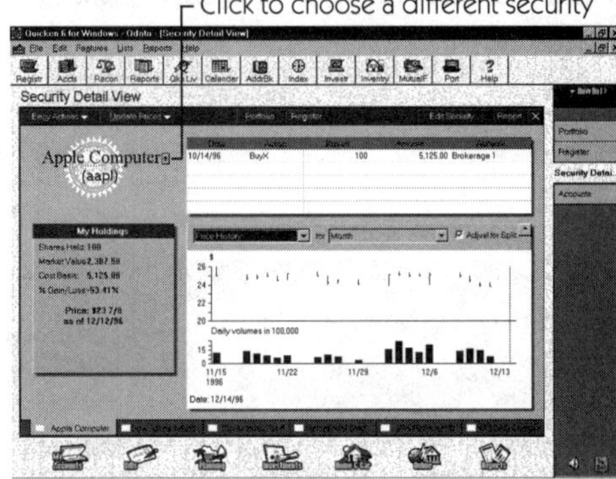

Figure 15.8 *If you prefer charts to raw data, switch to Security Detail View.*

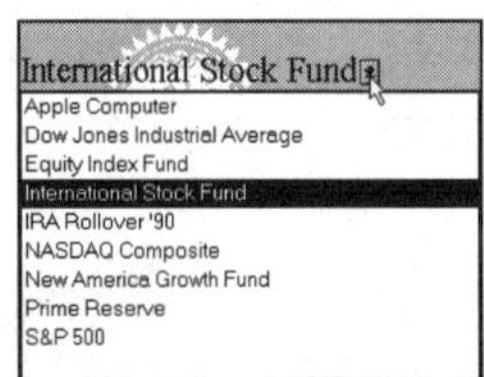

Figure 15.9 *Choose a security, mutual fund, portfolio, or index to view.*

Using the Display

There are two drop-down lists above the chart. You can view a security's price history or market value by choosing the appropriate option from the first list. Choose a date range from the second list.

If Price History is chosen, a long vertical bar marks the date being viewed. High, low, close, and volume figures for the day are shown at the bottom of the window. To see price information for another day, click that date on the chart.

When you choose Market Value, you can view investment value information for any date by moving the cursor over the line graph. To see a full-screen

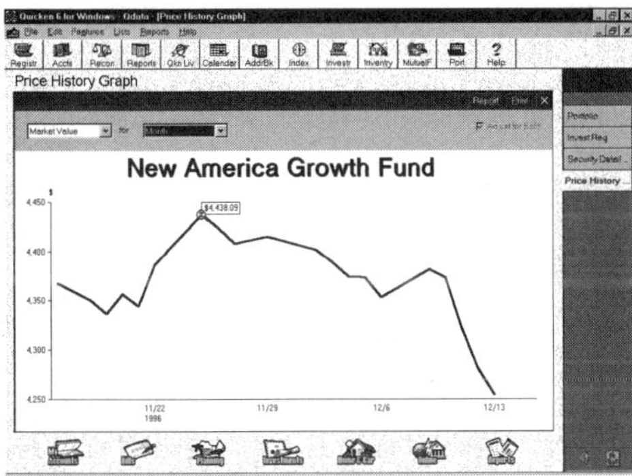

Figure 15.10 *Enlarging the graph makes it easier to view the information presented. Click the close button (X) to return to the normal display.*

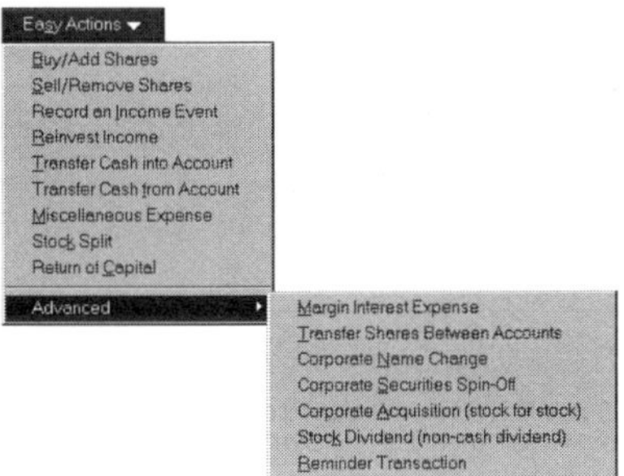

Figure 15.11 *Click the EasyActions button to display a menu of transaction types.*

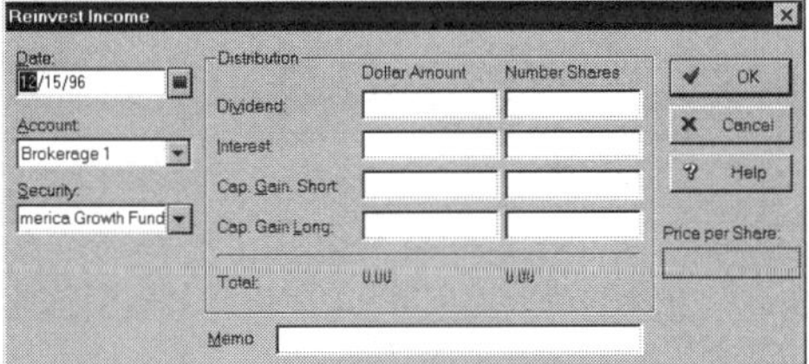

Figure 15.12 *One advantage of Security Detail View over using an account register is that you can record all transactions in easy-to-understand dialog boxes.*

version of the chart, click the up-arrow button in the upper-right corner of the chart (see **Figure 15.10**). To print the chart, click the Print button at the top of the window.

Recording Transactions

Transactions for the current security are displayed in the list at the top of the window. To edit a transaction, double-click it. A dialog box appears that is appropriate for that type of transaction.

To create a new transaction, choose an option from the EasyActions drop-down menu (see **Figure 15.11**). A transaction-specific dialog box appears (see **Figure 15.12**). Enter the requested information and click OK. The transaction is added to the list at the top of the window and is recorded in the account register.

✔ Tips

- You can rearrange the security name tabs at the bottom of the window by clicking and dragging.
- You can update prices or view/edit the price history for any security by following the instructions given in "Updating Security Prices" in the previous section of this chapter.
- As a convenience, you can alter basic information for a security (such as its trading symbol or name) by displaying the security and then clicking the Edit Security button at the top of the window.

The Investment Registers

To open an Investment Register (see **Figure 15.13**), click the Register button at the top of the Portfolio window or the Security Detail View window, or click the Investments icon in the activity bar and choose Use My Investment Register. If you have multiple investment portfolios, choose the one you wish to use by clicking a named tab at the bottom of the window.

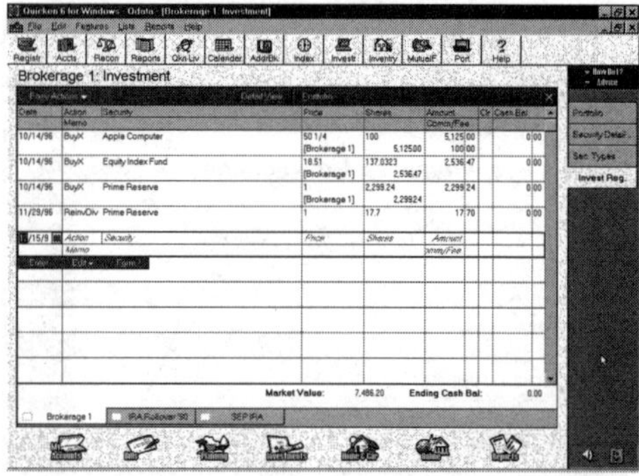

Figure 15.13 *A portfolio register looks and works like any other type of register. Note, however, that multiple investments can be stored in the same portfolio and, hence, in the same register.*

Like Security Detail View, the Investment Registers are used to record and edit security transactions. There are three ways to create a transaction:

- Create a transaction as you would in any other account register (a checking account, for example). Choose a type of transaction from the drop-down list in the Action field (see **Figure 15.14**) and choose a security from the Security field drop-down list.

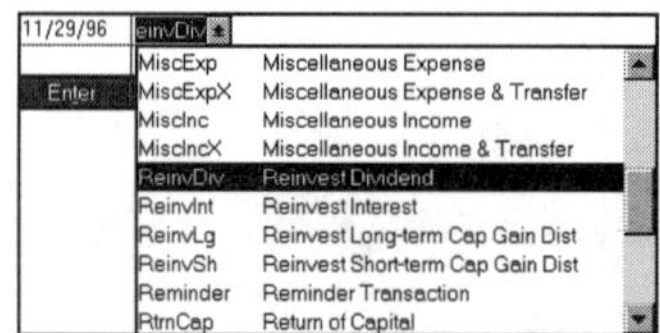

Figure 15.14 *This list parallels the one that appears in the EasyActions menu.*

- Choose a type of transaction by clicking the EasyActions button, and then fill in the dialog box that appears (as previously explained in "Security Detail View").
- To create a buy transaction, click the Form button beneath the record and then fill in the dialog box that appears.

  You can also click Form when editing a transaction. The specific dialog box that appears depends on the type of transaction being edited (see **Figure 15.15**).

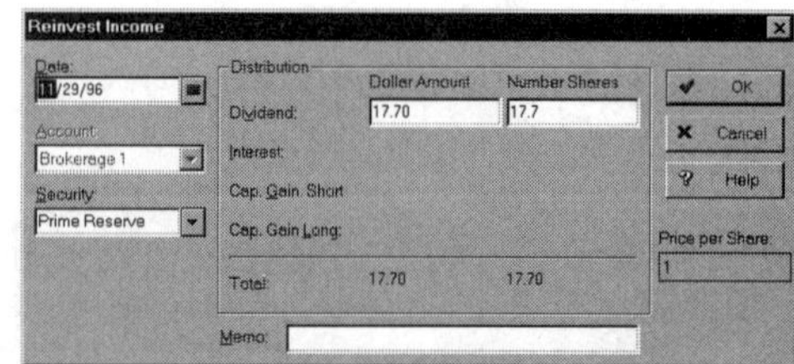

Figure 15.15 *Using a form to create or edit investment transactions is usually the simplest approach.*

Other Investment Activities

In addition to working in the Portfolio window, Security Detail View, and the Investment Registers, there are several other investment activities that you can perform in Quicken and its components.

Updating Share or Cash Balance

Rather than create transactions to adjust the number of shares in an account or a cash balance held in the account, you make these adjustments directly by choosing Update Share Balance or Update Cash Balance from the Investments submenu of the Features menu. Complete the dialog box that appears (see **Figure 15.16**).

Figure 15.16 *To update a share balance to match the current statement, specify a date, choose the name of the security from the drop-down list, and enter the new total number of shares.*

Creating Investment Reports

You can create several types of investment reports by selecting commands from the Investment submenu of the Reports menu. The Create Report dialog box appears (see **Figure 15.17**). To create the report, set options and click Create. For more information about creating and printing reports, see Chapters 17–18.

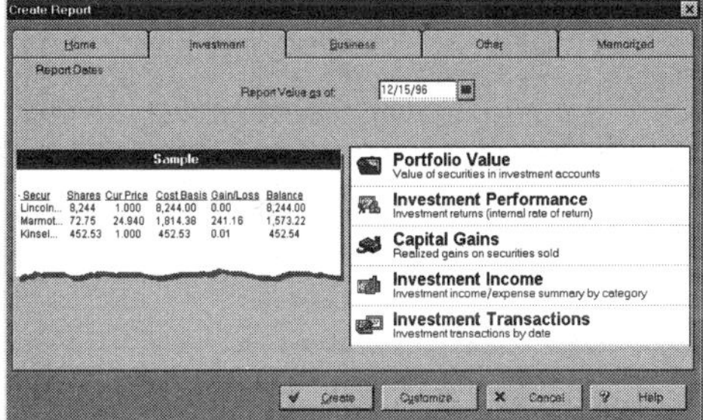

Figure 15.17 *Select a report type and set options in the Create Report dialog box.*

Choosing Mutual Funds

As their popularity continues to increase, it is becoming very difficult to select the *right* mutual fund. Mutual Fund Finder—a feature of Quicken Deluxe—enables you to rank funds according to your criteria.

To start Mutual Fund Finder, click the Mutual Funds (MutualF) button in the iconbar, choose Features ⇨ Investments ⇨ Mutual Fund Finder, or click the Investments icon in the activity bar and choose Research Mutual Funds. Mutual Fund Finder is a stand-alone application, so you also can choose it from the Start menu on the taskbar (Windows 95) or double-click its icon in the Quicken program group (Windows 3.1). The Mutual Fund Finder window appears (see **Figure 15.18**).

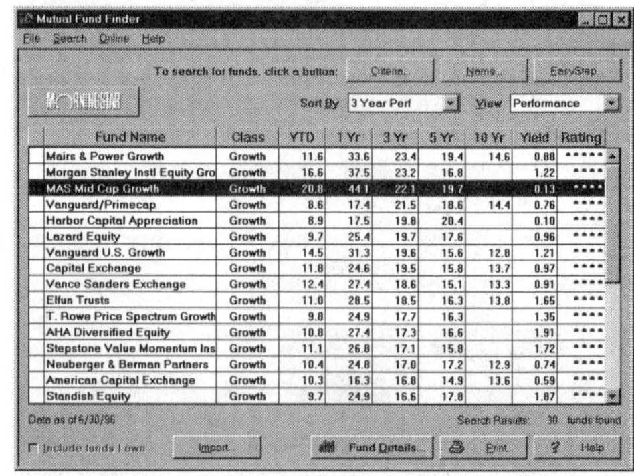

Fund Name	Class	YTD	1 Yr	3 Yr	5 Yr	10 Yr	Yield	Rating
Mairs & Power Growth	Growth	11.6	33.6	23.4	19.4	14.6	0.88	*****
Morgan Stanley Instl Equity Gro	Growth	16.6	37.5	23.2	16.8		1.22	****
MAS Mid Cap Growth	Growth	20.8	44.1	22.1	19.7		0.13	****
Vanguard/Primecap	Growth	8.6	17.4	21.5	18.6	14.4	0.76	****
Harbor Capital Appreciation	Growth	8.9	17.5	19.8	20.4		0.10	****
Lazard Equity	Growth	9.7	25.4	19.7	17.6		0.96	****
Vanguard U.S. Growth	Growth	14.5	31.3	19.6	15.6	12.8	1.21	****
Capital Exchange	Growth	11.8	24.6	19.5	15.8	13.7	0.97	****
Vance Sanders Exchange	Growth	12.4	27.4	18.6	15.1	13.3	0.91	****
Elfun Trusts	Growth	11.0	28.5	18.5	16.3	13.8	1.65	****
T. Rowe Price Spectrum Growth	Growth	9.8	24.9	17.7	16.3		1.35	****
AHA Diversified Equity	Growth	10.8	27.4	17.3	16.6		1.91	****
Stepstone Value Momentum Ins	Growth	11.1	26.8	17.1	15.8		1.72	****
Neuberger & Berman Partners	Growth	10.4	24.8	17.0	17.2	12.9	0.74	****
American Capital Exchange	Growth	10.3	16.3	16.8	14.9	13.6	0.59	****
Standish Equity	Growth	9.7	24.9	16.6	17.8		1.87	****

Figure 15.18 *Mutual Fund Finder.*

To find information on a particular fund or fund family, click the Name button, enter a search string or ticker symbol, and then click Search. To rank funds according to criteria, click the Criteria or the EasyStep button. Until you are familiar with the various criteria, you may find it simpler to use EasyStep (see **Figure 15.19**).

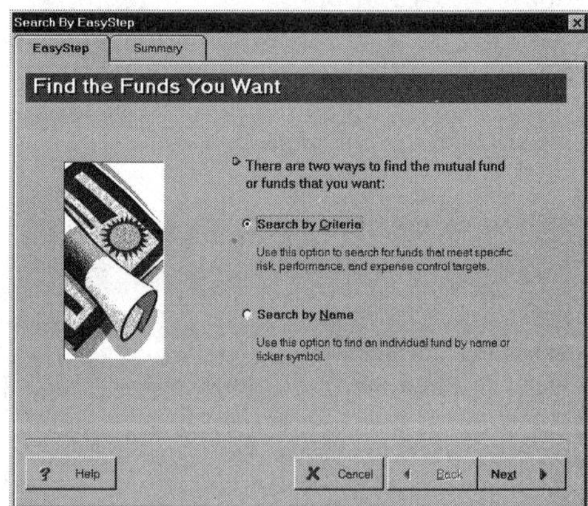

Figure 15.19 *EasyStep dialog boxes help you specify selection criteria.*

Once you have chosen a list of funds, specify sort criteria and fields to display by choosing options from the Sort By and View drop-down lists. To learn more about a particular fund, double-click it or select it and click Fund Details. The Fund Detail dialog box appears (see **Figure 15.20**). Click the Summary, Graph, or Prospectus tab, depending on the type of information you want.

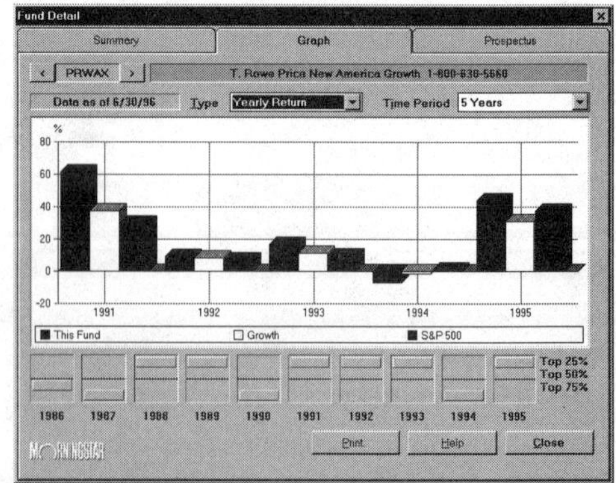

Figure 15.20 *This graph compares a fund's returns to those of the S&P 500 and other growth funds during the same period.*

To obtain a prospectus or other information directly from the fund, click the Prospectus tab and then click the Fund Family or Prospectus button. You are taken to the fund's page on the Internet. If you prefer, you can call the fund directly by dialing the number at the top of the Fund Detail dialog box.

Investor Insight

Investor Insight (see **Figure 15.21**) is an on-line based program included with Quicken Deluxe. You can use it download quotes, historical stock data, and financial news. To learn about Investor Insight, see Chapter 20.

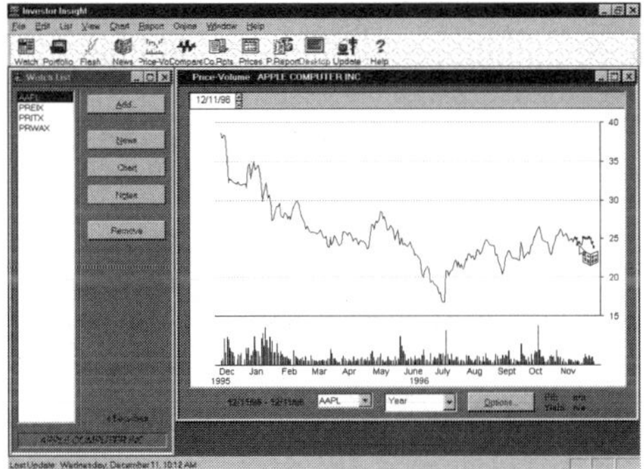

Figure 15.21 *Investor Insight.*

Mutual Fund Data Update — Hypertext link

Update information in the Quicken Mutual Fund Finder with the latest quarterly data.

Figure 15.22 *Click this hypertext link (the underlined text) to order a database update via modem.*

✔ Tips

- If you have a modem and access to the Internet, you can use Quicken Live to download price updates for the securities in your investment portfolio. See Chapter 19.
- Periodically, updates become available for the Mutual Fund Finder database. To order an update (for a small fee), choose Update Mutual Fund Data from the Online menu. You will connect to a Web site where you can find out what the most current version of the database is and, optionally, order the most recent update (see **Figure 15.22**).

Taxes

Quicken and Taxes

Although Quicken is not a tax program *per se*, you can use it to help minimize the amount of work you will have to do at tax time. Many tax programs can read Quicken data files. You can also create tax reports within Quicken that provide the totals you will need in order to complete your Federal and state tax returns.

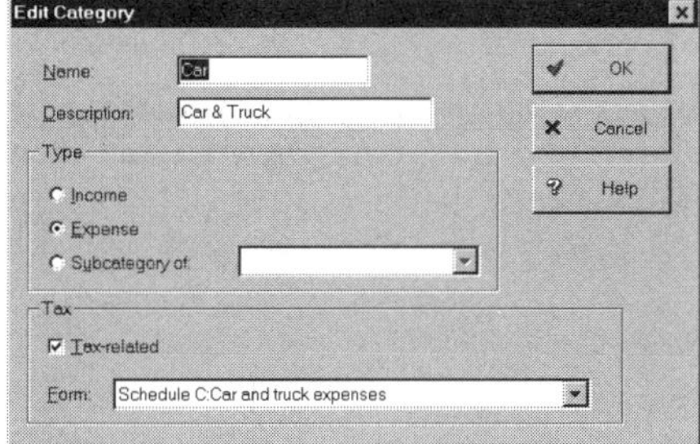

Figure 16.1 *To define a category as tax-related, open the Category & Transfer List window, select a category, and click Edit. Choose a tax line item from the drop-down Form list.*

If you want Quicken to track your tax data, all you have to do is assign tax links to your tax-related expense and income categories (as discussed in Chapter 3). For example, if you operate a business and have work-related auto expenses, you can create a category that is linked to the Car and Truck Expenses line item in Schedule C, as shown in **Figure 16.1**.

Quicken features that can help you manage the tax links and prepare for tax time include the following:

- *Tax Link Assistant.* Speeds up the process of assigning tax links to income and expense categories.
- *Deduction Finder.* Helps determine if you are taking all the deductions to which you are entitled.

- *Tax Planner.* Estimate your 1996 and 1997 taxes and create "what-if" scenarios.
- *Tax Reports.* View your taxable transactions in several useful report formats.

Tax Link Assistant

Rather than assign tax links on a piecemeal basis in the Category & Transfer List window, you can use Tax Link Assistant to speed up the process.

To use the Tax Link Assistant:

1. Choose Features ⇨ Taxes ⇨ Set Up for Taxes, or click the Tax Link button in the Category & Transfer List window. The Tax Link Assistant window appears, as shown in **Figure 16.2**.
2. Select a transaction category from the list in the left side of the window. The currently assigned tax link, if any, is displayed to the right of the category name.
3. From the list in the right side of the window, select a tax form line item to link to the current category.
4. Click Assign Line Item to Category.
5. To create additional tax links, repeat Steps 2–4. When you are finished, click OK.

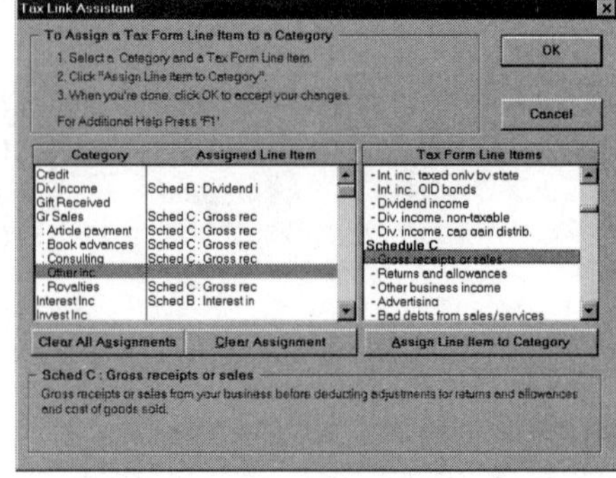

Figure 16.2 *You can quickly associate tax line items with categories in Tax Link Assistant.*

Deduction Finder

The IRS says that it wants you to take every deduction to which you are entitled. Have you? Are you sure?

DELUXE

Deduction Finder helps you find tax deductions that you may have overlooked. After you answer a series of Yes and No questions on a deduction topic, Deduction Finder states whether you may be eligible to take the deduction. If you wish, you can immediately create a Quicken expense category for the new deduction.

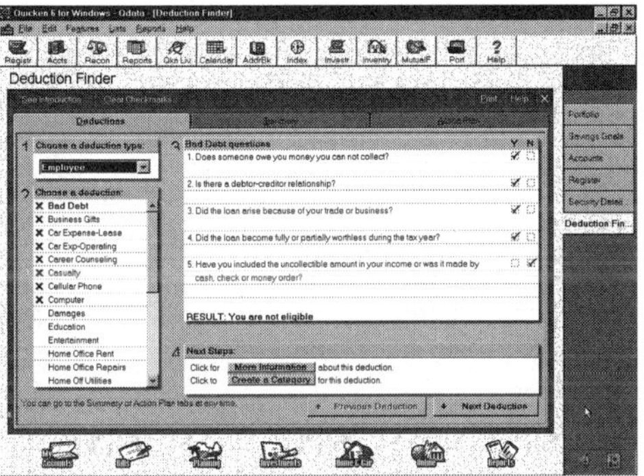

Figure 16.3 *The Deduction Finder window is divided into three numbered sections from which you choose deduction classes and topics, and then answer eligibility questions.*

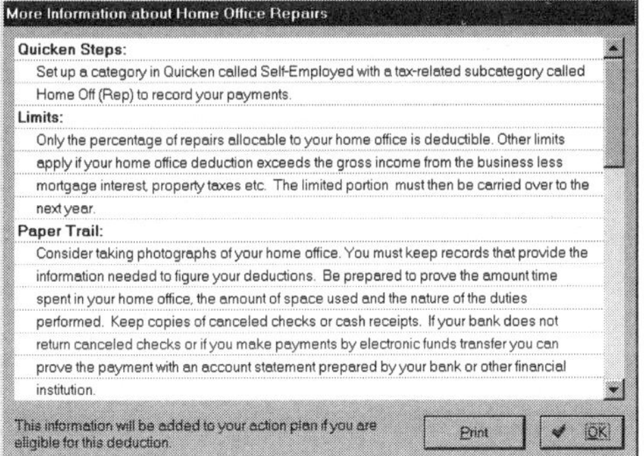

Figure 16.4 *The More Information dialog box explains what you should do to take advantage of the deduction.*

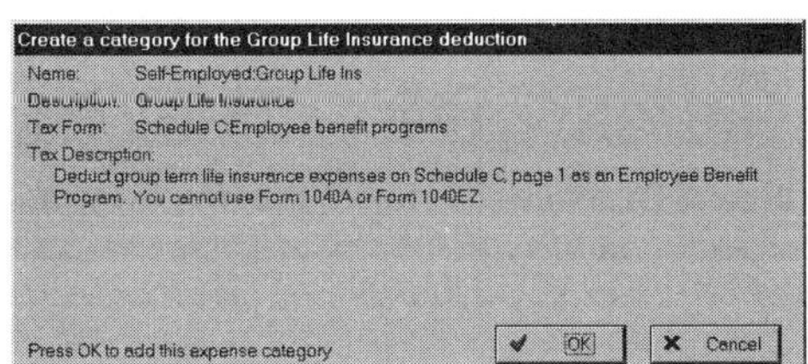

Figure 16.5 *Click OK to create the deduction category.*

To use Deduction Finder:

1. Choose Features ⇨ Taxes ⇨ Tax Deductions, or click the Planning icon in the activity bar and choose Identify Possible Tax Deductions. The Introduction to Deduction Finder dialog box appears. Read the instructions and click OK to dismiss it. Beneath the dialog box is the Deduction Finder window (see **Figure 16.3**).
2. Choose a class of deductions from the drop-down list in Section 1.
3. In Section 2, select the deduction topic that you want to explore.
4. Answer the questions posed in Section 3, clicking Yes or No for each one. Based on your answers, a recommendation is presented at the bottom of the window.
5. Repeat for additional deduction topics and classes that you want to examine.

You can move from topic to topic by clicking the Next Deduction and Previous Deduction buttons or by selecting topics from the list in Section 2.

You can get more information about the current deduction or create a new category for it by clicking More Information or Create Category, respectively (see **Figures 16.4–16.5**).

You can click the Summary Tab at any time to see how many deduction classes and specific topics you have addressed, as well as the number that you may be eligible to take. Click the Action Plan tab to receive instructions on how to take your new deductions.

Tax Planner

Tax Planner is an advanced calculator that you can use to estimate your 1996 or 1997 taxes, based on the data that you've entered in Quicken.

To use Tax Planner:

1. Choose Features ⇨ Taxes ⇨ Tax Planner, or click the Planning icon in the Activity Bar and choose Plan for Taxes. The Tax Planner window appears (see **Figure 16.6**).
2. Choose a filing status and tax year from the drop-down menus at the top of the window.
3. Click the Rates button. The Tax Rates for Filing Status dialog box appears (see **Figure 16.7**). Click a radio button to select 1996 or 1997 tax rates, and then click OK.
4. Click Quicken Data to import your year-to-date tax data from Quicken into Tax Planner. The data is read and the Preview Quicken Tax Data dialog box appears, as shown in **Figure 16.8**.
5. Each imported total can be *annualized* (averaged over the year) or *non-annualized* (the year-to-date amount is used). Double-click any item to toggle its state between annualized and non-annualized.
6. Make adjustments to the line item totals by entering numbers in the text boxes and clicking buttons (Business Income, for example). As you make changes, the figures are automatically recalculated.

You can also create two additional tax scenarios with Tax Planner and see how your taxes would differ.

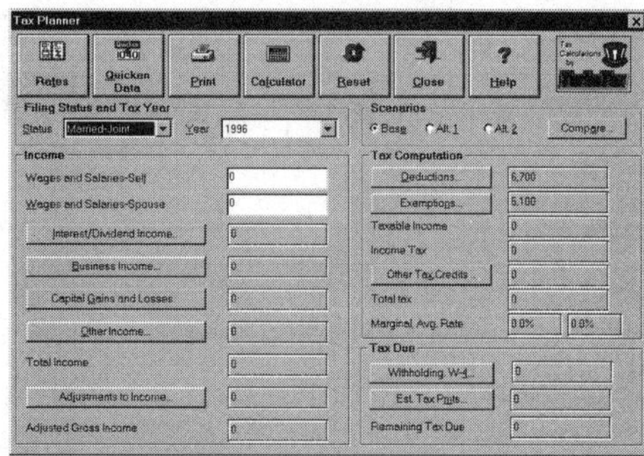

Figure 16.6 *The Tax Planner window.*

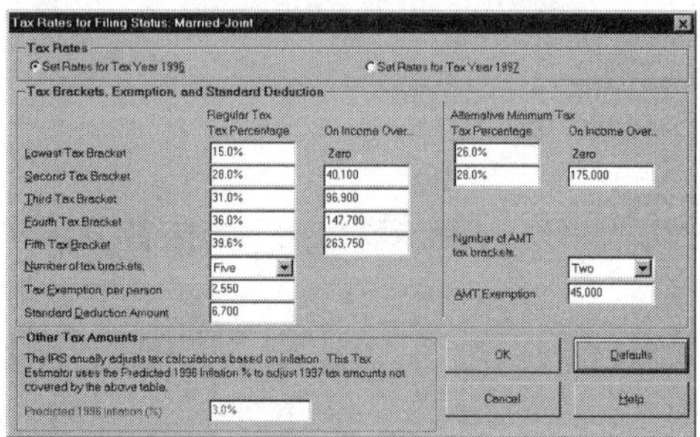

Figure 16.7 *Use the Tax Rates for Filing Status dialog box to set and adjust tax rates for various filing statuses.*

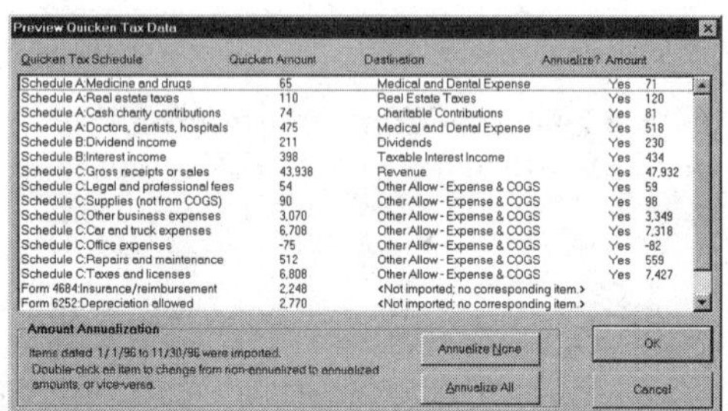

Figure 16.8 *The Preview Quicken Tax Data dialog box shows the initial figures on which the tax estimate will be based.*

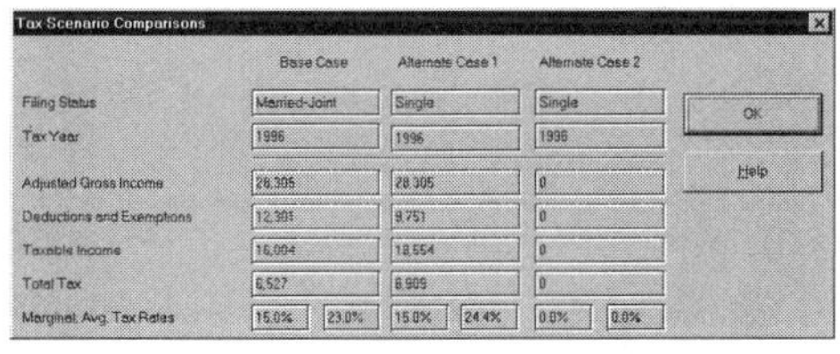

Figure 16.9 *The Tax Scenario Comparisons window shows how the base scenario and the two alternate tax strategies compare.*

To create additional tax scenarios:

1. A new scenario can be based on an existing scenario or created from scratch. To base it on an existing scenario, select that scenario by clicking its radio button, and then click a radio button for the new scenario (Alt. 1 or Alt. 2).

   You are asked if you want to "Copy current scenario?" Click Yes. To create the scenario from scratch, click No.

2. Edit the line item totals, if necessary. You can also change the filing status (to compare a joint return against married, filing separately, for example).

3. Click Compare. The Tax Scenario Comparisons window appears (see **Figure 16.9**), showing the differences between the three scenarios.

✔ Tips

- Tax information derived from annualized amounts is subject to error. And the shorter the period over which the data was collected, the greater the likelihood of error. For example, $2,000 in medical expenses in the first quarter does not mean that your annual total will be $8,000 (but it *will* be calculated that way). Better estimates will come near the end of your tax year.

- To clear the figures in one or all scenarios and begin again, click the Reset button.

Tax Reports

You can create three Quicken reports that you will find useful at tax time: Tax Summary, Tax Schedule, and Capital Gains.

Figure 16.10 *A Tax Summary Report.*

Tax Summary Report

Tax Summary is a year-to-date report that lists and subtotals all tax-related transactions by category (see **Figure 16.10**). To create the report, choose Reports ⇨ Home ⇨ Tax Summary.

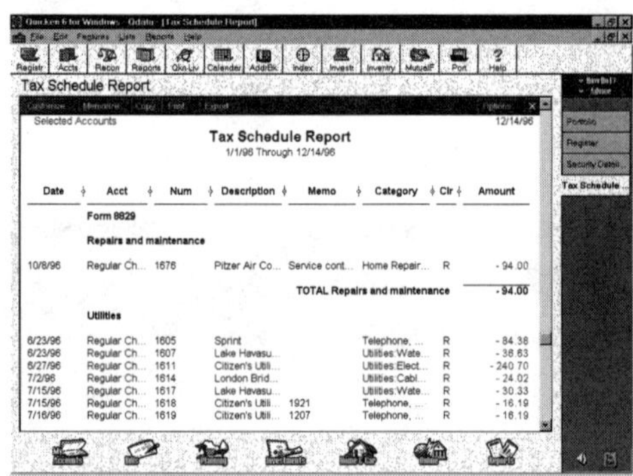

Figure 16.11 *A Tax Schedule Report.*

Tax Schedule Report

Tax Schedule is a year-to-date report that lists and subtotals all tax-related transactions by tax schedule line item, as shown in **Figure 16.11**. To create the report, choose Reports ⇨ Home ⇨ Tax Schedule.

Capital Gains Report

The Capital Gains report shows taxable gains on investments sold during the year. To create the report, choose Reports ⇨ Investment ⇨ Capital Gains.

✔ **Tip**

- When creating tax reports, be sure that the date range is correct. If the tax year is still in progress, choose Year to date or Current Year from the Report Dates drop-down list. If the tax year is over, choose Last Year.

  To learn more about creating and customizing reports, refer to Chapter 17.

Part IV: Reports and Graphs

Reports and Graphs

Quicken Report Capabilities

One of the great things about Quicken is that it enables you to effortlessly create dozens of useful reports and graphs to help illuminate your current financial situation. You can generate the following types of reports:

- *Account balances.* By displaying the Account List and choosing Print List from the File menu, you can generate a report that shows the balances for all selected accounts.
- *Register report.* You can create a transaction report for any account register.
- *Expense summary.* You can create a pie chart that shows expenses by category for any checking or credit card account.
- *EasyAnswer reports.* EasyAnswer reports and graphs are created by choosing from among a dozen different questions that you'd like to have answered (see **Figure 17.1**).
- *Snapshots.* You can display miniature graphs and text reports chosen from 18 possible categories (see **Figure 17.2**).
- *Home, Investment, Business, and Other.* More than two dozen reports and graphs can be chosen from the Reports menu (see **Figure 17.3**).

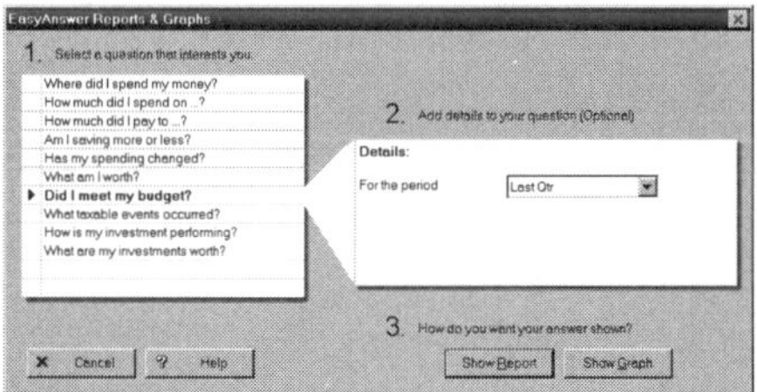

Figure 17.1 *To create an EasyAnswer report, all you have to do is pick the question to which you seek an answer.*

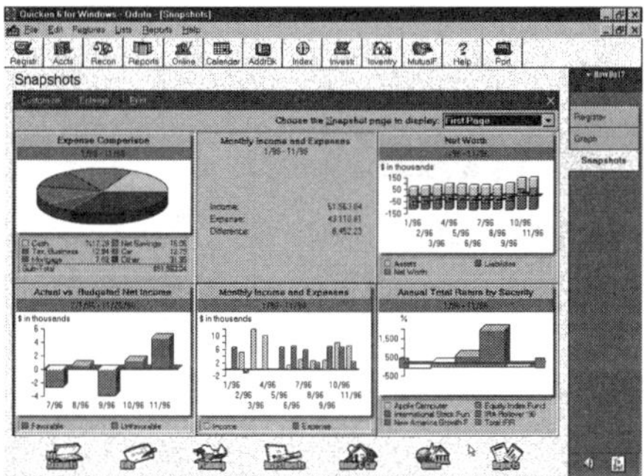

Figure 17.2 *Snapshots can display as many as six graphs and reports on a single screen.*

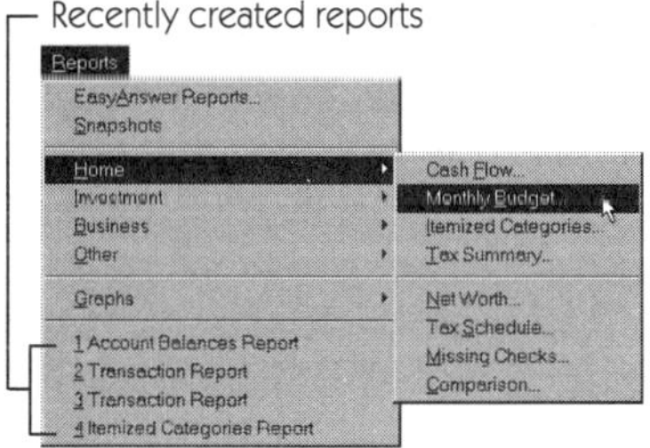

Figure 17.3 *Reports and graphs can be chosen from the Reports menu.*

You can create simple reports and graphs with a single button click or menu choice. And you can set default report settings that are used for every standard report.

In cases where the default settings do not meet your needs, you can customize reports by selecting a date range, sort order, specific categories, and other options to use. If you want to be able to quickly re-create a custom report, you can ask Quicken to memorize it.

You can generate a standard report in any of the following ways:

- Choose a specific report type or a general class of reports (such as EasyAnswer Reports or Snapshots) from the Reports menu.
- Click the Reports button in the top iconbar to choose a home, investment, business, or other report to create (see **Figure 17.4**).
- Click the Report button at the top of any window in which it appears. If multiple reports are available, you can choose one from the menu that appears (see **Figure 17.5**).
- Click the Reports icon in the activity bar and choose a report option from the pop-up menu that appears.

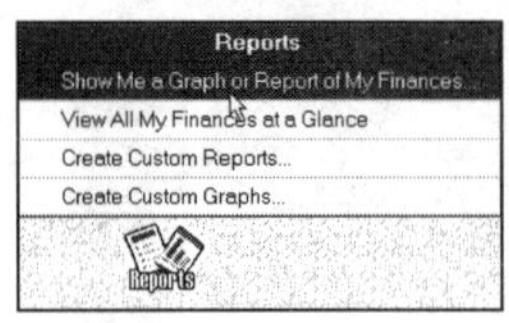

Figure 17.4 *Many of the commands in the Reports menu can also be executed by choosing commands from the Reports icon in the activity bar.*

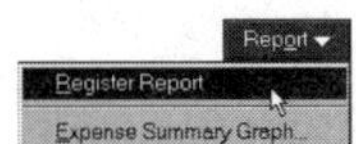

Figure 17.5 *Click the Report button at the top of any register window to generate a register report or expense summary graph.*

✓ **Tips**

- Reports and graphs can be printed or viewed on-screen. To learn about printing reports and graphs, see Chapter 18.
- Quicken lists the last four reports you created at the bottom of the Reports menu (refer to **Figure 17.3**).

Creating Reports and Graphs

You can create standard reports and graphs by performing the steps listed in the sections that follow.

Register Reports and Expense Summary Graphs

Register reports and expense summary graphs are simple to create. A register report is a list of transactions for a given register. (You can get a similar report by choosing Print Register from the File menu.) An expense summary graph is a pie chart that shows expenses by category for the current register.

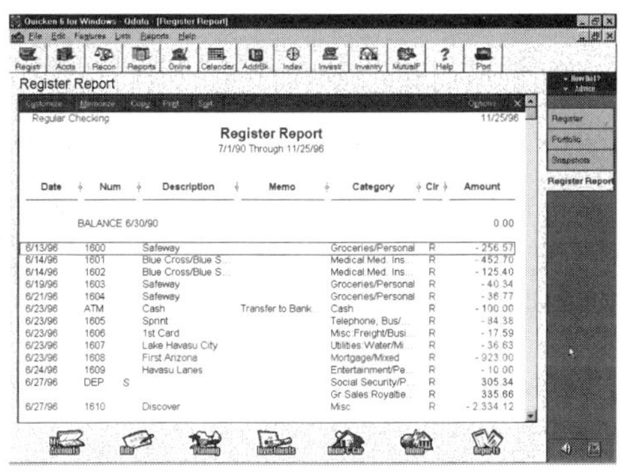

Figure 17.6 *A register report lists transactions for the current register.*

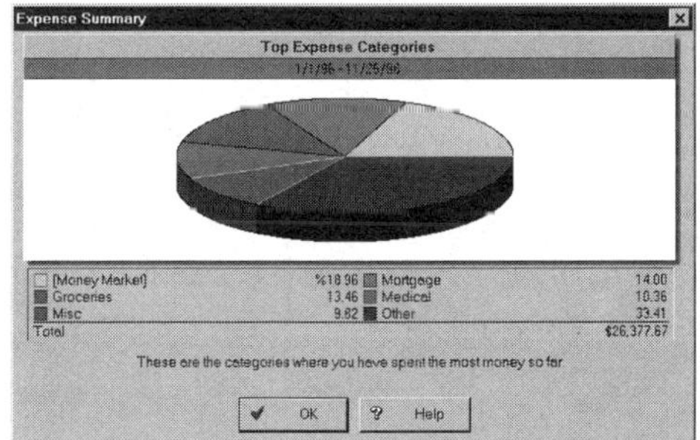

Figure 17.7 *Choose Expense Summary Graph to generate a pie chart that shows where you spent the most money from the current register.*

To create a register report or an expense summary:

1. Display the register for the account you wish to examine.
2. Click the Report button at the top of the register window and choose Register Report or Expense Summary Graph from the drop-down menu. The report (see **Figure 17.6**) or graph (see **Figure 17.7**) appears.

EasyAnswer Reports

EasyAnswer reports are aptly named. You don't have to understand accounting terms. All you need to do is choose a question that you want to have answered by a report or a graph.

To create an EasyAnswer report:

1. Choose EasyAnswer Reports from the Reports menu.

   or

1. Choose Show Me a Graph or Report of My Finances from the Reports icon in the activity bar (refer to **Figure 17.4**).

The EasyAnswer Reports & Graphs dialog box appears (refer to **Figure 17.1**).

2. In Section 1 of the dialog box, choose the question that you want the report to address.
3. In Section 2 of the dialog box, set report details, such as a date range or category to use. Listed options vary from one EasyAnswer report to the next.
4. In Section 3 of the dialog box, click Show Report or Show Graph. (Some EasyAnswer questions can only be presented as reports, some as graphs, and others as reports *or* graphs.) The report or graph is displayed (see **Figure 17.8**).

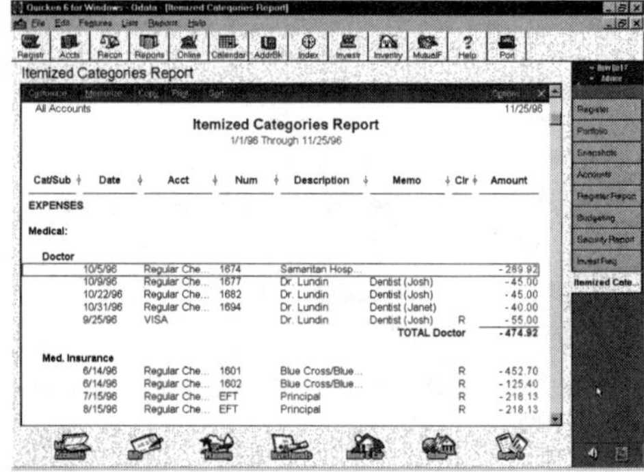

Figure 17.8 *You can create category-specific EasyAnswer reports. For example, this report shows only my family's year-to-date medical expenses.*

Snapshots

Snapshots are tiny reports and graphs that show how you're doing in several financial areas at the same time (see **Figure 17.9**). You can expand any snapshot to fill the window by double-clicking it or by selecting the snapshot and clicking the Enlarge button.

When you install Quicken, six default snapshot graphs and reports are automatically chosen for you. To display these snapshots or custom ones that you created, choose Snapshots from the Reports menu or choose View All My Finances at a Glance from the Reports icon in the activity bar.

The default snapshots may not suit your needs. You can customize snapshots in the following ways:

- Specify the number of snapshots that appear on each page.

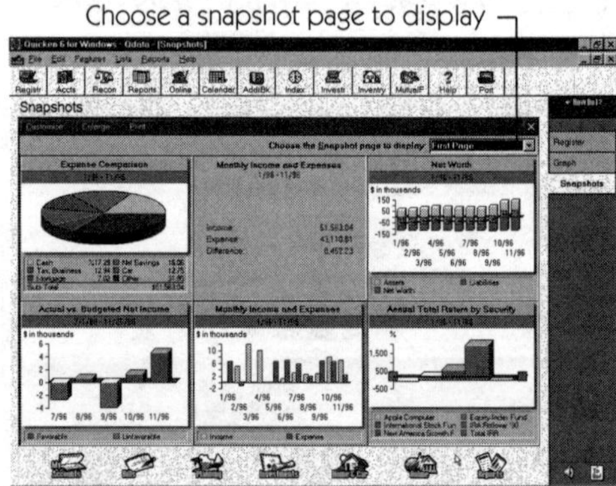

Figure 17.9 *Use snapshots to display some of your favorite reports and graphs.*

- Create additional pages of snapshots. To display a different page, choose the page's name from the drop-down list in the upper-right corner of the Snapshots window.
- Specify a different report or graph for each snapshot.
- Customize individual snapshots by specifying the accounts, categories, classes, and dates to use.

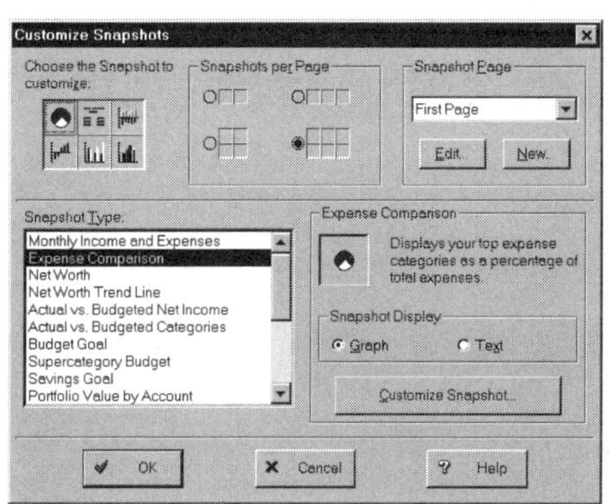

Figure 17.10 *You can customize the snapshot pages or the individual graphs and reports that are displayed.*

To customize a Snapshot page:

1. Display the Snapshots window and click the Customize button. The Customize Snapshots dialog box appears (see **Figure 17.10**).
2. *Optional:* You can display two, three, four, or six snapshots per page (the default is six). To select a different number, click a radio button in the Snapshots per Page area of the dialog box.
3. If there are multiple pages, choose the page that you want to change from the Snapshot Page drop-down list. To create a new snapshot page, click New.
4. A tiny representation of each snapshot on the current page is shown in the upper-left corner of the dialog box. Click an icon to select the snapshot that you want to change.
5. You can select a different type of report or graph for the current snapshot from the Snapshot Type scrolling list.
6. Specify a display preference for the current snapshot topic by clicking Graph or Text in the Snapshot Display area of the dialog box.

7. *Optional:* To change the settings for the selected report or graph, click Customize Snapshot. The Customize Snapshot dialog box appears (see **Figure 17.11**).

   Set a date range for the snapshot by choosing an option from the Graph Dates pop-up list or by entering dates in the From and To text boxes.

   To select specific accounts, categories, and classes to use when generating the snapshot, click the appropriate tab, and then click to add or remove item check marks. Only checked items are used.

   To include hidden accounts in the calculations, make sure that Show Hidden Accounts is checked.

   Click OK when you are finished making changes.

8. Repeat Steps 3–7 for any additional snapshots that you want to modify.
9. Click OK to save the changes, or click Cancel to ignore them.

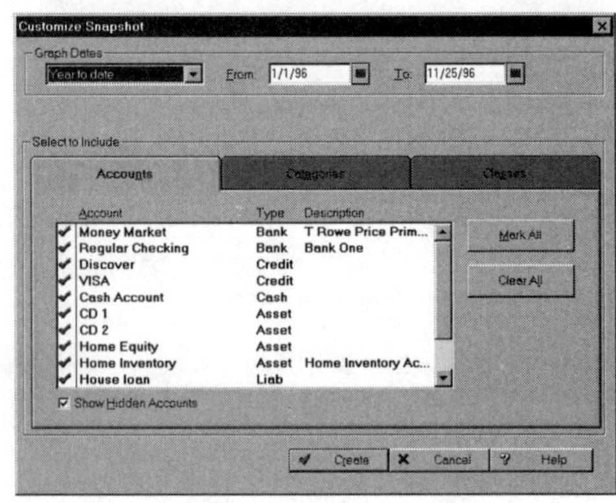

Figure 17.11 *You can customize a snapshot by choosing the dates, accounts, categories, and classes to include.*

Custom Reports

Quicken provides four groups of predefined custom reports that you can create: Home, Investment, Business, and Other.

To create a custom report:

1. Click the Reports icon in the activity bar and choose Create Custom Reports.

   or

1. Choose a report from the Home, Investment, Business, or Other submenu of the Reports menu.

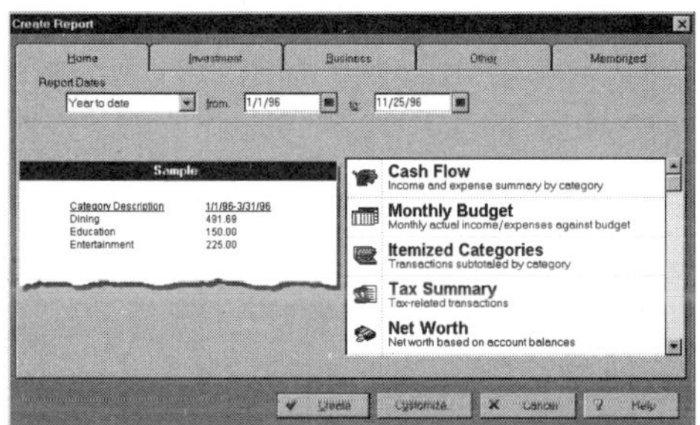

Figure 17.12 *You create custom reports in the Create Report dialog box. Report categories are displayed as tabs at the top of the dialog box.*

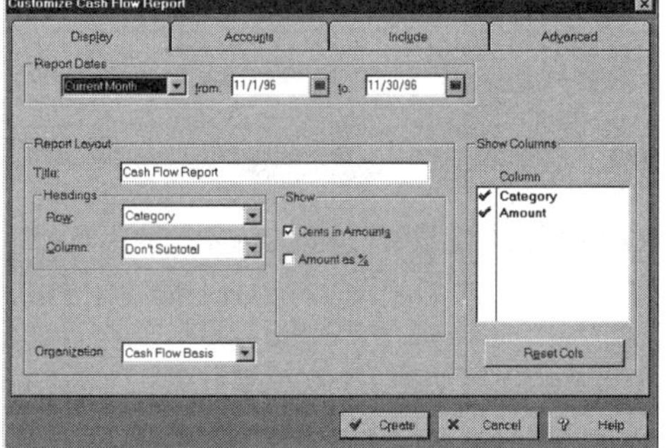

Figure 17.13 *You can customize many aspects of a report.*

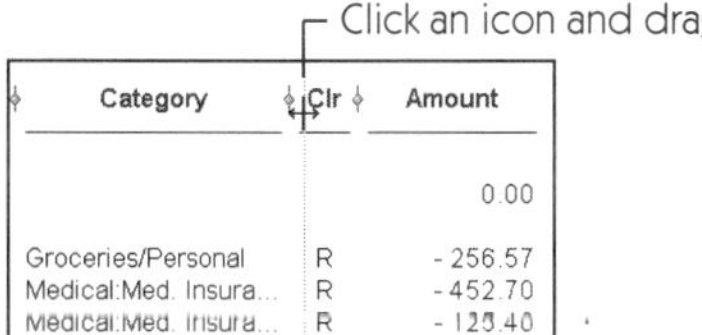

Figure 17.14 *To change a column's width, click the divider icon to the right of the column whose width you want to change.*

The Create Report dialog box appears (see **Figure 17.12**).

2. If the desired report isn't already selected, click a tab at the top of the dialog box to display a report category and then choose a report.
3. Set a date range for the report.
4. *Optional:* To view or change the standard options for the report, click Customize. The Customize Report dialog box appears (see **Figure 17.13**). For information about customizing reports, see "Customizing Reports," later in this chapter.
5. To display the report, click Create.

✔ Tips

- If you're not sure of the purpose of a particular report or what it looks like, choose "Reports, Examples" from the Help Index.
- You can change the column widths of some reports, such as the register report. Click the divider icon between any pair of column headings and then drag, as shown in **Figure 17.14**.
- If you're having trouble reconciling your checking account, you can create a missing checks report. Choose Reports ⇨ Home ⇨ Missing Checks. The report enables you to easily find duplicate checks and breaks in the numbering sequence.
- If your business operates on a fiscal year, you can base reports on your fiscal year. Specify the first month of your fiscal year by choosing Edit ⇨ Options ⇨ Quicken Program, and then click the Settings tab.

Default Report and Graph Settings

Quicken allows you to specify default settings to use when creating reports and graphs. Unless you override these settings with custom options, they are used whenever you create a standard report or graph.

To specify default report settings:

1. Choose Edit ⇨ Options ⇨ Reports or click the Options button at the top of any report window. The Report Options dialog box appears (see **Figure 17.15**).
2. Accounts and categories used in reports can be listed by name, by a text description that you assigned to the account or category, or by both name and description. Click radio buttons in the Account Display and Category Display sections to record your preferences.
3. Choose a Default Report Date Range and a Default Comparison Report Date Range from the drop-down lists. The former date range is used as the basis for standard reports; the latter range acts as the comparison period for reports that include comparisons. You can pick any preset range or choose Custom Date to specify a different range.
4. The meanings of the check boxes at the bottom of the dialog box are as follows:

   Skip Create Report Prompt. When you choose a report from the Home, Investment, Business, or Other submenu of the Reports menu, the Create Report dialog box appears (refer to **Figure 17.12**),

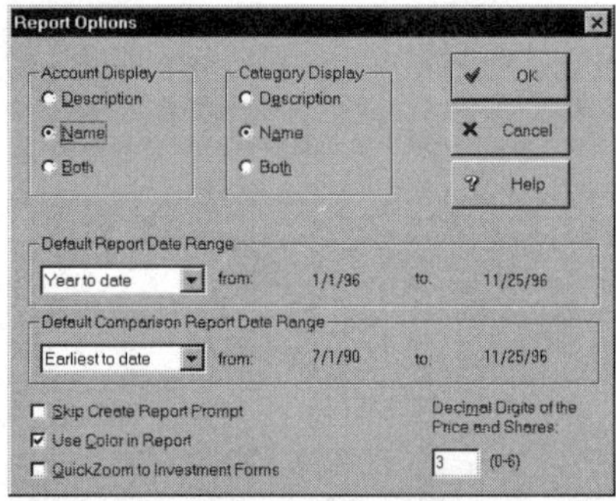

Figure 17.15 *Default report settings, such as the date range for the report, are set in the Report Options dialog box.*

Default Report and Graph Settings

enabling you to select a date range or a different report. If this box is checked, reports are created using the default date range(s) and appear without first displaying the Create Report dialog box.

Use Color in Report. Click to display titles and negative numbers in color.

QuickZoom to Investment Forms. When unchecked and you click a figure in an investment report with the QuickZoom tool, you zoom to the matching transaction line in the account register. When this option is checked, you zoom to the dialog box in which the transaction was recorded (see **Figure 17.16**).

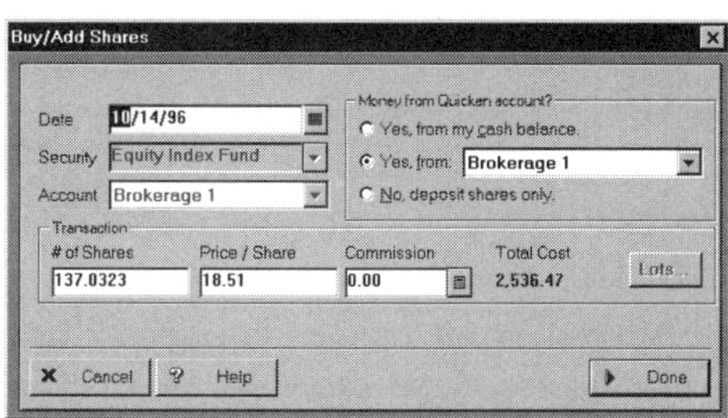

Figure 17.16 *Double-clicking a figure in an investment report can display the original dialog box for the transaction.*

5. Enter a number in the Decimal Digits text box to indicate the number of decimal places to display in share prices and quantities in portfolio reports.
6. Click OK to record the new report options.

To specify default graph settings:

1. Choose Edit ⇨ Options ⇨ Graphs or click the Options button at the top of any graph window. The Graph Options dialog box appears (see **Figure 17.17**).
2. The meanings of the options are as follows:

   Use Patterns Instead of Colors. When this option is checked, Quicken draws all graphs using black-and-white patterns. If you have a monochrome (non-color) monitor or are printing with a dot-matrix printer, you may wish to set

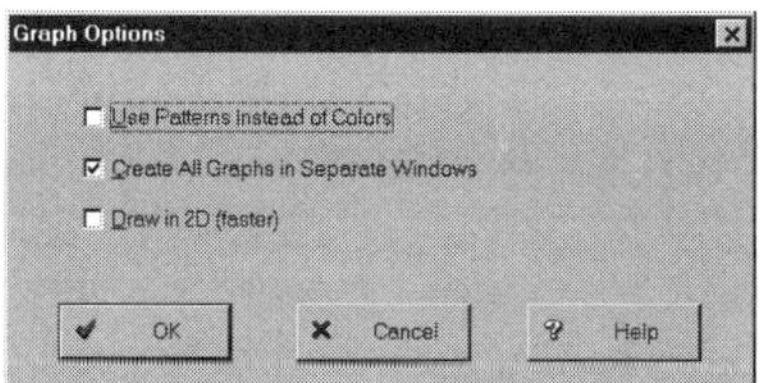

Figure 17.17 *Set default options for new graphs in the Graph Options dialog box.*

this option. However, you should note that when color graphs are displayed (unlike black-and-white graphs), they can be printed in grayscale on most laser and inkjet printers.

Create All Graphs in Separate Windows. Selecting some types of graphs results in a pair of graphs being created rather than only one. Such graphs can be displayed separately or in the same window.

Draw in 2D (faster). If you have a slow system, check this option to improve the speed with which graphs are displayed.

3. Click OK to record the new default graph settings.

Customizing Reports

Any report that you create using the standard settings can also be customized. For example, you can specify a different date range; choose accounts, categories, and types of transactions to include; and specify a title and sorting instructions.

To customize a report:

1. Create a report, and click the Customize button at the top of the report window.

   or

1. Click the Reports icon in the activity bar and choose Create Custom Reports, or click the Report button in the top iconbar. Select a report to create, and then click the Customize button.

   The Customize Report dialog box appears (see **Figures 17.18–17.21**).

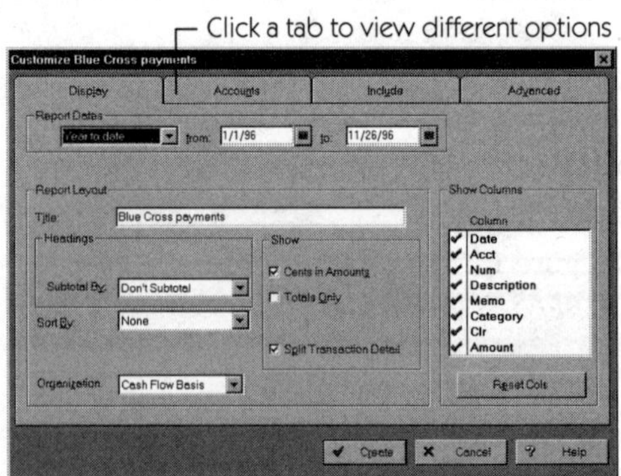

Figure 17.18 *Customization for most types of reports is done in this dialog box. The listed options vary slightly for different reports. These are the Display options.*

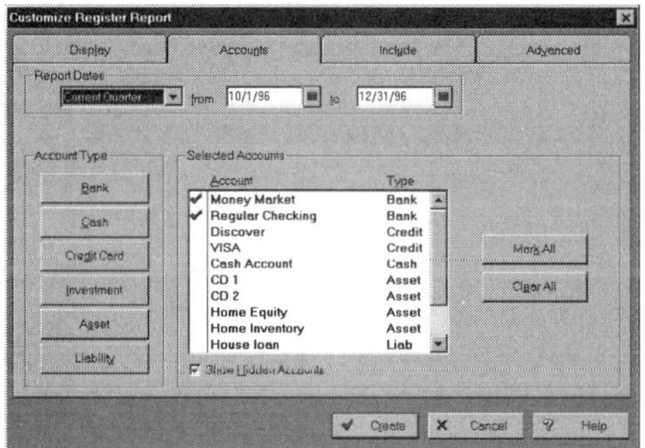

Figure 17.19 *Accounts options.*

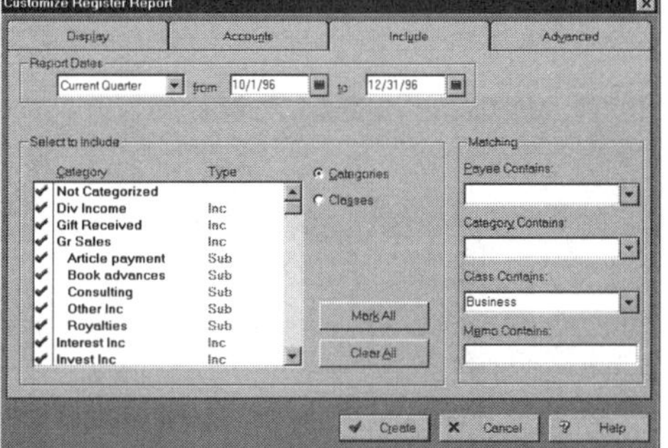

Figure 17.20 *Include options.*

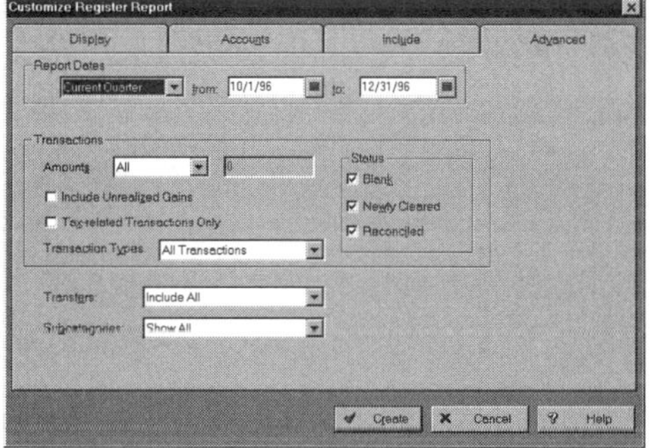

Figure 17.21 *Advanced options.*

The dialog box is divided into four parts: Display, Accounts, Include, and Advanced. You can view and change any set of options by clicking the appropriate tab at the top of the dialog box.

2. Click the Display tab to change the date range or title, specify sort and subtotal fields, or select columns to include.
3. Click the Accounts tab to specify accounts to include and ones to exclude.
4. Click the Include tab to select categories, classes, and supercategories to include. To include only specific transactions, choose options from the drop-down lists in the Matching area of the window.
5. Click the Advanced tab to specify the types of transactions to include.
6. Click the Create button to generate the report with the new options.

✔ Tips

- After creating a report, you can quickly display the Customize Report dialog box by double-clicking the report title or date range.
- You can set a new date range in any page of the Customize Report dialog box.
- You can select accounts to include by *type* (Bank, for example). Click the appropriate button(s) in the Accounts section of the dialog box.
- After creating a customized report, you may want Quicken to memorize the settings so they can be reused. See "Memorizing Reports" for instructions.

Memorizing Reports

Although you can create every report from scratch, you'll find the ability to memorize reports extremely useful. Any memorized report can later be recalled and displayed, using the original date range (last quarter, for example) or new dates.

To memorize a report:

1. Create the report that you want to memorize.
2. Click the Memorize button at the top of the report window, as shown in **Figure 17.22**. The Memorize Report dialog box appears (see **Figure 17.23**).
3. Type a title and description for the memorized report.
4. Set a date range for the memorized report by clicking a radio button. If you used a preset date range when you created the report, you can click *Named Range* to use the same relative date range (Current Month, for example). Click *Custom* to use the exact date range specified when you created the report (October 1996, for example). Click *None* to use the default date range set in the Report Options dialog box (see "Default Report and Graph Settings," earlier in this chapter).
5. *Optional:* Choose an icon to represent the memorized report. The icon appears beside the report name in the memorized reports list.
6. Click OK.

After memorizing one or more reports, it is simple to re-create, edit, delete, or customize the reports.

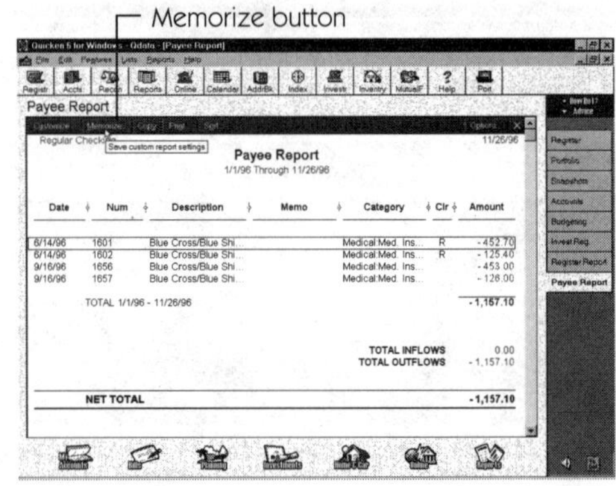

Figure 17.22 *Click Memorize to add a report to the roster of memorized reports.*

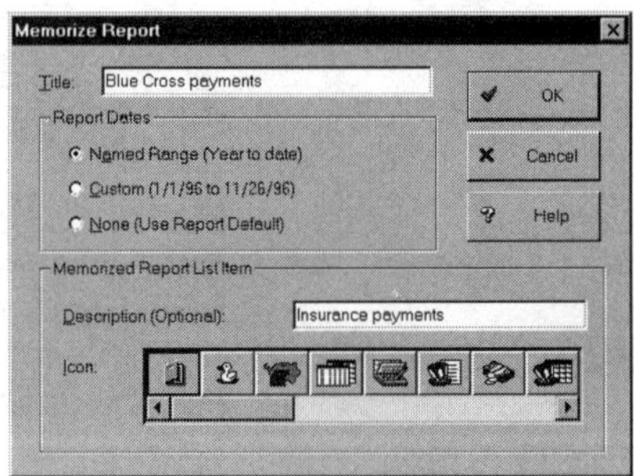

Figure 17.23 *When memorizing a report, the only required setting is that of the date range to use; all others are optional.*

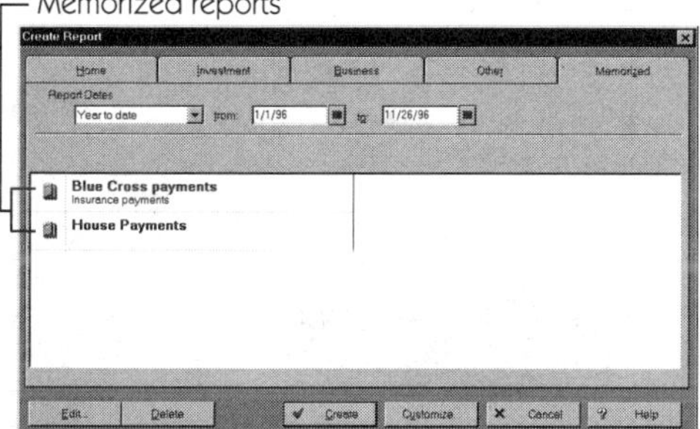

Figure 17.24 *Memorized reports are listed in the Memorized section of the Create Report dialog box.*

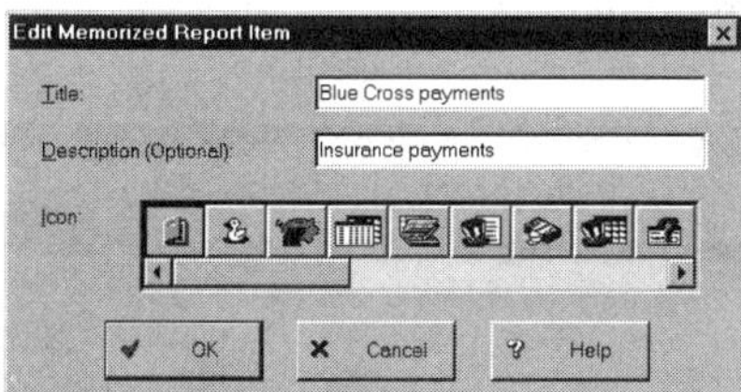

Figure 17.25 *Use the Edit Memorized Report Item dialog box to change the title, description, or icon for any memorized report.*

To re-create a memorized report:

1. Display the Create Report dialog box (see **Figure 17.24**) by choosing Memorized Reports from the Reports menu or by clicking the Reports icon in the Activity bar and choosing Create Custom Reports.
2. Click the Memorized tab at the top of the Create Report dialog box. All memorized reports are displayed in a scrolling list.
3. Select a report, change the date range (if desired), and click Create.

✔ Tips

- To remove a report from the memorized reports list, select the report and click Delete. To change the title, description, or icon for a memorized report, select the report, and click Edit. The Edit Memorized Report Item dialog box appears (see **Figure 17.25**).
- To further customize a memorized report, select it and click Customize. The Customize Report dialog box appears (refer to **Figures 17.18–17.21**). Click the tabs at the top of the dialog box to view or change the different classes of options. For help using the Customize Report dialog box, refer to "Customizing Reports," earlier in this chapter.

Using QuickZoom in Reports and Graphs

The QuickZoom magnifying glass (see **Figure 17.26**) can be used to get additional information about a line item in a report or a graph element. Double-clicking a graph element, for example, creates a second graph or a transaction report that provides additional detail for the graph element, as shown in **Figure 17.27**. You can double-click an element in a transaction report to view the original transaction, or double-click an element in a non-transaction report to see a new report that lists all related transactions.

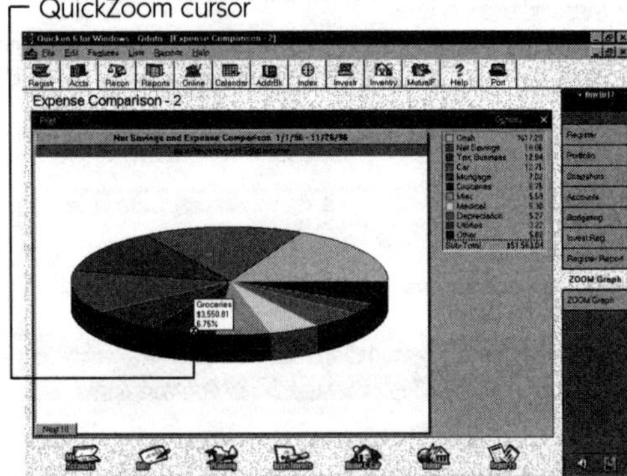

Figure 17.26 *You can double-click a slice of this expense categories chart to view additional details about a category.*

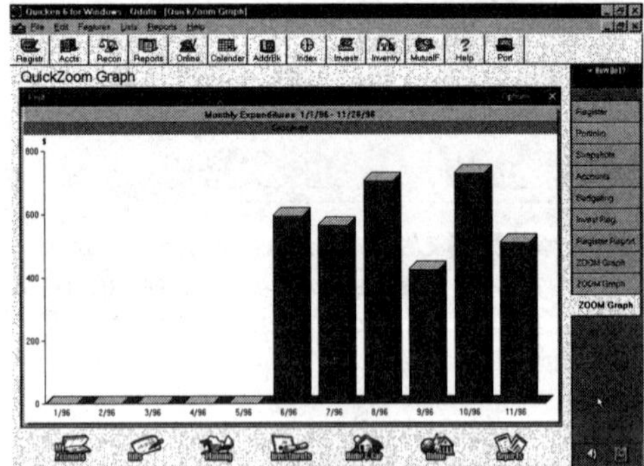

Figure 17.27 *This bar graph shows month-by-month expenditures for the zoomed category in the pie chart in Figure 17.26.*

18 Printing

Quicken Printing Essentials

If you have installed your printer in Windows, you can use Quicken's Print commands to print reports, budgets, lists, graphs, and checks. Printing involves just a few steps, and many of them need only be performed once.

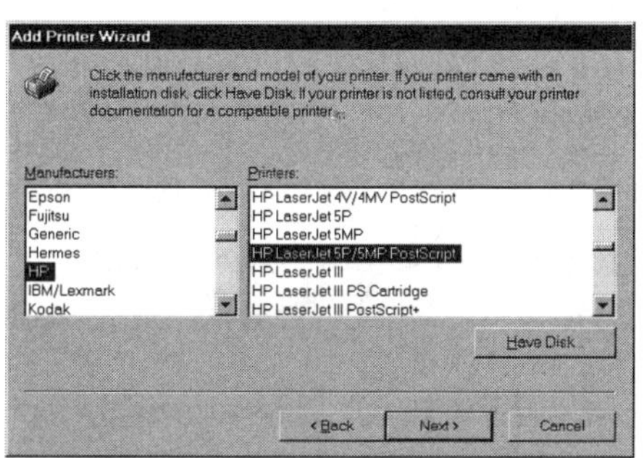

Figure 18.1 *To install a printer under Windows 95, open the Printers control panel and double-click Add Printer. The Add a Printer Wizard steps you through the installation process.*

First, you must let Windows know what printer you have and how it is connected to your computer. Normally, you install printers when you set up Windows. If you've changed printers or added a new one, you simply repeat the installation procedure for the new printer (see **Figure 18.1**). For help installing printers, refer to your Windows documentation.

Second, run the Printer Setup routine in Quicken. Printer Setup enables you to select a printer to use (if more than one is installed) and set basic options, such as the print margins, paper type, and fonts to use. Quicken has two Printer Setup commands—one for checks and one for printing everything else, such as lists, reports, and graphs.

Third, prepare something to be printed. You can generate a graph or report, create checks in the Write Checks window, or view a list. Then switch to the window in which the material to be printed is contained.

Fourth, select the Print command from the File menu or click the Print button at the top of the window. Review the current print settings, and click OK to send the data to the printer.

✔ **Tip**

■ The first and second steps (installing printers and running the Printer Setup routines) only need to be done once. Unless you change printers, paper, or decide that some of the settings are no longer optimal (the selected fonts, for instance), you can skip these steps on later print jobs.

The Printer Setup Commands

Depending on whether you plan to print reports or checks, you should perform one or both of the Printer Setup commands below—*before* you print for the first time. As shown in **Figure 18.2**, the File menu has two Printer Setup commands.

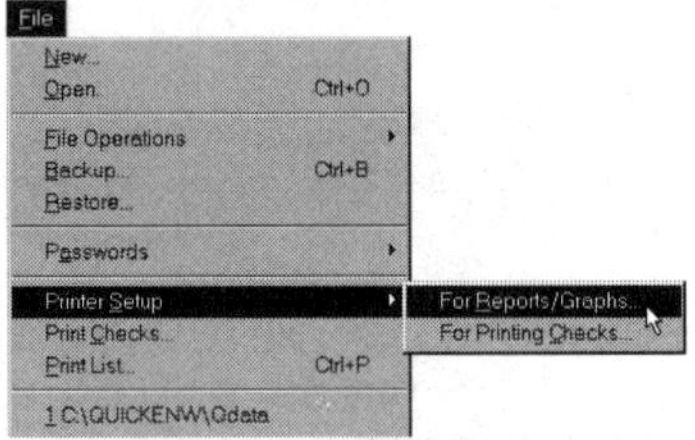

Figure 18.2 *There are two Printer Setup commands: one for reports and one for checks.*

To run Printer Setup for reports, lists, budgets, and graphs:

1. Choose File ➪ Printer Setup ➪ For Reports/Graphs. The Report Printer Setup dialog box appears (see **Figure 18.3**).

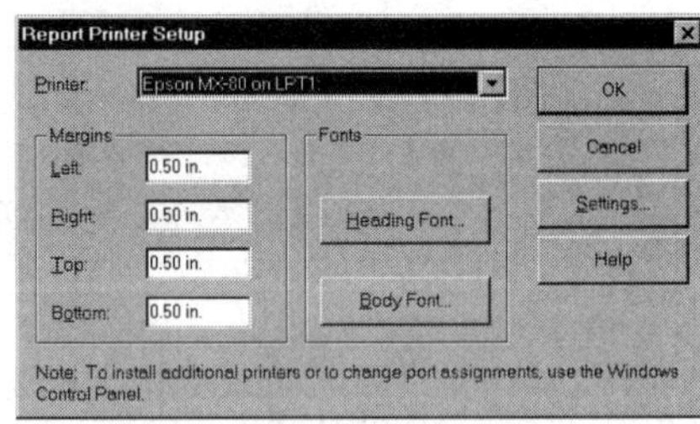

Figure 18.3 *The Report Printer Setup dialog box.*

2. Choose an installed printer from the Printer drop-down list. All reports, lists, and graphs will be printed on the chosen printer.
3. To alter the margin settings, type new numbers (in inches) in the Left, Right, Top, and Bottom boxes.
4. To set a font to be used when printing headings and body text, click the Heading Font or Body Font button. The dialog box shown in **Figure 18.4** appears. Select a font, style, and size from the three lists, and then click OK.

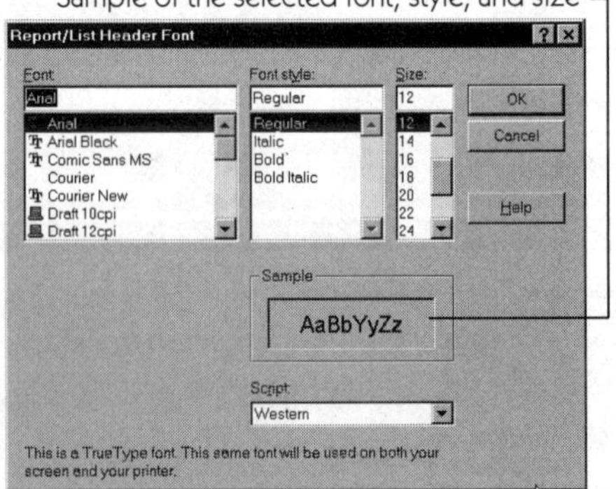

Figure 18.4 *You can select body and heading fonts from all fonts that are installed in Windows.*

5. To examine or change some of the printing properties of the current

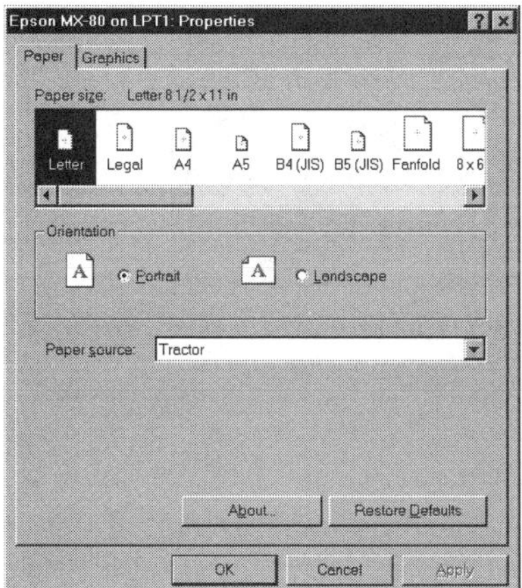

Figure 18.5 *You can select a paper type, orientation, and source in the Paper section of the Properties dialog box. Click the Graphics tab to change graphics settings.*

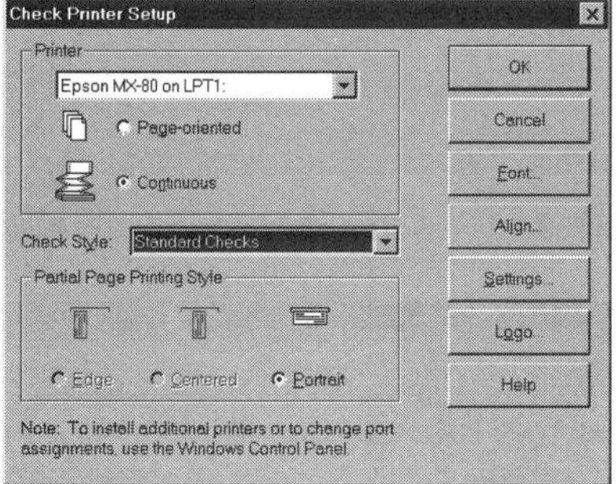

Figure 18.6 *Use the Check Printer Setup dialog box to set printer and paper-handling options for printing checks.*

printer, click Settings. A Properties dialog box specific to the current printer appears (see **Figure 18.5**).

6. Click OK to complete the setup.

To run Printer Setup for checks:

1. Choose File ⇨ Printer Setup ⇨ For Printing Checks. The Check Printer Setup dialog box appears, as shown in **Figure 18.6**.
2. Choose an installed Windows printer from the Printer drop-down list. All checks will be printed on the selected printer.
3. Indicate the types of checks you will be printing by clicking *Page-oriented* for checks that are in separate sheets (used by laser and inkjet printers) or *Continuous* (for tractor-feed/dot-matrix printers).
4. From the drop-down list, choose the Check Style that corresponds to the type of checks you purchased.
5. Choose a Partial Page Printing Style to indicate how partial pages are inserted into your printer. Normally, this is the same way that you position envelopes for printing.
6. Click the Font button to select a font to use for all printed text. The dialog box previously shown in **Figure 18.4** appears. Select a font, style, and size from the three lists, and then click OK.
7. To examine or change the printing properties of the current printer, click Settings. A Properties dialog box specific to the current printer appears (refer to **Figure 18.5**).

8. To print a personal logo on your checks, click the Logo button. The Check Logo dialog box appears (see **Figure 18.7**).

   To be used as a logo, a graphic must be saved or converted to Windows BMP format. Click File and select your logo file from its location on disk. The logo appears in the Selected Logo section of the dialog box. Click OK.

9. The manner in which you test and adjust printing alignment depends on the type of printer that you have. See "To set print alignment for page printers" and "To set print alignment for continuous-form printers," below.

10. Click OK to close the Check Printer Setup dialog box, completing the setup process.

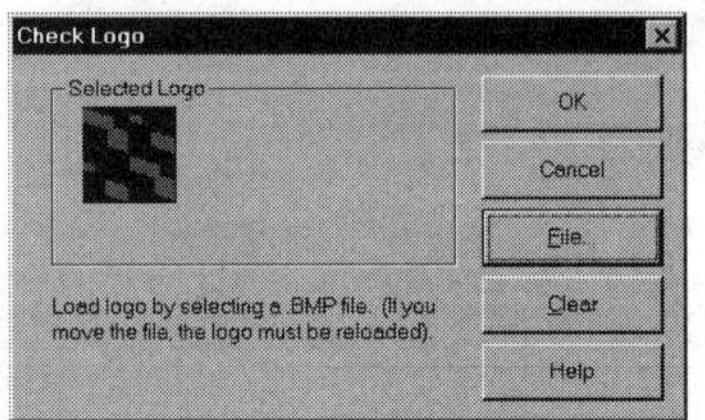

Figure 18.7 *You can add a personal logo that will print on each check.*

Aligning Checks in the Printer

When testing and adjusting alignment, the characteristics of your printer and check paper determine which sets of dialog boxes are presented. Dot-matrix printers usually print on continuous forms; lasers and most inkjet printers typically print on individual pages.

To set print alignment for page-oriented printers:

1. In the Check Printer Setup dialog box, click Align. The Align Checks dialog box appears (see **Figure 18.8**). Alignment is adjusted separately for full and partial pages.
2. Click the button for the alignment option that you want to test. The Fine Alignment dialog box appears (see **Figure 18.9**).

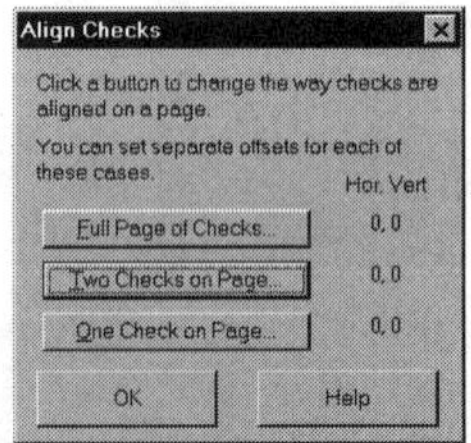

Figure 18.8 *Without adjustment, printing on the checks may not align properly.*

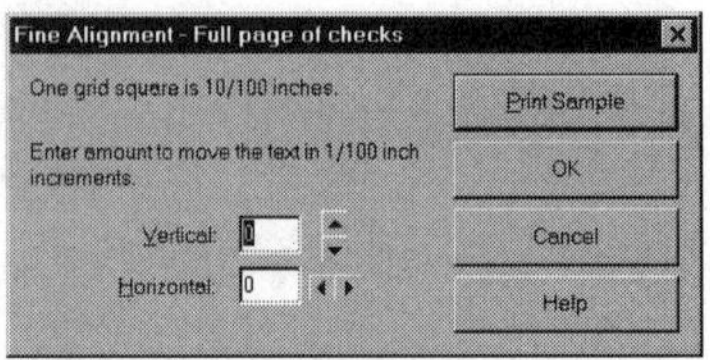

Figure 18.9 *Use the Fine Alignment dialog box to test and make small changes to check-printing alignment.*

The Printer Setup Commands

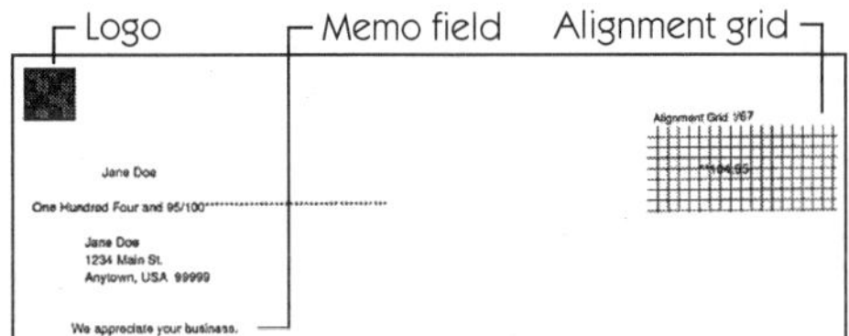

Figure 18.10 *To check printing alignment, place a sheet of checks under the sample and view them through a strong light.*

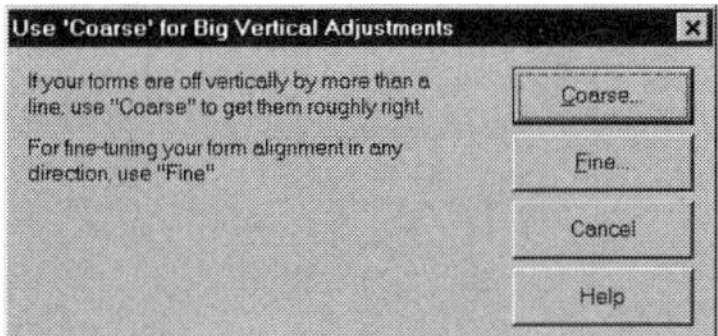

Figure 18.11 *There are two alignment options that you can use when printing continuous forms: Fine (for small adjustments) and Coarse (for big adjustments).*

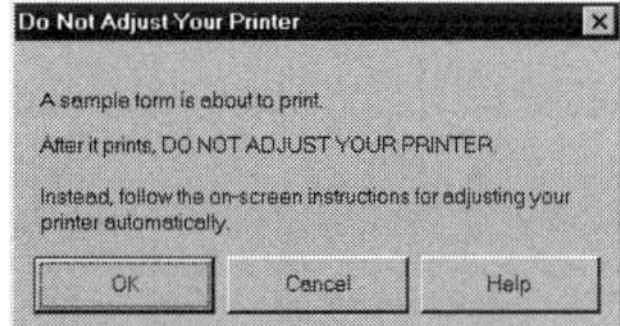

Figure 18.12 *When making large adjustments, Quicken presents a series of dialog boxes that step you through the process.*

3. Insert a page of sample checks or a blank sheet of paper into your printer, turn it on, and click Print Sample (see **Figure 18.10**). If necessary, adjust the vertical or horizontal alignment and print another sample. Repeat until the alignment is correct. Click OK.

4. Repeat Steps 2 and 3 for the other Checks on Page settings.

5. Close the Check Printer Setup dialog box.

To set print alignment for continuous-form printers:

1. In the Check Printer Setup dialog box, click Align. The dialog box shown in **Figure 18.11** appears.

2. To make large vertical adjustments, click Coarse. The dialog box shown in **Figure 18.12** appears. Click OK to print a sample, and then follow the on-screen instructions.

   When the Please Note Position dialog box appears, note the position of the checks in relation to a fixed part of the printer, such as the top of the printhead. On subsequent printings, you can use this information to align the checks.

   or

2. For smaller adjustments, click Fine. Turn on the printer and click Print Sample. If necessary, adjust the vertical or horizontal alignment and print another sample. Repeat until the alignment is correct.

3. Close the Check Printer Setup dialog box.

✔ **Tips**

- In Windows 95, another way to review printer settings is by opening the Printers control panel, selecting a printer icon, and choosing Properties from the File menu.
- If you have two or more printers, you can print reports on one and checks on the other, if you wish.

The Print Command

When you have a batch of checks or a report, list, or graph that you want to print, choose the relevant Print command from the File menu or click the Print button at the top of the current window.

Here are several important points about the Print command:

- The wording of the Print command changes depending on the window that is currently displayed. It may read Print Report, List, Register, Budget, or Graph, for instance.
- The Print Checks command is always available. However, you must first designate some checks to be printed in the Write Checks window or a register and then display that window. See "Printing Checks," later in this chapter, for instructions on setting print options.
- Before printing a report, summary, or list, you must display the appropriate Quicken window before choosing the Print command. See "Printing Reports," later in this chapter, for instructions on setting print options.
- Unlike printing reports, lists, and checks, graphs are immediately

sent to the printer. Be sure that the printer is on before choosing the Print Graph command. You can vary the quality of graph printouts by changing the printer settings (refer to **Figure 18.5**).

Printing Reports

Use the following steps when printing Quicken reports. For want of a better term, anything other than graphs and checks are referred to here as *reports*.

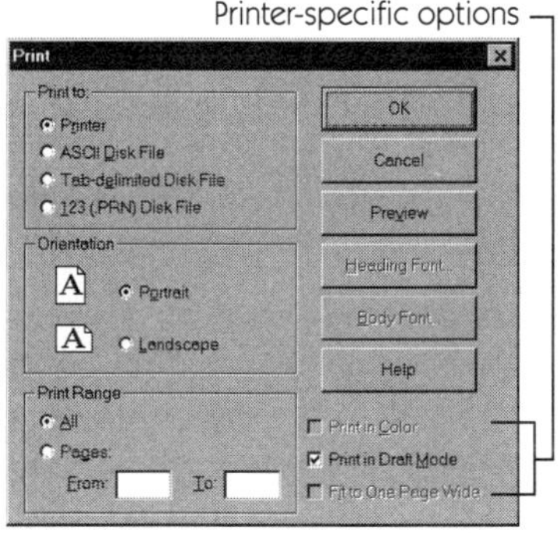

Figure 18.13 *When printing a report, list, or summary, the Print dialog box appears. You can use it to set a variety of options for the current print job.*

To print a report:

1. Display the report, list, or budget that you want to print.
2. Choose the Print command from the File menu, click the Print button at the top of the current window (if one is displayed), or press Ctrl P. The Print dialog box appears, as shown in **Figure 18.13**.
3. In the Print to section of the dialog box, click a radio button to indicate whether output should be sent to the printer or a print file. (Choose *ASCII* to create a standard text file; *Tab-delimited* to create a text file in which fields are separated by tabs; or *123* to create a Lotus 1-2-3 compatible worksheet file.)
4. In the Orientation section of the dialog box, click Portrait for a normal printout or Landscape to print sideways.
5. In the Print Range section of the dialog box, click All to print the entire report or list. To print only part of a report or list, click Pages and enter the starting and ending page numbers in the From and To text boxes.

6. To review the printout on-screen, click Preview. A window like the one shown in **Figure 18.14** appears. You can click buttons to change the magnification and view other pages.
7. Depending on the capabilities of the current printer, other options can be set to print in color, print in draft mode (for faster output), or compress the data horizontally so it fits within the current margins.
8. After setting options, click OK to begin printing or create a print file.

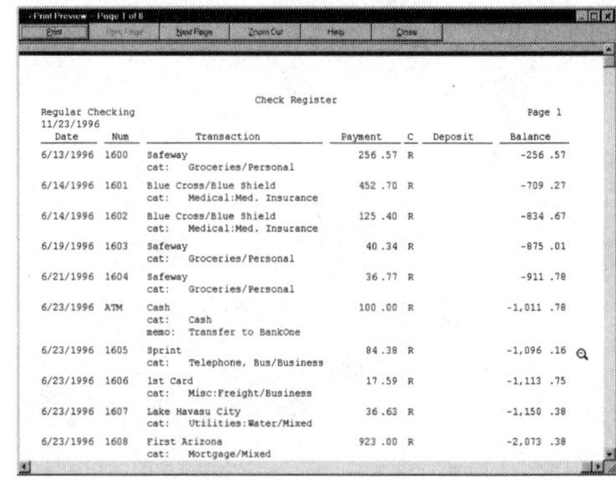

Figure 18.14 *Use the Preview option to see how a report will look before sending it to your printer.*

Printing Checks

Although checks designed for personal computer printers are more expensive than ones that you order from a bank, printing checks from within Quicken can save time and unnecessary duplication of effort.

To print checks:

1. Select the account from which the checks will be printed by changing to the Write Checks window or to the register for the account.
2. Choose Print Checks from the File menu. The Select Checks to Print dialog box appears, as shown in **Figure 18.15**.

   First Check Number refers to the number that will be assigned to the first check in this batch. If necessary, change the number so it matches the first prenumbered check in the printer.

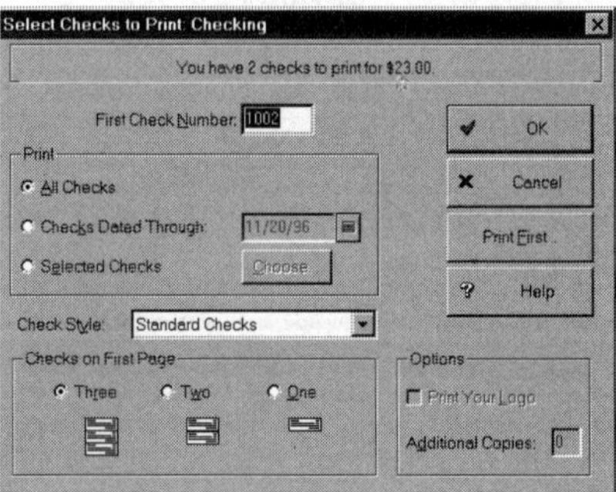

Figure 18.15 *Set check-printing options in the Select Checks to Print dialog box.*

3. In the Print section of the dialog box, click a radio button to print all waiting checks (All Checks), checks through a specific date (Checks Dated Through), or only

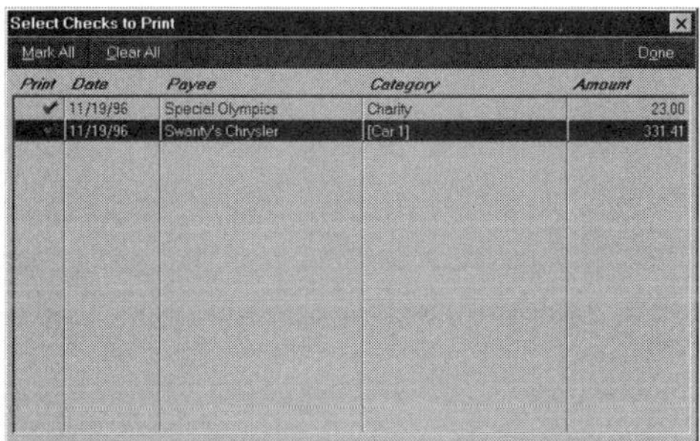

Figure 18.16 *Checks that will print are preceded by a check mark. Click to add or remove check marks.*

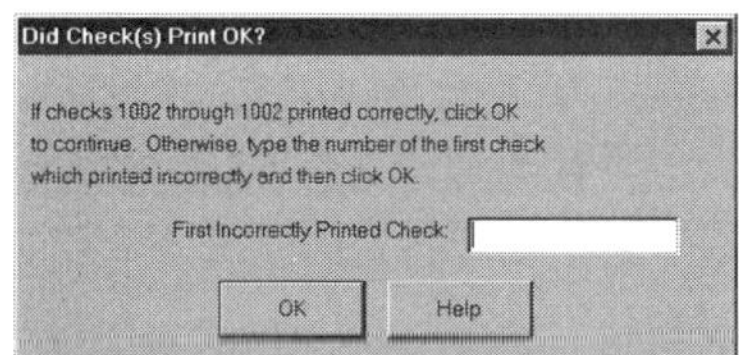

Figure 18.17 *This dialog box appears immediately after the selected checks are printed, enabling you to correct any printing errors.*

some of the waiting checks (Selected Checks). If you choose Selected Checks, the dialog box in **Figure 18.16** appears.

4. Make sure the check style is correct. If not, select another one from the Check Style drop-down list.
5. Click a radio button in the Checks on First Page section to indicate the number of remaining checks on the first page. Three is a full page; Two and One are partial pages.
6. *Optional:* If you have created a logo for your checks (see "To run Printer Setup for checks"), click the check box for Print Your Logo to add it to the checks.

   To print more than one copy of each check in this print run, enter a number in the Additional Copies text box. (This option allows you to print multipart voucher checks.)
7. To print only the first check in the batch, click Print First. To print the entire batch, click OK.
8. The dialog box shown in **Figure 18.17** appears. If there were no printing errors, click OK. Otherwise, enter the number of the first check that printed incorrectly so you can reprint them.

Printing Lists

For record-keeping purposes, you may find it helpful to print some of the lists you have created in Quicken.

To print a list:

1. Display the list you want to print by choosing it from the Lists menu.

2. Choose Print List from the File menu. The Print dialog box appears (refer to **Figure 18.13**).
3. Set print options and click OK.

Printing Graphs

To print a Quicken graph, display the graph on-screen and choose Print Graph from the File menu. Unlike other printing tasks, there is no preview mode and no Print dialog box. Immediately after issuing the Print command, the graph is sent to the printer.

Printing from Quicken Deluxe

Program components that are included only in Quicken Deluxe have their own Print and Printer Setup commands. To learn about printing with Financial Address Book, Home Inventory, and similar components, see the chapter in which each component is discussed.

✔ **Tip**

- When printing any type of report or graph, there are many options that you can set when creating the report or graph, such as the dates, records, or the categories to be included. To learn more about creating reports and setting options, see Chapter 17.

Part V:
On-Line Activities

Quicken Live

About Quicken Live

If you have a modem and Internet access (through an Internet service provider, an on-line information service, or a limited-access account from Intuit), you can use Quicken Live.

Quicken Live is a program component that helps you obtain financial information from the Internet. The parts of Quicken Live include:

- A hand-picked list of financial Web sites (Best of the Web).
- Quicken tips, news, and special offers from Intuit (What's New).
- On-line price quotes for stocks and mutual funds that you track in your Quicken portfolio.
- The Quicken Financial Network.
- Access to minor Quicken updates.

You can choose Quicken Live commands from the Online icon in the activity bar (see **Figure 19.1**) or from the Features ⇨ Online ⇨ Quicken Live (Internet) submenu (see **Figure 19.2**).

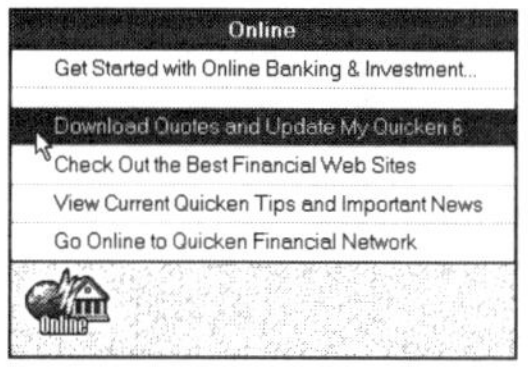

Figure 19.1 *Online commands in the activity bar.*

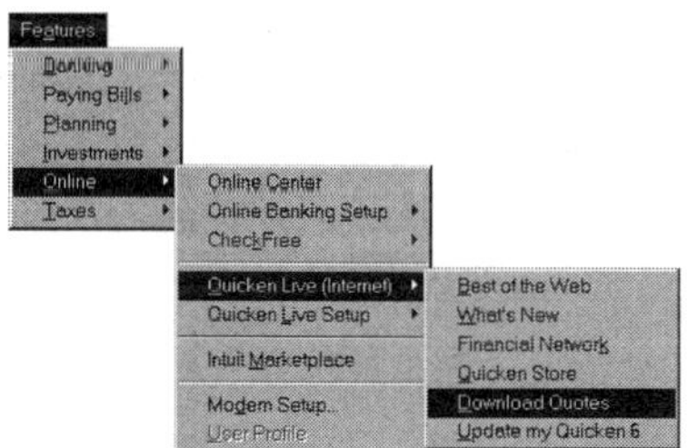

Figure 19.2 *Quicken Live commands.*

The first time you use a Quicken Live feature that requires an Internet connection, Quicken automatically begins an Internet configuration procedure, presenting a series of dialog boxes for you to complete. For instructions on setting up an Internet connection, refer to "Quicken Live Setup" in Chapter 4.

Best of the Web

If you're seeking financial information on the Internet, the Best of the Web is the first place to look. It lists and reviews dozens of personal finance Web sites. Best of the Web is provided by Excite, a popular Internet search site.

To open Best of the Web in Quicken, choose Features ⇨ Online ⇨ Quicken Live (Internet) ⇨ Best of the Web, or click the Online icon in the activity bar and choose Check Out the Best Financial Web Sites. The Quicken Live window opens to the Best of the Web section (see **Figure 19.3**).

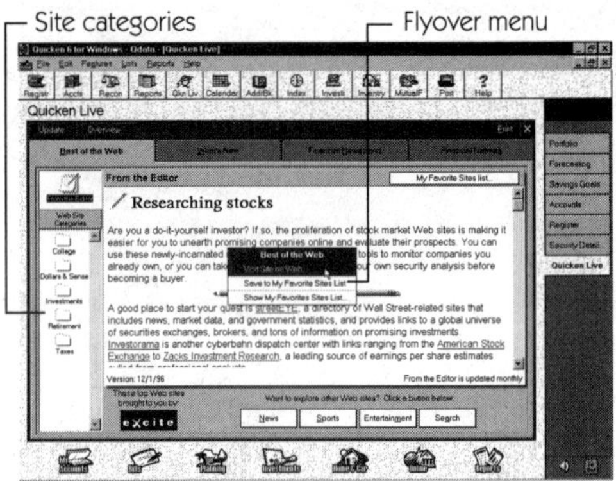

Figure 19.3 *The Quicken Live window is divided into sections, each represented by a tab. The Best of the Web is currently chosen.*

Visiting Web Sites

Web site names are shown in the scrolling text box as underlined text. If you move the cursor over the name of a financial site, a flyover menu appears (as shown in **Figure 19.3**). To go to the site, choose Visit Site on Web from the menu or click the underlined text.

To make it easy to find financial topics that interest you at the moment, Best of the Web is divided into categories. To view sites on a given topic, click a category icon in the scrolling list on the left side of the window.

Storing Favorite Sites

Any site that is listed in Best of the Web can be stored in a Favorite Sites List within Quicken (see **Figure 19.4**). To add a site to the list, move the cursor over its name in the Best of the Web window and choose Save to My Favorite Sites List from the flyover menu. To visit a favorite site, click the My Favorite Sites List button at the top of the window, select the site name from the list, and click Go to Site.

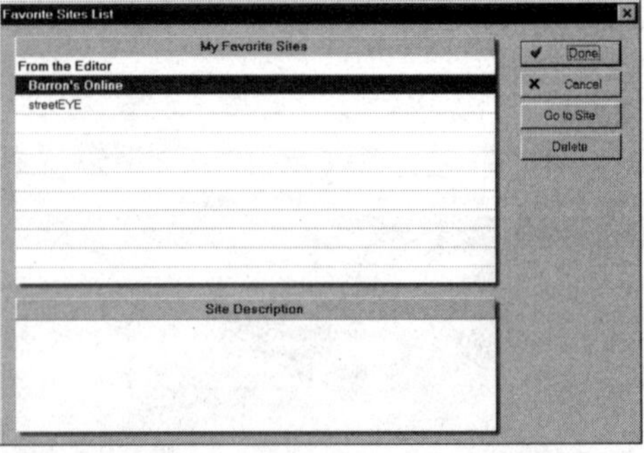

Figure 19.4 *To visit a favorite Web site, select it and click Go to Site. You can remove any site from this list by selecting it and clicking Delete.*

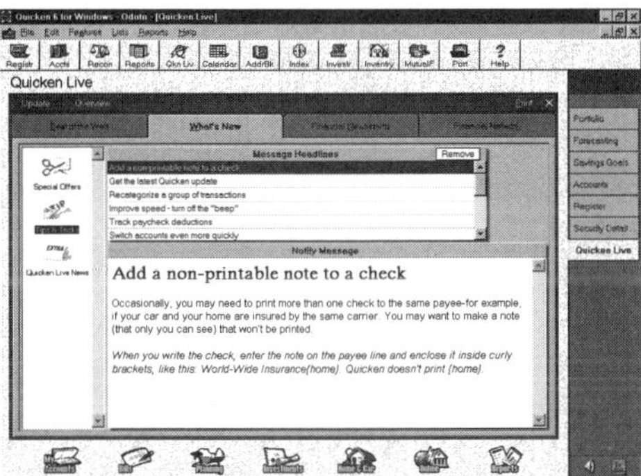

Figure 19.5 *The What's New section of Quicken Live.*

Quicken Tips and News

To view Quicken tips, news, and special offers from Intuit, click the What's New tab at the top of the Quicken Live window (see **Figure 19.5**). Choose the type of information you want to view by clicking a category icon in the left side of the window.

Although most of the information in What's New is intended to be read offline at your leisure, some text is linked to Web sites. To visit a site, click an underlined text string. To delete a tip, a news item, or an offer from Intuit, select its heading and click Remove.

The material in What's New can be brought up-to-date by going on-line with the Update My Quicken 6 command. For help using the Update feature, see "Updating with Quicken Live" at the end of this chapter.

Quicken Program Updates

Occasionally, Intuit may make changes to Quicken 6 by fixing bugs or adding minor features. Rather than requesting a set of update disks, you can use Quicken Live to download the updates over the Internet.

Each time that you use Quicken Live to connect to the Internet, a check is done to see if a Quicken update is available. If so, you are notified and can download it to your computer. For information on using Quicken Live to obtain program updates, see "Updating with Quicken Live" at the end of this chapter.

On-Line Quotes

Quicken Live can download current price quotes for stocks and mutual funds that are stored in your Quicken portfolio. Your holdings in Portfolio View are automatically adjusted to reflect the updated prices. For help with downloading quotes, see "Updating with Quicken Live" at the end of this chapter.

✔ Tips

- In addition to stocks and mutual funds, you can also track several popular stock indices.

  To add a stock index to your download list, change to Portfolio View, click the Update Prices button, and choose Get Online Quotes from the drop-down menu. The Online Quotes dialog box appears. Click New Security and enter one of the following indices in the Set Up Security dialog box (see **Figure 19.6**): Dow Jones 30 Industrial Average (INDU), New York Stock Exchange Composite (NYA.X), S&P 500 Composite (SPX.X), or NASDAQ Composite (COMPX).

  To view an index, switch to Security Detail View and choose the index from the drop-down security list (see **Figure 19.7**).

  Note that you can also track stocks and mutual funds that you *don't* own by following this procedure.

- If you hold mutual funds, wait until the exchanges close before downloading prices. Mutual fund prices are only updated at the end of each trading day.

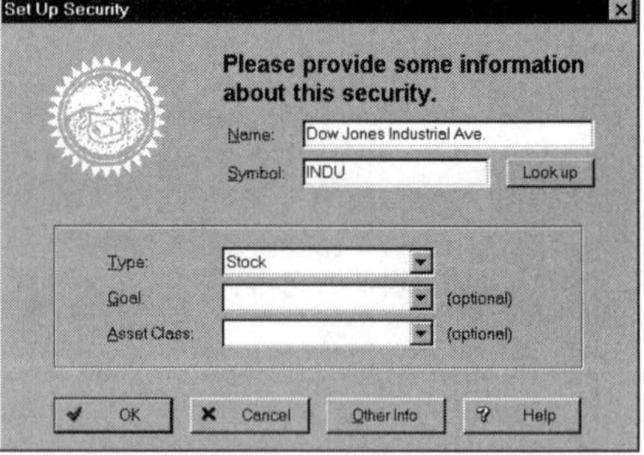

Figure 19.6 *Use the Set Up Security dialog box to create entries for stock indices that you wish to follow.*

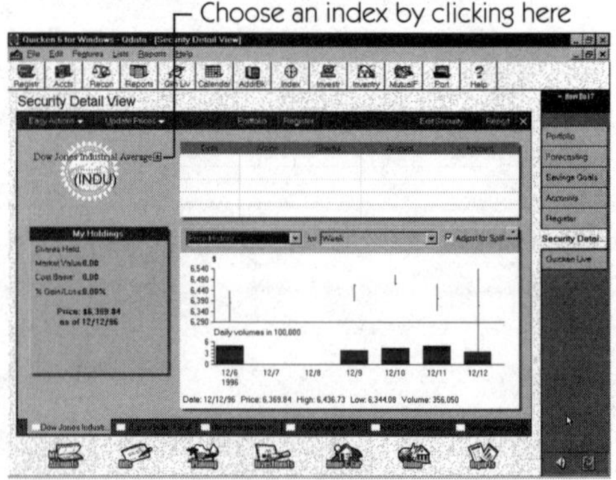

Figure 19.7 *You can examine stock indices in Security Detail View.*

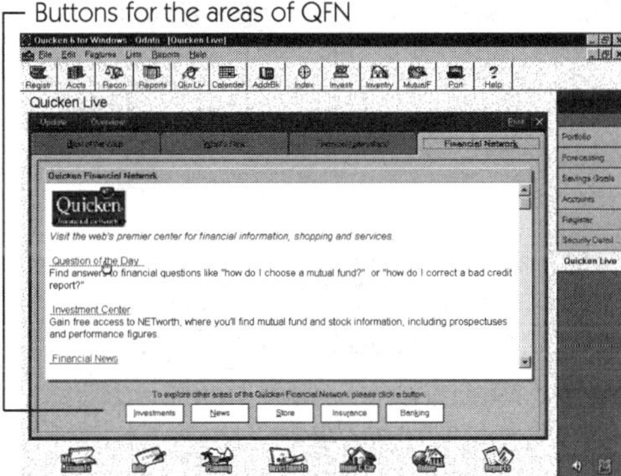

Figure 19.8 *You can click a button to go directly to any area of the QFN site.*

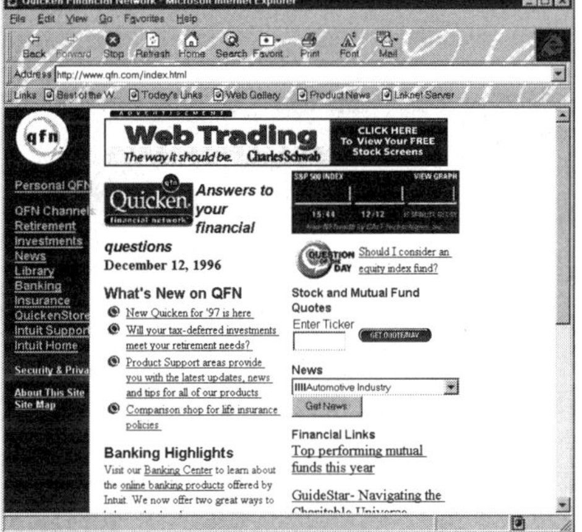

Figure 19.9 *The index (home) page for the Quicken Financial Network site.*

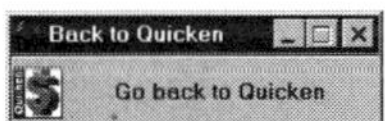

Figure 19.10 *Click in this window to return to Quicken.*

Quicken Financial Network

Through the Quicken Financial Network (QFN) site, you have access to financial news, insurance and on-line banking information, security prices, and the Quicken Store. To reach this Web site, perform any of the following actions:

- Click the Online icon in the activity bar, and choose Go Online to Quicken Financial Network.
- Choose Features ⇨ Online ⇨ Quicken Live (Internet), and then choose either Financial Network or Quicken Store.
- From the Quicken Live window (see **Figure 19.8**), click the Financial Network tab. Then click the button at the bottom of the window that corresponds to the part of QFN you want to visit, or click any underlined text in the window.

Quicken Live launches your browser and then displays the chosen Web page (see **Figure 19.9**). You can move from one area of the site to another by clicking underlined text or graphic links. Return to Quicken by clicking the icon in the tiny Back to Quicken window (see **Figure 19.10**).

✔ **Tip**

- The Back to Quicken window automatically appears whenever Quicken Live opens your browser.

Updating with Quicken Live

As shown in **Figure 19.11**, there are three types of information that you can update in Quicken Live: Online Quotes, Best of the Web, and What's New. In addition, the Update function always checks to see if there is an update to Quicken 6 and, if so, allows you to retrieve it.

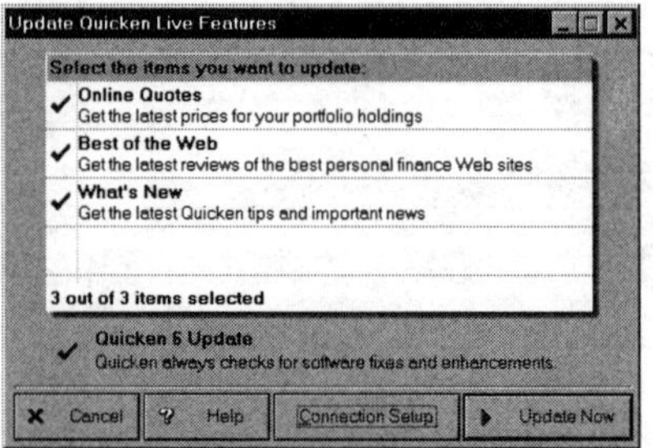

Figure 19.11 *The checked items will be downloaded from the Internet.*

To begin an update, choose one of the following commands:

- Choose Features ⇨ Online ⇨ Quicken Live (Internet), and then choose Download Quotes or Update My Quicken 6.
- Choose Download Quotes and Update My Quicken 6 from the Online icon in the activity bar.
- In Portfolio View, click the Update Prices button and choose Get Online Quotes.

Depending on the command chosen, the Update Quicken Live Features dialog box (refer to **Figure 19.11**) or the Online Quotes dialog box appears (see Figure **19.12**). In the latter case, you can modify the list of stock and fund prices that will be downloaded. When you're ready to continue, click Download. The Update Quicken Live Features dialog box appears.

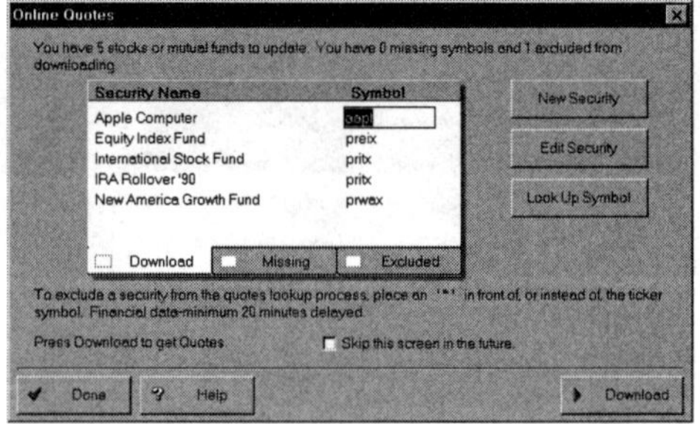

Figure 19.12 *Use the Online Quotes dialog box to specify stock and mutual fund prices to track with Quicken Live.*

Click to add or remove check marks, and then click Update Now. Quicken Live connects to the Internet, logs onto an Intuit site, downloads the chosen items, and then logs off. The Update Quicken Live Features dialog box now shows the items that were downloaded (see **Figure 19.13**). Double-click an underlined item to view it in Quicken.

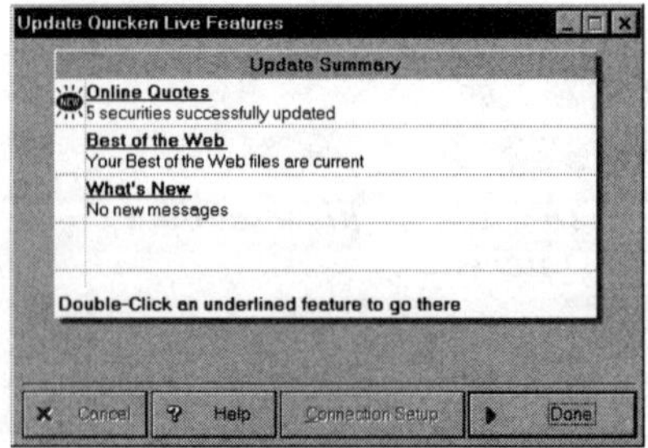

Figure 19.13 *The Update Quicken Live Features dialog box changes to show the results of the on-line session.*

Investor Insight

20

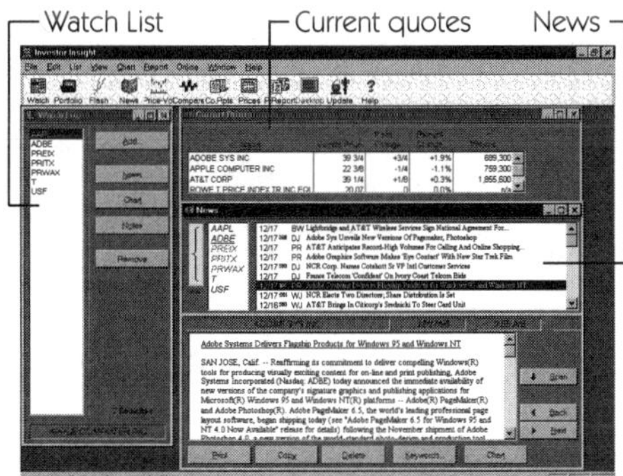

Figure 20.1 *Each Investor Insight component is displayed in a separate window. You can close or minimize windows to reduce the clutter.*

About Investor Insight

Quicken Deluxe includes a 30-day free trial of Investor Insight, a full-featured investment management and analysis program (see **Figure 20.1**). It can download quotes for all securities in your portfolio, as well as for others that you are considering as investments. The data can be charted in a variety of ways.

Investor Insight can also download news articles that mention securities of interest to you. These articles, along with detailed charts, can be combined into an attractive personal newsletter.

Starting Investor Insight

Because Investor Insight is a stand-alone program, it can be launched from the desktop or from within Quicken in the following ways:

- Choose Features ⇨ Investments ⇨ Investor Insight.
- Click the Investor Insight button (Investr) in the top iconbar.
- Click the Investments icon in the activity bar and choose Get Stock News, Prices and Research.
- From the Windows 95 desktop, choose Investor Insight from the Start menu in the taskbar.
- From the Windows 3.1 desktop, open the Quicken program group and click the Investor Insight icon.

To return to Quicken, choose Go to Quicken from the File menu.

Setting Up Investor Insight

Setting up is a three-step process. First, establish an account with Investor Insight. Second, set up portfolios and specify the investments that you want to track. Third, go on-line to retrieve current prices for your securities and to download historical data.

Creating an On-Line Account

To establish an account, click the Update button in the iconbar. Answer No when asked if you have an ID and password. The program dials through the modem and creates the account.

Building the Watch List

The Watch List (see **Figure 20.2**) is the list of stocks and mutual funds that you have chosen to follow with Investor Insight. You can track as many as 500 securities—whether you own them or not. Since portfolios can only contain securities that are in the Watch List, the Watch List is constructed first.

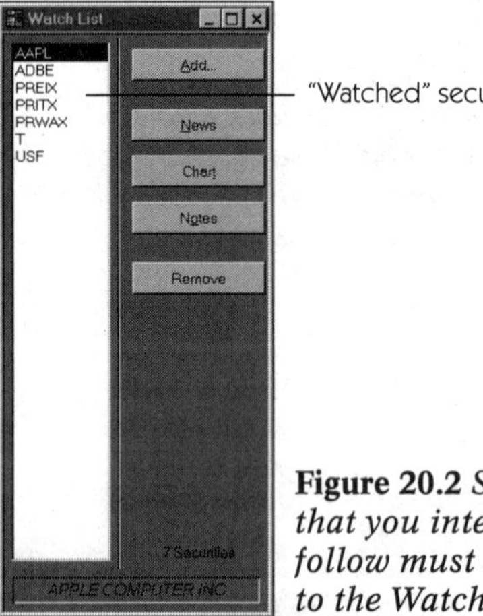

Figure 20.2 *Securities that you intend to follow must be added to the Watch List.*

To add a security to the Watch List:

1. Click Add. The Add Securities to Watch List dialog box appears (see **Figure 20.3**).
2. Click Symbol or Name in the Find By area of the dialog box, depending on how you want to search.
3. Type the security's name or symbol (as appropriate) in the Type Name text box. As you type, the list scrolls to the closest matching text.
4. Select the desired security, and click Add.

If you no longer wish to follow a given security, select it in the Watch List and click Remove.

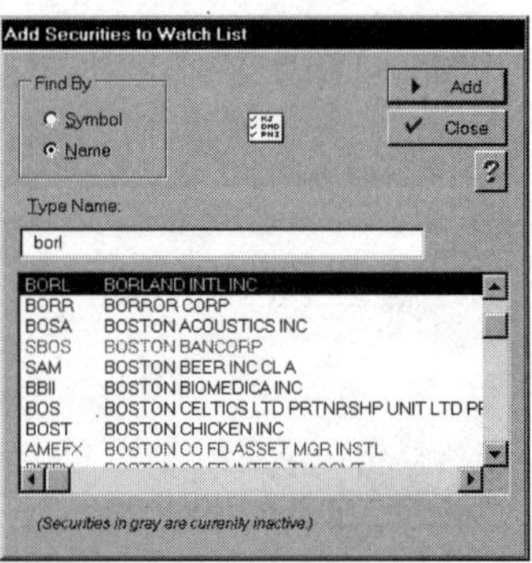

Figure 20.3 *Choose securities for the Watch List from this scrolling list.*

Importing Portfolios

The next step is to enter information about your investment portfolios. Although you can manually create portfolios, the simplest way to start is by importing the portfolios that you have already defined in Quicken.

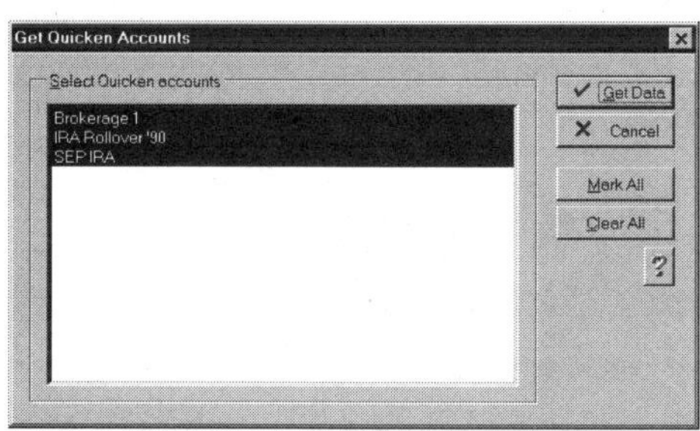

Figure 20.4 *Select Quicken investment accounts to import into Investor Insight.*

To import Quicken portfolios:

1. Choose Get Quicken Investments from the File menu. The Get Quicken Accounts dialog box appears (see **Figure 20.4**).
2. Select investment accounts that you want to import.
3. Click Get Data. The accounts are added to Investor Insight's Portfolio window as Quicken portfolios (marked with a [Q]).

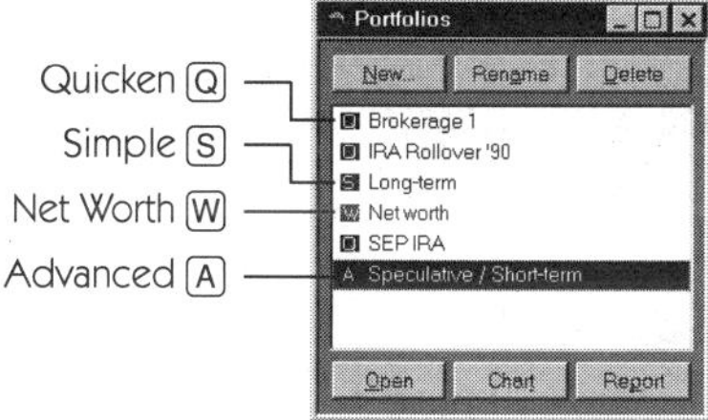

Figure 20.5 *Each type of portfolio is indicated by a different code letter.*

Manually Creating Portfolios

You can create three other kinds of portfolios (see **Figure 20.5**). A *simple portfolio* is based solely on current holdings. You cannot record transactions, such as buying or selling shares. A simple portfolio is best for static or lightly-traded securities.

An *advanced portfolio*, on the other hand, is ideal for tracking active investments. You can record buy and sell transactions, dividends, cash adjustments, stock splits, and so on.

Finally, you can create a single *net worth portfolio*, which combines all Quicken and advanced portfolios—enabling you to see all of your holdings at one time.

To create a new portfolio of any type, open the Portfolios window (click the Portfolio button in the iconbar or choose Portfolio List from the Lists menu), click the New button, and then choose stocks and/or mutual funds from the Watch List.

Updating Your Portfolios

To download current prices for the securities in your portfolios (as well as for unassigned ones in the Watch List), click the Update button in the iconbar or choose Update from the Online menu. The Download dialog box appears (see **Figure 20.6**).

Choose download options, and then click Update. The entire session occurs automatically (see **Figure 20.7**). When all requested actions have been completed, you are logged off the system.

✔ Tips

- Investor Insight normally requires you to have a 32-bit Internet connection and to be running Windows 95. If either condition is not met, you must use Investor Insight's private network to connect. To view or change your connection method, choose Settings from the Online menu (see **Figure 20.8**).
- Although you can't record transactions in a simple portfolio, you can update your holdings of any stock to reflect the new total shares. Open the simple portfolio, select the stock, click Edit, and then enter the total shares and the average share price.
- You can instruct the program to automatically download updates once a day or every so many hours. Choose Timer from the Online menu (see **Figure 20.9**). (The program must be running at the designated times for this to work.)

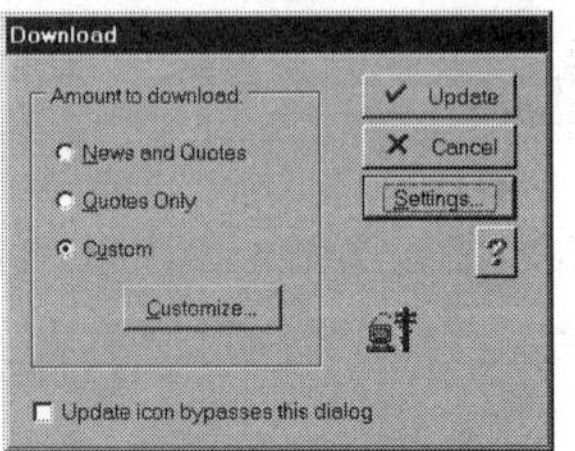

Figure 20.6 *In the Download dialog box, you can select items to download, check your connection settings, or specify custom downloading instructions.*

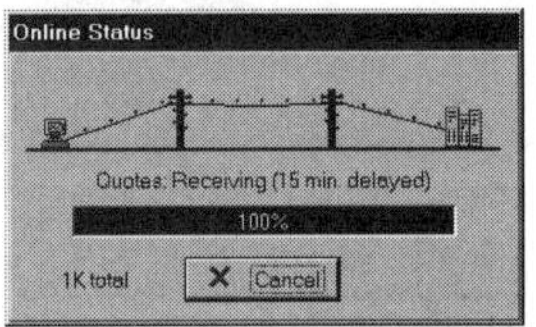

Figure 20.7 *You can follow the progress of the session by watching the Online Status dialog box.*

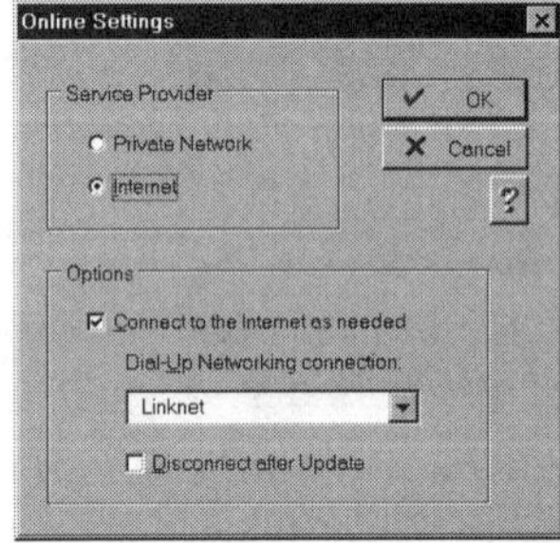

Figure 20.8 *The On-line Settings dialog box shows your connection method.*

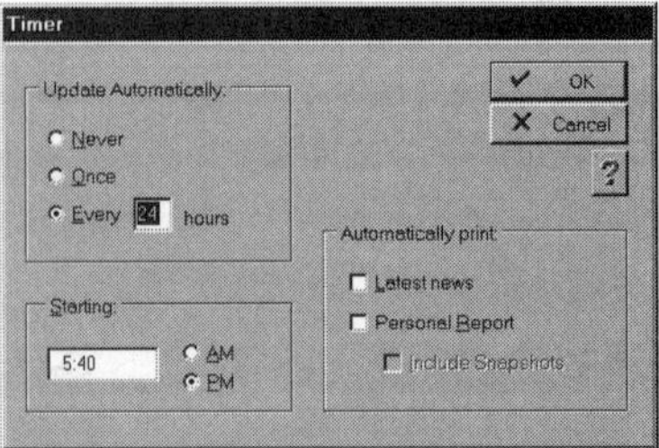

Figure 20.9 *Schedule automatic downloads in the Timer dialog box.*

Figure 20.10 *To view company news or financial data, choose a command from the Report menu.*

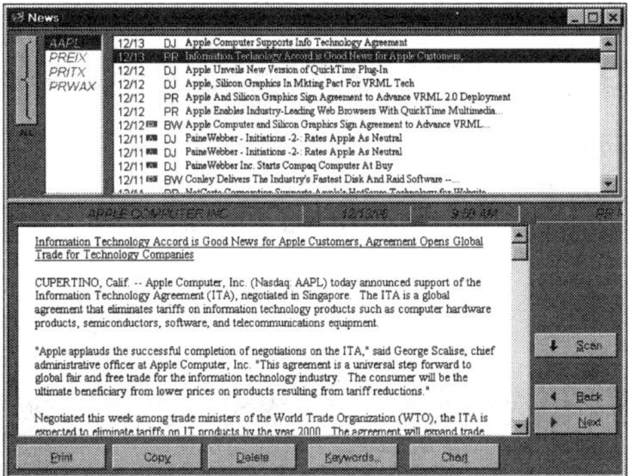

Figure 20.11 *Select a headline in the top of this window. The article text appears below. To view news for just one security, click its name in the upper-left corner of the window.*

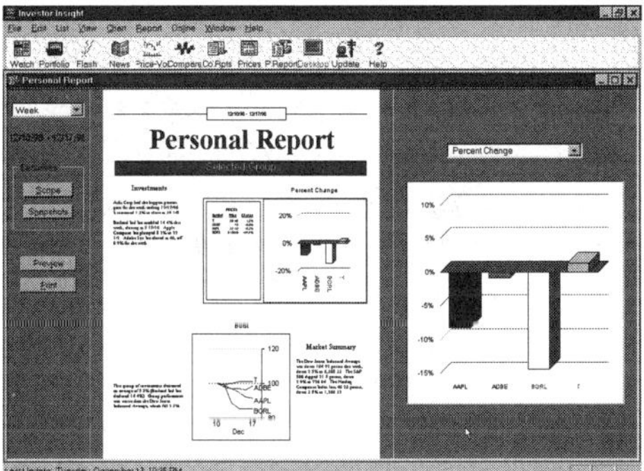

Figure 20.12 *You create personal reports in this window. Click Scope and Snapshots to select the securities to include.*

Analyzing Security Data

You can analyze securities in the Watch List by creating reports and charts and by ordering company profiles from Investor Insight.

Reports

As shown in **Figure 20.10**, Investor Insight can provide many types of financial information. You can create the following kinds of reports:

- *News.* Displays the News window (see **Figure 20.11**), listing recent news articles for the securities in the Watch List.
- *Flash Report.* Review today's trading highlights (the closing ticks for major stock indices and notification of any large changes in your portfolios or the securities in the Watch List).
- *Company Snapshot.* Headlines and news stories for stocks chosen from the Watch List.
- *Personal Report.* Newsletter-style custom report on selected securities. The report includes price data, charts, and news articles for a specified period (see **Figure 20.12**).
- *Current Prices.* View the most recent trading data for securities in the Watch List.
- *Historical Prices.* Review historical price and volume data for all securities in the Watch List. (Choose a stock to examine from the list at the top of the window.)

Charts

You can quickly generate a price/volume or price chart (see **Figure 20.13**) by double-clicking any stock or mutual fund in the Watch List. You can also create a price chart by double-clicking a security name in another window (such as a value report) or by clicking any Chart button.

To see charts for all or a subset of the securities in the Watch List, choose Comparative Charts from the Chart menu (see **Figure 20.14**). Double-click any thumbnail chart to expand it.

To display charts of the Dow Jones Industrial Average, the S&P 500, or the NASDAQ, choose Index Charts from the Chart menu.

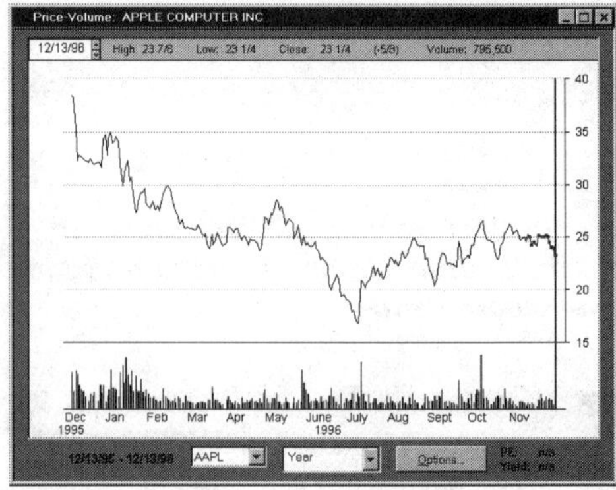

Figure 20.13 *When charting a stock or a mutual fund, you can specify the period to cover by clicking a drop-down list at the bottom of the window. Set other options by clicking the Options button.*

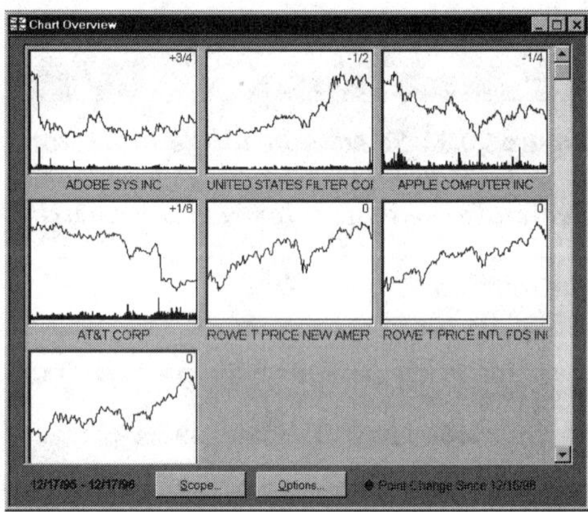

Figure 20.14 *The Chart Overview window can simultaneously show price charts for every security that you follow.*

Company Reports

For an added fee, you can order a detailed profile for any stock in the Watch List. (Currently, the first profile is free.)

To order a company report:

1. Click the Company Reports (Co. Rpts) button in the iconbar or choose Company Reports from the Report menu. The Company Reports dialog box appears.
2. Click the Order ($) button. The Order Company Report dialog box appears.
3. Highlight the report you want to order, and click Order. The chosen report will be downloaded the next time you run the Update procedure.

To examine the information in any downloaded company report, click the Company Reports (Co. Rpts) button

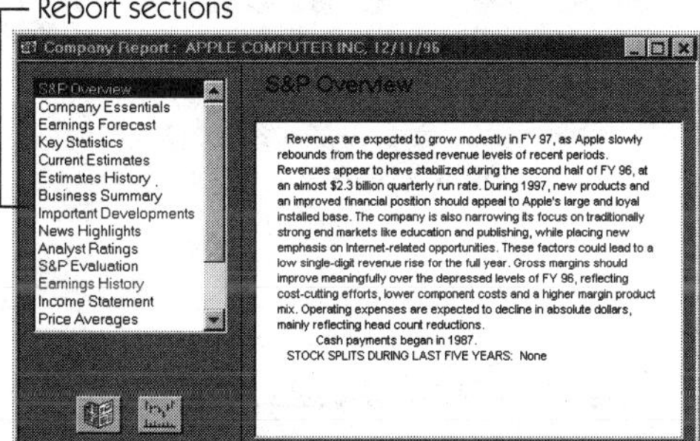

Figure 20.15 *To view different parts of a company report, click topics in the scrolling list.*

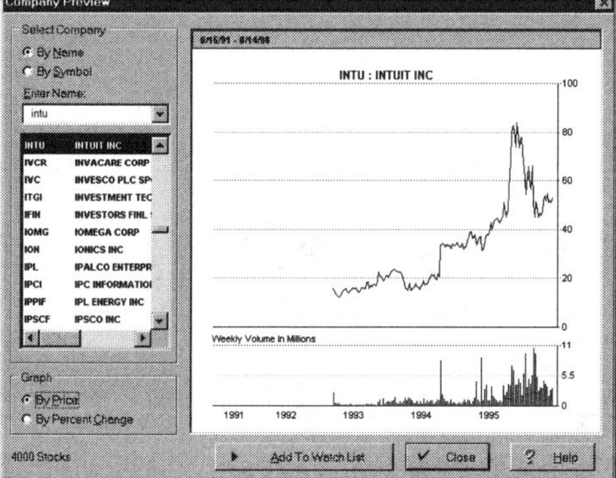

Figure 20.16 *The Company Preview window can display price/volume charts for 4,000 stocks.*

and click View (see **Figure 20.15**). You can open the News window to read recent articles that mention the security by clicking the left-most button at the bottom of the Company Report window. Click the other button to see a price chart.

✔ Tips

- Investor Insight contains a database of historical price information on 4,000 stocks. Although the data is only current through June 1996, you may find it helpful when deciding which stocks to investigate. Choose Company Preview from the Chart menu, and then enter the name or ticker symbol of the stock you want to examine, as shown in **Figure 20.16**.
- Double-click a portfolio name to see the current value of the securities it contains.
- You can further customize many charts by specifying a date range, selecting options to include, and so on. In the report window, click the Options button or select options from the drop-down menus.

  To help you spot trends or see how a security moves in relation to major indices, you can overlay a chart with a moving average or multiple stock indices.
- Click a red dot on any price chart to read news articles concerning the security that appeared on that date.
- Quicken 6 includes a sample company report for Intuit that you can examine to decide whether you want to buy additional reports.

Sharing Data with Quicken

Quicken and Investor Insight can share data, although it doesn't happen automatically. You can import the holdings in your Quicken portfolio into Investor Insight, saving you the trouble of re-creating the portfolio (as explained previously in this chapter in "To import Quicken portfolios"). And historical stock and mutual fund data can be imported from Investor Insight into Quicken so it can be displayed in Quicken charts (see **Figure 20.17**).

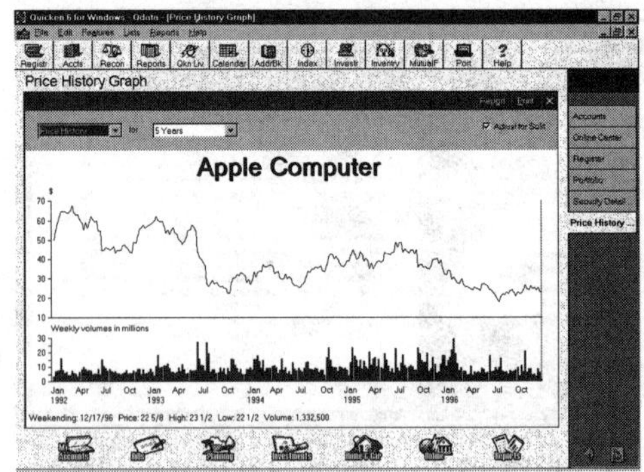

Figure 20.17 *After importing historical quotes into Quicken, you can create five-year price/volume charts in Quicken.*

To import historical data into Quicken:

1. In Quicken, switch to Portfolio view.
2. Highlight a stock or mutual fund in your portfolio.
3. Click the Update Prices button at the top of the window and choose Get Investor Insight Prices. The Import Investor Insight Quotes dialog box appears, as shown in **Figure 20.18**.
4. Choose a time period (up to five years) and a quote frequency from the drop-down lists, and click OK.

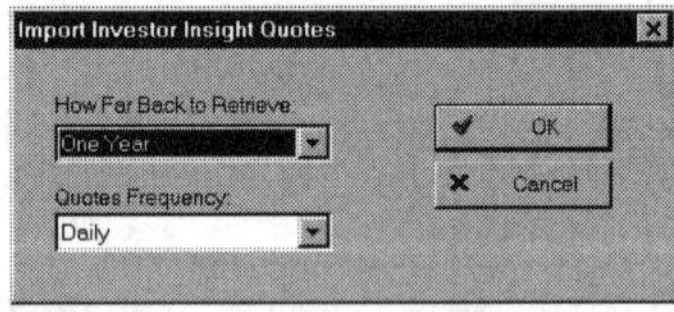

Figure 20.18 *To import Investor Insight historical quotes into Quicken, set options and click OK.*

✔ **Tip**

■ You can also import quotes into Quicken by right-clicking the name of a security in the Portfolio window and then choosing Import Historical Prices (see **Figure 20.19**).

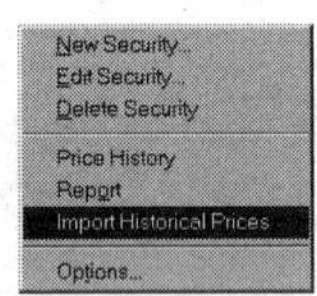

Figure 20.19 *Right-click any security name in your Quicken portfolio to bring up this menu.*

On-Line Banking and Payment

About On-Line Banking and Payment

Anyone with a modem can take advantage of Quicken's on-line banking and bill paying features.

On-line banking can be used to check your account balances, transfer funds between accounts at the same bank, and download transactions and compare them against your registers (see **Figure 21.1**). To apply for on-line banking, your bank must be one of the more than 40 institutions that offers it.

Figure 21.1 *On-line banking and payment activities are controlled from the Online Banking & Investment Center window.*

On-line bill paying, on the other hand, is available to everyone. (Intuit Services Corporation can provide this service if it is not offered by your bank.) It enables you to pay bills by creating transactions and transmitting them via modem.

As implied in the previous paragraphs, you can have on-line banking and bill paying, or you may have just one or the other. Accounts from which you can write checks (your checking and money market accounts, for example) may have both features enabled. Accounts that do not have check-writing privileges, however, cannot be used for on-line bill paying. You can have on-line accounts with multiple banks.

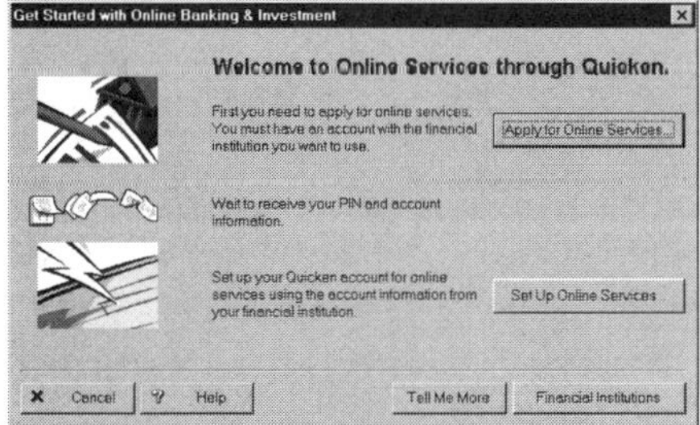

Figure 21.2 *Other than contacting your bank to see what services it offers, the entire registration can be done in the Get Started dialog box.*

After applying for on-line services by following the procedures described in "On-Line Banking and Bill Paying Setup" in Chapter 4 (see **Figure 21.2**), you are ready to conduct your first on-line session.

Your First On-Line Session

Rather than creating on-line payments, it's a good idea to use your first session to do nothing more than download the current transactions.

To conduct your first on-line session:

1. Choose Features ⇨ Online ⇨ Online Center. The Online Banking & Investment Center window appears (refer to **Figure 21.1**).
2. If you have accounts with multiple banks, be sure that the right bank is selected at the top of the window.
3. Click the Go Online button. The Instructions to Send dialog box appears.
4. Be sure that the instruction to download transactions is checked, and then click Send. The Change assigned PIN dialog box appears (see **Figure 21.3**).
5. The PIN that you received in the mail is a temporary one. The first time you connect, you must choose a new PIN.

   Enter the temporary and new PINs on the appropriate lines.
6. If you have an external modem, be sure that it is turned on. Click OK. Quicken dials through the modem, makes the connection, downloads transactions, and then disconnects. The Online Transmission Summary appears (see **Figure 21.4**).

✔ **Tip**

- For security reasons, Quicken does not store your new PIN. Because you must enter it each time that you connect, be sure to write it down.

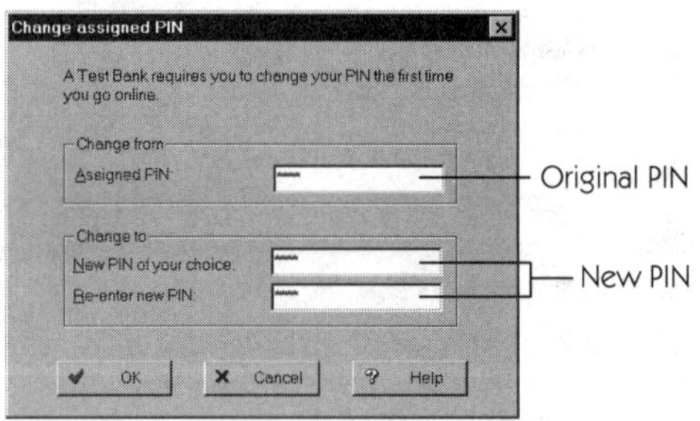

Figure 21.3 *Enter the PIN you received in the mail and a replacement PIN of your choosing on the appropriate lines.*

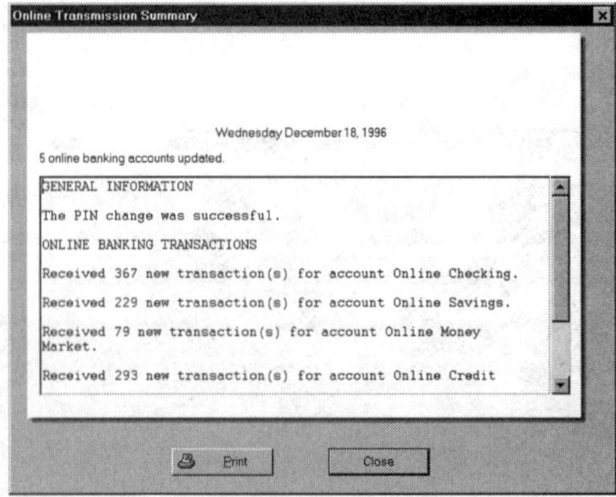

Figure 21.4 *The Online Transmission Summary dialog box lists all events that occurred during the session.*

On-Line Banking Essentials

With an on-line banking account, you can accomplish the following tasks:

- Download new transactions and record them in the appropriate account registers.
- Match transactions that have cleared the bank with those in your account registers and mark them as cleared.
- Transfer funds from one on-line account to another (at the same financial institution).

Downloading Transactions

Each day, new transactions—such as the checks you have written, deposits you have made, and so on—clear the bank. By regularly going on-line, you can download a list of all cleared and new transactions and update your on-line account balances.

To download transactions:

1. Choose Features ⇨ Online ⇨ Online Center. The Online Banking & Investment Center window appears (refer to **Figure 21.1**).
2. If you have on-line accounts with multiple financial institutions, be sure that the correct one is chosen from the drop-down list.
3. Click the Go Online button. The Instructions to Send dialog box appears (see **Figure 21.5**).
4. Be sure that Download transactions from *bank name* is checked, enter your new PIN, and click Send. Quicken dials through the modem, downloads all new and cleared transactions, and disconnects.

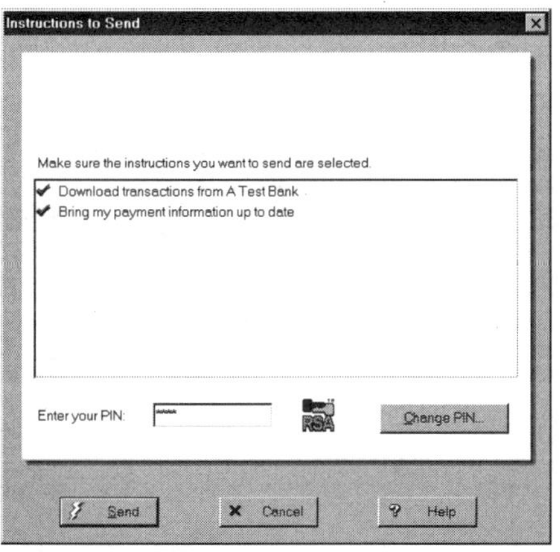

Figure 21.5 *The Instructions to Send dialog box lists all actions that are to be performed during the session. You can remove the check mark from any action.*

On-Line Banking Essentials

The Online Transmission Summary dialog box appears, listing all actions performed during the session (see **Figure 21.6**). The Online Banking & Investment Center window changes to show all new downloaded data (see **Figure 21.7**).

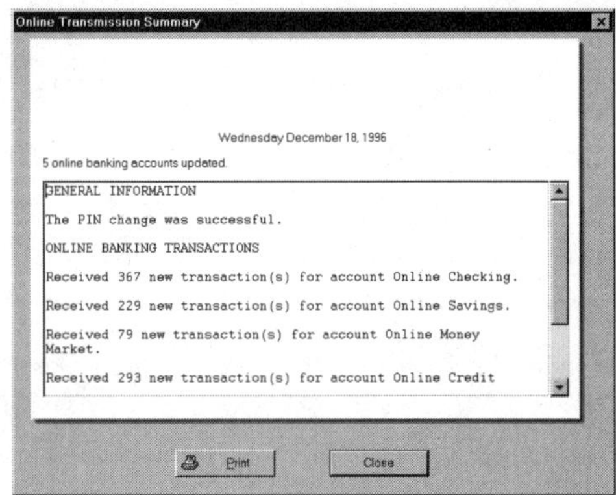

Figure 21.6 *This dialog box shows what transpired during the session.*

Recording the Matching and New Transactions

After downloading transactions, you can update all affected registers by marking the matching transactions as cleared and recording the new transactions.

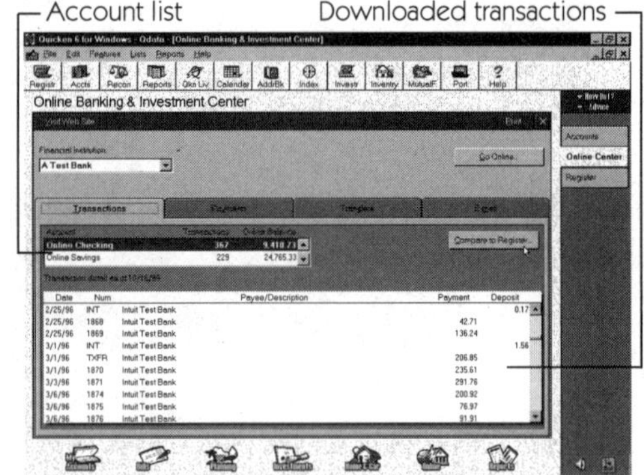

Figure 21.7 *Click the Transactions tab to see the most recent transactions for any on-line account.*

To update an account register:

1. Choose Features ⇨ Online ⇨ Online Center. The Online Banking & Investment Center window appears (refer to **Figure 21.7**).
2. Click the Transactions tab.
3. If you have more than one on-line account, choose an account from the scrolling Account list in the lower half of the window. Downloaded transactions are displayed for the chosen account.
4. Click Compare to Register. A modified version of the account register appears (see **Figure 21.8**). Initially, each of the downloaded transactions is designated as New or Matched. New transactions do not yet exist in the register; items marked as Matched *are* in the register, on the other hand.
5. To handle a Matched transaction, select it in the lower half of the window. Quicken displays the matching transaction in the register. If it is correct, click Accept.

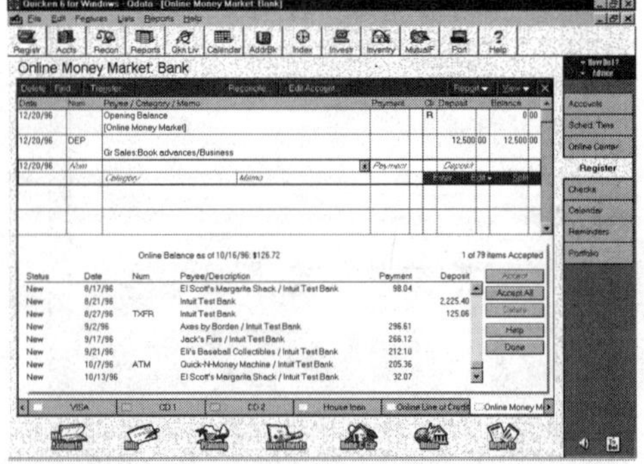

Figure 21.8 *Downloaded transactions are displayed in the lower half of the register window.*

The transaction designation now reads Accepted and the record is marked as cleared (c) in the register.

6. To handle a New transaction, select it in the lower half of the window and click Accept. The transaction is entered in the register.

   To complete the transaction, assign a category to it and then click the Enter button, click the Accept button, or press Return. The transaction designation changes to Accepted and the record is marked as cleared (c) in the register.

7. You can simultaneously accept all downloaded transactions for an account as correct by clicking the Accept All button. The transactions are copied to the register and marked as cleared (c). Edit the new transactions by assigning categories to them.

8. When you are finished, click Done. The register window is restored.

If you downloaded transactions for other on-line accounts, you can update their registers by returning to the Online Banking & Investment Center window and repeating Steps 3–8.

Transferring Funds

If you have more than one account at the same bank, you can use on-line banking to transfer funds between the accounts (moving money from savings to checking, for example).

To transfer funds between accounts:

1. Choose Features ⇨ Online ⇨ Online Center. The Online Banking & Investment Center window appears.

2. Click the Transfers tab (see **Figure 21.9**).
3. Choose an account to debit from the Transfer Money From drop-down list.
4. Choose an account to credit from the To drop-down list. Note the present balance for each account.
5. Enter the amount to transfer in the Amount text box.
6. Click Enter to record the transfer. It is now listed in the lower part of the window. The next time you log on, the transfer will be recorded.

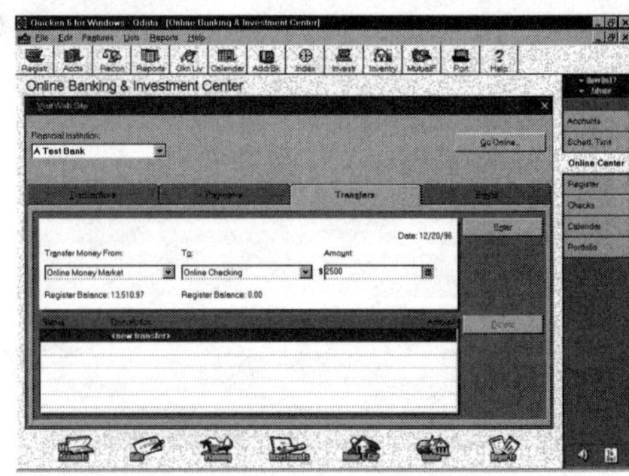

Figure 21.9 *Click the Transfers tab to move money between on-line accounts.*

✔ **Tips**

- You can change your PIN at the beginning of any on-line session. For security reasons, you may wish to do so periodically.

  The next time you are ready to connect, click Change PIN in the Instructions to Send dialog box (refer to **Figure 21.5**). The Change PIN dialog box appears (see **Figure 21.10**).

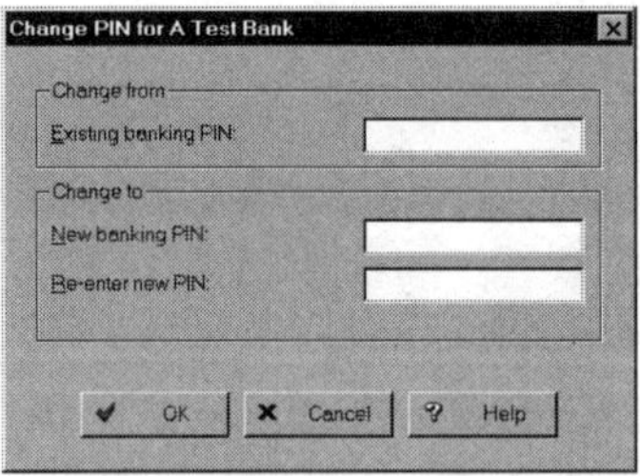

Figure 21.10 *Enter your current PIN and the new one in the appropriate text boxes.*

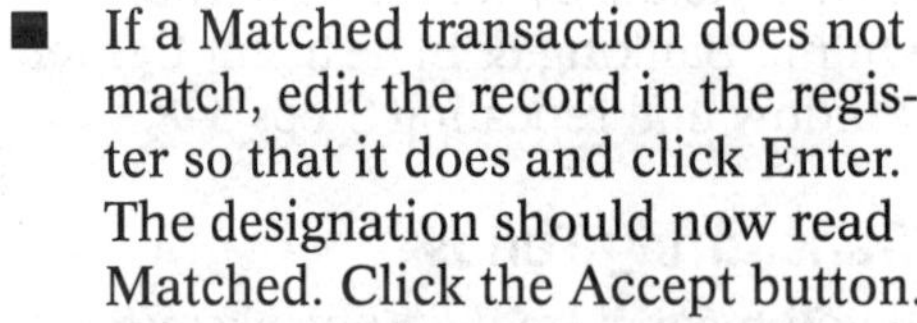

- If a Matched transaction does not match, edit the record in the register so that it does and click Enter. The designation should now read Matched. Click the Accept button.
- When you download transactions, the balances for your on-line accounts are also downloaded and can be viewed in the Account scrolling list (refer to **Figure 21.7**).
- When transferring funds, Quicken will not stop you from withdrawing more money than you actually have in the originating account. Be sure to check your balance.

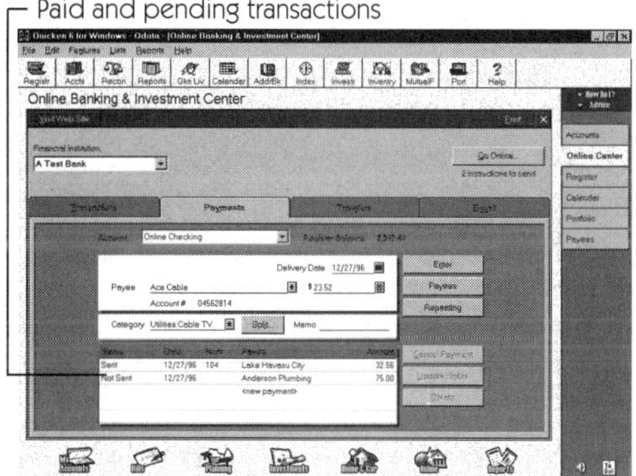

Figure 21.11 *Click the Payments tab to create payments from an on-line account.*

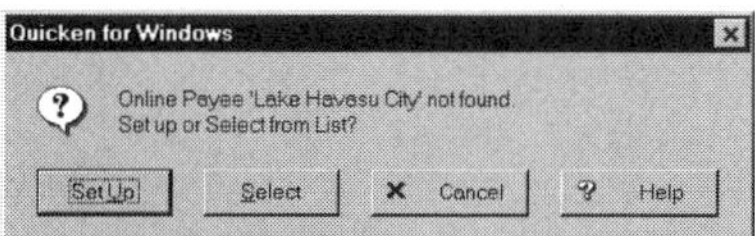

Figure 21.12 *If this is a new payee, this dialog box appears. Click Set Up to record address and account information for the new payee.*

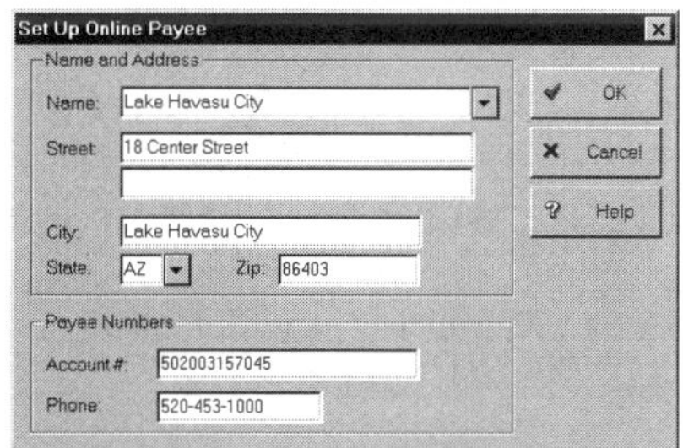

Figure 21.13 *Fill in the requested information for the new payee. Be sure to include a complete mailing address.*

On-Line Bill Paying

To pay bills from an on-line account, you create payment instructions in the Payments section of the Online Banking & Investment Center window. You can pay *anyone* from an on-line account, regardless of whether they can receive on-line payments directly. (Companies and individuals who cannot receive direct payments will be mailed a check.)

To pay a bill from an on-line account:

1. Choose Features ➪ Online ➪ Online Center. The Online Banking & Investment Center window appears.
2. Click the Payments tab (see **Figure 21.11**).
3. Choose the institution and the account from which the payment will be drawn.
4. Create the payment transaction as you would if you were in the Write Checks window. Choose a payee from the drop-down list.

   If the payee is not in the list, type the person or company's name on the Payee line. When you press Tab, the dialog box shown in **Figure 21.12** appears. Click Set Up, fill in the Set Up Online Payee dialog box (see **Figure 21.13**), and click OK.
5. Complete the transaction by filling in the amount, category, and so on, and then click Enter.

   The payment is added to the list (refer to **Figure 21.11**). When you connect, the payment will be transmitted and its status will change from Not Sent to Sent.

Repeating Payments

Like scheduling transactions in the Financial Calendar (see "Creating Transactions" in Chapter 7), you can create repeating on-line payments that are automatically made at regular intervals (every month, for example). A repeating payment can only be set up for bills that do not vary in amount or due date. A monthly cable TV bill, a mortgage, and ongoing equipment rentals are all good candidates for a repeating payment.

To create a repeating payment:

1. Click the Payments tab in the Online Banking & Investment Center window.
2. Click the Repeating button. The Create Repeating Online Payment dialog box appears, as shown in **Figure 21.14**.
3. Enter the information and click Authorize. Once transmitted, additional payments will automatically be made as they come due.

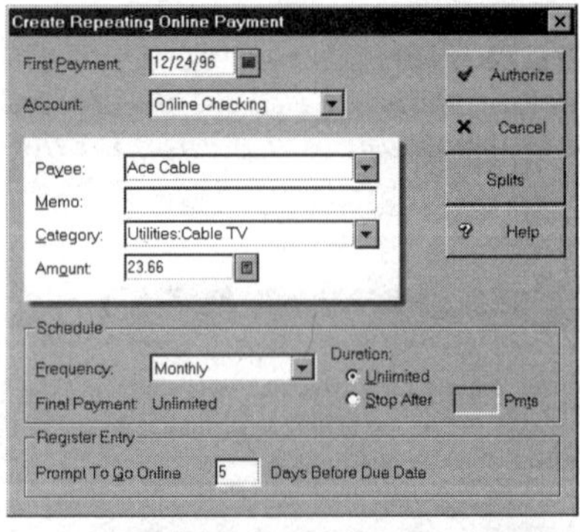

Figure 21.14 *Repeating payments are created in this dialog box.*

✔ Tips

- You can also create payments in the register of any on-line payment account. When creating the transaction, simply choose Send Online Payment from the pop-up list in the Num field.
- You can only send on-line payments to on-line payees. To view or modify the list of payees, choose Online Payees from the Lists menu.
- You can also view, edit, or create repeating payments in the Scheduled Transaction List window.

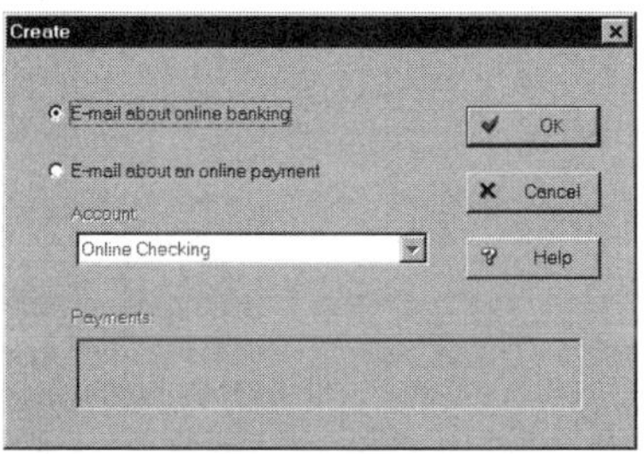

Figure 21.15 *Specify the subject of your message in the Create dialog box.*

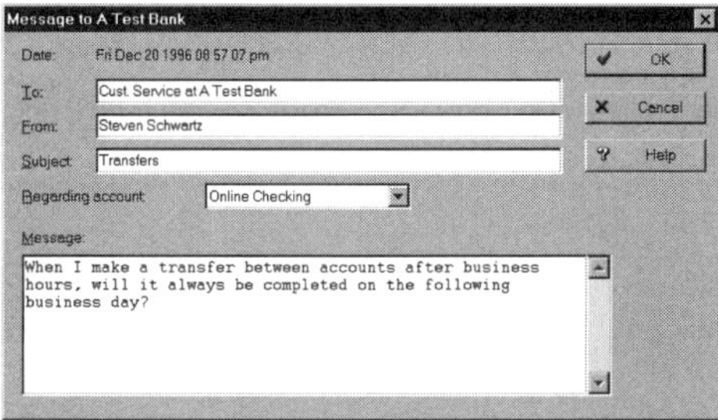

Figure 21.16 *When composing a message about on-line banking, this Message dialog box is used. Choose an account from the drop-down list, type the message, and click OK.*

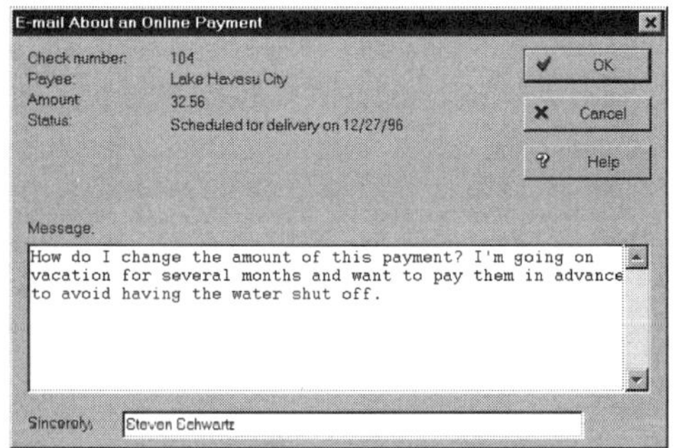

Figure 21.17 *When inquiring about an on-line payment, this dialog box is used. Enter a message and signature line, and then click OK.*

Sending E-mail

If you need to communicate with your bank or Intuit Services Corporation about an on-line banking or payment matter, you can compose and send electronic mail (e-mail) from Quicken.

To send an e-mail message:

1. Choose Features ⇨ Online ⇨ Online Center. The Online Banking & Investment Center window appears.
2. Click the E-mail tab, and then click the Create button. The Create dialog box appears (see **Figure 21.15**).
3. Click a radio button to indicate whether the message concerns on-line banking or an on-line payment. (In the latter instance, select the payment from those listed at the bottom of the dialog box.) Click OK. A message window appears (see **Figures 21.16–21.17**).
4. Type the message and click OK.

✔ Tip

- After you save an outgoing message, it cannot be edited. Instead, you must delete the original message and then create a new one.

  Rather than retype the message from scratch, open the original message by selecting it and clicking Read, select the message text, press Ctrl C to copy it to the clipboard, and then delete the message. Next, create a new message, press Ctrl V to paste the body text into the message, and make your edits.

Part VI:
Advanced Quicken

Customizing Quicken

Customization Options

Quicken can be customized to match the way you work. To set options for the program, choose Options from the Edit menu and then choose an option class, as follows:

- *Quicken Program.* Set QuickTabs options; backup prompt; calendar or fiscal year; Quicken or Windows keyboard mapping.
- *Register.* Set appearance options; specify a credit card alert limit.
- *Write Checks.* Select appearance options for printed checks; set notification and alert preferences.
- *Reports and Graphs.* These options are discussed in Chapter 17.
- *Reminders.* Set Billminder and Reminders to automatically appear; specify items to show and the number of days for advance notification.
- *Desktop.* Specify when to save the Quicken desktop.
- *Iconbar.* Customize the iconbar by adding, removing, and changing the appearance of icons; assign keyboard shortcuts.

✔ **Tips**

- Some Quicken windows, such as the on-screen reports, have Options and/or View buttons that enable you to customize the included elements or the manner in which the data is displayed.

- You can set some options, such as those for QuickFill, in several different Option dialog boxes.
- Although you can change options whenever you wish, you may want to wait until you're familiar with the way that Quicken works. The default option settings were carefully selected by Intuit to meet the needs of most users.

Quicken Program Options

To set general options for Quicken, choose Edit ⇨ Options ⇨ Quicken Program. The General Options dialog box appears. There are three sections in the dialog box, each represented by a labeled tab.

QuickTabs Options

QuickTabs are displayed on the side of the Quicken display. They list the names of all open windows (see **Figure 22.1**). You can switch to any window by clicking its QuickTab. When you close a window, its QuickTab is removed.

As shown in **Figure 22.2**, you can turn QuickTabs on or off (Show QuickTabs), display them on the left or right side of the screen (Position), and show or hide the activity bar at the bottom of the display (Show Activity Bar). You can use short or long commands in the activity bar menus (Use Short Commands on Activity Bar Menus), as shown in **Figure 22.3**.

You can choose any of 15 alternate color schemes for the display from the Quicken Color Scheme pop-up menu. Flyover help (the tiny labels that appear when the cursor is rested over an icon) can be turned on or off.

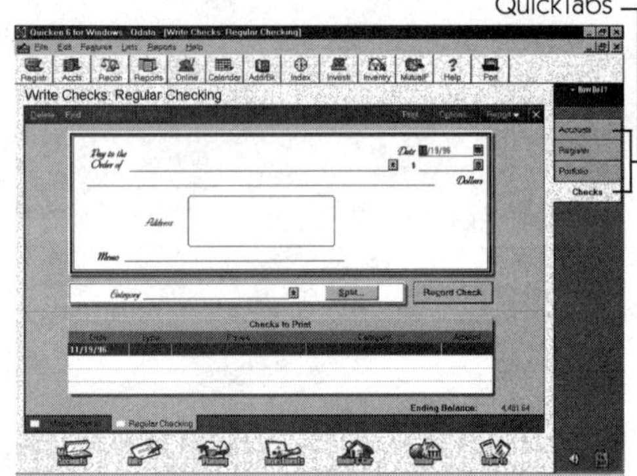

Figure 22.1 *QuickTabs are automatically added and removed as you open and close windows.*

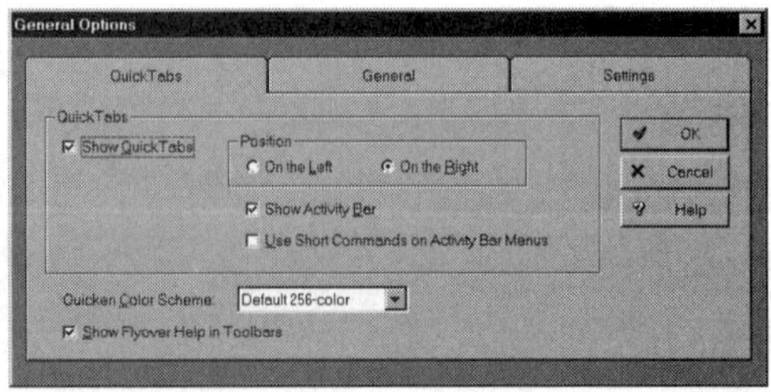

Figure 22.2 *The General Options dialog box (QuickTabs).*

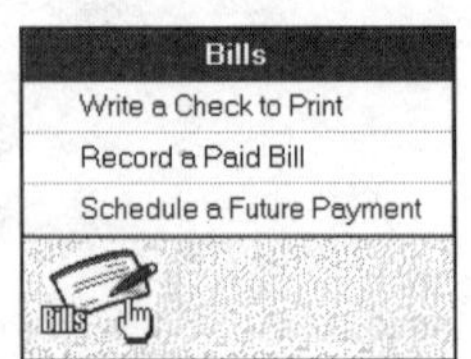

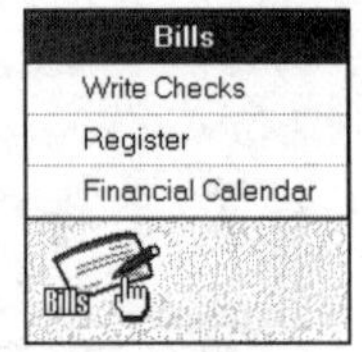

Figure 22.3 *The activity bar menus can display long (default) or short commands.*

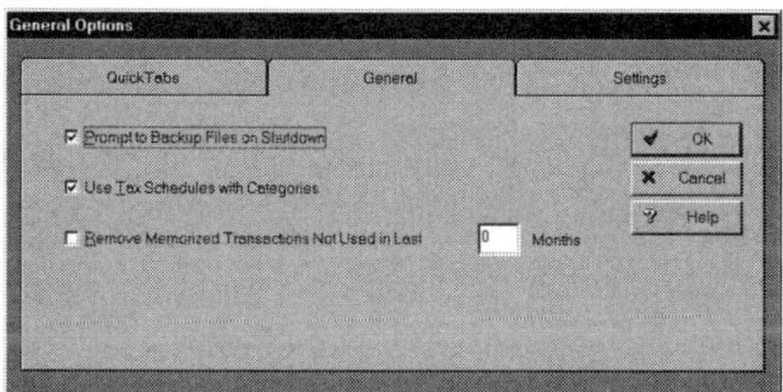

Figure 22.4 *The General Options dialog box (General).*

General Options

By default, Quicken reminds you to back up your data at the end of every third session (see **Figure 22.4**). You can turn this option off, if you wish. To alter the frequency with which the reminder is given, see "Changing the frequency of automatic backups..." in Quicken Help.

If you intend to generate tax reports, be sure that Use Tax Schedules with Categories is checked. This option enables you to associate a particular tax schedule and line item with any income or expense category.

If you pay bills to many different companies, the memorized transaction list expands rapidly. (You can create up to 2,000 memorized transactions. When this limit is reached, the feature is automatically turned off.) To slow the growth of the memorized transaction list, click Remove Memorized Transactions Not Used in Last... and then specify the number of months.

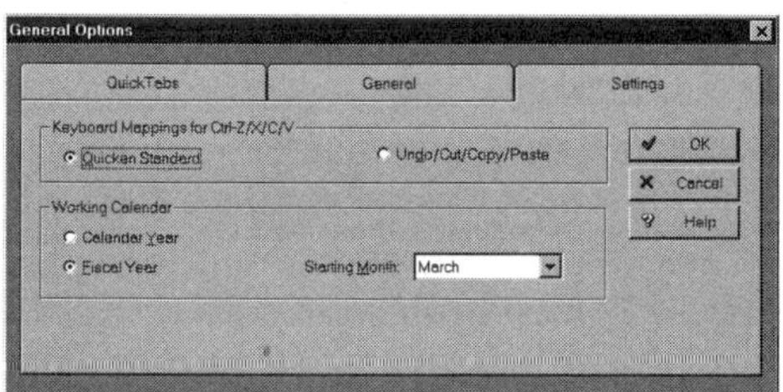

Figure 22.5 *The General Options dialog box (Settings).*

Settings Options

The Settings Options (see **Figure 22.5**) control two major areas of the program. By default, the normal Windows editing keyboard shortcuts are assigned to other Quicken commands. If you choose Undo/Cut/Copy/Paste mapping, the Ctrl Z, X, C, and V key combinations can be used for editing.

If you operate on a fiscal year rather than January–December, click Fiscal Year and choose the starting month of your year from the drop-down list.

Register Options

Like the Quicken Program Options, there are three categories of Register Options: Display, Miscellaneous, and QuickFill.

Display Options

Display Options (see **Figure 22.6**) govern the order in which some fields are displayed and the appearance of the register window.

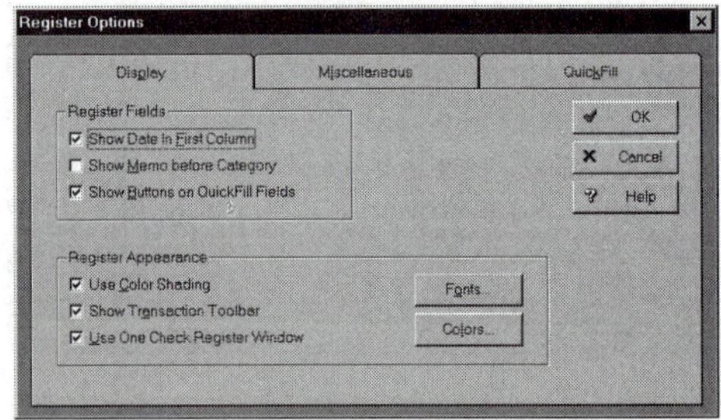

Figure 22.6 *The Register Options dialog box (Display).*

You can specify the order in which two sets of fields appear in records by adding or removing the check mark from Show Date in First Column and Show Memo before Category. To eliminate the buttons that appear in the Date, Payee, Amount, and Category fields, remove the check mark from Show Buttons on QuickFill Fields.

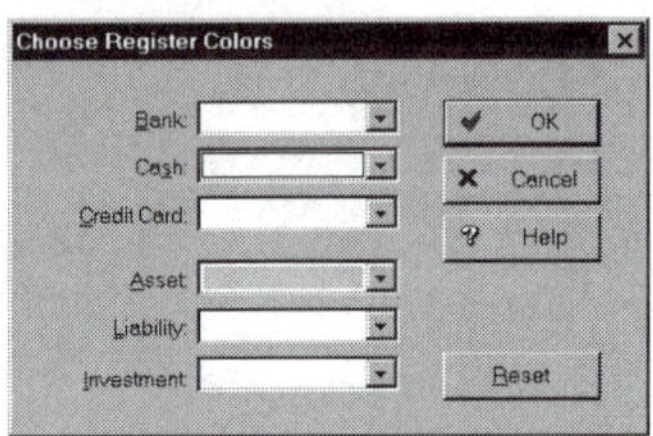

Figure 22.7 *You can pick a different color for each account type from the drop-down menus in the Choose Register Colors dialog box. Click Reset to revert to the standard colors.*

The Use Color Shading option associates a different background color with each type of account register. To pick other colors, click the Colors button (see **Figure 22.7**). To select a different font for displaying transaction text and register lists, click the Fonts button (see **Figure 22.8**).

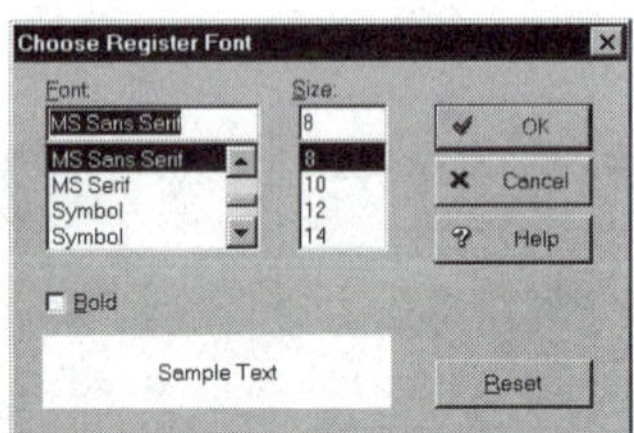

Figure 22.8 *You can choose a new font, size, and/or style for register text in the Choose Register Font dialog box. Click Reset to revert to the default font.*

To remove the Enter, Edit, and Split buttons from beneath the active transaction, turn off Show Transaction Toolbar. You can still use these commands by pressing [Return] or [Enter] for Enter and [Ctrl][S] for Split.

By default, as you switch from one account register to another, the new register takes the place of the previous one (Use One Check Register Window). To present each account register in its own window, remove the check mark from this option.

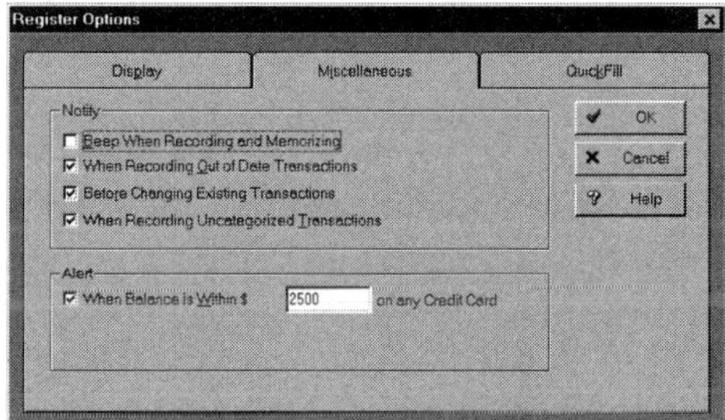

Figure 22.9 *The Register Options dialog box (Miscellaneous).*

Miscellaneous Options

The Miscellaneous section of the Register Options dialog box (as shown in **Figure 22.9**) is used to set register and account notification options.

Set options in the Notify portion of the dialog box to indicate when Quicken should beep or present a warning dialog box. If you want to be alerted when you are near the credit limit on a credit card, check the option for When Balance is Within $ and enter an amount in the text box.

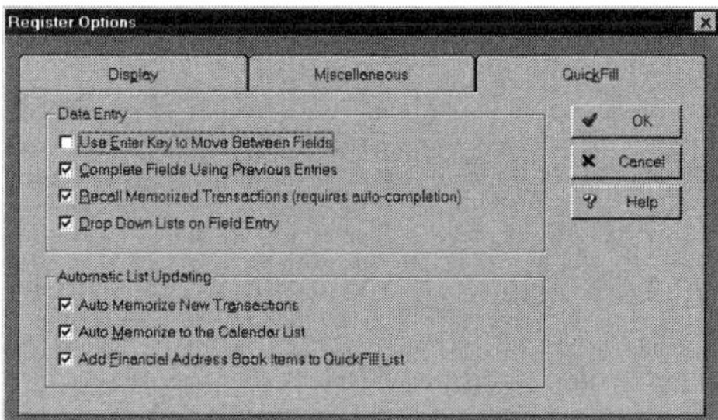

Figure 22.10 *The Register Options dialog box (QuickFill).*

QuickFill Options

Click the QuickFill tab in the Register Options dialog box (see **Figure 22.10**) to control whether QuickFill is used to complete transactions and to specify how memorized transactions work.

Normally, you use Tab to move from field to field within a transaction and press Enter to record it. To use *both* keys for between-field movement, check Use Enter Key to Move Between Fields.

The remaining Data Entry options work as a group, enabling Quicken to fill in many fields in a new transaction based on entries in the Memorized Transaction List.

Although you can manually add entries to the Memorized Transaction List, the fastest way is to set the option to Auto Memorize New Transactions. Whenever you create a transaction with a new payee, Quicken adds the entire transaction to the Memorized Transaction List. If you later create a new transaction to the same payee, the old details (Amount, Category, and Memo) are replaced by the new ones.

If you want to add new memorized transactions to the list in the Financial Calendar, enable the Auto Memorize to the Calendar List option. If you prefer to maintain greater control over the specific transactions that appear in the calendar list, turn this option off.

Names and addresses that you have manually recorded in the Financial Address Book can be added to the Memorized Transaction List by setting Add Financial Address Book Items to QuickFill List. However, if most of the manually added names are people with whom you do not do business (friends and colleagues, for example), you may prefer to turn this option off.

Check Options

The Check Options dialog box contains three sections: Checks, Miscellaneous, and QuickFill. For an explanation of QuickFill options, refer to “Register Options,” earlier in this chapter.

Checks Options

In the Checks section of the Check Options dialog box (see **Figure 22.11**), you can set a style for displaying the year in printed checks. Choose 4-digit Year (1997) or 2-digit Year (97).

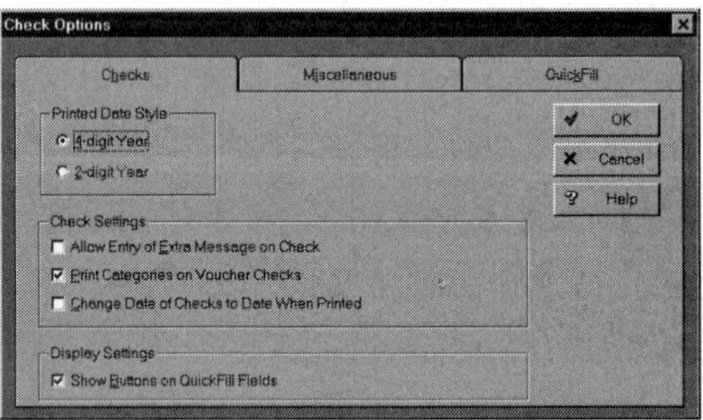

Figure 22.11 *The Check Options dialog box (Checks).*

To print a message line that cannot be seen through a check envelope window, set the option to Allow Extra Message on Check. This is particularly handy if you often record an account or Social Security number on your checks.

If you use voucher checks (ones with an attachment for printing additional details about the transaction) and you want to print category and split information on the voucher, set the option to Print Categories on Voucher Checks.

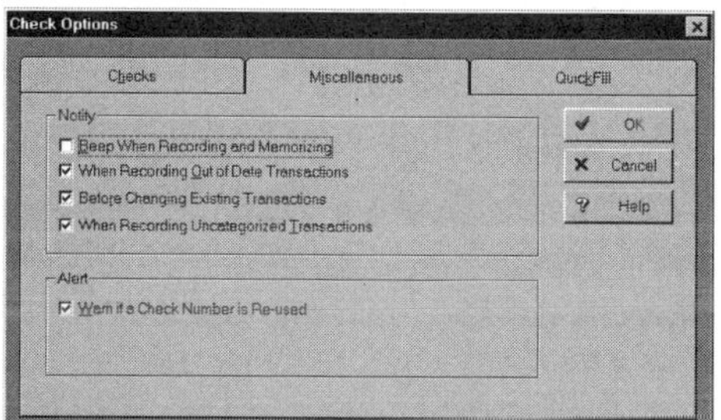

Figure 22.12 *The Check Options dialog box (Miscellaneous).*

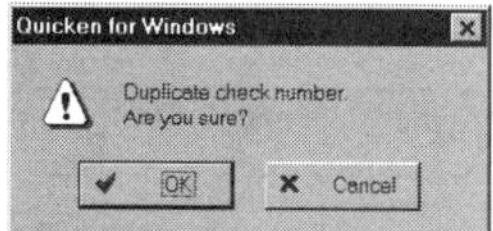

Figure 22.13 *This alert appears if you attempt to reuse a check number. You can still override it by clicking OK.*

By default, the date on a printed check matches the transaction date. However, you may prefer to set the option to Change Date of Checks to Date When Printed, particularly if you often postpone printing until you have a batch of checks that is ready.

Miscellaneous Options

Use the Miscellaneous section of the Check Options dialog box (see **Figure 22.12**) to set notification and alert options. The options in the Notify section are the same as the ones listed in the Register Options dialog box (refer to **Figure 22.9**).

To display an alert if you duplicate an existing check number (as shown in **Figure 22.13**), set the option to Warn If a Check Number is Reused.

✔ **Tip**

- All of the QuickFill options and the majority of the Miscellaneous options can also be set in the Register Options dialog box. Setting these options in *any* dialog box sets them for the entire program.

Report and Graph Options

Refer to the "Default Report and Graph Settings" section of Chapter 17 for an explanation of the report and graph options.

Reminder Options

You set options for Billminder and the Reminders window in the Reminder Options dialog box (see **Figure 22.14**).

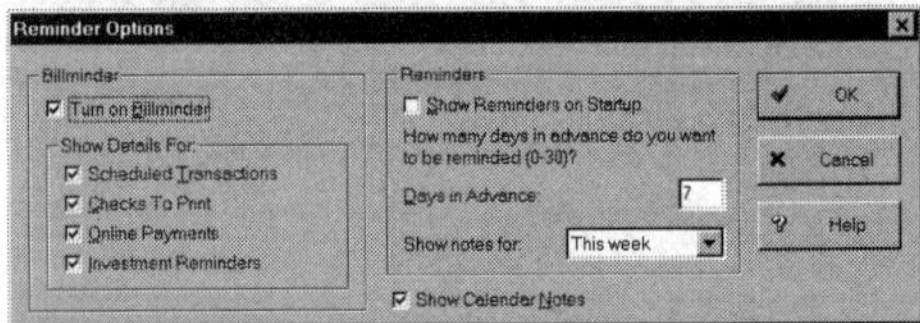

Figure 22.14 *The Reminder Options dialog box.*

When enabled, Billminder (see **Figure 22.15**) pops up at the start of any Windows session in which bills or other important financial events are pending. The options in the Show Details For part of the dialog box determine the types of events Billminder announces.

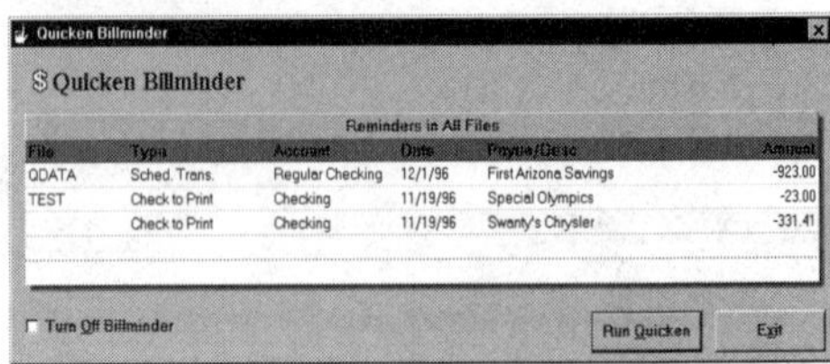

Figure 22.15 *Billminder automatically notifies you of pending financial events and transactions that are due.*

You can open the Reminders window at any time by clicking the To Do! icon, but it can also be set to open automatically at the start of any Quicken session in which there are pending transactions or calendar notes (Show Reminders on Startup). You can specify the number of days in advance that you want to be notified, whether notes from the Financial Calendar are displayed (Show Calendar Notes), and which notes will be listed.

Desktop Options

Use the Save Desktop dialog box (see **Figure 22.16**) to specify when the Quicken desktop is saved.

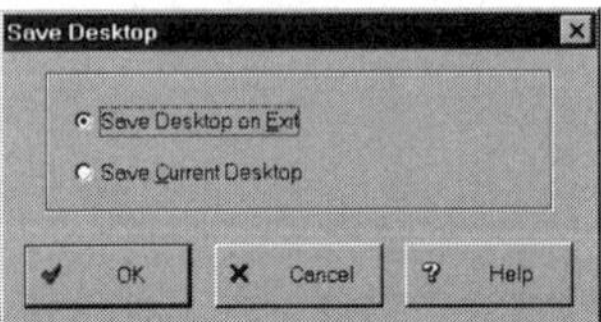

Figure 22.16 *The Save Desktop dialog box.*

Quicken normally begins each session by opening all windows that were open when you last quit from the program (Save Desktop on Exit). However, if there is a specific window arrangement that you always want to use, open those windows and choose Save Current Desktop. This setting remains in effect until you use the command to save a different desktop or you choose Save Desktop on Exit.

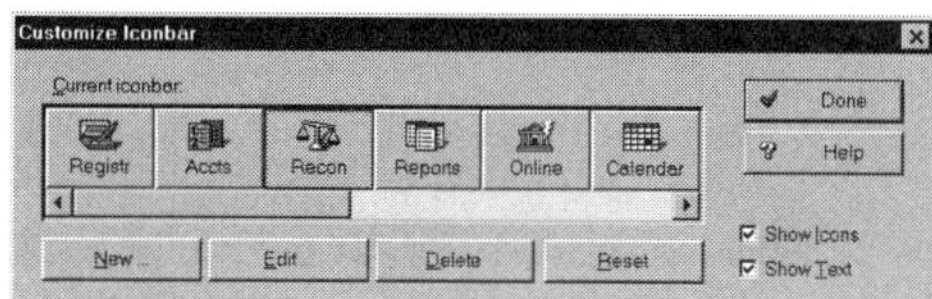

Figure 22.17 *The Customize Iconbar dialog box.*

Iconbar Options

You can change the icons in the top iconbar—as well as determine whether it is shown at all—in the Customize Iconbar dialog box (see **Figure 22.17**).

You can display iconbar buttons, their text labels, both, or neither by setting combinations of the Show Icons and Show Text options.

To remove an icon from the iconbar, select it in the Customize Iconbar dialog box, click Delete, and then confirm the deletion by clicking OK.

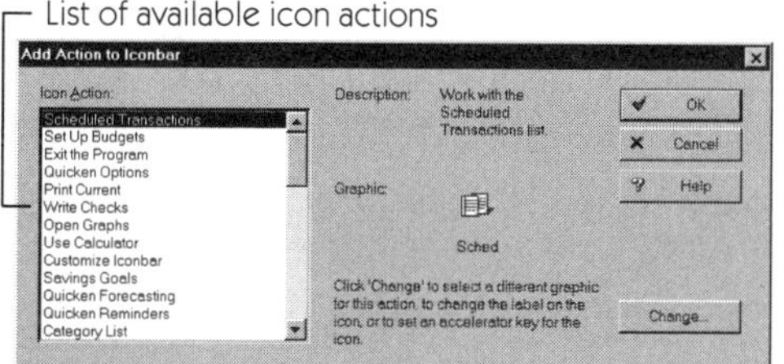

Figure 22.18 *All you have to do to add a new icon is pick one from this list.*

To add an icon to the iconbar:

1. In the Customize Iconbar dialog box, click New. The Add Action to Iconbar dialog box appears (see **Figure 22.18**).
2. Select an icon from the Icon Action list and click OK. The new icon is added to the end of the iconbar.

To replace an icon with another one, select the icon in the Customize Iconbar dialog box, click Edit, select a replacement icon, and click OK.

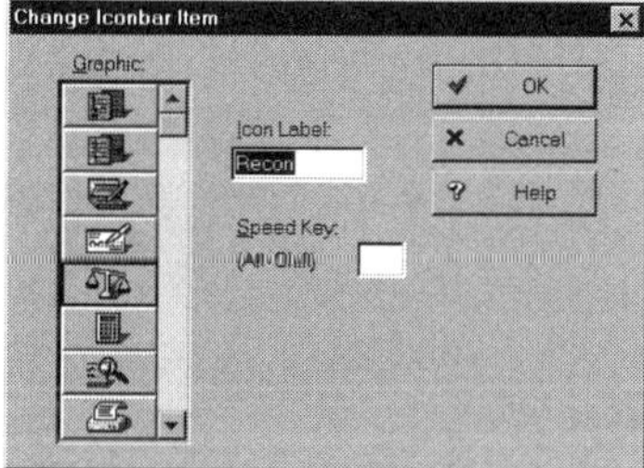

Figure 22.19 *Use the Change Iconbar Item dialog box to alter the appearance or label for an icon or to create a keyboard shortcut for it.*

You can further customize any icon by choosing a new graphic, creating a different text label, or associating a keyboard shortcut with it. To accomplish any of these tasks, select the icon in the Customize Iconbar dialog box, click Edit, and then click Change. The Change Iconbar Item dialog box appears (see **Figure 22.19**).

To change the graphic, select one from the Graphic list. To create a new label, enter it in the Icon Label text box. To associate a keyboard shortcut with the icon, type the key in the Speed Key text box. To later use the speed key, hold down Alt Shift and press the letter key that you associated with the icon.

✔ **Tips**

- If you seldom use the iconbar, you can remove it to gain some extra screen space.
- The Show Icons and Show Text options are put into effect immediately, as are changes made to the iconbar. There is no need to close the dialog box to see the effects of your changes.
- Don't worry about running out of room when adding new icons. If you add more than will fit, arrow buttons are added to the right and left sides of the iconbar—enabling you to scroll to icons that you can't see. (Once you reach this point, however, you've lost the much of the icons' easy accessibility.)
- After you've used Quicken for awhile, you should seriously consider editing the icons in the iconbar. You're certain to find some functions that you never use, and you can replace them with functions that you *do* use.
- When adding icons, consider adding functions that are buried in the program menus—particularly those that do not have keyboard shortcuts.

Quicken Solutions

About Quicken Solutions

If you've read the other 22 chapters of this book, you know how to use Quicken's features. But do you know how to use its features to accomplish the specific tasks you may encounter in everyday life?

That's what this chapter is all about. It explains how to use Quicken to solve real world, finance-related problems.

✔ **Tips**

- To use Quicken to perform tasks that are not specifically covered in this book or the manual, make sure you have a good understanding of Quicken's features. Then brainstorm about your specific needs to come up with creative solutions using the tools that Quicken provides.
- Unlike other chapters in this book, this chapter does not offer many step-by-step instructions. Instead, it presents lists of ideas and tips that you can explore on your own. Chapter references are provided to make it easy to find more information about the features mentioned.
- Some of the solutions in this chapter combine several Quicken features to get the job done. That's one of the things that this chapter stresses: thinking about Quicken's entire feature set and creatively combining features to achieve the desired result.

Quicken for Accountants

People with real-world accounting experience may find it difficult to adjust to Quicken. The reason? In making Quicken easy for non-accountants to use, Intuit removed or renamed many standard accounting concepts.

Debits and *credits* are called *payments, deposits, charges, increases,* and *decreases* to account balances. The term used varies by account type. This can be confusing if you are accustomed to thinking of debits as equity increases and credits as decreases. Accounts are discussed in Chapter 2.

Journals—used to record transactions in standard accounting systems—are replaced by *registers* (see **Figure 23.1**). While a register requires only one entry, two would be needed in a journal. Registers are discussed in Chapter 5.

Income and expense *accounts* are replaced by *categories* (see **Figure 23.2**). Categories do not have registers. They are discussed in Chapter 3.

Double-entry accounting requires balancing debit and credit entries in two or more accounts. In Quicken, you make single entries into registers. When you enter a transaction, the account is debited or credited, as appropriate. The assigned category (or categories, in the case of a split transaction) or a transfer account receives the balancing entry.

Rather than record transactions in an accounts payable journal, you write a check, dating it for when the payment is due or should be mailed. As a result, accounts payable is determined by totaling the unprinted checks for vendors. Check writing is discussed in Chapter 6.

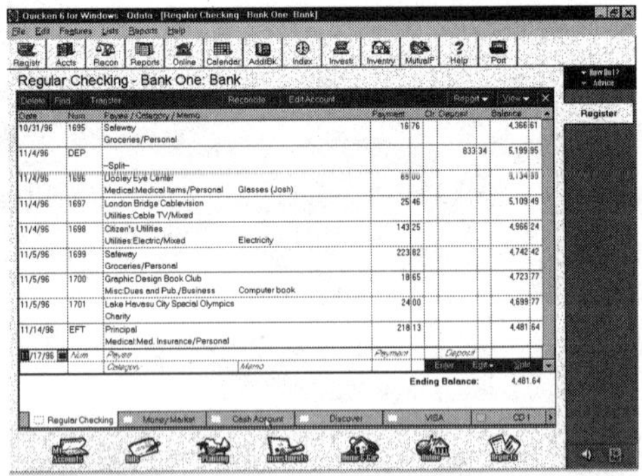

Figure 23.1 *Quicken uses registers like this one rather than journals.*

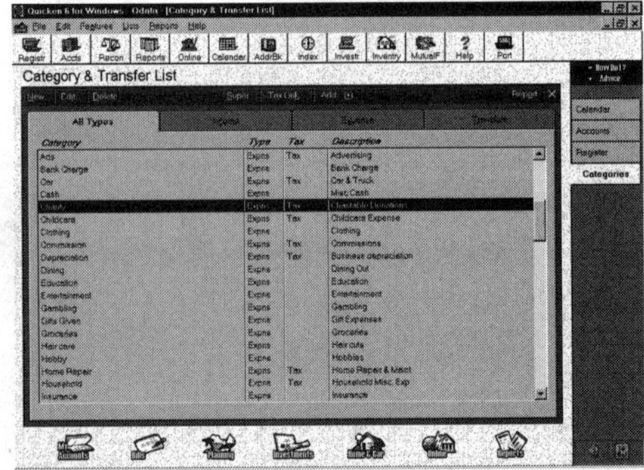

Figure 23.2 *Quicken uses categories rather than income and expense accounts.*

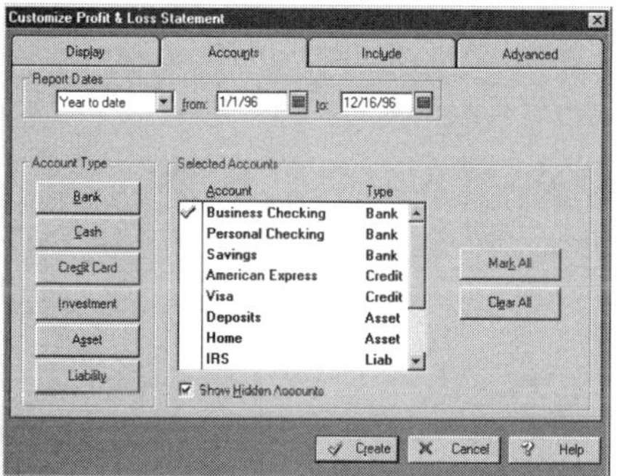

Figure 23.3 *With separate business and personal checking accounts, you can report transactions by account.*

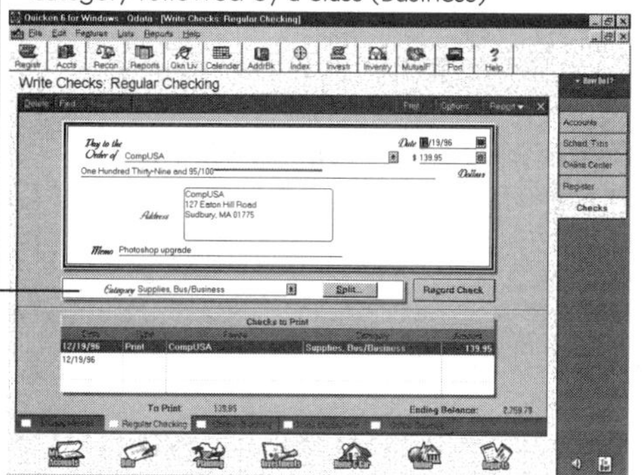

Figure 23.4 *To assign a class to a transaction, choose a category, enter a / and then type the class name.*

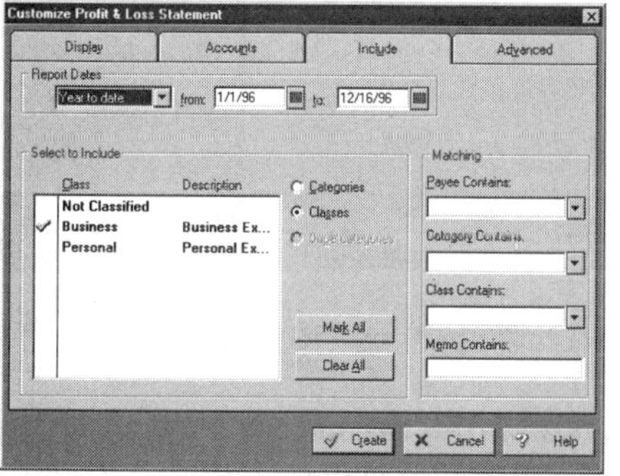

Figure 23.5 *If you assign a class to every transaction, you can create class-specific reports (as shown here).*

Tracking Business and Personal Expenses

If you use the same Quicken file to track personal and business expenses, it's important to be able to separate the expenses for business reporting and tax purposes. Quicken provides two ways to do this. You can keep separate checking accounts or define multiple expenditure classes.

If you maintain separate checking accounts for personal and business expenses, consider the following tips:

- Be sure to use the correct account when writing checks. Writing checks is discussed in Chapter 6.
- You can create custom reports that show expenses by account (see **Figure 23.3**). Custom reports are discussed in Chapter 17.
- You can pay yourself a salary by writing a check on one account and depositing it to the other or by using on-line banking to make electronic fund transfers. On-line banking is discussed in Chapter 21.

If you use classes to distinguish business from personal transactions, consider the following:

- Define classes for personal and business expenditures. Then assign each transaction you record to the appropriate class (see **Figure 23.4**). Creating and using classes are discussed in Chapters 3 and 5.
- You can create reports that show expenses by class (see **Figure 23.5**). Custom reports are discussed in Chapter 17.

Setting Up a Long-Term Savings Plan

Saving money for college, retirement, or some other event in the future isn't easy, especially if you don't know how much you need or how much you can afford to save. Here are some ideas to help you create and follow a long-term savings plan:

- Use Quicken's financial planning calculators (see **Figure 23.6**) to determine the amount of money you must save to reach your goal. The calculators that you will find most useful are the ones for Savings, College, and Retirement. The financial planning calculators are discussed in Chapter 12.
- Set up an accurate budget. It should include an affordable regular savings amount that is based on your financial planning calculations. Update the budget regularly so it always shows reasonable, accurate budget amounts. Budgeting is discussed in Chapter 10.
- Use the Financial Calendar to schedule regular deposits to your savings account (see **Figure 23.7**). If you have trouble putting away large sums of money, try small weekly deposits. The Financial Calendar is discussed in Chapter 7.
- You can make scheduled savings deposits via on-line banking or bill payment or by printing and depositing checks. On-line banking is discussed in Chapter 21; writing checks is discussed in Chapter 6.

Figure 23.6 *The Financial Planners.*

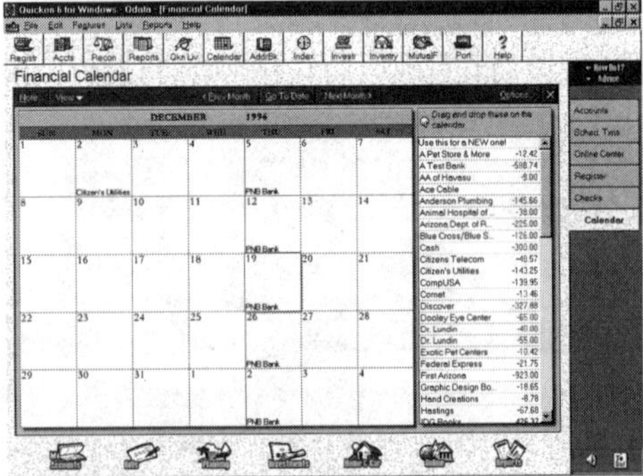

Figure 23.7 *You can use Quicken to schedule regular deposits to a savings or money market account.*

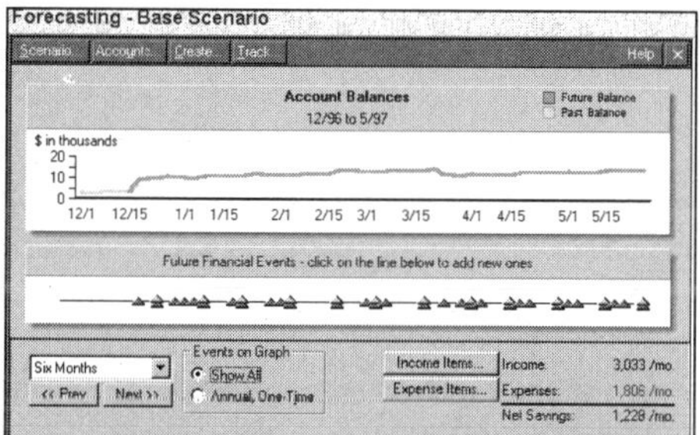

Figure 23.8 *Create a forecast to see when you can afford to make a big purchase.*

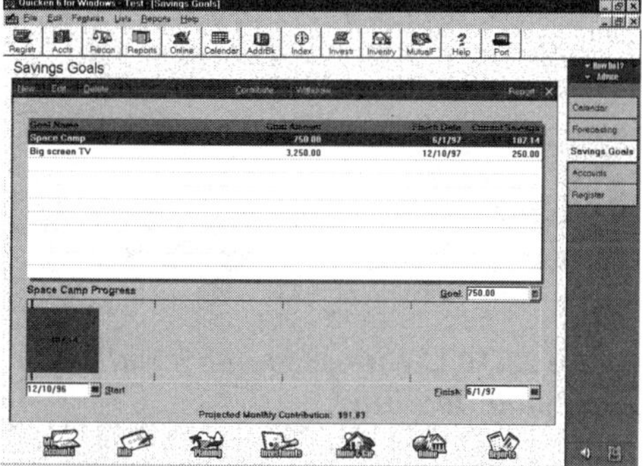

Figure 23.9 *You can create a Savings Goal to "hide" money from yourself.*

Planning a Cash Purchase

Making a large cash purchase or down payment on a home or car requires that you save money—often very quickly. Although you know the amount needed, you may need help putting it away or estimating when the funds will be available. The following are some ideas for achieving a short-term savings goal:

- Use Forecasting (see **Figure 23.8**) to chart your cash flow into the near future. If your forecast is accurate, you should be able to tell when you will have the necessary cash. Forecasting is discussed in Chapter 13.
- Create a savings goal (see **Figure 23.9**) to "hide" money from yourself. Savings goals are discussed in Chapter 13.
- If you create a savings goal, display progress bars so you can always see how close you are to achieving the goal. Progress bars are discussed in Chapter 10.
- Use ideas from the previous page to automatically save money in a savings account. If you're one of those people who simply spends whatever money you have, you can hide the savings account from view. Hiding accounts is discussed in Chapter 2.

✔ **Tip**

- You can also create a savings goal to hide a minimum required balance in your checking account. The cash reserve created by such a savings goal can also help assure that you will never bounce a check.

Preparing to Write a Will

If you have assets, you should have a will. It's as simple as that.

Creating a thorough will—with details about individual bequests—requires that you know what you own. The following Quicken features can help you take stock of your assets:

- Create asset accounts for major items, such as your home and car (see **Figure 23.10**). Creating asset accounts is discussed in Chapter 2.
- Periodically review asset values and make adjustments in the registers. If possible, get appraisals on valuable items. Updating an account balance is discussed in Chapter 8.

DELUXE

- Keep security values up-to-date by using Quicken Live or Investor Insight to obtain current quotes. Be sure to update your records to reflect purchases, sales, dividends, and so on. Managing a portfolio is discussed in Chapter 15; Quicken Live and Investor Insight are discussed in Chapters 19 and 20.

DELUXE

- Use Quicken Home Inventory to record information about household items (see **Figure 23.11**), especially those with real value. Home Inventory is discussed in Chapter 14.
- Use the reporting features of Quicken and Home Inventory to generate a net worth report and a list of your valuables. You can take these reports to your lawyer when you're ready to draft your will. Generating a net worth report is discussed in Chapter 13.

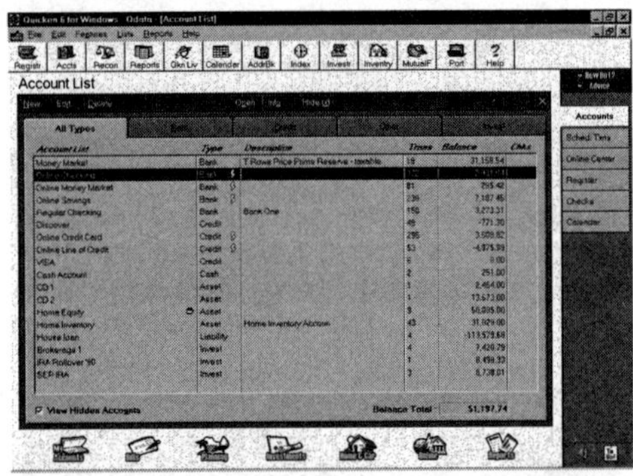

Figure 23.10 *Create accounts for all your assets and liabilities.*

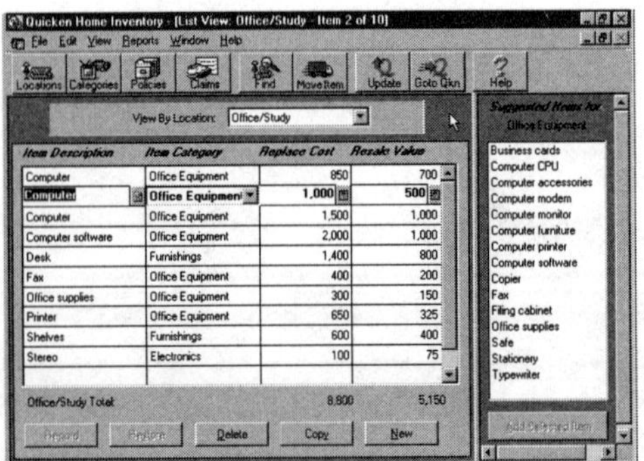

Figure 23.11 *Quicken Home Inventory makes it easy to keep track of everything in your home.*

Making Tax Time Easier

Nobody looks forward to tax time. Even if you're due a refund, completing a tax return is a time-consuming task that no one enjoys. And if you pay a tax preparer to do the job for you, it could cost hundreds of dollars!

If you use Quicken to keep track of your finances, you have the means to make tax time a lot easier and less expensive.

DELUXE

- Use Deduction Finder (see **Figure 23.12**) to look for additional deductible expenses. Deduction Finder is discussed in Chapter 16.
- When setting up categories, be sure to indicate which ones are tax-related, as well as the tax form and line on which each category should be recorded (see **Figure 23.13**). If you prefer, you can use the Tax Link Assistant to match categories to tax form line items. Creating categories is discussed in Chapter 3; using Tax Link Assistant is covered in Chapter 16.
- At tax time, generate a Tax Schedule report that summarizes categories by tax return line item and complete your return based on these reports. Even if your return is prepared by an accountant, providing the report may reduce the preparation fee. Generating a Tax Schedule report is discussed in Chapter 16.
- Use TurboTax to prepare your tax return. This Intuit program can automatically exchange data with Quicken and even prints the return for you!

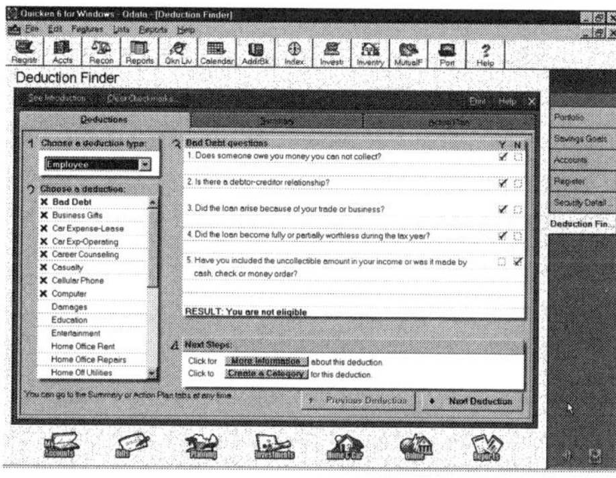

Figure 23.12 *Use Deduction Finder to determine if you missed some potential tax deductions.*

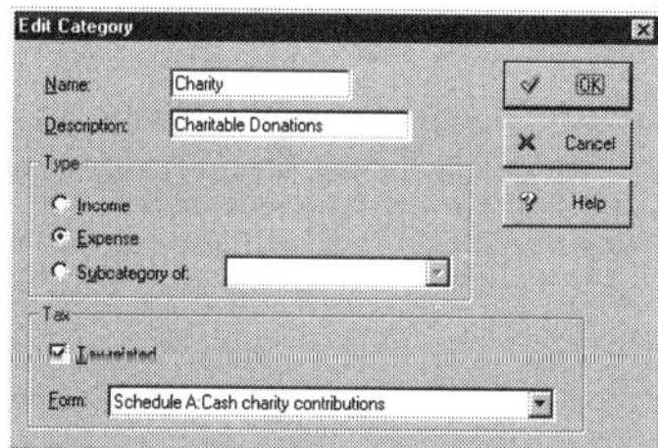

Figure 23.13 *You can specify a tax line item for each type of deductible expense.*

Tracking Reimbursable Medical Expenses

Medical expenses that are covered by your health insurance take time and effort to track. There are two concerns:

- You must track the bills submitted to your insurance provider for reimbursement. It's important to prevent any of them from "slipping through the cracks."
- For tax purposes, you must track the net amount of any medical expenses that you pay. This amount may be tax deductible.

You can use a Quicken asset account to serve both needs.

Using an asset account to track outstanding medical payments:

1. Set up an asset account for reimbursable medical expenses. Creating accounts is discussed in Chapter 2.
2. When paying a doctor's bill for a medical expense, use the reimbursable medical expenses account as a transfer account in the check writing form. This sets up a receivable for amounts due from your insurance company. Paying bills and using transfer accounts are discussed in Chapter 5.
3. Submit the paid medical bills and insurance forms to your insurance company. When you receive reimbursement from your insurance company, use the reimbursable medical expenses account to enter the following two transactions:

   Enter the amount of the payment as a deposit and as a reduction of

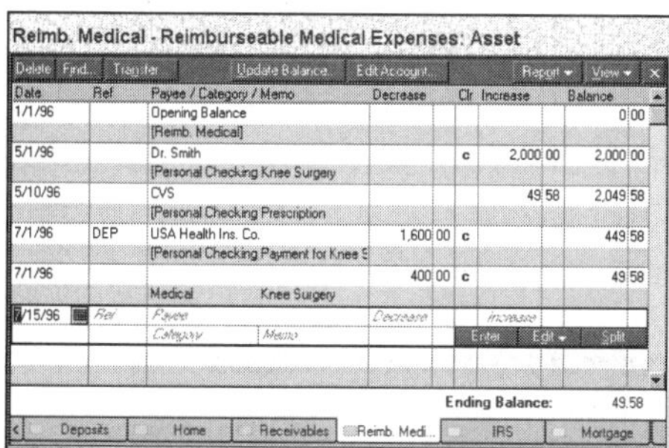

Figure 23.14 *You can create an asset account to track reimbursable medical expenses.*

the reimbursable medical expenses account.

Record the amount not paid for the bill as a reduction of the reimbursable medical expenses account, using your medical expenses category to complete the transaction.

4. Mark the entries for the bill, the payment, and the amount not paid as cleared.

Figure 23.14 shows an example of two bills: one (for Dr. Smith) paid and cleared and the other (for CVS) not yet paid. It's important to understand that once a bill has been paid by your insurance company, its balance should be "zeroed out" in the reimbursable medical expenses account and the amount you paid should be attributed to the medical expenses category.

✓ Tips

- Whenever possible, have medical providers bill your insurance company directly. You can then skip the accounting for reimbursable medical expenses and simply record the net amount you pay in the medical expenses category.
- If an expense is not reimbursable, simply record it in your medical expenses category.
- At tax time, generate a report of your medical expenses for possible deduction on Schedule A. Remember, the amount that you can deduct is limited by your income. Follow the instructions that come with your tax return or speak to your tax preparer for details.

Using Quicken Data in Other Programs

After data has been entered in Quicken, it can be exported and used in other programs. This makes it possible to reuse the data without reentering it. The following are some examples:

- Import transactions into a spreadsheet program to summarize the data and create custom graphs.
- Import Quicken accounts and category lists into a database program to create a custom chart of accounts.
- Use information from Quicken reports in word processing documents, such as annual reports or proposals.

Here is how to use Quicken data in other applications:

- Use the Export feature to create a file containing Quicken data. The QIF Export dialog box (see **Figure 23.15**) lets you specify the account and type of information to include. Exporting data from Quicken is discussed in Appendix B.

  Use the Import or Open command of the destination program to open the exported file. Check the manual that came with the program for information about working with files created by other applications.
- In Quicken, generate a report of the information you want to use. Then click the Copy button in the report window (see **Figure 23.16**) to copy the report to the clipboard. You can paste the report into a document created with another application.

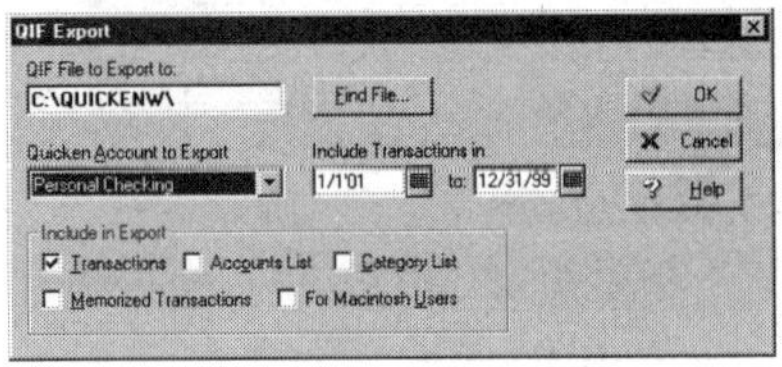

Figure 23.15 *Use the QIF Export dialog box to export Quicken data in a format that can be read by other programs.*

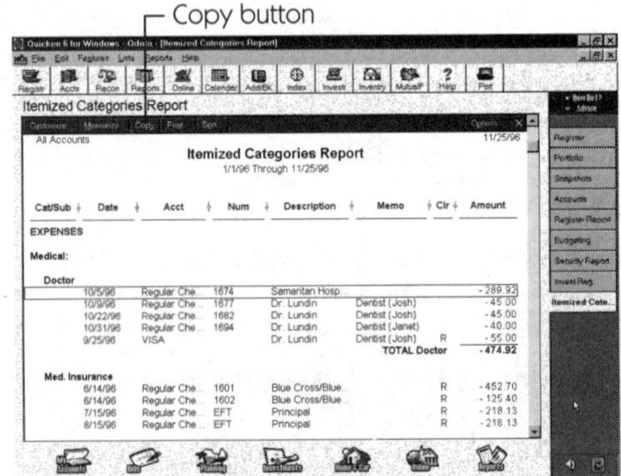

Figure 23.16 *When you click the Copy button in a report window, the report is copied to the clipboard.*

Appendices

Keyboard Shortcuts

You can perform common tasks in Quicken 6 by pressing a key or a combination of keys. These keyboard shortcuts can speed up your work and are often more convenient than searching for the associated menu command.

Table A.1. General Quicken Shortcuts

Task	Keyboard Shortcut	Menu Command
Open Quicken data file	Ctrl O	File ⇨ Open
Backup current data file	Ctrl B	File ⇨ Backup
Print	Ctrl P	File ⇨ Print
Use register	Ctrl R	Features ⇨ Banking ⇨ Use Register
Write checks	Ctrl W	Features ⇨ Paying Bills ⇨ Write Checks
Go to View Loans	Ctrl H	Features ⇨ Paying Bills ⇨ Loans
Go to Portfolio View	Ctrl U	Features ⇨ Investments ⇨ Portfolio View
Go to Financial Calendar	Ctrl K	
Display the Account List	Ctrl A	Lists ⇨ Accounts
Display the Category & Transfer List	Ctrl C	Lists ⇨ Category/Transfer
Display the Class List	Ctrl L	Lists ⇨ Class
Display the Memorized Transaction List	Ctrl T	Lists ⇨ Memorized Transaction
Display the Scheduled Transaction List	Ctrl J	Lists ⇨ Scheduled Transaction
Display the Security List	Ctrl Y	Lists ⇨ Investment ⇨ Security
Contextual help	F1	Help ⇨ Context Help

Table A.2. Quicken Editing Shortcuts

Task	Keyboard Shortcut	Menu Command
Cut selected text	Shift Del	Edit ⇨ Cut
Copy selected text	Ctrl Ins	Edit ⇨ Copy
Paste text from clipboard	Shift Ins	Edit ⇨ Paste
Find a transaction	Ctrl F	Edit ⇨ Find
New transaction	Ctrl N	Edit ⇨ Transaction ⇨ New
Delete current transaction	Ctrl D	Edit ⇨ Transaction ⇨ Delete
Insert transaction	Ctrl I	Edit ⇨ Transaction ⇨ Insert
Void current transaction	Ctrl V	Edit ⇨ Transaction ⇨ Void Transaction
Memorize current transaction	Ctrl M	Edit ⇨ Transaction ⇨ Memorize
Go to the selected transfer	Ctrl X	Edit ⇨ Transaction ⇨ Go To Transfer
Increase/decrease date or check number by one	+, -	
Set date to today, first of month, end of month, first of year, or end of year	T, M, H, Y, R	
Scroll the QuickFill list down/up	Ctrl ↓ or ↓, Ctrl ↑ or ↑	
Open/close Split Transaction window	Ctrl S, Ctrl Enter	
Copy data from the field above in Split Transaction window	'	
Complete a transaction	Enter or Ctrl Enter	
New account, security, or loan	Ctrl N	Edit ⇨ Account/Security/Loan ⇨ New
Edit account, security, or loan	Ctrl E	Edit ⇨ Account/Security/Loan ⇨ Edit
Delete account, security, or loan	Ctrl D	Edit ⇨ Account/Security/Loan ⇨ Delete

Table A.2. Quicken Editing Shortcuts (Continued)

Task	Keyboard Shortcut	Menu Command
Edit portfolio price history	Ctrl E	Edit ⇨ Portfolio ⇨ Edit Price History
Go to date (in portfolio)	Ctrl X	Edit ⇨ Portfolio ⇨ Go to Date
Increase/decrease a security price by one-eighth	+, -	
QuickZoom a report amount	Ctrl Z	

Table A.3. Register Navigation Shortcuts

Task	Keyboard Shortcut
Go to next/previous field in current transaction	Tab, Shift Tab
Go to same field in previous/next transaction	↑, ↓
Go to beginning/end of current field	Home, End
Go to first/last field in current transaction	Home Home, End End
Go to first/last transaction in the account	Ctrl Home, Ctrl End
Go to first/last transaction in the month	Ctrl Pg Up, Ctrl Pg Dn
Scroll up/down one screen	Pg Up, Pg Dn

Table A.4. Budget Navigation Shortcuts

Task	Keyboard Shortcut
Move one column to the right	Tab, →, or Enter
Move one column to the left	Shift Tab, ←, or Shift Enter
Scroll left/right one screen	Ctrl ←, Ctrl →
Move up/down one row in same column	↑, ↓
Go to first/last cell in current row	Home Home, End End
Go to first/last row in the budget	Ctrl Home, Ctrl End
Scroll up/down one screen	Pg Up, Pg Dn
Go to beginning/end of current field	Home, End
Undo the last amount entered in current field	Esc

Table A.5. Financial Address Book Shortcuts

Task	Keyboard Shortcut	Menu Command
Open address book file	Ctrl O	File ➪ Open
Print the address book	Ctrl P	File ➪ Print
Cut selected text	Ctrl X	Edit ➪ Cut
Copy selected text	Ctrl C	Edit ➪ Copy
Paste text from clipboard	Ctrl V	Edit ➪ Paste
Undo last editing command	Ctrl Z	
New address record	Ctrl N	Edit ➪ New
Edit selected address record	Ctrl E	Edit ➪ Edit
Delete selected address record	Ctrl D	Edit ➪ Delete
Move organization data into Name fields	Ctrl M	Edit ➪ Move Organization into Names
Search the address book	Ctrl S	Edit ➪ Search
Move to next/previous address in list	↓, ↑	
Move to first/last address in list	Home, End	
Move up/down one screen in list	Pg Up, Pg Dn	
Move to next/previous address field	Tab, Shift Tab	
Move to beginning/end of current field	Home, End	
Move one word left/right in current field	Ctrl ↑ or Ctrl ←, Ctrl ↓ or Ctrl →	
Contextual help	F1	Help ➪ Context Help

Table A.6. Quicken Home Inventory Shortcuts

Task	Keyboard Shortcut	Menu Command
New inventory item	Ctrl N	File ➪ New
Open inventory file	Ctrl O	File ➪ Open
Print current report	Ctrl P	File ➪ Print
Go to Quicken	Ctrl Q or Alt Q	File ➪ Goto Quicken
Cut selected text	Ctrl X	Edit ➪ Cut
Copy selected text	Ctrl C	Edit ➪ Copy
Paste text from clipboard	Ctrl V	Edit ➪ Paste
Delete current item	Ctrl D or Alt D	
Record changes to item	Alt C	
Undo last editing command	Ctrl Z	
Increase/decrease amount by $50	+, -	
Increase/decrease date by one day	+, -	
Set date to today, first of month, end of month, first of year, or end of year	T, M, H, Y, R	
Drop down location list, calendar, or calculator (in appropriate field)	Alt ↓	
Switch between detail and list views	Ctrl L	
Switch between list or detail view and the suggested items list	F6	
Move to next/previous inventory item	↓, ↑	
Move up/down one screen in list	Pg Up, Pg Dn	
Move to next/previous inventory field	Tab, Shift Tab	
Move to beginning/end of field	Home, End	
Move one word left/right in field	Ctrl ↑ or Ctrl ←, Ctrl ↓ or Ctrl →	
Contextual help	F1	Help ➪ Context Help

File Operations

About File Operations

Most Quicken file operations are either automatic (such as saving changes to data) or are seldom used (deleting or renaming a data set, for example). In this appendix, you'll learn how to manage your Quicken data files in those rare instances when it is necessary.

To initiate a file operation, choose a command from the File menu or from the File Operations submenu of the File menu (see **Figure B.1**).

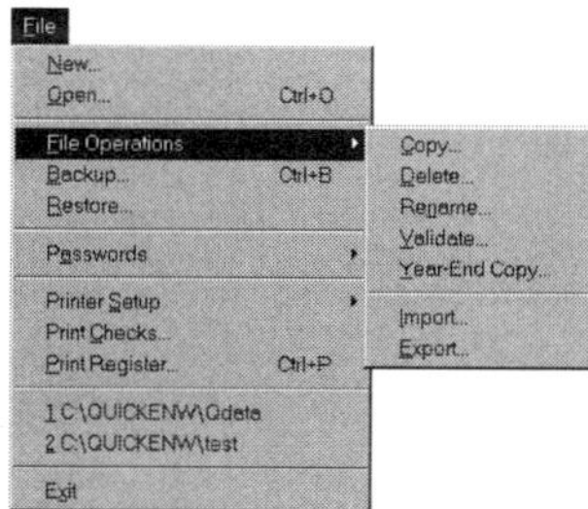

Figure B.1 *All user-initiated file operations are performed by selecting a command from the File menu.*

Making Backups

Quicken protects against data loss by automatically saving changes as they are made. (There are no Save or Save As commands with which to contend.) However, this does nothing for you if the hard drive on which the data is stored happens to fail. In order to fully protect your Quicken data, you should also make regular *backups* (exact copies of the data).

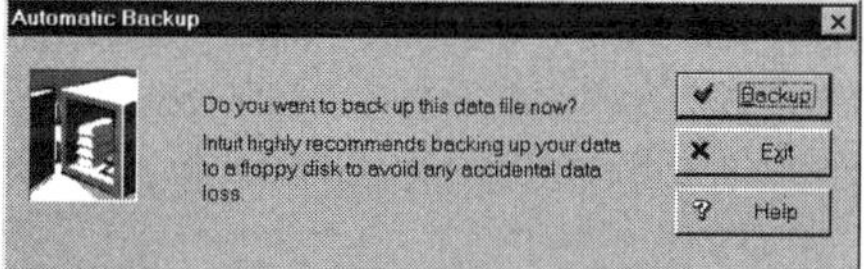

Figure B.2 *At regular intervals, Quicken suggests that you back up your data.*

To back up Quicken data:

1. Quicken regularly suggests that you back up your data (see **Figure B.2**). Click Backup to begin the backup procedure.

   or

1. To begin a manual backup, choose Backup from the File menu.

   The Select Backup Drive dialog box appears (see **Figure B.3**).

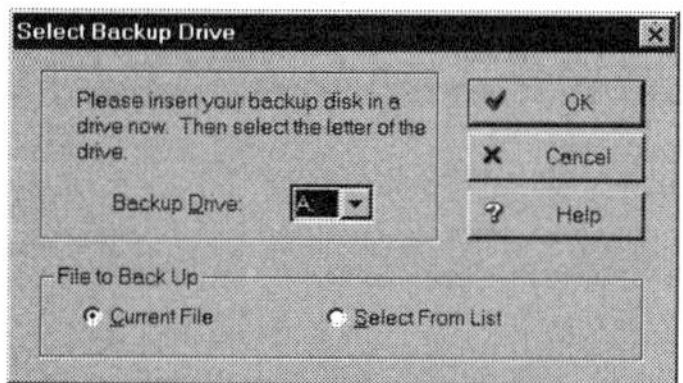

Figure B.3 *Set backup options in the Select Backup Drive dialog box.*

2. Select a target drive for the backup from the drop-down list.

   To afford the greatest protection, you should back up onto a floppy disk, a removable cartridge, or any media other than your internal hard disk.

3. To back up the current Quicken data file, click Current File and then click OK.

   or

3. To back up a different data file (if you have created multiple users for the program), click Select From List. A file dialog box appears in which you can choose the correct data file. Click OK to continue.

4. Insert a formatted disk into the drive chosen in Step 2. The backup commences.

5. When the backup is done, the dialog box shown in **Figure B.4** appears. Click OK. You can now remove the backup disk and store it in a safe place.

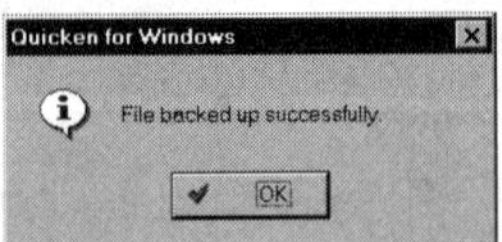

Figure B.4 *Click OK to complete the backup.*

✔ Tips

- To protect against major disasters, such as theft and fire, it's a good idea to store a backup at another location (in a safety deposit box, for example).
- If making a backup is a good idea, making *several* is better. Floppy disks can also fail, and they do so at a higher rate than hard disks. You may want to make several backups, and then rotate them on a daily or weekly basis. You can archive some or all of the backup disks as an added precaution.

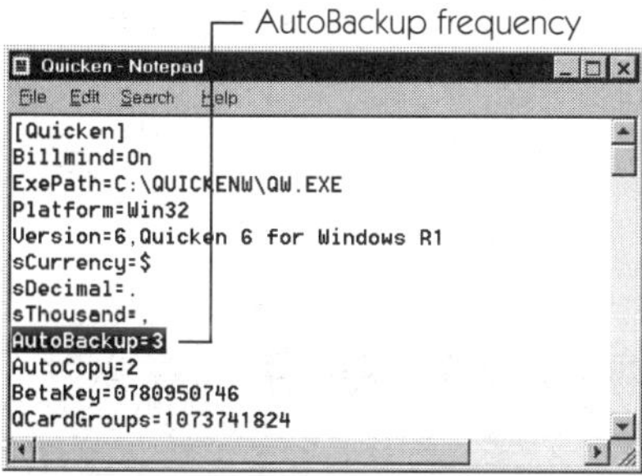

Figure B.5 *Change the number to the right of AutoBackup to alter the frequency with which Quicken suggests a backup.*

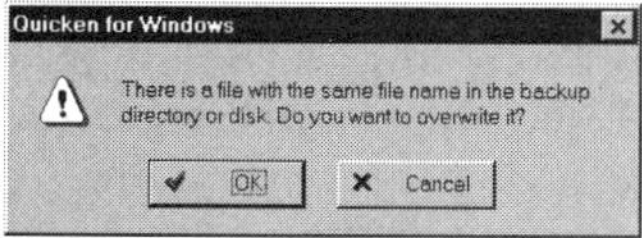

Figure B.6 *Click OK to use the current disk. Click Cancel to use a different disk.*

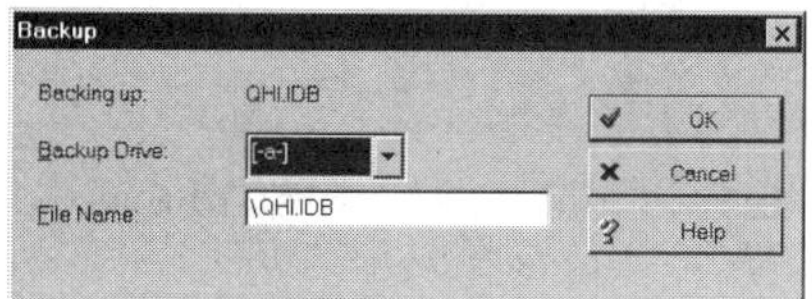

Figure B.7 *Quicken Home Inventory automatically selects the correct file to back up (QHI.IDB).*

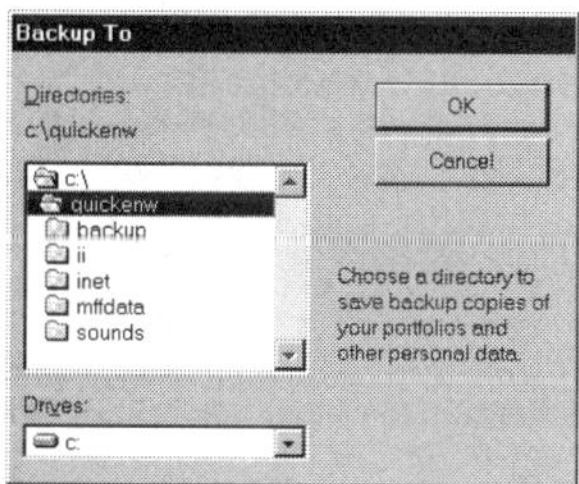

Figure B.8 *Investor Insight uses another procedure to perform backups. Rather than select the file to back up, you choose the folder in which to store the backup. As is done in Quicken, you can select a floppy as the target drive.*

- The frequency with which automatic backups are suggested is determined by the AutoBackup setting in the Quicken.ini file (found in the Windows directory). The default setting is **3**, indicating that a backup is suggested every third time that you quit from Quicken. To change this setting, open Quicken.ini in Notepad, change the number (see **Figure B.5**), and save the file.
- You can reuse a backup disk to perform additional backups. Note that doing so causes the previous backup set to be overwritten.

  If you reuse a backup disk, the dialog box shown in **Figure B.6** appears. Click OK to reuse the current disk.

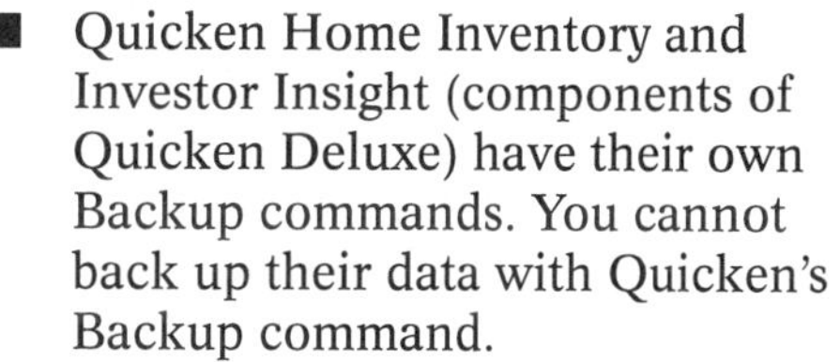

- Quicken Home Inventory and Investor Insight (components of Quicken Deluxe) have their own Backup commands. You cannot back up their data with Quicken's Backup command.

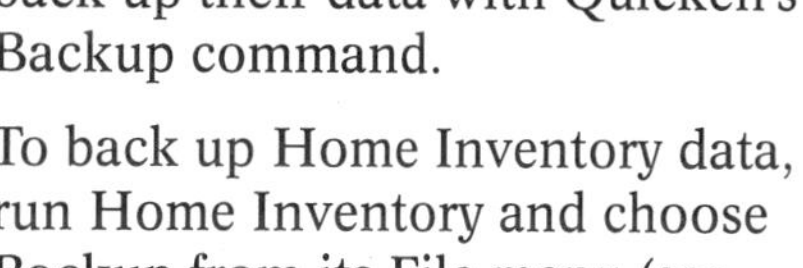

  To back up Home Inventory data, run Home Inventory and choose Backup from its File menu (see **Figure B.7**).

  To back up Investor Insight data, run the program, choose Backup Portfolios from its File menu, and select a folder in which to make the backup (see **Figure B.8**).
- Until the files get very large, you can use the same floppy to store backups for all three programs.

Restoring a Backup

If a data file is corrupted and cannot be repaired, you can restore the most recent backup.

To restore a backup:

1. Choose Restore from the File menu. The Restore Quicken File dialog box shown in **Figure B.9** appears.
2. Navigate to the drive that contains the backup disk (usually A: or B:).
3. Select the name of the backup data file (Qdata, for example), and click OK.
4. If a Quicken data file by the same name is currently open, the dialog box shown in **Figure B.10** appears. Click OK to replace the file with the backup.

✔ Tips

- You will have to reenter any changes that you made to the data since the backup. The more often you make backups, the less data you risk losing.
- You can use the Restore command to move Quicken data from one computer to another. If you get a new computer, for example, you can install Quicken on it and then use Restore to re-create the data. All transactions, account information, categories, and classes are restored.

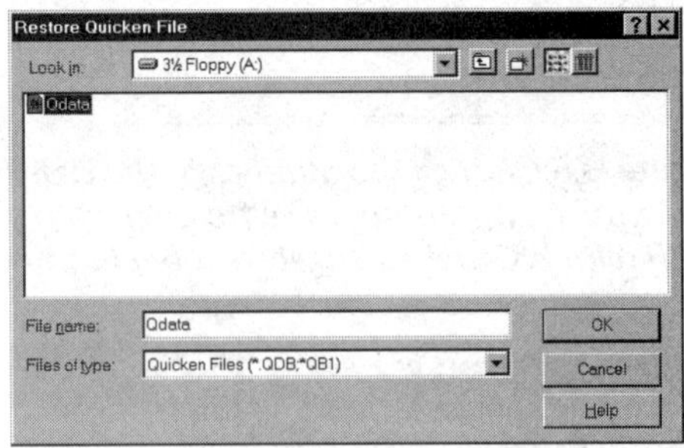

Figure B.9 *Select the file to restore from the Restore Quicken File dialog box.*

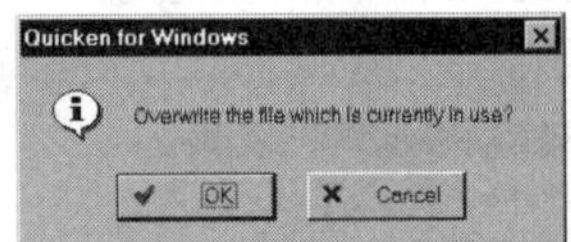

Figure B.10 *If a file is currently in use, click OK to replace that file with the backup, or click Cancel if you change your mind.*

Validating a Quicken File

If Quicken is having difficulty opening a data file, you can use the Validate command to determine if the file is corrupted. If the damage isn't serious, Validate may be able to repair the file.

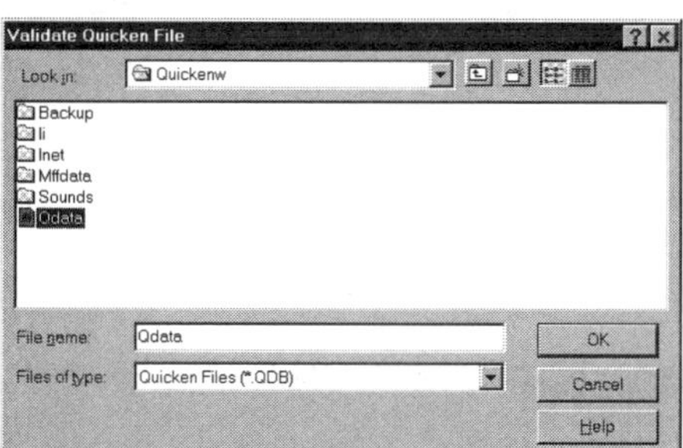

Figure B.11 *By default, the Validate command displays the folder in which Quicken is installed. If your data file is in a different folder, use normal Windows procedures to switch to that folder.*

To validate a data file:

1. Choose File ⇨ File Operations ⇨ Validate. The Validate Quicken File dialog box appears, as shown in **Figure B.11**.
2. Select the data file that you wish to validate, and click OK. (Note that if you only have a single data file, its name is normally Qdata.)

   Quicken checks the integrity of the data and attempts to repair it, if necessary.

Renaming Data Files

You can rename Quicken data files, if you wish.

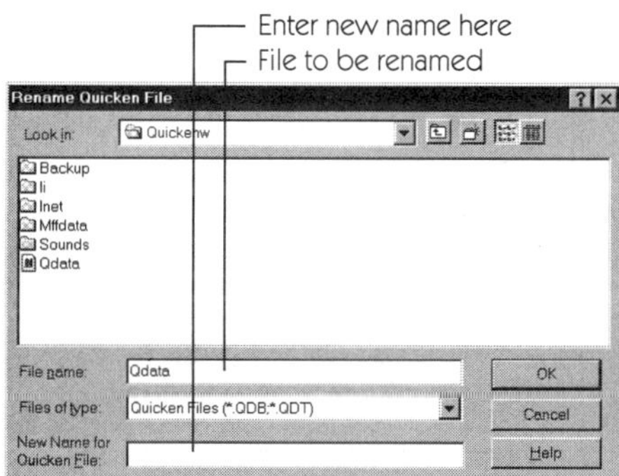

Figure B.12 *Renaming a file is done in a modified version of the normal file dialog box.*

To rename a data file:

1. Choose File ⇨ File Operations ⇨ Rename. The Rename Quicken File dialog box appears, as shown in **Figure B.12**.
2. Select Qdata or another data file from the file list. The chosen file appcars in the File Name text box.
3. Type a new name in the New Name for Quicken File text box.
4. Click OK to rename the file as indicated.

Deleting Data Files

To eliminate old or unwanted data, you can delete a Quicken data file—eliminating all records. After deleting, you can either create a new data file or restore a backup.

To delete a data file:

1. Choose File ⇨ File Operations ⇨ Delete. The Delete Quicken File dialog box appears.
2. Select Qdata (or another data file that you want to delete), and then click OK.
3. If the file selected in Step 2 is currently open, the dialog box shown in **Figure B.13** appears. Click OK to continue or Cancel to quit.
4. The dialog box shown in **Figure B.14** appears. To complete the deletion, type Yes in the text box and then click OK.

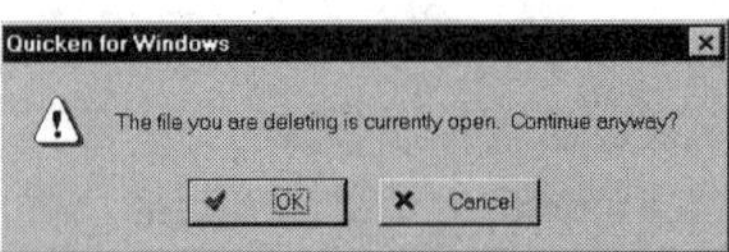

Figure B.13 *If the chosen file is currently open, this dialog box appears.*

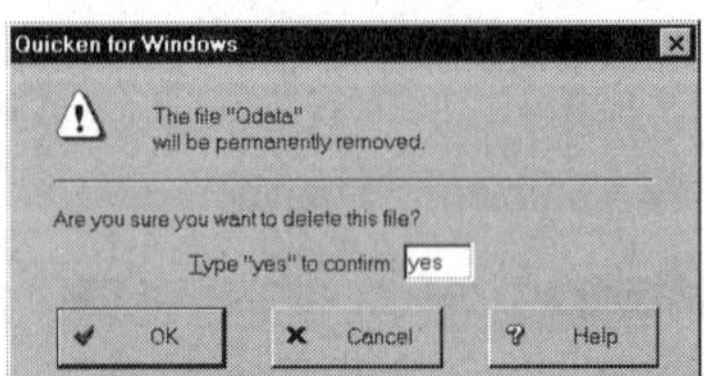

Figure B.14 *You must type Yes to confirm a file deletion.*

✔ **Tip**

- If you want to delete only *part* of a data set, use the Copy command.

Copying Data Files

Use the Copy command to create a new data file that includes only a subset of the current transactions.

To copy a data file:

1. Open the data file from which you intend to copy.
2. Choose File ⇨ File Operations ⇨ Copy. The Copy File dialog box appears (see **Figure B.15**).
3. In the Name text box, enter the name of the new file.

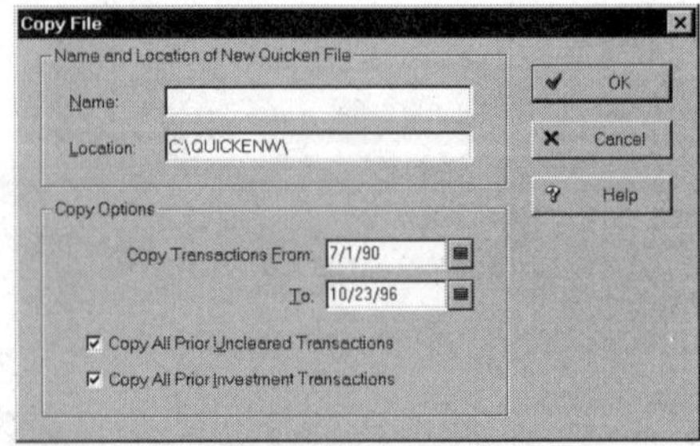

Figure B.15 *Set copy options in the Copy File dialog box.*

4. *Optional:* In the Location text box, Quicken enters the path of the current Quicken folder. You can change the location to another folder, if desired.

5. *Optional:* Change the date range for the transactions you want to include in the new file, if desired.

6. Decide whether you want to include uncleared account transactions and/or uncleared portfolio transactions *prior* to the Copy Transactions From date. Set the check boxes accordingly.

   When you include prior uncleared transactions, Quicken totals them and uses the total as the account's opening balance.

7. Click OK to create the new file. The File Copied Successfully dialog box appears (see **Figure B.16**).

8. Select the file that you want to use by clicking Original file or New copy, and then click OK.

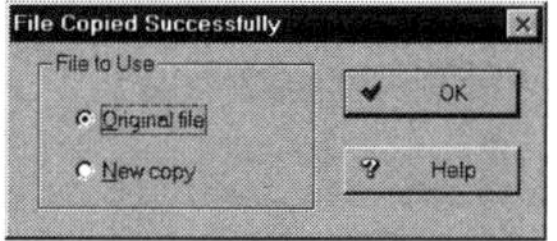

Figure B.16 *Select the file that you now want to use.*

✔ **Tips**

- To create a data file with no transactions that still contains your categories, memorized transactions, scheduled transactions, and transaction groups, set a date range that is *after* today's date and clear the two check boxes.

- If you accept all the default settings, the copy made is identical to the original file.

Starting a New Year

Quicken offers several options for starting a new year. You can:

- *Archive a copy of the previous year's data.* This option leaves the current data file intact, enabling you to continue to make multi-year comparisons.
- *Clear all data prior to the new year.* This option also saves a copy of the current data file, but removes all old transactions. (In general, this option is not recommended. In particular, it should not be used if you use on-line banking to update your credit accounts because old payee information is also cleared.)
- *Do nothing at all.* You are not required to archive your data or to remove old transactions. You can continue working with Quicken as you always have.

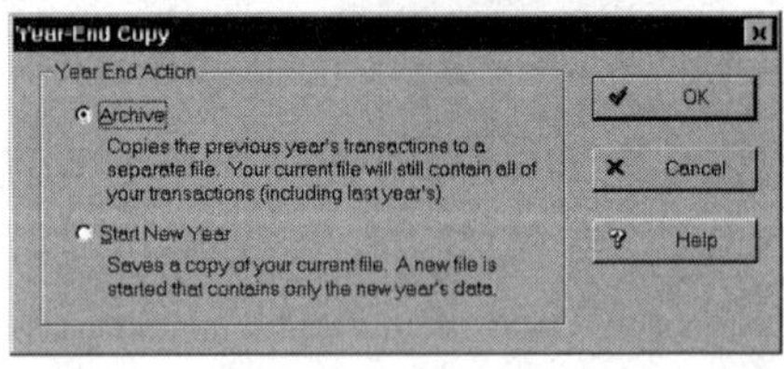

Figure B.17 *You can make a copy of (Archive) or remove (Start New Year) last year's data in the Year-End Copy dialog box.*

To archive last year's data:

1. Choose File ⇨ File Operations ⇨ Year-End Copy. The Year-End Copy dialog box appears, as shown in **Figure B.17**.
2. Click the Archive radio button, and then click OK. The Archive File dialog box appears (see **Figure B.18**).
3. By default, the archival file is named *current filename*, followed by the year of the archived transactions (e.g., Qdata96). You can assign a different name to the file by entering it in the Archive Old Data to File text box.
4. Select a location for the archive. The current directory is proposed.

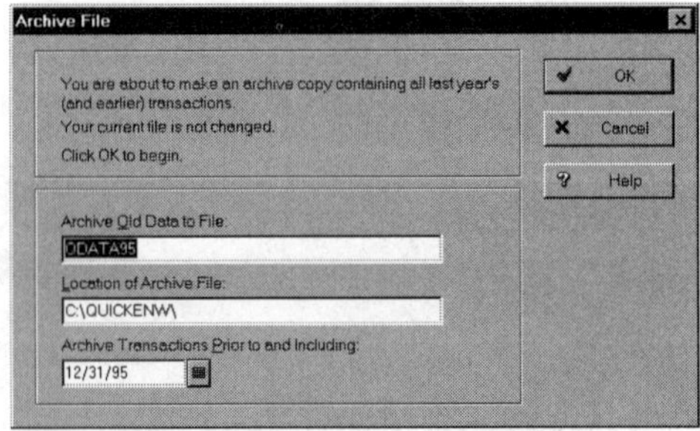

Figure B.18 *Specify a name, location, and transaction dates to be included in the archive.*

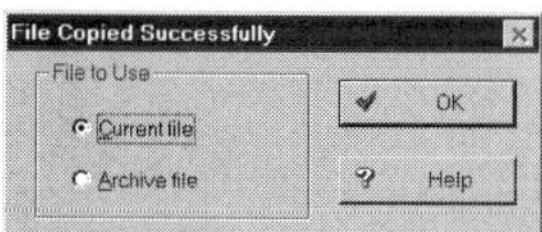

Figure B.19 *You can either use the current file or the archive. (Normally, you'll want to use the current file.)*

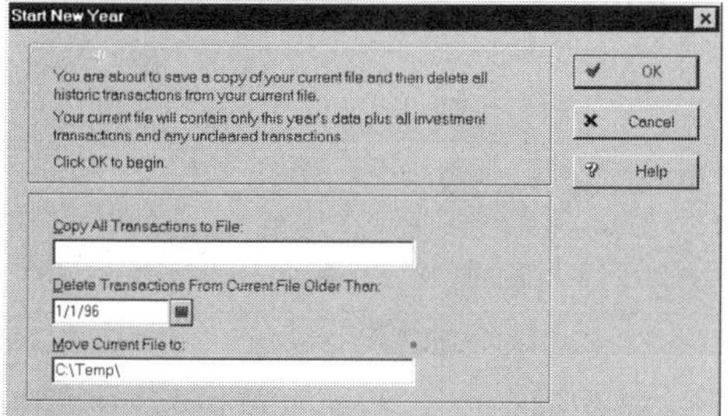

Figure B.20 *Options for removing old transactions from the current file are presented in the Start New Year dialog box.*

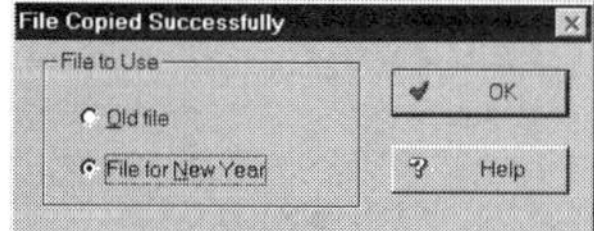

Figure B.21 *Select the file that you now want to use. Normally, this is the File for New Year.*

5. Select an end date for transactions to be included in the archive.
6. Click OK. The archive is created, and the dialog box shown in **Figure B.19** appears.
7. Decide whether you want to use the current file or the archive, and then click OK.

To clear all old data:

1. Choose File ⇨ File Operations ⇨ Year-End Copy. The Year-End Copy dialog box appears, as previously shown in **Figure B.17**.
2. Click the Start New Year radio button, and then click OK. The Start New Year dialog box appears (see **Figure B.20**).
3. As part of this procedure, Quicken makes a backup copy of the current file. Enter a name for this file in the Copy All Transactions to File text box.
4. In the Move Current File to text box, enter a path for the backup file that you are about to create.
5. Specify which transactions to eliminate from the current file by setting a date in the middle box.
6. Click OK. The backup copy is created, the selected transactions are removed from the current file, and the dialog box shown in **Figure B.21** appears.
7. Decide whether you want to use the current file (File for New Year) or the archive (Old file), and click OK.

Password-Protecting Data

If security is an issue for you, there are two ways that you can protect your Quicken data:

- *File password*. You can set a password for the entire data file. Unless the password is known, the file cannot be opened.
- *Transaction password*. You can protect transactions that occurred prior to a specific date. If you close your books each month (a common accounting practice), creating a transaction password prevents anyone from inadvertently altering the closed transactions.

Setting a Password

The following sets of steps explain how to set file and transaction passwords. Each password can contain up to 16 characters, including spaces.

To set a file password:

1. Choose File ⇨ Passwords ⇨ File. The Set Up Password dialog box appears (see **Figure B.22**).
2. Enter the password twice—once in each text box—and click OK.

The next time you run Quicken or attempt to open the protected data file, a dialog box prompts for the password (see **Figure B.23**).

To set a transaction password:

1. Choose File ⇨ Passwords ⇨ Transaction. The Password to Modify Existing Transactions dialog box appears (see **Figure B.24**).
2. Enter the password twice—once in each of the top two text boxes

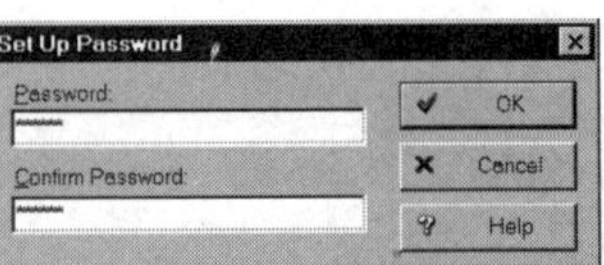

Figure B.22 *You create a file password in the Set Up Password dialog box.*

Figure B.23 *The Quicken Password dialog box automatically appears each time you use or manually open a password-protected Quicken data file.*

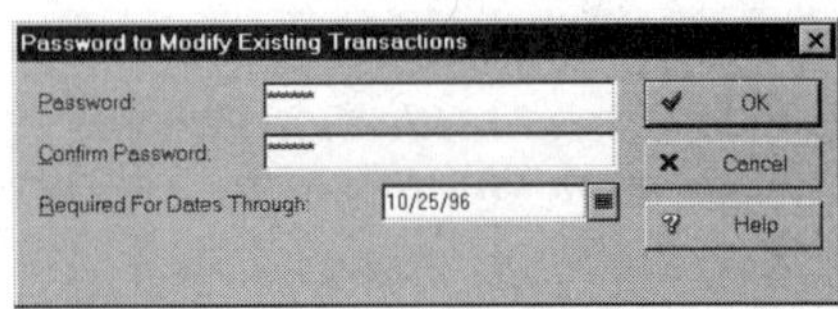

Figure B.24 *To set a transaction password, enter the password, confirm it, and then set an end date for the transactions to be covered.*

Password-Protecting Data

Figure B.25 *A Quicken Password dialog box appears whenever you try to alter a protected transaction. Enter the password and click OK to continue, or click Cancel to leave the transaction unchanged.*

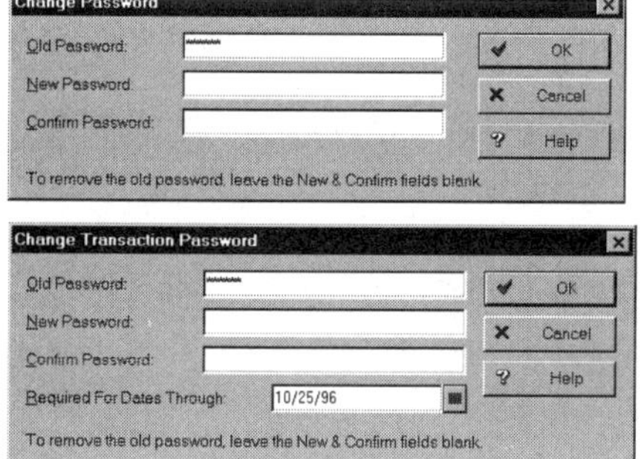

Figure B.26 *Slightly different dialog boxes appear when you change a file password (top) or a transaction password (bottom).*

3. Set a date for the last transaction to be covered by the password, and then click OK.

Whenever you attempt to modify a protected transaction, a dialog box prompts you for the password, as shown in **Figure B.25**.

Changing or Removing Passwords

Quicken also enables you to change or remove an existing password. Note that you must know the current password to perform either action.

To remove or change a password:

1. Choose File or Transaction from the Passwords submenu of the File menu, depending on the type of password you want to change or remove. One of the dialog boxes shown in **Figure B.26** appears.
2. Enter the current password in the Old Password text box.
3. To change the password, enter a new password in the New Password and Confirm Password text boxes. (When changing a transaction password, you can also specify a different set of transactions to protect by selecting a new date.)

   or

3. To remove the password, leave the New Password and Confirm Password text boxes blank.

✔ Tips

- Letter case is ignored in passwords. Thus, *Snappy* and *snappy* are treated as the same password.
- If you have multiple Quicken files, each data set can have its own file

and/or transaction password. For example, you could have two data files, each with a different password or one with a password and one without.

- If you forget a password, Intuit Technical Support can recover it for you.

Exporting/Importing Data

Quicken uses a file format called *QIF* (Quicken Interchange Format) for exporting and importing data. If you have another financial program that can export its data as a QIF file, it can be merged with your current Quicken data (enabling you to quickly add information about your portfolio or a money market account, for example). Programs that can export QIF files include Microsoft Money, Simply Money, and Money Counts (via a conversion utility).

To import another program's data into Quicken 6:

1. Use the other program's Export command or similar procedure to create a QIF file for the account you want to transfer into Quicken.
2. In Quicken, open the file that will receive the data. If the file does not already contain an account to receive the new data, create the account now.
3. Choose Import from the File Operations menu of the File menu. The QIF Import dialog box appears (see **Figure B.27**).
4. Set the following transfer options: the pathname of the file to be imported, the account to receive

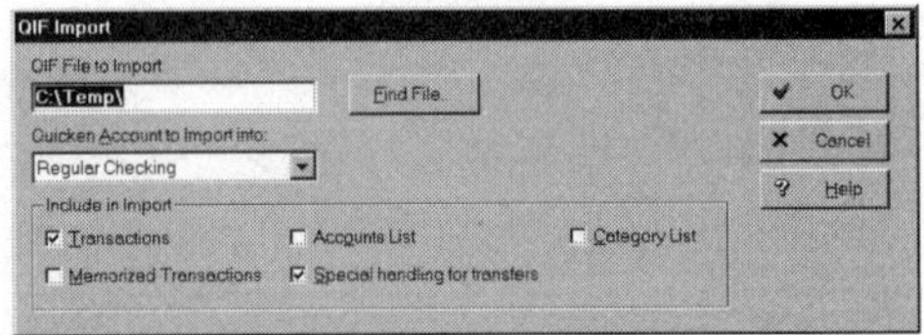

Figure B.27 *Set import options in the QIF Import dialog box.*

the data, and the specific elements to be imported.

5. Click OK to import the data.

You can also export account data from one Quicken file (all transactions for a checking account, for instance), and then import it into a different file on the same or on another computer.

To export Quicken data:

1. Open the Quicken file from which the account data is to be exported.

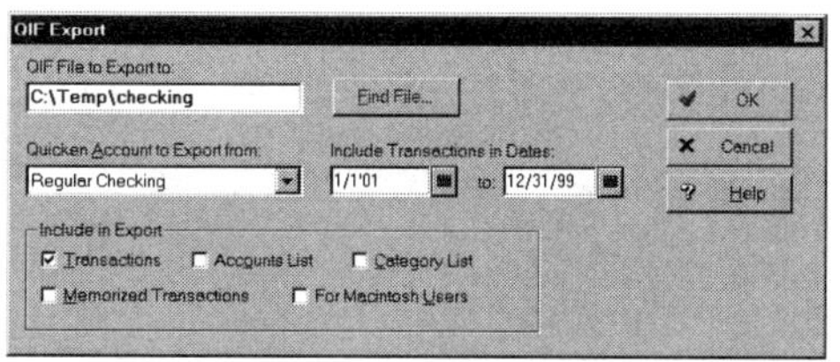

Figure B.28 *Exported data can include all transactions from the chosen account or a date-based subset of transactions.*

2. Choose File ⇨ File Operations ⇨ Export. The Export QIF dialog box appears (see **Figure B.28**).

3. Set the following transfer options: the pathname of the export file to be created, the account from which the data is to be exported, the date range of the transactions to be included, and the specific elements to be exported.

5. Click OK to create the export file.

6. To import the data into the other Quicken file, follow the instructions in "To import another program's data into Quicken 6," beginning with Step 2.

Finally, you can print Quicken reports or lists to disk so that they can be read by other programs. You might want to export report data so that you can do additional analyses in a spreadsheet, embed a report in a desktop publishing document or presentation, or use another program to create graphs or charts that are not available in Quicken.

To export a Quicken report or list:

1. Generate the Quicken report that you want to export, or display the list that you want to export.
2. Choose Print command from the File menu. The Print dialog box appears, as shown in **Figure B.29**. (The wording of the Print command varies, depending on what you are printing.)
3. In the Print to section of the dialog box, choose the type of print file to be made: *ASCII Disk File* (a text file that uses spaces to separate fields/columns); *Tab-delimited Disk File* (a text file that uses tabs to separate fields/columns; a common choice when importing data into a database program); or *123 (.PRN) Disk File* (a text file that can be imported into a Lotus 1-2-3 compatible spreadsheet program).
4. Click OK. The Create Disk File dialog box appears (see **Figure B.30**).
5. Set a name and location for the print file. (Regardless of the file type selected, the filename will have a .TXT extension). Click OK to generate the print file.

   Figure B.31 shows the output from a tab-delimited print file.

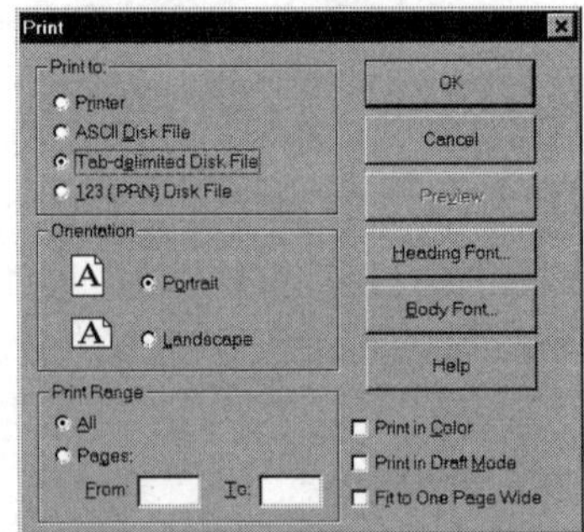

Figure B.29 *The Print to section of the Print dialog box contains several options for making a print file.*

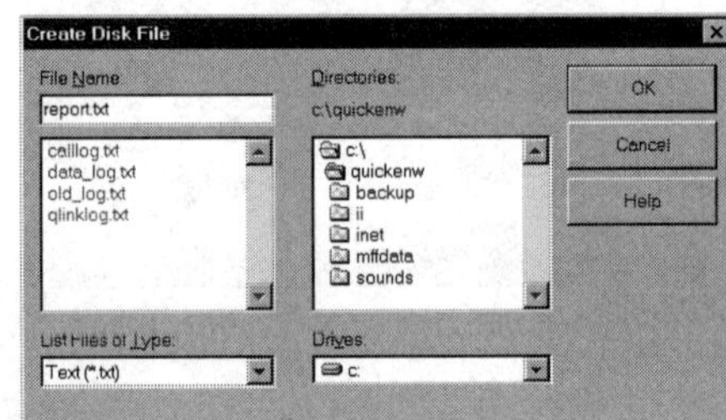

Figure B.30 *Name and choose a location for the output file in the Create Disk File dialog box.*

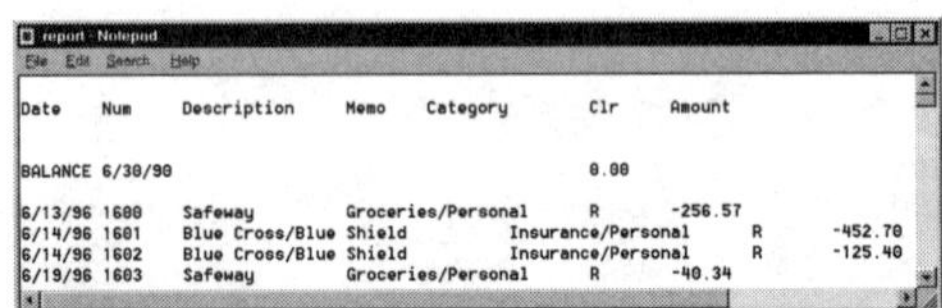

Figure B.31 *A typical print file opened in Notepad.*

Ordering Supplies

About Quicken Supplies

Many users print their checks from within Quicken. By using preprinted checks and window envelopes from Intuit, you can make short work of the monthly bills.

Inside the Quicken box is a copy of the Checks Catalog. You can order checks and other supplies in these ways:

- *Mail.* Fill out the postage-paid order form, and drop it in the mail.
- *Quicken Checks Customer Service.* You can place phone orders at 800-433-8810 (U.S.) or 800-268-5779 (Canada).
- *Fax.* Fill out the order form, and fax it to Intuit at 206-925-9301.
- *Intuit Marketplace.* This Quicken feature (see **Figure C.1**) can help you place supply orders via modem or mail.

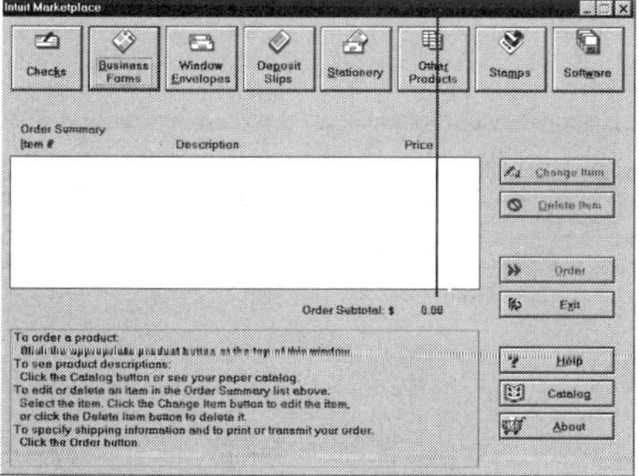

Figure C.1 *When you invoke Intuit Marketplace, this dialog box appears. As items are added to the order, a running total is calculated.*

Using Intuit Marketplace

Whether you intend to place an order by mail or modem, you can use Intuit Marketplace to create the order. This program feature steps you through the process of ordering checks and forms, while providing extensive on-line help.

To learn more about the products, you can click the Catalog button. Click Help for assistance with any part of the ordering process.

To place an order:

1. Choose Features ⇨ Paying Bills ⇨ Order Checks.

   or

1. Choose Features ⇨ Online ⇨ Intuit Marketplace.

   The Intuit Marketplace window appears (refer to **Figure C.1**).

2. Choose a type of item to purchase by clicking a button at the top of the Intuit Marketplace window.

3. A series of dialog boxes appears in which you are prompted for information, such as the type of printer you have; your name, address, and bank account number; and so on.

   As an example, **Figures C.2–C.4** show the dialog boxes that appear when ordering a business form.

4. In the final dialog box, click OK to add the item to the order, click Cancel to return to the Intuit Marketplace window without adding the item to the order, or click Back to change the information that you entered for the item.

   If you click OK, the item is added to the order and the subtotal is updated to reflect the cost of the new item.

5. Repeat Steps 2–4 as necessary, adding other items to the order. If you want to remove an item, select it in the Order Summary list and click Delete Item.

6. To process the order, click the Order button in the Intuit Marketplace window. The Payment and Delivery dialog box appears, as shown in **Figure C.5**).

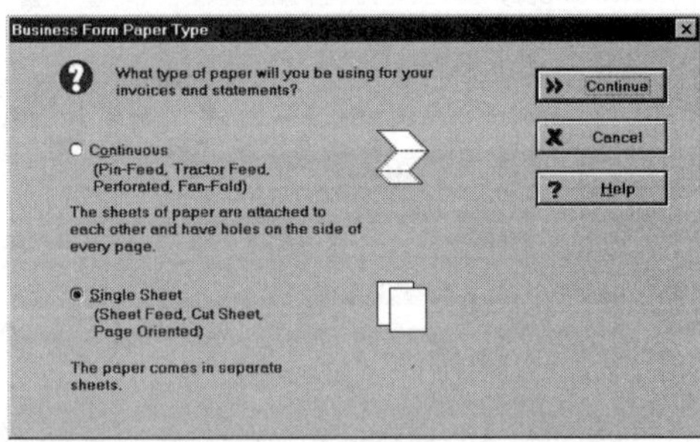

Figure C.2 *First, select a paper type.*

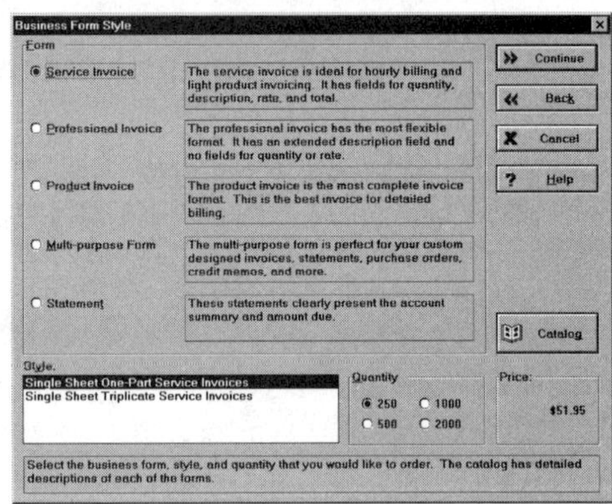

Figure C.3 *Choose a form type, style, and quantity in the Business Form Style dialog box.*

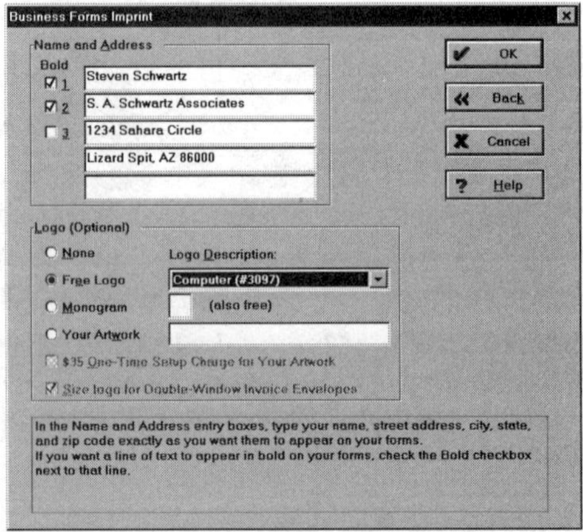

Figure C.4 *Enter personalization information in the Business Forms Imprint dialog box.*

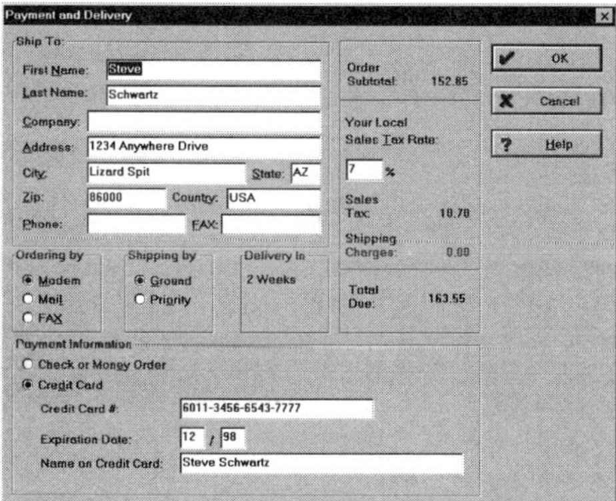

Figure C.5 *Complete this form, and choose a method of ordering (modem, mail, or fax).*

Figure C.6 *The Preview Order dialog box enables you to examine the contents of your order before you transmit or print it.*

7. Fill in the requested data, and choose a method of delivering the information to Intuit: modem, mail, or fax. Click OK. The Preview Order dialog box appears (see **Figure C.6**).

8. Examine the order in the scrolling pane. If it is correct, click Transmit (when the delivery method is Modem) or Print (when using Mail or Fax).

   If you discover an error, click Back. If you change your mind about ordering at this time, click Cancel.

✔ Tips

- The kind of paper supplies you should order are dictated by the type of printer you own. If you have a laser or inkjet printer, choose *single-sheet* products. If you have a dot-matrix printer, choose *continuous* products. (Although single-sheet forms can also be used in many dot-matrix printers, continuous-form products are usually easier to manage.)
- Similarly, multipart forms (referred to as *duplicate* or *triplicate*) are meant to be used in dot-matrix printers.
- If you have a laser or ink-jet printer, it can be very difficult (or impossible) to print partial sheets—after printing one or two checks from a page, for example. Consider buying a set of *forms leaders* (Item #6349) that you can attach to the partial pages, enabling them to be printed. A similar product (Item #7897) is available for continuous-form printers.

- Although Intuit is the leading vendor of paper supplies for Quicken, it is not the *only* vendor. Ask your current paper supply company about the availability of Quicken-compatible checks and forms.
- If you cancel or click the close box for an Intuit Marketplace order, the current order is not discarded. The chosen items are stored. You can place the order at a later date by returning to the Intuit Marketplace window.
- You can also run Intuit Marketplace from the taskbar in Windows 95. Click the Start button, and choose Intuit Marketplace from the Quicken folder (see **Figure C.7**).

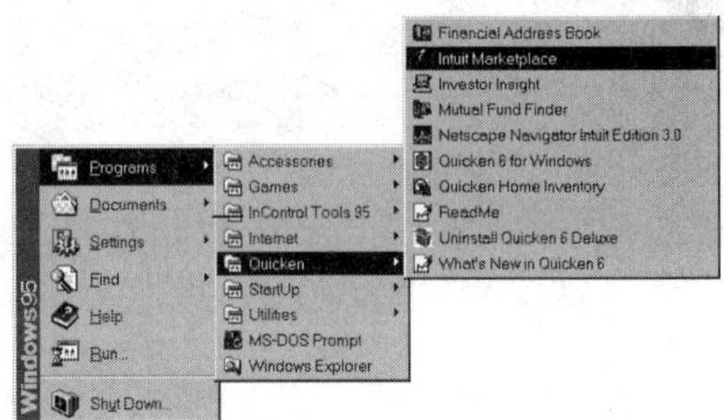

Figure C.7 *You can run Intuit Marketplace without launching Quicken.*

Index

C

D

E

F

G

H

I

P

Q

R

S

T

U

V

W